the ECOLOGICAL REVOLUTION

THE ECOLOGICAL REVOLUTION

making peace with the planet

by JOHN BELLAMY FOSTER

MONTHLY REVIEW PRESS
New York

Library of Congress Cataloging-in-Publication Data

Foster, John Bellamy.
   The ecological revolution : making peace with the planet / John Bellamy
Foster.
        p. cm.
   ISBN 978-1-58367-179-5 (pbk.) — ISBN 978-1-58367-178-8 (cloth)
   1. Human ecology. 2. Environmentalism. I. Title.
   GF41.F67 2009
   304.2'8—dc22

2009009109

Monthly Review Press
146 West 29th Street, Suite 6W
New York, NY 10001

5 4 3 2 1

Contents

PREFACE 7

INTRODUCTION: The Ecological Revolution 11

PART ONE: THE PLANETARY CRISIS

1. The Ecology of Destruction 39

2. Ecology: The Moment of Truth 55

3. Rachel Carson's Ecological Critique 67

4. Peak Oil and Energy Imperialism 85

5. The Pentagon and Climate Change 107

6. The Jevons Paradox:
   Environment and Technology under Capitalism 121

7. A Planetary Defeat:
   The Failure of Global Environmental Reform 129

PART TWO: MARX'S ECOLOGY

8. Marx's Ecology in Historical Perspective 143

9. Marx's Theory of Metabolic Rift:
   Classical Foundations for Environmental Sociology 161

10. Capitalism and Ecology: The Nature of the Contradiction . . . 201

11. *The Communist Manifesto* and the Environment 213

12. Ecological Imperialism: The Curse of Capitalism 233

PART THREE: ECOLOGY AND REVOLUTION

13. Envisioning Ecological Revolution 253

14. Ecology and the Transition from Capitalism to Socialism 265

NOTES 279

INDEX 319

Preface

My premise in this book is that we have reached a turning point in the human relation to the earth: all hope for the future of this relationship is now either revolutionary or it is false. In *Making Peace with the Planet*, from which the subtitle for this book was taken, Barry Commoner wrote: "If the environment is polluted and the economy is sick, the virus that causes both will be found in the system of production."[1] Today, the sickness of both environment and economy—and the fact that the common cause is to be found in the capitalist mode of production—can no longer be doubted. It is this that makes ecological revolution necessary.

The principal aim of *The Ecological Revolution* is to provide what Raymond Williams once called "resources for a journey of hope." Historical materialism is indispensable for such a journey because of its unceasing commitment to the confrontation of reality with reason. It is, as Ernst Bloch explained in *The Principle of Hope*, the "coldest detective" and the most fervent believer in a "concrete utopia."

To be sure, it is not hope so much as necessity that must drive us at present. As Bertolt Brecht explained in his poem "Buddha's Parable of the Burning House," we cannot afford to sit in a burning house while the flames lick the rafters and singe our brows and question whether a new house is possible. We must abandon the old structure and seek to build a new one.[2]

Ironically, one common criticism that has been directed against the revolutionary environmental outlook offered here is that it is devoid of hope, since it requires going beyond the existing capitalist system.[3] However, the view that the historical journey of humanity is over and that the prevailing mode of production is inviolable—even when faced with an impending collapse of the world's ecosystems and of human civilization, placing in question the continued existence of humanity itself—can only lead to despair, since it offers no conceivable way out of today's closing circle.

In contrast, the struggle for ecological revolution is firmly rooted in "the principle of hope." Here, the development of human freedom and the evolution of the human relation to nature is only just the beginning. The entire history of humanity's cultural evolution can be conceived as one of punctuated equilibrium, with revolutions leading at critical points to new forms of social organization. We cannot say that the current attempt at radical transformation in the human social relation to the earth (and in humanity's self-relation) will succeed. But we do know that hundreds of millions, perhaps billions, of people, will struggle for such an outcome in the century before us.

The Ecological Revolution was written over a period of a dozen years. All of the chapters, aside from the introduction, are based on previously published articles. However, each has been adapted, and most have been substantively revised, for this book. They have been organized in such a way as to generate a single, coherent argument. Certain key themes and tools of analysis, such as Marx's concept of metabolic rift and the Jevons paradox, appear repeatedly throughout the following pages. These should be viewed as key connecting links in the analysis, demonstrating why and how we should and can struggle for a more sustainable ecological and social order.

I was fortunate, early in the stage of my ecological studies that is represented by this book, to get to know Brett Clark, who came to the Department of Sociology at the University of Oregon to do graduate studies in environmental sociology, and with whom I have worked closely ever since. Brett, now a professor of sociology at North Carolina State University, coauthored four of the chapters in this book, in their original form: Chapter 2, "Ecology: The Moment of Truth"; Chapter 3, "Rachel

Carson's Ecological Critique"; Chapter 6, "The Jevons Paradox: Environment and Technology Under Capitalism"; and Chapter 12, "Ecological Imperialism." He has helped me at every point in this work. My colleague and close friend in the University of Oregon sociology department, Richard York, coauthored chapter 2, along with Brett and myself, and has left a deep and indelible impact on my thinking on questions of ecology, evolution, and capitalism. Much of this book derives from work done in conjunction with Paul Burkett in the period since the late 1990s. Paul's books *Marx and Nature* and *Marxism and Ecological Economics* are essential readings in this area, and can be seen as companion volumes to this and my other previous ecological works: *The Vulnerable Planet, Marx's Ecology,* and *Ecology Against Capitalism.*

Others too have contributed enormously to this book. At *Monthly Review,* I have been privileged to be able to draw on the invaluable help and inspiration of a talented group of close friends: Michael Yates, now director of Monthly Review Press, John Mage, John Simon, Claude Misukiewicz, Martin Paddio, Fred Magdoff, Yoshie Furuhashi, Victor Wallis, and, most recently, Scott Borchert. John Mage, in particular, has been Bloch's "coldest detective," giving me the enormous benefits of sharp criticism and untiring support from the beginning.

I have also benefited from working with Rebecca Clausen, Hannah Holleman, Ryan Jonna, Philip Mancus, and Stefano Longo, a brilliant group of graduate students at the University of Oregon during the years when I was writing this book. They provided new questions and new ways of thinking—and in the cases of Hannah and Jonna, in particular, direct help in the development of my work.

In my trips abroad, a number of friends and associates have offered their support. Among these I would especially like to thank Patrick Bond, in South Africa, where what is now chapter 7 was presented; Peter Dickens, in England, where chapter 8 was presented; Nildo Ouriques and Catarina Gewehr, in Brazil, where chapter 1 was presented; and Peter Boyle, Dave Holmes, Terry Townsend and Ariel Salleh, in Australia, where chapter 14 was first presented.

Robert McChesney, through his staunch friendship, support, and the example he has provided, has had a deep influence on all of my political and intellectual pursuits over the last thirty-five years.

Finally, the sense of a revolutionary journey of hope that pervades this book has entered my own daily life largely thanks to Carrie Ann Naumoff. *The Ecological Revolution* is dedicated to Carrie Ann. Her lifelong struggles in the legendary Hoedads tree-planting collective, as a defender of the struggles of workers, and as a teacher, community organizer, and family member, embody the commitment to sustainability, community, and equality that constitutes the essence of what I am calling here "the ecological revolution."

The Ecological Revolution

We need the concept of "enough."
—Niles Eldredge, *Life in the Balance*[1]

We live in a time in which the confrontation of reality with reason requires us to ask apocalyptic questions: Is the planet facing a major ecological collapse? Is civilization on the edge of the abyss? Is the survival of the human species itself in doubt? What makes the raising of these questions rational and necessary, today, is that scientific research is consistently telling us that if current trends continue, even for a century, the results for the earth and its inhabitants will be a collapse of the world as we know it. Indeed, in less than a generation, perhaps as little as a decade, ecological tipping points, associated with the rapid disintegration of ice sheets in West Antarctica and Greenland, the disappearance of Arctic sea ice, the thawing of frozen tundras, and vanishing glaciers in the Himalayas and elsewhere, could be reached, seeding vast changes in the climate and in ecosystems, endangering countless human beings and innumerable species. Consequently, it is now widely recognized that an ecological revolution—a massive and sudden change in the relation of humanity to the earth—is necessary.

In her book *Ecological Revolutions*, Carolyn Merchant defined "ecological revolutions" as "major transformations in human relations with nonhuman nature. They arise from changes, tensions, and contradictions that develop between a society's mode of production and its ecology, and between its modes of production and reproduction."[2] Society today is clearly facing such a major transformation in its mode of production and its ecological regime in response to the contemporary crisis of the earth.

Yet, this only leads us to another question: What kind of ecological revolution? There are of course numerous answers. But a central premise of this book is that these can be divided into two main approaches. The first of these is best described as an eco-industrial revolution—a new industrial revolution that seeks almost entirely by technological means, such as more efficient energy systems, to create the basis for sustainable capitalist development.[3] This green industrial revolution is often conceived by its proponents as a form of "ecological modernization," in which the rich countries lead the way in developing ecological innovations as new market opportunities. Where technological innovations, such as increased energy efficiency, are concerned no barrier is seen as too great. But aside from technology, virtually nothing in the social organization of society will change in this vision. The commitment to unlimited accumulation of capital and to an order that places artificially generated private wants over individual and social needs is unaltered. Indeed, "going green" is often seen as a way of vastly expanding commodity production and sales opportunities in a competitive and nationalist race for economic growth and dominance. It thus remains within the main "possessive-individualist" assumptions of the current social order.[4]

The second approach—the one I advance in this book—is that of a more radical, eco-social revolution, which draws on alternative technologies where necessary, but emphasizes the need to transform the human relation to nature and the constitution of society at its roots within the existing social relations of production. This can be accomplished only through a process of sustainable human development. This means moving decisively in the direction of egalitarian and communal forms of production, distribution, exchange, and consumption, thus breaking with the logic of the dominant social order. Rather than further widening the rift in the human/nature metabolism that characterizes the contemporary world economy, the goal is to return to more organic, sustainable social-ecological relations. Such changes involve a civilizational shift based on a revolution in culture, as well as economy and society.

What is, ultimately, at issue in this approach is finding a way beyond the capitalist system of production, or the current destructive phase of historical civilization, replacing it brick by brick with a fundamentally different edifice. Although this necessarily involves radical changes in technology, the emphasis here is on changing the wider social relations of production, since these, not technology as such, are the problem. As Lewis Mumford, the greatest social ecologist that the United States has yet produced, emphasized, we are faced with a problem of "technics and human development," with the latter standing for the question of the sustainable development of human beings and their broader social relations.[5]

This more social, as opposed to merely industrial, approach constitutes, in the argument presented in this book, the only genuine approach to ecological revolution. The attempt to solve our problems merely by technological, industrial or "free market" means, divorced from fundamental social relations, is futile. At the crux of the ecological problem of today is capitalism as a civilizational project that has reached a dead end. Although representing a great advance over earlier forms of production, the capital accumulation system—including the externalization of social costs on the poor, less developed countries, and the planet at large that goes with this system of accumulation—has increasingly become a hindrance to human development and even to the survival of humanity (along with most "higher" species).

Given that the dire nature of ecological problems is now very widely, if not yet universally, recognized, the conflict between these two opposing approaches to ecological revolution can now be considered the central problem facing environmental social science today. This is not a debate about technology or non-technology, industrialism or non-industrialism. Rather it is a dispute over whether capitalism can accommodate the necessary ecological changes—or whether, alternatively, it is a system that for a combination of material reasons (economic, social, and environmental) has finally reached its limits. The case for a genuine ecological and social revolution, in line with Marx's general conception of a revolutionary situation, lies in the fact that "all the productive forces" for which the existing mode of production is "sufficient," and that are compatible with sustain-ability, have been developed, requiring a revolutionary shift in the social relations of production and society as a whole.[6]

A GREEN INDUSTRIAL REVOLUTION

It has become commonplace today, as noted above, to observe that we are threatened by ecological collapse and even the demise of civiliza-tion. "Extreme global warming may not be a survival crisis for humani-ty as a species," Mark Lynas has written in his *Six Degrees*, "but it will certainly be a survival crisis for most humans unfortunate enough to inhabit a rapidly warming planet, and that situation is surely bad enough."[7] It is now clear that it is "business-as-usual," i.e., capitalism as we know it, which is chiefly at fault for this rapidly accelerating plane-tary catastrophe. Yet we are led to believe by thinkers stretching across the political divide between right and left that the problem goes no deeper than the system's narrowly conceived technological characteris-tics. Increased efficiency is seen as the proverbial free lunch, allowing unending exponential growth of the economy, without expanding the exploitation of the earth.

The confused state of mind that frequently accompanies this issue can be illustrated by quoting a passage from historian David Christian's *Maps of Time: An Introduction to Big History*. Recognizing the severity of the ecological crisis facing the world, and attributing this to the expansion of capitalism, Christian nonetheless observes:

> We have seen that capitalism is the driving force of innovation in the mod-ern world, and capitalist economies depend on increasing production and sales. Is that growth incompatible with sustainability? The answer is unclear, but there are reasons for thinking that capitalism may well man-age to coexist with at least some of the early stages of a transition to sus-tainability. One is that capitalist economies need increasing profits more than increasing production—and profits can be made in many ways, some of which are compatible with a sustainable economy. . . . There is no absolute contradiction between capitalism and sustainability.[8]

Such views suggest that sustainability, at least in its early stages, may be within the reach of the present economic and social order. Yet they skirt the main issues, doing violence to centuries of the development of social science. To argue vaguely that capitalism "may well manage to coexist with at least some of the early stages of a transition to sustainability" is to avoid the question of whether its logic as a system is a help or a hindrance to such a necessary transition, and indeed whether it is compatible with the later stages of the transition. To suggest that "capitalist economies need increasing profits more than increasing production" is to imply that the two can somehow be decoupled—and to ignore the dire consequences for the vast majority of the world's population of a shift toward profits not accompanied by a growth of production. In terms of the existing order, this would mean an intensification of the failed neoliberal phase of capitalist development: economic stagnation accompanied by a state-directed redistribution of income to the top (the only way profits can increase if the economic pie is not growing), resulting in vastly increased exploitation, inequality, unemployment, and poverty. To profess that profits can be made off of information that is somehow separated from production is what is known as the "myth of the paperless office," and has been repeatedly shown to be false.[9] To associate the drive to innovation exclusively with capitalism is wrongly to attribute to a specific economic formation the creative drive of human beings and human culture and civilization in general.

Lastly, the proposition that there is "no absolute contradiction between capitalism and sustainability" is true only in the very limited sense that there is no insurmountable barrier, in each and every instance, between the capitalist market and shifts toward sustainability in particular areas. Things are altogether different, however, when *capitalism as a universalizing system* is viewed against the backdrop of *the earth as a planetary system*. Capitalism as a world economy, divided into classes and driven by competition, embodies a logic that accepts no boundaries on its own expansion and its exploitation of its environment. The earth as a planet, in contrast, is by definition limited. This is an absolute contradiction from which there is no earthly escape.

Those who wish to deny any lasting conflict between the existing economic and social order and ecology promise unending technological mira-

cles linked to the market. The "black box" of technology, as economists like
to refer to it, is presented as a magical answer that defies both social science
(what we know about capitalism as social system), and science (i.e., physics
and ecological science itself). Tasks that might be accomplished quite rapidly by moving away from the narrow, restrictive goals of the accumulation
of capital, the proliferation of economic waste, and the promotion of pos-
sessive-individualism are to be reached by technological silver bullets still to
be developed. Improved engineering, we are led to believe, can solve all
problems, without altering social structure or human behavior.

Such strategies are designed to guide society perpetually along the
edge of the cliff, in line with the growth of a planetary risk economy, rather
than to pull back from the precipice altogether.[10] Sustainable development is turned into engineering, with the help of improved technology,
the maximum exploitation of the earth (and human beings) that can be
undertaken in the present without exceeding the absolute ecological limits of the planet. Accumulation of capital is viewed as an enterprise based
on risk, and this is extended to ever more risky wagers on the future of the
biosphere, generating a global risk society.

It is a defining characteristic of the green industrial revolution argument that the bounds of change are strictly set by the horizon of capitalism. The capitalist engine itself and its inherent destructiveness are seldom questioned. Worries are confined largely to the quantity and quality
(cleanliness) of its fuel, its efficiency as a motor, and the emissions that it
releases. The narrow technocratic nature of these answers has less to do
with their efficacy in solving the problem than in establishing legitimacy
for the system of production by ensuring that all wider, non-technocratic
solutions are forever off-limits.

This view is increasingly embraced by both liberal exponents of affir-
mative government and free market conservatives. Indeed, leading cheer-
leaders of globalization and neoliberalism such as *New York Times*
columnist Thomas Friedman and conservative politician and pundit
Newt Gingrich have recently joined those promoting the idea of such a
new green industrial revolution. Friedman argues in his best-selling *Hot,
Flat, and Crowded: Why We Need a Green Revolution—And How It Can
Renew America* that the world is facing growing demands on ecological
resources. These are emerging as a result of rising world population

together with what he calls the shift toward "flatness"—standing for the claim that globalization places the whole world increasingly at the same competitive level, rooted in the growth of the industrial classes in China, India, and other "emerging" economies. For Friedman these two demographic factors, population growth and "flatness," have added appreciably to the burdens imposed on the world ecology, manifested primarily in global warming (the "hot" element in his title). There are now, he says, "too many Americans," i.e., too many people in the world approaching American levels of consumption. The answer, he argues, is population control mechanisms aimed primarily at the poor countries, plus a new green technological revolution (not to be confused with the earlier agribusiness Green Revolution), modeled on the eighteenth century industrial revolution but with an emphasis now on clean energy and energy efficiency.

For Friedman this is the core of today's global competitive race. If the United States and U.S. corporations can lead the way in developing such technologies, he argues, it will reestablish U.S. global dominance and simultaneously solve the problems of: (1) enhancing growth and prosperity; (2) building a strong military; (3) putting "petrodictators" in their place; and (4) mitigating climate change. A green industrial revolution thus promises to solve all of the world's most pressing problems, reconciling globalization with the earth, while also reestablishing U.S. dominance. Friedman's "green revolution," he tells his readers, "is not your grandfather's green movement anymore. This is Code Green. It's about national power" (read: ecological imperialism). Moreover, green technology represents "the mother of all markets."

The essence of Friedman's fantasy of green technological revolution is an abundance of "clean electrons." "No single solution," he writes,

> would defuse more of the Energy-Climate Era's problems at once than the invention of a source of abundant, clean, reliable, and cheap electrons. Give me abundant, clean, reliable, and cheap electrons, and I will give you a world that can continue to grow without triggering unmanageable climate change. Give me abundant, clean, reliable, and cheap electrons, and I will put every petrodictator out of business. Give me abundant, clean, reliable, and cheap electrons, and I will end deforestation

from communities desperate for fuel and I will eliminate any reason to drill in Mother Nature's environmental cathedrals. Give me abundant, clean, reliable, and cheap electrons, and I will enable millions of the world's poor to get connected, to refrigerate their medicines, to educate their women, and to light up their nights.[11]

Similar technocratic and market-fetishizing arguments have been advanced by Newt Gingrich and Terry Maple in *A Contract with the Earth*, in which they contend that new technologies arising from entrepreneurial capitalism will allow for mitigation of and adaptation to climate change, and provide the basis for a whole new era of U.S.-led economic advance based on green technology. Rejecting both government regulation and the "elitist politics of big business" they claim that investments that "stoke the competitive fire" of entrepreneurial capitalism can generate a conservative-based revolution in sustainable development.[12]

Contract with the Earth relies heavily on the investment approach to environmental problems propagated by Ted Nordhaus and Michael Shellenberger in their influential book *Break Through*. Nordhaus and Shellenberger claim that the old environmentalism based on a "doomsday discourse" is dead and what is replacing it is a new "third way" environmentalism or post-environmentalism with a can-do emphasis on investment in eco-technology. "The transition to a clean-energy economy should be modeled," they write, "not on pollution control efforts, like the one on acid rain, but rather on past investments in infrastructure, such as railroads and highways." Economic growth is promoted as the first value and environmental protection as a secondary value that can be achieved mainly through technological breakthroughs that are also "pro-growth." They thus steer away from a focus principally on drastically slowing down or even halting climate change—even with respect to the role of the United States and other great powers that represent the major sources of global greenhouse gas emissions. A serious attempt to limit or even lower the concentration of greenhouse gases in the atmosphere, they suggest, represents too much of a threat to the capital-centered accumulation strategy. Rather they argue for a much heavier emphasis on adaptation through such measures as "building higher seawalls and levees or identifying new water supplies for regions likely to be affected by drought."

Under what Nordhaus and Shellenberger call the "investment-centered agenda" the goal is to overcome "the dead weight of the pollution paradigm" and the "politics of limits" and replace this with a transformed "energy economy." The chief object is to "bring the *real* cost of clean energy below that of fossil fuels," leaving other areas of the economic and social order untouched. This can be expedited as part of the neoliberal globalization regime, represented by the World Bank, the IMF, and the WTO.[13]

More sophisticated versions of this same green industrial revolution strategy have been articulated for some time by a school of environmental sociologists—the best known representative of which is the Dutch sociologist Arthur Mol—operating under the banner of "ecological modernization." The chief claim of such perspectives is that "the sustainability of capitalism" is possible—so ecological revolution is about modernization of the existing system rather than a radical transformation of the mode of production. The capitalist economy, it is contended, can "dematerialize" through reduction in throughputs of energy and raw materials utilized in production.[14]

Yet, while it is true that energy and resource-use efficiency have continually risen along with the advance of production, the overall result has not been to reduce the consumption of energy and materials. This is because efficiency gains under a capitalist economy result in further accumulation and economic expansion, with the increase in scale typically overwhelming gains in efficiency (a phenomenon known as the "Jevons Paradox"). Moreover, what appear to be environmental gains are often the result of simply shifting the problems elsewhere—from rich to poor regions and countries. Ecological modernization has thus not prevented the rapid overall rise in ecological destruction.

Ironically, one of the main faults of purely technological approaches to ecological revolution is that they are too narrow in their concept of technology, focusing only on those very limited technological solutions that would allow economic expansion and the accumulation of capital to proceed unaltered, unrestricted by the limits of the earth system. The primary purpose of such "modernizing" technology is to perpetuate the current treadmill of production rather than to solve ecological problems. Hence, insofar as such narrowly focused eco-technological, i.e., energy-efficient and resource-saving, innovations do emerge, they are quickly undermined by the very expansion of the economic system that they enable, and which is the ultimate goal.[15] Moreover, given the unlimited growth aspirations of capital and its increasing weight on the earth, the new technologies that are supposed to overcome these contradictions run up against the challenge of transcending physics itself (the entropy law). Hence, one is left with Friedman's science fantasy of infinite, clean, reliable electrons that will magically solve all problems. (Not surprisingly, Friedman is a strong supporter of nuclear power as a solution, which he describes as "reliable and clean," downplaying its immense ecological and social dangers.)[16]

Ignored in all of this is the much wider universe of technologies, many of which are not new, nor high-tech, available to meet social needs and ecological restoration *if the existing political economy did not confine technology and its employment to certain, restrictive parameters*. "The contemporary use of machines," Marx wrote, "is one of the relations of our present economic system, but the way in which machinery is utilised is totally distinct from the machinery itself. Powder is powder whether used to wound a man or to dress his wounds."[17] How and why particular technologies, which exist in abundance, are used or not used within human production and consumption is at least as important as the introduction of new technologies themselves—and depends to a very large extent on the social-economic relations of production. Solar power alternatives have been available for years but have been restricted by the fact that they are in many cases less profitable (how does one put a meter on the sun?) than less ecologically sound alternatives.[18]

In terms of climate change, the most serious industrial and technological danger at present is coal-fired plants, which in the United States emit more carbon dioxide into the atmosphere than the entire U.S. transportation system. Friedman deals with this problem by pointing to coal-sequestration technology that is still being developed. So-called "clean coal" is thus presented as the magic answer. Such a strategy of decarbonization of the power grid primarily through carbon sequestration and "clean coal" would probably not be accomplished in the United States prior to the second half of the century at best—and, indeed, might not in the end prove practical under the existing system of economic relations, where externalization of environmental costs is a built-in reality. Yet the more radical ecological solution that seeks an immediate closing down of coal-fired plants and their replacement by solar, wind, and other forms of renewable power—coupled with alterations on the demand-side through a transformation of social priorities—is viewed by the vested interests as completely undesirable. A serious shift in favor of such genuine environmental alternatives is thus completely incompatible with Friedman's green industrial revolution. Since promoting the needs of the powers that be is the first principle in his green technological revolution, he sees no alternative to Big Coal (except perhaps Big Nuclear Power). It is necessary, we are told, to put our faith chiefly in the development of the new carbon-sequestration technologies, while bridging the gap in the meantime with an "efficiency surge."[19]

Needless to say, this policy, favored as well by Obama, of maintaining for the time being existing coal-fired plants, and their displacement only gradually by "clean coal" technology (requiring entirely new plants and equipment) as that becomes economically practical, has serious environmental drawbacks. "The largest single producer of carbon dioxide in the United States," according to University of Montana climate scientist Steve Running, a lead author of the most recent United Nations Intergovernmental Panel on Climate Change report, "is coal fired power plants." It therefore follows that "from a climate point of view—not taking into account any economics—the best thing you can do is close down coal plants all across the country as soon as possible." Moreover, coal-sequestration technology, even if feasible on the scale required, invariably carries heavy environmental costs associated with coal mining and coal use, *plus* long-term threats associated with possible leakages of sequestered carbon.[20] As NASA's James Hansen, the leading U.S. climatologist, writes: "The dirtiest trick that governments play on their citizens is the pretense that they are working on 'clean coal' or that they will build power plants that are 'capture-ready' in case technology is ever developed to capture all pollutants. The trains carrying coal to power plants are death trains. Coal-fired power plants are factories of death."[21]

The foregoing suggests that technocratic choices, frequently based on futuristic notions, are more often than not about the requirements of the profit-system than about the environmental efficacy of the technology itself. Such choices involve trying to square the circle to avoid any real reckoning with social, economic, and environmental realities. "To say that 'science and technology *can* solve all our problems, in the long run,'" István Mészáros wrote in *Beyond Capital*,

> is much worse than believing in witchcraft; for it tendentiously ignores the devastating social embeddedness of present-day science and technology. In this respect, too, the issue is not *whether* or *not* we use science and technology for solving our problems—for obviously we must—but whether or not we *succeed* in radically *changing* their *direction* which is at present narrowly determined and circumscribed by the self-perpetuating needs of profit maximization.[22]

THE ECONOMICS OF EXTERMINISM

Excessive technological optimism in present-day society is tied to what might be called "the economics of exterminism." In the modern economic system of monopoly-finance capital, in which concentrated capital, economic stagnation, and the growth of debt and speculation are the dominant elements of the accumulation process, technology is viewed first and foremost as a means with which to amass wealth.[23] It is thus disproportionately directed at reducing labor costs and the maximization of surplus. The system is energy-intensive as opposed to labor-intensive, even at the cost of the environment, employment, and human welfare. Economic efficiency in this system of production is seen as efficiency in generating profits rather than sustaining people and the earth. The accumulation drive of the system, as John Maynard Keynes noted, makes "avarice and usury . . . our gods."[24] In such an economy, no rational accounting is possible, since costs are everywhere socialized—imposed on the environment and the majority of human beings in order to maximize private gain. The penetration of waste within the production process, as Thorstein Veblen first pointed out, becomes "rational" insofar as it increases markets and hence the marketability of goods.[25] Nature and human beings, insofar as they are not incorporated into the market, are valueless—and to the extent that they are incorporated into the prevailing economic system their value lies solely in their abstract existence as commodities. The *quid pro quo* that is supposed to underlie this mode of production—its abstract promise of equal exchange and the mutual benefit of all—is belied everywhere outside of its own abstract justification. "Capitalism," as the ecological economist K. William Kapp wrote, "must be regarded as an economy of unpaid costs, 'unpaid' in so far as a substantial proportion of the actual costs of production remain unaccounted for in entrepreneurial outlays; instead they are shifted to, and ultimately borne by, third persons or by the community as a whole."[26]

Where the treadmill of accumulation becomes society's sole goal, nothing means anything but growth, and growth is primarily growth in profits and wealth for a relative few. It is not surprising, therefore, that economics is the dominant social science and that economics and economists assume command of all attempts to address ecological problems, while at the same time constituting the main source of skepticism aimed at all attempts to promote egalitarian, ecological ends.

Indeed, mainstream economics itself is little more than the self-reinforcing ideology of capitalism itself—or what John Kenneth Galbraith in his final book called *The Economics of Innocent Fraud*.[27] Such ideological legitimation takes priority over reason, leading to absurd results. The egoistic pursuit of insatiable wants trumps planetary ecological preservation. Thus, we are faced with something akin to David Hume's great paradox of the passions: "Where a passion is neither founded on false suppositions, nor chuses means insufficient for the end, the understanding can neither justify nor condemn it. 'Tis not contrary to reason to prefer the destruction of the whole world to the scratching of my finger."[28]

As a contemporary example of this, leading neoclassical economists addressing climate change, such as William Cline, William Nordhaus, Lawrence Summers, and Nicholas Stern, have repeatedly proposed holding back on strongly combating global warming. They prescribe accepting levels of carbon concentration in the atmosphere (550-700 ppm or higher) that greatly exceed those deemed catastrophic by most climatologists—on the possessive-individualist grounds that serious attempts to stabilize climate change at lower levels in order to save the life on the planet as we know it would be too economically costly.[29]

This has resulted in an unbridgeable chasm between mainstream economists and climatologists. Economists claim that vast changes in the climate of the earth—on an order that previously would have been associated with geological time but taking place over a mere century— would produce only a minuscule change in the economy, hardly affecting world output. In approaching the issue of climate change, they thus tend to lean toward inaction or at most slow action, promoting adaptation over mitigation. They characteristically contend that technological substitution for natural resources through "efficient markets," which will also serve to spur growth, is the only answer. Much of this is based on the practice in orthodox economics of heavily discounting the future—an approach that runs directly counter to promoting the sustainability of the world for future generations.[30]

The chronic incapacity of orthodox economics to envision the full implications of the ecological problem was brought out in an exchange in *Science* magazine in 1992-1993 in which Yale economist William Nordhaus projected that the loss to gross world output in 2100 due to the continuation of the current trends would be insignificant (about 1 percent)—*even though the continuation of business-as-usual could lead, according to the UN Intergovernmental Panel on Climate Change, to a 6°C (10.8°F) rise in average global temperature, which for scientists was nothing short of calamitous.* On the basis of his model of the economic effects of global warming, Nordhaus argued that attempts at "emissions stabilization and climate stabilization are projected to be *worse than inaction*" (italics added). Yet climatologists were at the same time insisting that apocalyptic conditions threatened. One physical scientist, responding to a survey of economists and scientists conducted by Nordhaus in 1994 for the *American Scientist*, claimed that there was a 10 percent chance under present circumstances of the complete destruction of civilization. Such views are now, a decade and a half later, much more frequently voiced by scientists, who are very concerned that the dangers are accelerating and time is running out.

As Stanford biologist and climate scientist Stephen Schneider, writing in 1997 in his *Laboratory Earth,* summed up the situation: "Most conventional economists . . . thought that even this gargantuan climate change—equivalent to the scale of the change from an ice age to an interglacial epoch in a hundred years, rather than thousands of years—would have only a few percent impact on the world economy. In essence, they accept the paradigm that society is almost independent of nature."[31]

Despite the fact that Nordhaus himself has now tripled his projections of the losses to global output in 2100 attributable to climate change from 1 to 3 percent, it remains relatively insignificant in his conception. On this basis, he persists in arguing against any strenuous attempt to stabilize emissions this century. He proposes instead what he calls an "optimal path" in economic terms that would simply slow down the growth of carbon emissions, but would lead eventually (in the following century) to carbon concentrations of 700 ppm, presenting the possibility of global average temperature increases approaching 6°C above preindustrial levels—a level that Lynas in his *Six Degrees* compares to the sixth circle of hell in Dante's *Inferno*.[32] Indeed, at a level of carbon concentration well short of this, 500 ppm (associated with global warming of up to 3.8°C), "a conservative estimate for the number of species that would be exterminated (committed to extinction)," according to James Hansen, director of NASA's Goddard Institute for Space Studies, "is one million."[33]

To the extent that orthodox economists like Nordhaus support doing something about climate change, their favored solution (other than the black box of technology) is "cap and trade," or a market-based attempt to regulate carbon emissions. Such schemes, however, always involve various ways to buy out of the emissions reductions and have had little or no effectiveness. Thus there has been an increase in carbon emissions in countries that are part of the Kyoto process, which relies on a cap and trade system for controlling carbon emissions, that is not very different from that of the United States, which failed to go along with Kyoto. Support for such measures by economists has more to do with the fact that they create new markets and new means to accumulate than their actual efficacy at addressing global warming. The more radical approach of a carbon tax at well head and point of entry, with 100 percent of the revenue from the tax being redistributed to the public monthly on a per person basis (with children receiving half shares), as suggested by James Hansen, is an anathema to orthodox economists, since it sets ecological priorities first, above those of capital accumulation.[34]

Such failure by mainstream economists to comprehend or take seriously ecological limits is deeply rooted. Robert Solow, who was to receive the Bank of Sweden's Nobel Memorial Prize in Economics Sciences, once stated in the *American Economic Review*: "If it is very easy to substitute [by technological means] other factors for natural resources, then there is in principle no 'problem.' The world can, in effect, get along without natural resources, so exhaustion is just an event, not a catastrophe." Known as the "weak sustainability hypothesis," the assumption here is that through the development of new technological products it is possible to substitute for all natural services. This contrasts with the "strong sustainability hypothesis" advocated by ecologists, which asserts that nature provides irreplaceable critical ecological services for which there is no substitute.

There is no doubt that the weak sustainability hypothesis, preferred by most economists, seriously underestimates the rapidly accelerating dangers to the earth system. Climate warming gases are now being emitted at much faster rates than scientists had predicted. Christopher Field of the Carnegie Institution for Science recently declared, at the annual meeting of the American Association for the Advancement of Science, that carbon emissions since 2000 have been rising at 3.5 percent a year as compared with 0.9 percent a year in the 1990s. "It is now," he said, "outside the entire envelope of possibilities" projected by the United Nations International Governmental Panel on Climate Change in its 2007 report.[35]

The earth-endangering ecological trend represented by today's business-as-usual, which is now virtually impossible to deny, has compelled the vested interests to place all of their bets on new revolutionary technology—since systemic social change is off-limits. This has given rise to a new set of global environmental engineers, who promise either to engineer a new energy-efficient production technology without altering the basic parameters of the system or, more ambitiously, to "geoengineer" the entire planet. As Schneider noted:

Robert Frosch, a former administrator of NASA and then vice president of research at General Motors, went so far as to calculate how many battleship cannons aimed skyward and loaded with dust bombs targeted on the stratosphere it would take to reflect away enough sun-

light to offset warming from a CO_2 doubling. The annual costs of this
geoengineering project were in the tens of billions, but less than the
cost of fuel taxes, he argued.[36]

Similarly, the well-known physicist Freeman Dyson has proposed
that we alleviate the problems of global warming by replacing a quarter
of the trees in the world's forests with genetically engineered carbon-
eating trees.[37]

Faced with the real, present-day dilemmas of oil dependence and climate change, John Holdren, Obama's top advisor for science and technology, has asked "what should be done?" Holdren's answers are entirely technological, since, as he implies, slowing economic growth or even
changing the economic organization of society is not really an option in
the existing order. He thus specializes in promoting hypothetical "win-
win" technological solutions to be induced through government subsidies to private business: enhancing energy research; promoting promis-
ing innovations and securing financing to make them commercially
viable; making sure that improved energy technologies are diffused; creating a global managerial framework; and ensuring partnership between
the public and private sectors.

There is no doubt that an emphasis on the development of green technologies is needed. But what is missing, necessarily, from such a policy
vision is the recognition that real and rapid ecological change can only be
achieved by altering the economic and social order, and that the population as a whole needs to reshape society as a whole. Many of the technologies that are seen by futuristic technocrats such as Holdren as providing
the answers are not in existence. Nevertheless, immediately available
solutions such as conservation and alterations in the organization of production and consumption (for example, the promotion of mass transit
over the private automobile—or even more radical measures to constrain
the role of marketing in promoting wasteful consumption), no matter how
viable, are not included in Holdren's "what should be done," since these
would interfere with the accumulation system.[38]

In 1980, the British Marxist historian E. P. Thompson wrote a cautionary essay for *New Left Review* entitled "Notes on Exterminism, The
Last Stage of Civilization." Although directed particularly at the growth of

nuclear arsenals and the dangers of global holocaust by those means in the final phase of the Cold War, Thompson's thesis was also concerned with the larger realm of ecological destruction wrought by the system. German ecologist Rudolf Bahro later commented on Thompson's ideas in his *Avoiding Social and Ecological Disaster*, explaining: "To express the exterminism-thesis in Marxian terms, one could say that the relationship between productive and destructive forces is turned upside down. Marx had seen the trail of blood running through it, and that 'civilisation leaves deserts behind it.'" Today this ecologically ruinous trend has been extended to the entire planet, with capitalism's proverbial "creative destruction" being transformed into a destructive creativity endangering both humanity and life in general.[39]

"The dream that man can make himself godlike by centering his energies solely on the conquest of the external world," Lewis Mumford wrote in *The Condition of Man*, "has now become the emptiest of dreams: empty and sinister." The result is a kind of "economics of exterminism" in which the worst aspects of biology, economics, technology, and social organization are brought together.[40] Today, making war on the planet is fought primarily by technological means, pointing toward exterminism. In contrast, the task of making peace with the planet is a question not mainly of technology, but of changing social relations, pointing toward sustainability and coevolution.

ECOLOGICAL AND SOCIAL REVOLUTION

What distinguishes a genuine ecological revolution from a green industrial revolution is primarily social agency. Green industrial revolution is conceived, as we have seen, as a top-down attempt at a technological shift, led by ecologically modernizing elites, but without a popular uprising that would challenge the economic, social, cultural, and environmental norms of capitalist society. The goal of the vested interests is to keep social change in relation to the environmental challenge contained within the limits acceptable to the system, even at the risk of endangering the entire planet. This means restricting direct social involvement in such change, leaving it mainly in the hands of technocrats.

In contrast, a genuine ecological revolution, able to transform the relations between the mode of production and the ecology, would be associated with a wider *social*, not merely *industrial*, revolution, emanating from the great mass of the people. Like all social revolutions, it would question every aspect of society down to its roots. It would necessarily reestablish economics as *political* economy, subject to class revolt and public intervention, while transforming this, in line with today's necessity, into an *ecological* political economy. As Roy Morrison put it in his *Ecological Democracy*, an eco-social revolution would mean: "the rise of a new political economy, one rooted in . . . respect for the interdependence of social, political, and economic realms, and their connection to the encompassing social and natural ecologies."[41]

It is impossible to provide a blueprint for such a social and ecological revolution. Yet there are elements in the past and present that can provide us with insights and broad principles. Mumford defined some of the crucial requirements, in 1944, in *The Condition of Man*. Such an ecological and social transformation would necessarily be rooted in what he called "basic communism":

> During the last generation there has been a steady shift from individual demands, satisfied mainly by machine industry as an incident in the creation of profits and dividends, to collective demands expressed in goods and services that are supplied by the community to all of its citizens. This process I have elsewhere called basic communism: it applies to the whole community the standards of the household and distributes benefits according to need, not according to ability or productive contribution. Education, recreation, hospital services, public hygiene, art, have all increased in importance in every national economy: they represent collective needs that cannot be left to the automatic working out—or failure—of the laws of commercial supply and demand. Such a change in the human goals of production is essential for the full use of natural, technical, and scientific resources.[42]

Mumford attached his notion of "basic communism" to what John Stuart Mill, in his self-defined "socialist" phase, had presented as the challenge of a "stationary state" (a no-growth economy). Classical liberal political economists from Ricardo to Mill saw the stationary state as the inevitable result of the slowing down over time of accumulation, largely because of land and resource scarcities. For Mill, however, this was not a tragedy. "It is scarcely necessary to remark," he wrote,

> that a stationary condition of capital and population implies no station-ary state of human improvement. There would be as much scope as ever for all kinds of mental culture, and moral and social progress; as much room for improving the Art of Living, and much more likelihood of its being improved, when minds ceased being engrossed by the art of getting on. Even the industrial arts might be as earnestly and successfully culti-vated, with this sole difference, that instead of seeking no purpose but the increase of wealth, industrial pursuits would produce their legitimate effect, that of abridging labour.[43]

In developing his idea of "basic communism" as the aim of an organic revolution in society, Mumford took the example of the Works Progress Administration during Roosevelt's New Deal, the most radical labor pro-gram ever to emerge in the United States, and the broader concept of wealth creation that it involved. "In vital and essential human needs," he wrote, "the United States created less wealth during the boom period of the nineteen-twenties than it did in the strained years of depression, when the public works program and the WPA cleared out slums, restored run-down lands, rehabilitated forests, and introduced art and drama into communities sunk in destitution." For Mumford a socially and ecological-ly balanced economy would not be geared to endless acquisition and waste but "would translate energy into leisure and leisure into life."[44]

As Mumford observed, in the preface to the 1973 edition of *The Condition of Man,* it was time to transcend the dream of "the now-obso-lete economy based on a yearly increase of the gross national product . . . maintained only by war or augmented preparations for war, which would absorb by sheer waste the inflated surplus that the capitalist economy had never learned to distribute equitably—or to liquidate without bringing on economic depression. Moreover, a pseudo-stabilization by 'finance, insurance, and corporate monopolies' might frustrate a more viable social method for achieving dynamic equilibrium."

Capitalism's *ecological* failures, Mumford argued, were related to its *economic* failures. It had been built on three forms of expansion: land expansion, population expansion, and industrial expansion. All three had reached their limits as a strategy of wealth creation, falling into ecological and economic contradictions. The closing of the global frontier and the increasing population pressures on the earth meant the end of the long wave of outward colonization of territories and the environment. Continuation of capitalist economic industrialization was now possible only through a waste economy and at direct cost to life. "A period of stabilization on a planetary basis," he contended, "was now at hand." Beginning in the fourteenth century, the world had been dominated by "the rise of capitalism, militarism, scientism, and mechanization." Now it needed to give way to social and cultural forces of broader orientation that put life itself at the center—or it would descend into a passive and active barbarism worse than anything the world had ever seen.

A stable, balanced, and "life-centered" economy would require a rise in the income of workers, and a shift toward leisure, community, and the arts of living. Material wealth, in a rich society such as the United States, was not the problem but rather it was the use of such wealth. As Shelley had said, under existing social conditions, "the accumulation of the materials of external life exceed the quantity of the power of assimilating them to the internal laws of human nature."[45]

The solution to the "external crisis," for Mumford, required that the "internal crisis" of capitalist society be addressed: the alienation of humanity. The answer to this was the development of a society oriented to the creation of the "organic person," or a system of sustainable human development. This meant the creation of social forms that presented the opportunity for balance in the human personality. Rather than the promotion of the asocial traits of humanity, the emphasis would be on the creation of the social and collective characteristics. Each human being would be "in dynamic interaction with every part of his environment."[46]

For revolutionary environmental sociologists the long-term answers to problems of sustainability involve the rebuilding of human community (and communities of communities), consciously incorporating a dynamic, interdependent relation to nature. From an ecological and humanistic perspective, the concept of community points, as Herman Daly and John

Cobb insisted in *For the Common Good*, to a social order with definite "communal" characteristics. The goal is a way of life in which people are not isolated individuals but identify with and relate to each other through their larger relations of neighborliness, friendship, and interdependence, as "persons-in-community." It involves extensive collective participation in decision making, and thus requires, at its highest level of development, what the great early communist François Babeuf called a "society of equals," a system of substantive equality.[47] A community that is actively *communal* in this sense can arise only out of a strong social bond—in line with Mumford's "basic communism" and Marx's ideal of "from each according to his ability, to each according to his need"—dissolving mere individual economic exchange.[48] A sustainable community of this kind demands the cultivation of a sense of place and an extension of the community ethic to what Aldo Leopold called a "land ethic," incorporating the surrounding ecology. Such a broad conception of social and ecological community is clearly revolutionary in the context of today's possessive-individualist society.[49]

THE ELEMENTARY TRIANGLE OF ECOLOGY

As I explain throughout this book, it was Marx who saw most clearly how the material contradictions of capitalism—both economic and ecological—arise out of the way in which labor is organized in possessive-individualist society. Indeed, "labour," he explained, is "first of all, a process between man and nature, a process by which man, through his own actions, mediates, regulates and controls the metabolism between himself and nature." The distortion, estrangement, and ultimate destruction of that metabolism under capitalism constituted a "rift" in the irrevocable metabolism between human beings and nature, a "metabolism prescribed by the natural laws of life itself." Such alienation of nature was inextricable from the alienation of humanity and from the sharp division between town and country. For Marx socialism/communism pointed to a society of associated producers who "govern the human metabolism with nature in a rational way . . . with the least expenditure of energy and in conditions most worthy and appropriate for their human nature."[50]

Hugo Chávez's notion of the "elementary triangle of socialism," which he has used to articulate a new socialism for the twenty-first century in the context of Venezuela's Bolivarian Revolution, closely follows Marx's notion of a society of associated producers. For Chávez the elementary triangle of socialism consists of: (1) social ownership; (2) social production organized by workers; and (3) satisfaction of communal needs. Socialism requires the solving of these three problems simultaneously or it will cease to be sustainable.

It is clear that at the root of this *elementary triangle of socialism*, for Marx, was what could be called the *elementary triangle of ecology* (related specifically to human ecology) prescribed by the natural laws of life itself: (1) social use, not ownership, of nature; (2) rational regulation by the associated producers of the metabolism between human beings and nature; and (3) the satisfaction of communal needs—not only of present but also future generations. "Even an entire society, a nation, or all simultaneously existing societies taken together," he wrote, "are not the owners of the earth. They are simply its possessors, its beneficiaries, and have to bequeath it in an improved state to succeeding generations as *boni patres familias* [good heads of the household]." Marx's conception of the future, as Paul Burkett has demonstrated, was therefore one of sustainable human development, in which the elementary triangles of socialism and ecology converge, becoming one and the same.[51]

If a capitalist economy is inherently geared to the growth of private profits and accumulation, socialism from the beginning—both utopian socialism and classical Marxism—was primarily about control over production by the associated producers, the rational planning of production to meet social needs, and equitable distribution. Its emphasis was on use-values (i.e., concrete needs) rather than expansion of exchange-value. Communal and qualitative values were seen as replacing the institutionalized greed of Adam Smith's "invisible hand." Although expansion of production was certainly part of the early socialist analysis, it always took second place to control of production by the associated producers and human development.

In this respect, the Soviet Union—though the result of a socialist-led revolution and a break with capitalism—deviated sharply from the defining aims of socialism in making production for its own sake the main goal of society, while imposing a new kind of exploitative class structure beginning in the 1930s. Emphasizing the forced drafting of labor and resources, this form of society promoted the degradation of both labor and the environment, and ultimately prepared the way for its own demise.[52] However, the failures of Soviet-type societies have had the long-term effect of returning socialism to its classical roots, and to a more radical, egalitarian, and ecological vision.

The emphasis within classical Marxism on sustainable human development, rather than economic expansion for its own sake, as the goal of society made it possible for a Marxist economist, such as Paul Sweezy, to go beyond both most of today's ecological economists and the arguments of most radical environmental sociologists. Sweezy pointed out that what was needed ecologically was an about-face in the economic-ecological processes in the rich economies—in order both to reduce the overall economic footprint on the earth and to make space for poorer economies to carry out needed development. As he put it in his 1989 article, "Capitalism and the Environment," "what is essential to success is a reversal, not merely a slowing down, of the underlying trends of the last few centuries." This reversal of existing trends could, he suggested, be accomplished while improving the quality of life, given the waste, exploitation, and alienation built into the present social order. A genuine ecological revolution would be both a social and a cultural revolution. It would need to generate equality at every level of global society while organizing production rationally in terms of genuine needs.[53]

All of this suggests that ecological and socialist revolutions, if carried to their logical conclusions, are necessary and sufficient conditions of each other. The socialist goal of transcending the alienation of humanity is impossible to achieve to any considerable extent unless it coexists with the goal of transcending the alienation of nature. Likewise, the ecological goal of transcending natural alienation is impossible to attain without addressing social alienation. Socialism is ecological, ecologism is socialist or neither can truly exist.

Such a deep understanding of the necessary social revolution goes back to the utopian socialist roots of socialism. But the existence today of actual societies that are simultaneously seeking to forge a socialism for the twenty-first century and also a new ecological society, of which the greatest examples today are to be found in the periphery of the capitalist world—Cuba, Venezuela, Bolivia, Ecuador, Kerala in India, Nepal—has demonstrated already that the organic world is in reach in a truly revolutionary struggle for human and ecological liberation.

A genuine ecological revolution, the present book argues, thus requires an end to the destructive metabolism of capitalism, embracing in its place a new communal metabolism encompassing all of humanity and the earth. Today, I believe, there is no higher wisdom, and no higher necessity. As Evo Morales, socialist president of Bolivia, observed on November 28, 2008:

> As long as we do not change the capitalist system for a system based on complementarity, solidarity, and harmony between the people and nature, the measures that we adopt will be palliatives that will [be] limited and precarious in character. For us, what has failed is the model of "living better," of unlimited development, industrialization without frontiers, of modernity that deprecates history, of increasing accumulation of goods at the expense of others and nature. For that reason we promote the idea of Living Well, in harmony with other human beings and with our Mother Earth.[54]

PART ONE

the planetary crisis

CHAPTER ONE

The Ecology of Destruction

I would like to begin my analysis of what I am calling here "the ecology of destruction" by referring to Gillo Pontecorvo's 1969 film *Burn!*[1] Pontecorvo's epic film can be seen as a political and ecological allegory intended for our time. It is set in the early nineteenth century on an imaginary Caribbean island called "Burn." Burn is a Portuguese slave colony, with a sugar production monoculture, dependent on the export of sugar as a cash crop to the world economy. In the opening scene, we are informed that the island got its name from the fact that the only way that the original Portuguese colonizers were able to vanquish the indigenous population was by setting fire to the entire island and killing everyone on it, after which slaves were imported from Africa to cut the newly planted sugarcane.

Sir William Walker, played by Marlon Brando, is a nineteenth-century British agent sent to overthrow the Portuguese rulers of the island. He instigates a revolt amongst the numerous black slaves, and at the same time arranges an uprising by the small white colonial planter class seeking independence from the Portuguese crown. The goal is to use the slave revolt to defeat Portugal, but to turn actual rule of the island over to the white planter class, which will then serve as a comprador class subservient to British imperialists.

Walker succeeds brilliantly at his task, convincing the victorious army of former slaves and their leader José Dolores to lay down their arms after the Portuguese have been defeated. The result is a neocolony dominated by the white planters—but one in which the *de facto* rulers, in accordance with the laws of international free trade, are the British sugar companies. Walker then departs to carry out other intelligence tasks for the British admiralty—this time in a place called Indochina.

When the film resumes in 1848 ten years have passed. A revolution has again broken out on the island Burn led by José Dolores. Sir William Walker is brought back from England as a military advisor, but this time as an employee of the Antilles Royal Sugar Company, authorized by Her Majesty's government. His task is to defeat this new rebellion of the former slaves. He is told by the oligarchy ruling the island that this should not be difficult since only ten years have passed and the situation is the same. He replies that the situation may be the same but the problem is different. In words that seem to echo Karl Marx, he declares: "Very often between one historical period and another, ten years suddenly might be enough to reveal the contradictions of a whole century."

British troops are brought in to fight the insurgents, who are waging a relentless guerrilla war. To defeat them Walker orders the burning down of all the plantations on the island. When the local representative of the British sugar interests objects, Walker explains: "That is the logic of profit. . . . One builds to make money and to go on making it or to make more sometimes it is necessary to destroy." This, he reminds his interlocutor, is how the island Burn got its name. Nature on the island has to be destroyed, so that labor can be exploited on it for hundreds of additional years.

My intention here is not to recount the entirety of Pontecorvo's extraordinary film, but to draw out some important principles from this allegory that will help us to understand capitalism's relation to nature. Joseph Schumpeter famously praised capitalism for its "creative destruction."[2] But this might be better seen as the system's destructive creativity. Capital's endless pursuit of new outlets for class-based accumulation requires for its continuation the destruction of both pre-existing natural conditions and previous social relations. Class exploitation, imperialism, war, and ecological devastation are not mere unrelated accidents of history but interrelated, intrinsic features of capitalist development. There has always been the danger, moreover, that this destructive creativity would turn into what István Mészáros has called the "destructive uncontrollability" that is capital's ultimate destiny. The destruction built into the logic of profit would then take over and predominate, undermining not only the conditions of production but also those of life itself. Today, it is clear that such destructive uncontrollability has come to characterize the entire capitalist world economy, encompassing the planet as a whole.[3]

THE EARTH SUMMITS: 1992 AND 2002

It is a characteristic of our age that global ecological devastation seems to overwhelm all other problems, threatening the survival of life on earth as we know it. How this is related to social causes and what social solutions might be offered in response have thus become the most pressing questions facing humanity. The world has so far convened two major earth summits: in Rio de Janeiro, Brazil, in 1992 and Johannesburg, South Africa, in 2002. These summits took place a mere ten years apart. Yet they can be seen as lying in the dividing line separating one historical period from another, revealing the contradictions of an entire century—the twenty-first.

The 1992 Earth Summit in Rio, organized by the United Nations Conference on Environment and Development, represented the boundless hope that humanity could come together to solve its mounting global ecological problems. The late 1980s and early 1990s were a period in which the global ecological crisis penetrated the public consciousness. Suddenly, there were grave concerns about the destruction of the ozone layer, global warming, and the rising rate of species extinctions resulting from planetary destruction of ecosystems. In June 1988, James Hansen, Director of the NASA Goddard Institute for Space Studies, testified before the U.S. Senate Energy and Natural Resources Committee, presenting evidence of global warming due to the emission of carbon dioxide and other greenhouse gases into the atmosphere.

That same year, the United Nations set up a new international organization, the Intergovernmental Panel on Climate Change (IPCC), to address global warming.

A new ideology of world unity pervaded the Rio summit. The Gulf War of 1991 and the demise of the Soviet Union later in the same year had given rise to the then dominant rhetoric of a "new world order" and of "the end of history." The world, it was said, was now one. The recent passage of the Montreal Protocol, placing restrictions on the production of ozone-depleting chemicals, seemed to confirm that the world's economically dominant countries could act in unison in response to global environmental threats. The site chosen for the Earth Summit, Brazil, home to the Amazon, was meant to symbolize the planetary goal of saving the world's biodiversity. The summit's principal document, known as *Agenda 21,* was intended to launch a new age of sustainable development for the twenty-first century.

The mood of the second earth summit, the World Summit on Sustainable Development in Johannesburg, could not have been more different than the first. Rio's hope had given way to Johannesburg's dismay. Rather than improving over the decade that had elapsed, the world environment had experienced accelerated decline. The planet was approaching catastrophic conditions, not just with respect to global warming, but also in a host of other areas. Sustainable development had turned out to be about sustaining capital accumulation at virtually any ecological cost. All the rhetoric ten years earlier of a "new world order" and the "end of history"—it was now clear to many of the environmentalists attending the Johannesburg summit—had simply disguised the fact that the real nemesis of the global environment was the capitalist world economy.

The site of the Johannesburg summit had been chosen partly to symbolize the end of apartheid, and hence the advent of significant world social progress. Yet critics at the second summit raised the issue of global ecological apartheid, emphasizing the destruction wrought on the environment by the rich nations of the North in ways that disproportionately affected the global South. The ecological imperialism of the center of the capitalist world economy was symbolized by Washington's refusal to ratify the Kyoto Protocol on limiting greenhouse gas emissions generating global warming. Significantly, U.S. President George W. Bush declined to attend the Earth Summit. Instead, at the very moment that debates were taking place in Johannesburg on the future of the world's ecology, the Bush administration seized the world's stage by threatening a war on Iraq, ostensibly over weapons of mass destruction—though to the world's environmentalists assembled in Johannesburg it was clear even then that the real issue was oil.[4]

In fact, a new historical period had emerged in the ten years since the Rio summit. The world had witnessed what Paul Sweezy in 1994 called "the triumph of financial capitalism" with the transformation of monopoly capital into what might be called global monopoly-finance capital.[5] By the end of the twentieth century, capitalism had evolved into a system that was if anything more geared to rapacious accumulation than ever before, relatively independent from its local and national roots. Global financial expansion was occurring on top of a world economy that was stagnating at the level of production, creating a more unstable and more viciously inegalitarian order, dominated by neoliberal economics and financial bubbles. Declining U.S. hegemony in the world system, coupled with the demise of the Soviet Union, induced repeated and increasingly naked U.S. attempts to restore its economic and political power by military means.

Meanwhile, global warming and other crucial environmental problems had crossed critical thresholds. The question was no longer whether ecological and social catastrophes awaited but how great these would be. For those (including myself) in Johannesburg in 2002, watching the U.S. president prepare for war in the petroleum-rich Persian Gulf while the planet was heating up from the burning of fossil fuels, the whole world seemed on fire.

THE DESTRUCTION OF THE PLANET

In the years that have elapsed since the second earth summit it has become increasingly difficult to separate the class and imperial war inherent to capitalism from war on the planet itself. At a time when the

United States is battling for imperial control of the richest oil region on earth, the ecology of the planet is experiencing rapid deterioration, marked most dramatically by global warming. Meanwhile, the neoliberal economic restructuring emanating from the new regime of monopoly-finance capital is not only undermining the economic welfare of much of humanity, but is also, in some regions, removing such basic ecological conditions of human existence as access to clean air, drinkable water, and adequate food. Ecologists who once warned of the possibility of future apocalypse now insist that global disaster is on our doorstep.

Bill McKibben, author of *The End of Nature,* declared in his article "The Debate Is Over" in the November 17, 2005, issue of *Rolling Stone* magazine that we are now entering the "*Oh Shit*" era of global warming. At first, he wrote, there was the "*I wonder what will happen?*" era. Then there was the "*Can this really be true?*" era. Now we are in the *Oh Shit* era. We now know that it is too late to avert global disaster entirely. All we can do is limit its scope and intensity. Much of the uncertainty has to do with the fact that "the world . . . has some trapdoors—mechanisms that don't work in straightforward fashion, but instead trigger a nasty chain reaction."[6]

In his book, *The Revenge of Gaia,* influential scientist James Lovelock, best known as the originator of the Gaia hypothesis, has issued a grim assessment of the earth's prospects based on such sudden chain reactions.[7] Voicing the concerns of numerous scientists, Lovelock highlights a number of positive feedback mechanisms that could—and in his view almost certainly will—amplify the earth warming tendency. The destructive effect of increasing global temperatures on ocean algae and tropical forests (on top of the direct removal of these forests) will, it is feared, reduce the capacity of the oceans and forests to absorb carbon dioxide, raising the global temperature still further. The freeing up and release into the atmosphere of enormous quantities of methane (a greenhouse gas twenty-four times as potent as carbon dioxide) as the permafrost of the arctic tundra thaws due to global warming, constitutes another such vicious spiral. Just as ominous, the reduction of the earth's reflectivity as melting white ice at the poles is replaced with blue seawater is threatening to ratchet-up global temperatures.[8]

In Lovelock's cataclysmic view, the earth has probably already passed the point of no return and temperatures are destined to rise eventually as much as 8° C (14° F) in temperate regions. The human species will survive in some form, he assures us. Nevertheless, he points to "an imminent shift in our climate towards one that could easily be described as Hell: so hot, so deadly that only a handful of the teeming billions now alive will survive."[9] He offers, as the sole means of partial salvation, a massive technical fix: a global program to expand nuclear power facilities throughout the earth as a limited substitute to the carbon-dioxide-emitting fossil fuel economy. The thought that such a Faustian bargain would pave its own path to hell seems scarcely to have crossed his mind.

Lovelock's fears are not easily dismissed. James Hansen, who did so much to bring the issue of global warming to world attention, has recently issued his own warning. In an article entitled "The Threat to the Planet," Hansen points out that animal and plant species are migrating throughout the earth in response to global warming—though not fast enough in relation to changes in their environments—and that alpine species are being "pushed off the planet." We are facing, he contends, the possibility of mass extinctions associated with increasing global temperature, comparable to earlier periods in the earth's history in which 50 to 90 percent of living species were lost.

The greatest immediate threat to humanity from climate change, Hansen argues, is associated with the destabilization of the ice sheets in Greenland and Antarctica. A little more than 1° C (1.8° F) separates the climate of today from the warmest interglacial periods in the last half million years when the sea level was as much as sixteen feet higher. Further, increases in temperature this century by around 2.8° C (5° F), if business-as-usual continues, could lead to a long-term rise in sea level by as much as eighty feet, judging by what happened the last time the earth's temperature rose this high—three million years ago. "We have," Hansen says, "at most ten years—not ten years to decide upon action but ten years to alter fundamentally the trajectory of greenhouse gas emissions"—if we are to prevent such disastrous outcomes from becoming inevitable. One crucial decade, in other words, separates us from irreversible changes that could produce a very different world.

The contradictions of the entire Holocene—the geological epoch in which human civilization has developed—are suddenly being revealed in our time.[10]

In the *Oh shit* era, the debate, McKibben says, is over. There is no longer any doubt that global warming represents a crisis of earth-shaking proportions. Yet, it is absolutely essential to understand that this is only one part of what we call *the* environmental crisis. The global ecological threat as a whole is made up of a large number of interrelated crises and problems that are confronting us simultaneously. In my 1994 book, *The Vulnerable Planet*, I started out with a brief litany of some of these, to which others might now be added:

> Overpopulation, destruction of the ozone layer, global warming, extinction of species, loss of genetic diversity, acid rain, nuclear contamination, tropical deforestation, the elimination of climax forests, wetland destruction, soil erosion, desertification, floods, famine, the despoliation of lakes, streams, and rivers, the drawing down and contamination of ground water, the pollution of coastal waters and estuaries, the destruction of coral reefs, oil spills, overfishing, expanding landfills, toxic wastes, the poisonous effects of insecticides and herbicides, exposure to hazards on the job, urban congestion, and the depletion of nonrenewable resources.[11]

The point is that not just global warming but many of these other problems as well can each be seen as constituting a global ecological crisis. Today, every major ecosystem on the earth is in decline. Issues of environmental justice are becoming more prominent and pressing everywhere we turn. Underlying this is the fact that the class/imperial war that defines capitalism as a world system, and that governs its system of accumulation, is a juggernaut that knows no limits. In this deadly conflict the natural world is seen as a mere instrument of world social domination. Hence, capital by its very logic imposes what is in effect a scorched earth strategy. The planetary ecological crisis is increasingly all-encompassing, a product of the destructive uncontrollability of a rapidly globalizing capitalist economy, which knows no law other than its own drive to exponential expansion.

TRANSCENDING BUSINESS-AS-USUAL

Most climate scientists, including Lovelock and Hansen, follow the IPCC in basing their main projections of global warming on a socioeconomic scenario described as "business-as-usual." The dire trends indicated are predicated on our fundamental economic and technological developments and our basic relation to nature remaining the same. The question we need to ask then is what actually is business-as-usual? What can be changed and how fast? With time running out, the implication is that it is necessary to alter business-as-usual in radical ways in order to stave off or lessen catastrophe.

Yet the dominant solutions—those associated with the dominant ideology, i.e., the ideology of the dominant class—emphasize minimal changes in business-as-usual that will somehow get us off the hook. After being directed to the growing planetary threats of global warming and species extinction, we are told that the answer is better gas mileage and better emissions standards, the introduction of hydrogen-powered cars, the capture and sequestration of carbon dioxide within production, improved conservation, and voluntary cutbacks in consumption. Environmental political scientists specialize in the construction of new environmental policy regimes, embodying state and market regulations. Environmental economists talk of tradable pollution permits and the incorporation of all environmental factors into the market to ensure their efficient use. Some environmental sociologists (my own field) speak of ecological modernization: a panoply of green taxes, green regulations, and new green technologies, even the greening of capitalism itself. Futurists describe a new technological world in which the weight of nations on the earth is miraculously lifted as a result of digital "dematerialization" of the economy. In all of these views, however, there is one constant: the fundamental character of business-as-usual is hardly changed at all.

Indeed, what all such analyses intentionally avoid is the fact that business-as-usual in our society, in any fundamental sense, means the capitalist economy—an economy run on the logic of profit and accumulation. Moreover, there is little acknowledgement or even appreciation of the fact that the Hobbesian war of all against all that characterizes capitalism requires for its fulfillment a universal war on nature. In this sense, new technology cannot solve the problem since it is inevitably used to further the class war and to increase the scale of the economy, and thus the degradation of the environment. Whenever production dies down or social resistance imposes barriers on the expansion of capital, the answer is always to find new ways to exploit and degrade nature more intensively. To quote, once again, Pontecorvo's *Burn!*: "That is the logic of profit. . . . One builds to make money and to go on making it or to make more sometimes it is necessary to destroy."

Ironically, this destructive relation of capitalism to the environment was probably understood better in the nineteenth century—at a time when social analysts were acutely aware of the issue of revolutionary changes taking place in the mode of production and how this was transforming the human relation to nature. As a result, environmental sociologists of the more radical stamp in the United States, where the contradiction between economy and ecology nowadays is especially acute, draw heavily on three interrelated ideas derived from Marx and the critique of capitalist political economy dating back to the nineteenth century: (1) the treadmill of production; (2) the second contradiction of capitalism; and (3) the metabolic rift.

The first of these, the *treadmill of production*, describes capitalism as an unstoppable, accelerating treadmill that constantly increases the scale of the throughput of energy and raw materials as part of its quest for profit and accumulation, thereby pressing on the earth's absorptive capacity. "Accumulate, Accumulate!" For capital, Marx wrote, "that is Moses and the prophets!"[12]

The second of these notions, the *second contradiction of capitalism*, is the idea that capitalism, in addition to its primary economic contradiction stemming from class inequalities in production and distribution, also undermines the human and natural conditions (i.e., environmental conditions) of production on which its economic advancement ultimately rests. For example, by systematically removing forests we lay the grounds for increasing scarcities in this area—the more so to the extent that globalization makes this contradiction universal. This heightens the overall cost of economic development and creates an economic crisis for capitalism based on supply-side constraints on production.[13]

The third notion, the *metabolic rift*, suggests that the logic of capital accumulation inexorably creates a rift in the metabolism between society and nature, severing basic processes of natural reproduction. This raises the issue of the ecological sustainability—not simply in relation to the scale of the economy, but also, and even more importantly, in the form and intensity of the interaction between nature and society under capitalism.[14]

I shall concentrate on the third of these notions, the metabolic rift, since this is the most complex of these three socio-ecological concepts, and the one that has been the focus of my own research in this area, particularly in my book *Marx's Ecology*. Marx was greatly influenced by the work of the leading agricultural chemist of his time, Justus von Liebig. Liebig had developed an analysis of the ecological contradictions of industrialized capitalist agriculture. He argued that such industrialized agriculture, as present in its most developed form in England in the nineteenth century, was a robbery system, depleting the soil. Food and fiber were transported hundreds—even in some cases thousands—of miles from the country to the city. This meant that essential soil nutrients, such as nitrogen, phosphorus, and potassium, were transported as well. Rather than being returned to the soil these essential nutrients ended up polluting the cities, for example, in the degradation of the Thames in London. The natural conditions for the reproduction of the soil were thus destroyed.

To compensate for the resulting decline in soil fertility the British raided the Napoleonic battlefields and the catacombs of Europe for bones with which to fertilize the soil of the English countryside. They also resorted to the importation of guano on a vast scale from the islands off the coast of Peru, followed by the importation of Chilean nitrates (after the War of the Pacific in which Chile seized parts of Peru and Bolivia rich in guano and nitrates). The United States sent out ships throughout the oceans searching for guano, and ended up seizing ninety-four islands, rocks, and keys between the passage of the 1856 Guano Islands Act and 1903, sixty-six of which were officially recognized as U.S. appurtenances and nine of which remain U.S. possessions today.[15] This reflected a great crisis of capitalist agriculture in the nineteenth century that was only solved in part with the development of synthetic fertilizer nitrogen early in the twentieth century—and which led eventually to the overuse of fertilizer nitrogen, itself a major environmental problem.

In reflecting on this crisis of capitalist agriculture, Marx adopted the concept of metabolism, which had been introduced by nineteenth-century biologists and chemists, including Liebig, and applied it to socio-ecological relations. All life is based on metabolic processes between organisms and their environment. Organisms carry out an exchange of energy and matter with their environment, which are integrated with their own internal life processes. It is not a stretch to think of the nest of a bird as part of the bird's metabolic process. Marx explicitly defined the labor process as the "metabolic interaction between man and nature." In terms of the ecological problem, he spoke of "an irreparable rift in the interdependent process of social metabolism," whereby the conditions for the necessary reproduction of the soil were continually severed, breaking the metabolic cycle. "Capitalist production," he wrote, "therefore only develops the techniques and the degree of combination of the social process of production by simultaneously undermining the original sources of all wealth—the soil and the worker." Marx saw this rift not simply in national terms but as related to imperialism as well. "England," he wrote, "has indirectly exported the soil of Ireland, without even allowing its cultivators the means for replacing the constituents of the exhausted soil."

This principle of metabolic rift obviously has a very wide application and has in fact been applied by environmental sociologists in recent years to problems such as global warming and the ecological degradation of the world's oceans.[16] What is seldom recognized, however, is that Marx went immediately from a conception of the metabolic rift to the necessity of *metabolic restoration*, arguing that "by destroying the circumstances surrounding that metabolism, which originated in a merely natural and spontaneous fashion, it [capitalist production] compels its systematic restoration as a regulative law of social reproduction." The reality of the metabolic rift pointed to the necessity of the restoration of nature, through sustainable production.

It is this dialectical understanding of the socio-ecological problem that led Marx to what is perhaps the most radical conception of socio-ecological sustainability ever developed. Thus, he wrote in the third volume of *Capital*:

> From the standpoint of a higher socio-economic formation, the private property of individuals in the earth will appear just as absurd as the private property of one man in other men. Even an entire society, a nation, or all simultaneously existing societies taken together, are not owners of the earth. They are simply its possessors, its beneficiaries, and have to bequeath it in an improved state to succeeding generations, as *boni patres familias* [good heads of the household].

For Marx, in other words, the present relation of human beings to the earth under private accumulation could be compared to slavery. Just as "private property of one man in other men" is no longer deemed acceptable, so private ownership of the earth and nature by human beings (even whole countries) must be transcended. The human relation to nature must be regulated so to guarantee its existence "in an improved state to succeeding generations." His reference to the notion of "good heads of the household" hearkened back to the ancient Greek notion of household or *oikos* from which we get both "economy" (from *oikonomia* or household management) and "ecology" (from *oikologia* or household study). Marx pointed to the necessity of a more radical, sustainable relation of human beings to production in accord with what we would now view as ecological rather than merely economic notions. "Freedom, in this sphere," the realm of natural necessity, he insisted, "can consist only in this, that socialized man, the associated producers, govern the human metabolism with nature in a rational way, bringing it under their collective control . . . accomplishing it with the least expenditure of energy."[17]

The destructive uncontrollability of capitalism, emanating from its dual character as a system of class and imperial exploitation and as an enslaver and destroyer of the earth itself, was thus well understood by Marx. With regard to the film, *Burn!*, we saw how the exploitation of human beings was tied to the destruction of the earth. Relations of domination changed but the answer remained the same: to burn the island as a means of winning the class/imperial war. Today, a few hundred people taken together own more wealth than the income of billions of the world's population. To maintain this system of global inequality a global system of repression has been developed and is constantly put in motion. And, along with it, vast new systems of destructive exploitation of the earth, such as modern agribusiness, have evolved.

SOCIAL REVOLUTION AND METABOLIC RESTORATION

Pontecorvo's film *Burn!*, about revolution in the Caribbean, reaches its climax in the year 1848, a revolutionary year in real-world history. In 1848, Marx famously observed in his speech on free trade: "You believe perhaps, gentlemen, that the production of coffee and sugar is the natural destiny of the West Indies. Two centuries ago, nature, which does not trouble herself about commerce, had planted neither sugarcane nor coffee trees there."[18] Much of what we take as natural is the product of capitalism. Indeed, we are brought up believing that capitalist market relations are more natural, more incontrovertible, than anything within nature. It is this way of thinking that we have to break with, if we are to restore our relation to the earth: if we are to invert the metabolic rift. The only answer to the ecology of destruction of capitalism is to revolutionize our productive relations in ways that allow for a metabolic restoration. But this will require a break with capitalism's own system of "socio-metabolic reproduction," i.e., the logic of profit.[19]

What such a revolutionary break with today's business-as-usual offers is, of course, no guarantee but the mere possibility of social and ecological transformation through the creation of a sustainable, egalitarian and socialist society. Lovelock's "revenge of Gaia"—what Frederick Engels in the nineteenth century called the "revenge" of nature, now writ large on a planetary scale—will not be automatically overcome simply through a rupture with the logic of the existing system.[20] Yet such a rupture remains the necessary first step in any rational attempt to save and advance human civilization. Burn is no longer an island; it stands for the entire world, which is heating up before our eyes.

At the end of Pontecorvo's film, José Dolores is killed, but his revolutionary spirit lives on. The strategy of destroying nature to enslave humanity, we are led to believe, will not work forever. Today, Latin America is reawakening to the revolutionary spirit of Bolivar and Che—a spirit that has never perished. But we now know—what was seldom understood before—that a revolutionary transformation of society must also be a revolutionary restoration of our metabolic relation to nature: equality and sustainability must coevolve if either is to emerge triumphant. And if we are to survive.

CHAPTER TWO

Ecology: The Moment of Truth

It is impossible to exaggerate the environmental problem facing humanity in the twenty-first century. Nearly fifteen years ago one observer noted: "We have only four decades left in which to gain control over our major environmental problems if we are to avoid irreversible ecological decline."[1] Today, with a quarter-century still remaining in this projected timeline, this appears to have been too optimistic. Available evidence now strongly suggests that, under a regime of business-as-usual, we could be facing an irrevocable "tipping point" with respect to climate change within a mere decade.[2] Other crises—such as species extinction;[3] the rapid depletion of the oceans' bounty; desertification; deforestation; air pollution; water shortages and pollution; soil degradation; the imminent peaking of world oil production (creating new geopolitical tensions); and a chronic world food crisis—all point to the fact that the planet as we know it and its ecosystems are stretched to the breaking point. The moment of truth for the earth and human civilization has arrived.

To be sure, it is unlikely that the effects of ecological degradation in our time, though enormous, will prove "apocalyptic" for human civilization within a single generation, even under conditions of capitalist business-as-usual. Measured by normal human life spans, there is doubtless considerable time still left before the full effect of the current human degradation of the planet comes into play. Yet the period remaining in which we can *avert* future environmental catastrophe, before it is essentially out of our hands, is much shorter. Indeed, the growing sense of urgency of environmentalists has to do with the prospect of various tipping points being reached as critical ecological thresholds are crossed, leading to the possibility of a drastic contraction of life on earth.

Such a tipping point, for example, would be an ice-free Arctic, which could happen within two decades or less (some scientists believe as early as 2013). Already, in summer 2007, the Arctic lost *in a single week* an area of ice almost twice the size of Britain. The vanishing Arctic ice cap means an enormous reduction in the earth's reflectivity (albedo), thereby sharply increasing global warming (a positive feedback known as the "albedo flip"). At the same time, the rapid disintegration of the ice sheets in West Antarctica and Greenland points to rising world sea levels, threatening coastal regions and islands.[4]

In 2008, James Hansen, director of NASA's Goddard Institute for Space Studies and the leading U.S. climatologist, captured the state of the existing "planetary emergency," with respect to climate change:

> Our home planet is dangerously near a tipping point at which human-made greenhouse gases reach a level where major climate changes can proceed mostly under their own momentum. Warming will shift climatic zones by intensifying the hydrologic cycle, affecting freshwater availability and human health. We will see repeated coastal tragedies associated with storms and continuously rising sea levels. The implications are profound, and the only resolution is for humans to move to a fundamentally different energy pathway within a decade. Otherwise, it will be too late for one-third of the world's animal and plant species and millions of the most vulnerable members of our own species.[5]

According to environmentalist Lester Brown in his *Plan B 3.0*: "We are crossing natural thresholds that we cannot see and violating deadlines that we do not recognize. Nature is the time keeper, but we cannot see the clock. . . . We are in a race between tipping points in the earth's natural systems and those in the world's political systems. Which will tip first?"[6] As the clock continues to tick and little is accomplished, it is obvious that decisive and far-reaching changes are required to stave off ultimate disaster. This raises the question of more revolutionary social change as an ecological as well as social necessity.

Yet, if revolutionary solutions are increasingly required to address the ecological problem, this is precisely what the existing social system is guaranteed *not* to deliver. Today's environmentalism is aimed principally at those measures necessary to lessen the impact of the economy on the planet's ecology *without* challenging the economic system that in its very workings produces the immense environmental problems we now face. What we call "*the* environmental problem" is in the end primarily a problem of political economy. Even the boldest establishment economic attempts to address climate change fall far short of what is required to protect the earth—since the "bottom line" that constrains all such plans under capitalism is the necessity of continued, rapid growth in production and profits.

THE DOMINANT ECONOMICS OF CLIMATE CHANGE

The economic constraint on environmental action can easily be seen by looking at what is widely regarded as the most far-reaching establishment attempt to date to deal with *The Economics of Climate Change* in the form of a massive study issued in 2007 under that title, commissioned by the UK Treasury Office.[7] Subtitled the *Stern Review*, after the report's principal author Nicholas Stern, a former chief economist of the World Bank, it is widely viewed as the most important and most progressive mainstream treatment of the economics of global warming.[8] The *Stern Review* focuses on the target level of carbon dioxide equivalent (CO_{2e}) concentration in the atmosphere necessary to stabilize global average temperature at no more than 3°C (5.4°F) over pre-industrial levels. (CO_{2e} refers to the six Kyoto greenhouse gases—carbon dioxide [CO_2], methane, nitrous oxide, hydrofluorocarbons, perfluorocarbons, and sulfur hexafluoride—all expressed in terms of the equivalent amount of CO_2. While CO_2 concentration in the atmosphere today is 387 parts per million [ppm], CO_{2e} is around 430 ppm.)

The goal proposed by most climatologists has been to try to prevent increases in global temperature of more than 2°C (3.6°F) above pre-industrial levels, requiring stabilization of atmospheric CO_{2e} at 450 ppm. Beyond that level all sorts of positive feedbacks and tipping points are likely to come into play, leading to an uncontrollable acceleration of climate change. Indeed, James Hansen and other climatologists at NASA's Goddard Institute for Space Studies have recently argued: "If humanity wishes to preserve a planet similar to that on which civilization developed and to which life on Earth is adapted, paleoclimate evidence and ongoing climate change suggest that CO_2 will need to be reduced from its current 385 ppm to at most 350 ppm."[9] The *Stern Review*, however, settles instead for a global average temperature increase of no more than 3°C (a threshold beyond which the environmental effects would undoubtedly be absolutely calamitous), which it estimates can likely be achieved if CO_{2e} in the atmosphere were stabilized at 550 ppm, roughly double pre-industrial levels.

Yet the *Stern Review* acknowledges that current environmental sensitivities "imply that there is up to a one-in-five chance that the world would experience a warming in excess of 3°C above pre-industrial [levels] even if greenhouse gas concentrations were stabilised at today's level of 430 ppm CO_{2e}." Moreover, it goes on to admit that "for stabilisation at 550 ppm CO_{2e}, the chance of exceeding 3°C rises to 30–70%." Or as it states further on, a 550 ppm CO_{2e} suggests "a 50:50 chance of a temperature increase above or below 3°C, and the Hadley Centre model predicts a 10% chance of exceeding 5°C [9°F] even at this level." A 3°C increase would bring the earth's average global temperature to a height last seen in the "middle Pliocene around 3 million years ago." Furthermore, such an increase might be enough, the *Stern Review* explains, to trigger a shutdown of the ocean's thermohaline circulation that warms Western Europe, creating abrupt climate change, and thereby plunging Western Europe into Siberian-like conditions. Other research suggests that water flow in the Indus may drop by 90 percent by 2100 if global average temperatures rise by 3°C, potentially affecting hundreds of millions of people. Studies by climatologists indicate that at 550 ppm CO_{2e} there is more than a 5 percent chance that global average temperature could rise in excess of 8°C (14.4°F). All of this suggests that a stabilization target of 550 ppm CO_{2e} could be disastrous for the earth, as we know it, as well as for its people.

Why then, if the risks to the planet and civilization are so enormous, does the *Stern Review* emphasize attempting to keep global warming at 3°C by stabilizing CO_{2e} at 550 ppm (what it describes at one point as "the upper limit to the stabilisation range")? To answer this it is necessary to turn to some additional facts of a more economic nature.

Here it is useful to note that an atmospheric concentration level close to 550 ppm CO_{2e} would result by 2050, if greenhouse gas emissions simply continued at present levels without any increases in the intervening years. However, as the *Stern Review* itself notes, this is unrealistic, under business-as-usual, since global greenhouse gas emissions can be expected to continue to increase on a "rapidly rising trajectory." Hence, an atmospheric CO_{2e} level of 550 ppm, under more realistic assumptions, would be plausibly reached by 2035. This would increase the threat of 750 ppm CO_{2e} (or more) and a rise in global average temperature in excess of 4.3°C (7.7°F) within the next few decades after that. (Indeed, IPCC scenarios include the possibility that atmospheric carbon could rise to 1,200 ppm and global average temperature by as much as 6.3°C [11.3°F] by 2100.)

To counter this business-as-usual scenario, the *Stern Review* proposes a climate stabilization regime in which greenhouse gas emissions would peak by 2015 and then drop 1 percent per year after that, so as to stabilize at a 550 ppm CO_{2e} (with a significant chance that the global average temperature increase would thereby be kept down to 3°C).

But, given the enormous dangers, why not aim at deeper cuts in greenhouse gas emissions, a lower level of atmospheric CO_{2e} and a smaller increase in global average temperature? After all, most climatologists have been calling for the stabilization of atmospheric CO_{2e} at 450 ppm or less, keeping the global temperature increase at about 2°C above pre-industrial levels. Hansen and his colleagues at NASA's Goddard Institute have now gone even further, arguing that the target should be 350 ppm CO_2.

The *Stern Review* is very explicit, however, that such a radical mitigation of the problem *should not be attempted*. The costs to the world economy of ensuring that atmospheric CO_{2e} stabilized at present levels or below would be prohibitive, destabilizing capitalism itself. "Paths requiring very rapid emissions cuts," we are told, "are unlikely to be economically viable." If global greenhouse gas emissions peaked in 2010, the annual emissions reduction rate necessary to stabilize atmospheric carbon at 450 ppm, the *Stern Review* suggests, would be 7 percent, with emissions dropping by about 70 percent below 2005 levels by 2050. This is viewed as economically insupportable.

Hence, the *Stern Review*'s own preferred scenario, as indicated, is a 550 ppm target that would see global greenhouse gas emissions peak in 2015, with the emission cuts that followed at a rate of 1 percent per year. By 2050 the reduction in the overall level of emissions (from 2005 levels) in this scenario would only be 25 percent. (The report also considers, with less enthusiasm, an in-between 500 ppm target, peaking in 2010 and requiring a 3 percent annual drop in global emissions.) Only the 550 ppm target, the *Stern Review* suggests, is truly economically viable because "it is difficult to secure emission cuts faster than about 1% per year except in instances of recession" or as the result of a major social upheaval, such as the collapse of the Soviet Union.

Indeed, the only actual example that the *Stern Review* is able to find of a sustained annual cut in greenhouse gas emissions of 1 percent or more, coupled with economic growth, among leading capitalist states was the United Kingdom in 1990–2000. Due to the discovery of North Sea oil and natural gas, the United Kingdom was able to switch massively from coal to gas in power generation, resulting in a 1 percent average annual drop in its greenhouse gas emissions during that decade. France came close to such a 1 percent annual drop in 1977–2003, reducing its greenhouse gas emissions by .6 percent per year due to a massive switch to nuclear power. By far the biggest drop for a major state was the 5.2 percent per year reduction in greenhouse gas emissions in the former Soviet Union in 1989–98. This, however, went hand in hand with a social-system breakdown and a drastic shrinking of the economy. All of this signals that any reduction in CO_{2e} emissions beyond around 1 percent per year would make it virtually impossible to maintain strong economic growth— the bottom line of the capitalist economy. Consequently, in order to keep the treadmill of profit and production going the world needs to risk environmental Armageddon.[10]

ACCUMULATION AND THE PLANET

None of this should surprise us. Capitalism since its birth, as Paul Sweezy wrote in "Capitalism and the Environment," has been "a juggernaut driven by the concentrated energy of individuals and small groups single-mindedly pursuing their own interests, checked only by their mutual competition, and controlled in the short run by the impersonal forces of the market and in the longer run, when the market fails, by devastating crises." The inner logic of such a system manifests itself in the form of an incessant drive for economic expansion for the sake of class-based profits and accumulation. Nature and human labor are exploited to the fullest to fuel this juggernaut, while the destruction wrought on each is externalized so as to not fall on the system's own accounts.

"Implicit in the very concept of this system," Sweezy continued, "are interlocked and enormously powerful drives to both creation and destruction. On the plus side, the creative drive relates to what humankind can get out of nature for its own uses; on the negative side, the destructive drive bears most heavily on nature's capacity to respond to the demands placed on it. Sooner or later, of course, these two drives are contradictory and incompatible." Capitalism's overexploitation of nature's resource taps and waste sinks eventually produces the negative result of undermining both, first on a merely regional, but later on a world and even planetary basis (affecting the climate itself). Seriously addressing environmental crises requires "a reversal, not merely a slowing down, of the underlying trends of the last few centuries." This, however, cannot be accomplished without economic regime change.[11]

With climate change now more and more an establishment concern, and attempts to avert it now increasingly institutionalized in the established order, some have pointed to the "death of environmentalism" as an oppositional movement in society.[12] However, if some environmentalists have moved toward capitalist-based strategies in the vain hope of saving the planet by these means, others have moved in the opposite direction: toward a critique of capitalism as inherently ecologically destructive. A case in point is James Gustave Speth. Speth has been called the "ultimate insider" within the environmental movement. He served as chairman of the Council on Environmental Quality under President Jimmy Carter, founded the World Resources Institute, co-founded the Natural Resources Defense Council, was a senior adviser in Bill Clinton's transition team, and administered the United Nations Development Programme from 1993 to 1999. At present, he is dean of the prestigious Yale School of Forestry and Environmental Studies. Speth is a winner of Japan's Blue Planet Prize.

Recently, however, in his *Bridge at the Edge of the World: Capitalism, the Environment, and Crossing from Crisis to Sustainability,* Speth has emerged as a devastating critic of capitalism's destruction of the environment. In this radical rethinking, he has chosen to confront the full perils brought on by the present economic system, with its pursuit of growth and accumulation at any cost. "Capitalism as we know it today," he writes, "is incapable of sustaining the environment." The crucial problem from an environmental perspective, he believes, is exponential economic growth, which is the driving element of capitalism. Little hope can be provided in this respect by so-called "dematerialization" (the notion that growth can involve a decreasing impact on the environment), since it can be shown that the expansion of output overwhelms all increases in efficiency in throughput of materials and energy. Hence, one can only conclude that "right now . . . growth is the enemy of [the] environment. Economy and environment remain in collision." Here, the issue of capitalism becomes unavoidable. "Economic growth is modern capitalism's principal and most prized product." Speth favorably quotes Samuel Bowles and Richard Edwards's *Understanding Capitalism,* which bluntly stated: "Capitalism is differentiated from other economic systems by its drive to accumulate, its predisposition toward change, and its built-in tendency to expand."

The principal environmental problem for Speth then is capitalism as the "operating system" of the modern economy. "Today's corporations have been called 'externalizing machines.'" Indeed, "there are fundamental biases in capitalism that favor the present over the future and the private over the public." Quoting the system's own defenders, Paul Samuelson and William Nordhaus, in the seventeenth edition of their textbook on *Macroeconomics,* Speth points out that capitalism is the quintessential "Ruthless Economy," engaged "in the relentless pursuit of profits."

Building on this critique, Speth goes on to conclude in his book that: (1) "today's system of political economy, referred to here as modern capitalism, is destructive of the environment, and not in a minor way but in a way that profoundly threatens the planet"; (2) "the affluent societies have reached or soon will reach the point where, as Keynes put it, the economic problem has been solved . . . there is enough to go around"; (3) "in the more affluent societies, modern capitalism is no longer enhancing human well-being"; (4) "the international social movement for change—which refers to itself as 'the irresistible rise of global anti-capitalism'—is stronger than many imagine and will grow stronger; there is a coalescing of forces: peace, social justice, community, ecology, feminism—a movement of movements"; (5) "people and groups are busily planting the seeds of change through a host of alternative arrangements, and still other attractive directions for upgrading to a new operating system have been identified"; and (6) "the end of the Cold War . . . opens the door . . . for the questioning of today's capitalism."

Speth does not actually embrace socialism, which he associates, in the Cold War manner, with Soviet-type societies in their most regressive form. Thus, he argues explicitly for a "nonsocialist" alternative to capitalism. Such a system would make use of markets (but not the self-regulating market society of traditional capitalism) and would promote a "New Sustainability World" or a "Social Greens World" (also called "Eco-Communalism") as depicted by the Global Scenario Group. The latter scenario has been identified with radical thinkers like William Morris (who was inspired by both Marx and Ruskin). In this sense, Speth's arguments are not far from that of the socialist movement of the twenty-first century, which is aimed at the core values of social justice and ecological sustainability. The object is to create a future in which generations still to come will be able to utilize their creative abilities to the fullest, while having their basic needs met: a result made possible only through the rational reorganization by the associated producers of the human metabolism with nature.[13]

Such rational reorganization of the metabolism between nature and society needs to be directed not simply at climate change but also at a whole host of other environmental problems. No single issue captures the depth and breadth of what we call "the environmental problem," which encompasses all of these ecological contradictions of our society and more. If we are facing a "moment of truth" with respect to ecology

today, it has to do with the entire gamut of capitalism's effects on natural
(and human) reproduction. Any attempt to solve one of these problems
(such as climate change) without addressing the others is likely to fail,
since these ecological crises, although distinct in various ways, typically
share common causes. Only a unified vision that sees human production
as not only social, but also rooted in a metabolic relation to nature, will
provide the necessary basis to confront an ecological rift that is now as
wide as the planet.

WHY NOT?

In 1884, William Morris, one of the great creative artists, revolutionary
socialist intellectuals, and environmental thinkers of the late nineteenth
century, wrote an article entitled "Why Not?" for the socialist journal
Commonweal. He was especially concerned with the fact that most people, including many socialists in his time, in rebelling against the evils of
capitalism, tended to picture the future in terms that were not that far
removed from many of the worst, most environmentally and humanly
destructive, aspects of capitalism itself. "Now under the present Capitalist
system," Morris observed,

> it is difficult to see anything which might stop the growth of these horri-
> ble brick encampments; its tendency is undoubtedly to depopulate the
> country and small towns for the advantage of the great commercial and
> manufacturing centres; but this evil, and it is a monstrous one, will be no
> longer a necessary evil when we have got rid of land monopoly, manufac-
> turing for the profit of individuals, and the stupid waste of competitive
> distribution.

Looking beyond the "terror and the grinding toil" in which most people were oppressed, Morris argued, there was a need to recognize other
ends of social existence: most notably "the pleasure of life to be looked
forward to by Socialists." "Why," he asked:

> should one third of England be so stifled and poisoned with smoke that
> over the greater part of Yorkshire (for instance) the general idea must be

that sheep are naturally black? And why must Yorkshire and Lancashire rivers run mere filth and dye?

Profits will have it so: no one any longer pretends that it would not be easy to prevent such crimes against decent life: but the 'organizers of labour,' who might better be called 'organizers of filth,' know that it wouldn't pay; and as they are for the most part of the year safe in their country seats, or shooting—crofters' lives—in the Highlands, or yachting in the Mediterranean, they rather like the look of the smoke country for a change as something, it is to be supposed, stimulating to their imaginations concerning—well, we must not get theological.

In rejecting all of this, Morris asked was it not possible to create a more decent, more beautiful, more fulfilling, more healthy, less hell-like way of living, in which all had a part in the "share of earth the Common Mother" and the sordid world of "profit-grinding" was at last brought to an end? Why not?[14]

CHAPTER THREE

Rachel Carson's Ecological Critique

Rachel Carson was born just over one hundred years ago in 1907. Her most famous book, *Silent Spring,* published in 1962, is often seen as marking the birth of the modern environmental movement. Although an immense amount has been written about Carson and her work, the fact that she was objectively a "woman of the left" has often been downplayed. Today, the rapidly accelerating planetary ecological crisis, which she more than anyone else alerted us to, calls for an exploration of the full critical nature of her thought and its relation to the larger revolt within science with which she was associated.

Carson was first and foremost a naturalist and scientist. But she was propelled by her understanding of the destructive ecological forces at work in modern society into the role of radical critic. A recent biography attempts to capture this in its title: *The Gentle Subversive.* The principal causes of ecological degradation, Carson insisted, were "the gods of profit and production." The chief obstacle to a sustainable relation to the environment lay in the fact that we live "in an era dominated by industry, in which the right to make a dollar at any cost is seldom challenged."[1]

Silent Spring was directed against the chemical industry and its production of deadly pesticides. Carson combined the best scientific information then available with the skills of a great writer, and had an extraordinary effect in raising public concern over this issue. Yet, despite a number of victories, Carson and those who followed in her footsteps lost the war against synthetic pesticides, which she preferred to call "biocides." Although she conceded that there were some situations where the application of such chemicals might be appropriate, she strongly believed "the elimination of the use of persistent toxic pesticides should be the goal"— as stated in the 1963 report on pesticides of the President's Science Advisory Committee, which she regarded as a "vindication" of her views. Chemical control needed to be replaced wherever practicable by biological control (organic methods relying on natural enemies of the pests). She called this, in the concluding chapter of her book, "The Other Road." Nevertheless, except for the banning of a few of the most deadly toxins such as DDT, the chemical industry triumphed, seeing an expansion of the production of this class of chemicals.[2]

This growing use of synthetic pesticides had nothing to do with the rational application of science. Although the chemical industry and their allies attempted to demonstrate that Carson made mistakes and exaggerated the dangers of pesticides in her arguments, her research has generally stood the test of time. Moreover, the questions she raised about the accumulation of these dangerous chemicals in living organisms are today even more relevant. She was especially concerned about the long-term, widespread effects of such biocides, which were being used in ever greater quantities, were persistent in the environment, and drifted uncontrollably, often concentrating in organisms in areas far removed from the point of introduction. She accurately predicted that dependence on synthetic pesticides would result in a pesticide treadmill as organisms evolved rapidly into more resistant forms requiring either higher doses or new biocides. "The chemical war," she wrote, "is never won, and all life is caught in its violent crossfire."

By the late 1980s, the production of pesticide active ingredients, much of it destined for U.S. farms, had increased to more than twice that of the early 1960s when Carson wrote *Silent Spring*. In 1999, over one hundred million U.S. households applied some type of pesticide to their homes, lawns, and gardens. Many such chemicals on the market today have not been adequately tested. Meanwhile U.S. agribusiness has continued to produce and export banned pesticides to other countries. Some of the food imported to the United States from abroad is grown using these substances.

In the last decade and a half, the main focus of concern with regard to pesticides and related chemicals has shifted from cancer and the potential for genetic mutations—both of which remain among the biggest dangers of these chemicals—to the disruption of the endocrine system, affecting a myriad of bodily functions. Numerous pesticides mimic the female hormone estrogen, and research has suggested that they can reduce fertility, produce testicular and breast cancer, and malform the genital organs. Serious questions are being raised about the complex and still little understood effects of these chemicals on animal and human reproductive systems. Between the early 1970s and the early 1990s the incidence of testicular cancer in the United States increased by about 50 percent; while the last half-century or so has seen a drop worldwide in sperm counts by about 50 percent.

Attention has also turned to other synthetic chemicals introduced into the environment in countless products. Over seventy thousand synthetic chemicals are used in commerce, while only 10 to 20 percent of these chemicals have been systematically tested. The failure to adequately test or limit the use of such chemicals more than forty-five years after the publication of *Silent Spring* makes Carson's book of continuing importance for that reason alone.[3]

But Carson's attack on synthetic pesticides is not her most notable achievement. Rather it is her wider, ecological critique, challenging the whole nature of our society, which is so important today. Carson is better understood if we recognize that she was not simply an isolated figure as is often supposed, but was part of a larger revolt among scientists and left thinkers in the 1950s and 1960s arising initially from concerns over the effects of nuclear radiation. Alarm about aboveground nuclear tests and the harmful effects of radiation, coupled with fears of nuclear war, spurred scientists, emanating primarily from the left, to raise searching questions about the destructiveness of our civilization. From this work, the modern ecology movement emerged.

RADIATION AND ECOLOGY

Carson's discussions of the effects of pesticides on living things drew heavily upon earlier discoveries by scientists regarding radiation. She repeatedly referred, in *Silent Spring* and elsewhere, to the breakthroughs in the 1920s of the U.S. geneticist H. J. Muller, who was the first to discover that exposure of organisms to radiation could generate genetic mutations. As she explained to the National Council of Women of the United States in October 1962, two weeks after the publication of her book:

> When I was a graduate student at Johns Hopkins University, studying under the great geneticist H. S. Jennings, the whole biological community was stirring with excitement over the recent discovery of another distinguished geneticist, Professor H. J. Muller, then at the University of Texas. Professor Muller had found that by exposing organisms to radiation he could produce those sudden changes in hereditary characteristics that biologists call mutations.
>
> Before this it had been assumed that the germ cells were immutable—immune to influences in the environment. Muller's discovery meant that it was possible for many, by accident or design, to change the course of heredity, although the nature of the changes could not be controlled.
>
> It was much later that two Scottish investigators discovered that certain chemicals have a similar power to produce mutations and in other ways to imitate radiation. This was before the days of the modern synthetic pesticides, and the chemical used in these experiments was mustard gas. But over the years it has been learned that one after another of the chemicals used as insecticides or as weed-killers has power to produce mutations in the organisms tested or to change or damage the chromosome structure in some other way.[4]

As Carson observed in *Silent Spring*, "among the herbicides are some that are classified as 'mutagens,' or agents capable of modifying the genes, the materials of heredity. We are rightly appalled by the genetic effects of radiation; how, then, can we be indifferent to the same effect in chemicals that we disseminate widely in our environment?"[5]

Muller, who was to be awarded the Nobel Prize in physiology or medicine in 1946 for his discoveries, was a complex figure, who had a long history as a socialist and a critic of capitalism. He had been a faculty adviser to the Texas branch of the National Student League in the early

1930s and helped in the sponsoring and editing of its publication *Spark*, named after Lenin's *Iskra*. Muller went to the Soviet Union in 1933 to work in the advanced genetic laboratories there, but came into conflict with the regime in the context of the Lysenko controversy and ran directly afoul of Stalin. He served in the international brigades in the Spanish Civil War and worked with the Canadian doctor Norman Bethune, later a hero of Mao's China.

Although Muller was to become a very strong opponent of the Soviet Union under Stalin (due to the closing down of the genetic institute he had helped set up and the murder of some of his close friends and colleagues), he retained many of his critical beliefs, including faith in socialism. He held on to his earlier dialectical understanding that emphasized "the complicated processes ('movements' in the Marxian sense) whereby . . . objects are interrelated to one another and undergo their development"; such a dialectical approach he argued was crucial to the "realization of the complex realities of matter, especially of living matter, of its inter-connectedness."[6]

The receipt of the Nobel Prize for work on the genetic effects of radiation shortly after the dropping of the bombs on Hiroshima and Nagasaki made Muller a public figure. He frequently warned of the long-term dangers of radioactive fallout from nuclear war (and also nuclear tests), helping to raise public concern in this area, and running into conflict with the Atomic Energy Commission, which saw him as an obstacle to the full expansion of nuclear armaments. Muller was later to be the most prestigious scientific defender of Carson's *Silent Spring*. In a review for the *New York Herald Tribune*, coinciding with the publication of her book, he called it "a smashing indictment that faces up to the disastrous consequences, for both nature and man, of the chemical mass-warfare that is being waged today indiscriminately against noxious insects, weeds, and fungi." However, the real importance, he suggested, of *Silent Spring* lay in the profound understanding that it conveyed of the interconnections within nature and between nature and society: in "the enlightenment it brings the public regarding the high complexity and interrelatedness of the web of life in which we have our being."[7]

Muller was one of the eleven prominent intellectuals who signed the Russell-Einstein letter, leading to the Pugwash Conference in 1957 that addressed the control of nuclear weapons. He was a signatory along with thousands of other scientists of the 1958 petition to the United Nations initiated by the Nobel Prize–winning chemist Linus Pauling (with the support of biologist Barry Commoner), calling for an end to nuclear weapons testing.

When the cloud of secrecy surrounding the fallout problem lifted in 1954, the scientific community was able to study the extent of environmental degradation and contamination caused by nuclear weapons tests. Such work required the expertise of biologists, geneticists, ecologists, pathologists, and meteorologists, who explored the effects of radiation on plants and animals, as well as the movement of radioactive materials through the atmosphere, ecosystems, and food chains. Nuclear testing had joined the world's population in a common environmental fate, as radioactive fallout was distributed globally by wind, water, and living creatures. Human-made radioactive isotopes, such as strontium-90, iodine-31, cesium-137, and carbon-14, were introduced into the global environment, and from this point on, became part of the bodily composition of humans and all life. Different radioactive elements had distinct properties and posed unique threats to people and the environment. Plants and animals took up such materials, which were passed on through the food chain. Strontium-90 was built into children's bones and teeth, cesium-137 concentrated in muscles, and iodine-131 was embedded in thyroid glands, each increasing the risk of cancer. Linus Pauling pointed to the myriad biological threats associated with carbon-14 lodged in all the tissues in the body.

In studying the effects of radioactive substances on food chains, the concepts of bioaccumulation and biological magnification were established—and later became intimately identified with Carson's *Silent Spring*. Bioaccumulation refers to a process whereby a toxic substance is absorbed by the body at a rate faster than it is lost. For instance, strontium-90 is a radioactive isotope that is chemically similar to calcium and can accumulate in the bones, where it can cause genetic mutations and cancer. Biological magnification occurs when a substance increases in concentration along the food chain. An example of this occurred when radionuclides discharged into the Columbia River in trace amounts from the Hanford nuclear facility in Washington State were discovered to increase in order of magnitude as they were passed along in the food chain. A number of variables influence such biological magnification, such as the length of the food chain, the rate of bioaccumulation within an organism, the half-life of the nuclide (in the case of radioactive substances), and the concentration of the toxic substance in the immediate environment. Ecologist Eugene Odum noted that due to biological magnification it was possible to release an "innocuous amount of radioactivity and have her [nature] give it back to us in a lethal package!" Carson herself pointed to how biological magnification resulted in dangerously high burdens of strontium-90 and cesium-137 in the bodies of Alaskan Eskimos and Scandinavian Lapps at the terminal end of a food chain that included lichens and caribou.

In the 1961 edition of *The Sea Around Us*, Carson, who was deeply involved in protesting the dumping of radioactive wastes in the oceans, raised the pregnant question, "What happens then to the careful calculation of a 'maximum permissible level' [of radioactivity]? For the tiny organisms are eaten by larger ones and so on up the food chain to man. By such a process tuna over an area of a million square miles surrounding the Bikini bomb test developed a degree of radioactivity enormously higher than that of the sea water."

The Castle Bravo hydrogen-bomb detonation at Bikini Atoll in March 1954, which Carson referred to here, was one of sixty-seven nuclear tests carried out by the United States in the Marshall Islands between 1946 and 1958, and the most notorious in its effects. The size of the blast—fifteen megatons, equivalent to a thousand times the bomb dropped on Hiroshima—was more than twice what was expected. Radioactive fallout rained down on inhabited areas of the Marshall Islands and on a Japanese fishing boat, the *Lucky Dragon*, some eighty nautical miles from Bikini (and contaminated ocean life over a vast region), creating an international controversy as the United States denied responsibility.[8]

A key figure linking the scientific critique of nuclear fallout and environmental contradictions in general to social movement struggles, and one with whom Carson closely identified, was the biologist and socialist Barry Commoner. In 1956, Commoner discussed with his friend and Marxist activist, Virginia Brodine, the possibility of organizing a campaign to get milk tested for strontium-90, modeled after the earlier pure milk campaign organized by St. Louis women. This led to the formation in April 1958 of the Greater St. Louis Citizens Committee for Nuclear Information (CNI). Known as the Committee for Environmental Information after 1963, it brought scientists (the "technical division" of the CNI) together with activists. The CNI soon initiated its famous Baby Tooth Survey to examine babies' teeth for strontium-90. Carson praised Commoner's critique of the system's failure to address problems such as air pollution before a new potentially dangerous technology was introduced. In her 1963 speech on "Our Polluted Environment," she underscored the importance of the CNI's research on the effects of radioactive fallout.[9]

CARSON AND ECOSYSTEM ECOLOGY

Another very important influence on Carson's environmental thinking was the rise of ecosystem ecology and the new developments in evolutionary theory in her day. Ecology at this time was still a young field. The key concept of "ecosystem" had been introduced only a few decades prior in 1935 by the British ecologist Arthur Tansley. Tansley was a Fabian-style socialist who had studied under the leading Darwinian biologist of his day, E. Ray Lankester. Lankester was an adamant materialist, an early, sharp critic of ecological degradation, and a young friend of Karl Marx—who was present at Marx's funeral.

In the late 1920s and 1930s, when Tansley was writing, the new field of ecology was dominated by teleological conceptions (emphasizing the purposiveness of nature, emanating from final causes) associated with the work of Frederick Clements in the United States and Jan Christian Smuts and his associates in South Africa. (Smuts, who served as South African Prime Minister, was one of the principal figures in establishing the preconditions for the apartheid system.) Incensed by the idealistic and racist interpretations of ecology propounded by Smuts and his followers, Tansley developed the concept of "ecosystem" as a materialist alternative to Smuts's teleological "holism." "Though the organisms may claim our primary interest," he wrote, "we cannot separate them from their special environment, with which they form one physical system. . . . These *ecosys-*

tems, as we may call them, are of the most various kinds and sizes. They form one category of the multitudinous physical systems of the universe, which range from the universe as a whole down to the atom." Tansley was deeply concerned with "the destructive human activities of the modern world." "Ecology," he argued, "must be applied to conditions brought about by human activity," and for this purpose the ecosystem concept, which situated all life within the larger material environment and penetrated "beneath the forms of the 'natural' entities," was the essential form of analysis.[10]

Another of the founders of modern ecosystem analysis was the British zoologist Charles Elton, a close associate of Tansley's, whose work was to be fundamental to the development of Carson's ecological critique. Elton was famous for his pioneering 1927 work *Animal Ecology*. However, it was a work published in 1958, *The Ecology of Invasions by Animals and Plants*, in which he employed the new ecosystem concept that was to inspire much of the wider argument of *Silent Spring*. In a powerful ecological condemnation of synthetic pesticides, Elton declared that "this astonishing rain of death upon so much of the world's surface" was largely unnecessary and threatened "the very delicately organized interlocking system of populations" in a given ecosystem. There were "other and more permanent methods of safeguarding the world's organic wealth" that emphasized complexity and diversity rather than biological simplification. The unthinking use of "chemical warfare" on living things, he contended, following the U.S. ecologist and environmentalist Aldo Leopold, reflected the failure of a system based on economic values that had no place for the larger values of a biotic community. He stressed that these actions might one day be looked upon as we now do on "the excesses of colonial exploitation." Carson quoted Elton's statement on "the rain of death" in her April 1959 letter to the *New York Times* in which she opened her attack on pesticides; she was to quote it again in *Silent Spring* as the leitmotiv of her chapter "Indiscriminately from the Skies."[11]

Elton's analysis had provided the foundation for the work of Carson's friend and associate, Robert Rudd, a professor of zoology at the University of California at Davis. Carson first contacted Rudd in April 1958 to get help with her pesticide research, and to obtain some of his publications on the subject. He visited her with his children at her Maine

cottage in July and the two struck up a strong friendship and a close working relationship.

Rudd was a sophisticated left thinker with a deep sense of the ecology, sociology, and political economy of the pesticide issue. When he met
Carson he had already started his own book on the subject funded by the
Conservation Foundation. In 1959 he wrote two articles for *The Nation*:
"The Irresponsible Poisoners" in May and "Pesticides: The *Real* Peril"
in July. "The Irresponsible Poisoners" argued that the use of deadly pesticides such as DDT was based on a misplaced emphasis on production
over all other values. "Overproduction has settled on us like a plague. . . .
Chemical use to increase production is continually stressed; and few
stop to inquire 'Why?'" In "Pesticides: The *Real* Peril," he contended
that the key reason that such chemicals were needed and also the leading
effect of their use—in a kind of self-reinforcing vicious circle—was the
extreme "simplification" imposed on the environment by industrial agriculture. Asked why there was an increasing reliance on such deadly
chemicals, "an ecologist would answer . . . simplification of the ecosystem, [which] is the result of most current production practice in the
United States." The only effective way of dealing with the problem was,
therefore, to change the production practice: to "cultivate ecological
diversity" and reliance on biological control. "For the good of us all,
chemical techniques must give way to ecological emphasis. The cultivation of ecosystem diversity will yield crop safety, sustained productivity,
[and] reduction of chemical hazards." The emerging system of global
agribusiness needed to be questioned at the outset: "Our export of
American agricultural 'know-how' may be doing the 'favored' countries
an ultimate disservice."

Carson drew extensively on Rudd's research in two of the chapters of
Silent Spring ("And No Birds Sang" and "Rivers of Death"). Rudd's
Nation articles also helped inspire Murray Bookchin's first work on ecol-
ogy, *Our Synthetic Environment*, published in 1962 (the same year as
Silent Spring) under the pseudonym Lewis Herber.

Rudd's ecosystem-based critique of the pesticide industry and
agribusiness as a whole was so thoroughgoing that he found himself
under attack by the vested interests and his own university position was
jeopardized. Unlike Carson, he was not an independent writer but a uni-

versity professor at a land grant college dependent on publications and peer evaluation for promotion. His magnum opus, *Pesticides and a Living Landscape*, was completed before Carson's *Silent Spring*. But the corporate publisher to which the Conservation Foundation gave the manuscript turned it down as a "polemic." The manuscript was then offered to the University of Wisconsin Press where eighteen reviewers including the entire university entomology department went over it—with the result that it ended up with the record for the largest number of reviewers for that press and the decision on whether to publish it was a protracted one. Consequently, *Pesticides and a Living Landscape* was not published until 1964, the year of Carson's death. The book was reviewed over 200 times, overwhelmingly favorably, but Rudd lost a promotion at the University of California at Davis and his career was threatened. He was dismissed without notice or cause in 1964 from his position at the university's Agricultural Experiment Station.

There is no doubt that *Pesticides and a Living Landscape* was a brilliant work and a devastating critique of existing environmental practice. Rudd explored in depth the larger systematic issues related to the transformation of ecosystems associated with the application of pesticides that Carson, whose main object was to bring the deadly nature of pesticides themselves before the public, was unable fully to address. According to Rudd, "the general problem" could be succinctly stated:

> Crop systems are necessarily ecologically simplified for economical production of marketable foods and fibers. The frequent consequence is an unbalanced ecosystem in which a few species of organisms increase beyond thresholds of numbers that we can tolerate. By definition these species then become pests. . . . Production and [pest] protection are parts of the same cloth. They cannot be biologically separated. . . . We can no longer afford to dismiss piecemeal the "separate" problems that arise from uncontrolled chemicals in living environments. There are no separate problems.

With respect to the risks to human beings from pesticides, Rudd pointed out that "it would be embarrassing for our 'experts' to learn that significant effects do occur in the long term. One hundred and eighty million human guinea pigs [in the United States] would have paid a high price for their trust."

For Carson, the ecosystem concept emerged as the basis of a radical challenge to the notion of the human domination of nature. The modern discovery of "the fact that man, like all other living creatures, is part of the vast ecosystems of the earth, subject to the forces of the environment," she argued, was on a par with (and ultimately inseparable from) Darwin's theory of evolution. The obvious corollary of such an evolutionary-ecological view was that "man is affected by the same environmental influences that control the lives of all the many thousands of other species to which he is related by evolutionary ties."[12]

Crucial in forming Carson's ecological critique were the new developments in evolutionary theory and in the theory of life's origin. A materialist explanation of the origin of life had been introduced in 1924, when the Soviet biochemist A. I. Oparin developed the hypothesis that life had arisen prior to the presence of oxygen in the atmosphere (allowing the sun's rays to operate more effectively to promote life on earth) from a body of water gradually enriched in organic molecules, later referred to as the "Oparin ocean" or "primordial soup." Somehow life emerged when these molecules clustered together and then self-organized into a chemical system capable of self-replication. Similar ideas were developed separately in 1929 by the British biologist and Marxist J. B. S. Haldane, who was one of the major figures in the development of the neo-Darwinian synthesis linking Darwin's evolutionary theory to the new field of genetics. This general approach to the origins of life was pushed forward experimentally in the early 1950s by the Chicago chemist Harold Urey and his student Stanley Miller, who succeeded in producing amino acids, the building blocks of proteins, by passing a spark through water under such primitive earth conditions replicated in a laboratory. Carson was clearly affected by this new influential scientific theory of the origin of life and the unified evolutionary-ecological perspective it generated. Her book *The Sea Around Us* commenced with the sea as the setting "for the creation of life from non-life."

One of the fundamental conceptions of this theory of the origin of life, going back to Oparin and Haldane (and derived from V. I. Vernadsky's conception of the biosphere), was that life had itself altered the atmosphere by generating oxygen and the ozone layer, making such spontaneous creation of new life from non-life no longer possible. Carson, in her talk on "The Pollution of Our Environment," placed enormous importance on this point and its significance for an ecological critique, arguing that:

> From all of this we may generalize that, since the beginning of biological time, there has been the closest possible interdependence between the physical environment and the life it sustains. The conditions on the young earth produced life; life then at once modified the conditions of the earth, so that this single extraordinary act of spontaneous generation could not be repeated. In one form or another, action and interaction between life and its surroundings has been going on ever since.
>
> The historic fact has, I think, more than academic significance. Once we accept it we see why we cannot with impunity make repeated assaults upon the environment as we do now. The serious student of earth history knows that neither life nor the physical world that supports it exists in little isolated compartments. On the contrary, he recognizes that extraordinary unity between organisms and the environment. For this reason he knows that harmful substances released into the environment return in time to create problems for mankind. . . . The branch of science that deals with these interrelations is Ecology. . . . We cannot think of the living organism alone; nor can we think of the physical environment as a separate entity. The two exist together, each acting on the other to form an ecological complex or an ecosystem.[13]

Such complex, evolving ecosystems were highly dynamic entities. Consequently, the changes they were undergoing were frequently unforeseen until it was too late.

Throughout her work Carson stressed the evolutionary character and interconnectedness of the natural world. It was this that gave her naturalistic writings their breathtaking quality. In an insightful analysis of Carson's sea trilogy—*Under the Sea Wind* (1941), *The Sea Around Us* (1951), and *The Edge of the Sea* (1955)—together with *Silent Spring*, Mary McCay has traced this quality in Carson's writing to her fundamental concept, introduced early on in her work, of "material immortality." As

Carson wrote in 1937 in her article "Undersea," the various forms of life are "redissolved into their component substance," as a result of "the inexorable laws of the sea." Consequently, "individual elements are lost to view, only to reappear again and again in different incarnations in a kind of material immortality." As a scientist, Carson approached the natural world from a materialist standpoint, rejecting all non-naturalistic explanations. Once when her mother said to her that God had created the world, she replied, "Yes and General Motors created my Oldsmobile. But *how* is the question." The evolution of a complex web of life was everything.[14]

ECOLOGY AS A RADICAL FORCE

Carson's intense study of ecosystem ecology, in the context of her work on *Silent Spring*, heightened this materialist understanding and turned it into a radical force. At the time of her death, she had a book contract to undertake a philosophical examination of ecology and she was collecting material for a scientific study of evolution. The two subjects were obviously connected in her mind and were undoubtedly to form the basis of a thoroughgoing critique of the present human relation to the earth.[15]

This put her in direct conflict with the powers that be. For the dominant economic interests, as her editor and biographer Paul Brooks observed, "the really scary thing" was that Carson "was questioning the whole attitude of industrial society toward the natural world. This was heresy and this had to be suppressed." Carson herself was well aware that her radical ecological perspective was placing her at odds with a system geared to expansion of private production at all costs. In the process of writing *Silent Spring*, she studied John Kenneth Galbraith's *Affluent Society*, which had raised the question of private wealth and public squalor, i.e., the external diseconomies of the market system, whereby social and environmental costs were imposed on society and nature.[16]

In responding to the attacks on *Silent Spring*, Carson complained of the "enormous stream of propaganda" blocking rational science and ecological values. She railed against the tax subsidies given for corporate lobbyists, and attacked the large private grants to universities through which corporations tried to purchase a "scientific front" for their operations.

Behind all of this lay the question she continually raised: "What happens . . . when the public interest is pitted against large commercial interests?"

Carson had no doubt that there was an irreconcilable conflict between economic and environmental interests within contemporary society. Thus, she complained of the promotion of extreme "intensivism" in production in the search for greater profits, particularly as it related to the maltreatment of animals. The economic system, she emphasized in line with Rudd, was geared toward "overproduction" at the expense of the environment. In our society, dominated by material acquisition, life was destroyed because business was "blinded by the dollar sign." Indeed, "the modern world," she declared, "worships the gods of speed and quantity, and of the quick and easy profit, and out of this idolatry monstrous evils have arisen." She added that "the struggle against the massed might of industry is too big for one or two individuals . . . to handle"—a view that clearly called for the formation of an environmental movement to counter the power of industry.[17]

What appeared to anger the chemical industry more than anything else about Rachel Carson's book was that she chose to begin *Silent Spring* with a literary device: "A Fable for Tomorrow"; the tale of "a town . . . where all life seemed in harmony with its surroundings," and which unthinkingly, almost unbeknownst to itself, introduced chemicals of destruction into its midst. For Carson "a grim specter" was haunting modern industrial, acquisitive society, threatening to silence the spring. Her fable was clearly "for tomorrow" in two senses: it represented both an unprecedented threat to all life, and the possibility of overcoming it. The worst society could do would be to stand still in the face of such a threat. Giving evidence of her broad progressivism, she wrote elsewhere: "the changes and the evolution of new ways of life are natural and on the whole desirable."[18]

Today, many of the same problems that Carson pointed out persist, often in more potent forms. This has to be the case for a system that by its very nature must grow (at a rate exceeding population growth) in order to stay out of severe crises, and in which producing more and more profit is the motive force propelling the economy. An example of how economic priorities override ecological approaches can be seen in the case of strawberry growers in California, who can't make as much money if they rotate crops and take land out of strawberries. Thus, they "need" to use a bio-cide, methyl bromide (which also acts to deplete the protective atmos-pheric ozone layer at fifty times the level of CFCs), in order to kill soil-borne pests that would be well taken care of by a more ecological approach to growing strawberries. To give an idea of how significant the problem of pesticide use continues to be, in 2006 some 64 percent of the fresh produce and 59 percent of the processed fruits and vegetables test-ed by the U.S. Department of Agriculture contained detectable levels of pesticide residues.[19]

Likewise, producers of agricultural animals using factory farms, in which animals are crowded together under inhumane conditions, "must," we are told, routinely use antibiotics (a form of pesticide, of course) to try to keep the animals growing reasonably fast. This leads not only to antibi-otic residue in meat but also to the development of antibiotic-resistant microbes. Raising animals in a less dense and more humane system, only using antibiotics when animals actually get sick, leads to higher produc-tion costs and hence is rejected by market principles—what Carson called "the gods of profits and production." Although there is a developing pub-lic interest in organically raised agricultural products and "humanely" raised animals, these are still niche markets.

The U.S. government has been particularly sympathetic to the desires of business to maintain as free a hand as possible in continuing to intro-duce new chemicals into the environment. It has, therefore, opposed mandating the removal of potential hazards. As pointed out in a 2007 *New York Times* article: "The United States has held on to its original 30-year-old chemical regulatory systems, which make it difficult for agencies to ban chemicals or require industry testing. While the government has worked with the industry on a voluntary basis to study as many as 2,000 chemicals and phase out certain ones, it has required the study of only 200 chemicals and restricted the use of only 5 since 1976."[20]

Beyond these persistent problems associated with the introduction of synthetic chemicals into our environment, there remains the wider set of ecological perils that Carson addressed. It was this larger ecological cri-tique, which challenged the whole nature of the modern production sys-tem, that represented her most enduring contribution. Far from being the quiet, demure, establishment figure that we often hear of today, Carson in reality represented a defiant, radical voice. As a scientist and a writer, she went beyond the bounds of what is allowed in "polite circles" and thus alerted and energized the public. When attacked by industry, she stood her ground, and went to the root of the issue. She urged us, and particularly those responsible for raising and educating children, to reject "the sterile preoccupation with things that are artificial, the alienation from the sources of our strength."[21]

Carson spent most of her adult life discovering and lovingly describing the "sea around us." But as her ecological critique developed, perceiving the destructiveness of the social encounter with the environment, she sought not merely to explain the world but to change it.

CHAPTER FOUR

Peak Oil and Energy Imperialism

The rise in overt militarism and imperialism, at the outset of the twenty-first century, can plausibly be attributed to a considerable extent to attempts by the dominant interests of the world economy to gain control over diminishing world oil supplies.[1] Beginning in 1998, a series of strategic energy initiatives were launched in national security circles in the United States in response to: (1) the crossing of the 50 percent threshold in U.S. importation of foreign oil; (2) the disappearance of spare world oil production capacity; (3) concentration of an increasing percentage of all remaining conventional oil resources in the Persian Gulf; and (4) looming fears of peak oil.

The response of the vested interests to this world oil supply crisis was to construct what Michael Klare in *Blood and Oil* has called a global "strategy of maximum extraction."[2] This required that the United States as the hegemonic power, with the backing of the other leading capitalist states, seek to extend its control over world oil reserves with the object of boosting production. Seen in this light, the invasion and occupation of Afghanistan (the geopolitical doorway to Western access to Caspian Sea Basin oil and natural gas) following the 9/11 attacks, the 2003 invasion of Iraq, the rapid expansion of U.S. military activities in the Gulf of Guinea in Africa (where Washington sees itself as in competition with Beijing), and the increased threats now directed at Iran and Venezuela—all signal the rise of a dangerous new era of energy imperialism.

THE GEOPOLITICS OF OIL

In April 1998 the United States, for the first time, imported the majority of the petroleum it consumed. The crossing of this threshold pointed to a very rapid growth in U.S. foreign oil dependency. At the same time, fears that the world would soon reach peak oil production became increasingly prominent, assuming a high profile behind the scenes in establishment discussions. A key event was the publication in *Scientific American,* in March 1998, of "The End of Cheap Oil" by retired oil industry geologists Colin J. Campbell and Jean H. Laherrère. "The End of Cheap Oil" predicted that world oil production would peak "probably within 10 years." The Campbell and Laherrère article and the question of peak oil immediately drew the attention of the International Energy Agency (IEA), the OECD's energy organization, in its *World Energy Outlook* of 1998. The IEA claimed that even adopting the pessimists' assumptions on the real extent of world oil reserves and the existence of a bell-shaped production curve (but without the sharp oil price hike suggested by Campbell), its own long-term supply model "would not peak until around 2008–2009." Employing the IEA's own assumptions on reserves, moreover, would push the peak back around a decade further.[3] This, however, was still far from distant. The peaking of United Kingdom North Sea oil production in 1999 (Norwegian production peaked two years later) added a still greater sense of urgency.

Matthew Simmons, CEO of the Houston-based energy investment banking firm Simmons and Company International and a member of the National Petroleum Council and the Council on Foreign Relations, published an article in *Middle East Insight,* in 1999, in which he emphasized the "far faster" depletion of major oil fields arising from high-extraction technology. Rather than extending the life of oil fields as previously supposed, the introduction of this technology most likely accelerated their depletion. Referring to oil fields "brought into production since 1970," Simmons noted that "almost all of these new fields have already reached peak production and are now experiencing rapid rates of decline. . . . And when the stable base of old, but giant, fields also starts to deplete," he asked, "what will this do to the world's average depletion rate?"[4]

In 2000 Simmons's concerns regarding diminishing oil supply led to his becoming an energy advisor for George W. Bush's presidential campaign. As he recounted it in a February 2008 interview, he had "pulled aside" Bush's "first cousin" in early March 2000 to tell him of an earlier conversation he had had with an assistant to Secretary of Energy Bill Richardson, who had been sent to examine the spare oil production capacity of the OPEC countries. As Simmons reported to Bush's cousin:

> I said, "When you have someone who is the head of U.S. oil policy call you and [say 'shit!'] about five times in 20 seconds, this is so much worse than what they've warned us about." I said, "Between now and the election, if this all breaks out and Bush is misinformed, he can mispronounce every head of state in the world, but this, this will sink you." And that dragged me into helping create the comprehensive energy plan put forth by Bush when he was running.[5]

Simmons was a member of the Bush-Cheney Energy Transition Advisory Committee, advising on the growing oil constraints. His 2005 book, *Twilight in the Desert: The Coming Saudi Oil Shock and the World Economy*, which argued that the Saudi oil production peak was imminent, has become one of the most influential works propounding the peak oil notion.[6]

The Energy Information Administration (EIA) of the U.S. Department of Energy conducted a full assessment of the peak oil issue as early as July 2000, considering a number of scenarios. As opposed to those who saw the peak occurring "as early as 2004" the EIA concluded that "world conventional oil production may increase two decades or more before it begins to decline." The analysis itself, however, was not altogether reassuring to the vested interests, since it suggested that a world oil peak could be reached as early as 2021.[7]

These concerns with regard to world oil supply, which began to penetrate the corridors of power in the 1998–2001 period, led to a wide-ranging debate within the inner circles in the United States about the nature of the oil extraction problem and the strategic means with which to alleviate it. This was increasingly integrated with wider issues on the expansion of the U.S. empire raised by groups such as the Project for a New American Century.[8]

In July 1998, the Center for Strategic and International Studies (CSIS) launched its "Strategic Energy Initiative," at the urging of former Chairman of the Senate Armed Services Committee Sam Nunn and former Secretary of Defense (and former Secretary of Energy) James R. Schlesinger. In November 2000, the Strategic Energy Initiative issued a three volume report, *The Geopolitics of Energy into the 21st Century*, with Nunn and Schlesinger as co-chairs. It stressed that the Persian Gulf would have to expand its energy production "by almost 80 percent during 2000–2020" in the face of rising demand and declining oil production elsewhere in the world in order to meet world energy needs.

The question of a world oil peak in the decade 2000–10 was also examined, focusing on the arguments of Campbell and Laherrère and Simmons. The CSIS Strategic Energy Initiative officially rejected the notion that the world oil peak would be reached as early as 2010. Nevertheless, its report took the peak oil issue extremely seriously. As the "only superpower" the United States, it declared, had "special responsibilities for preserving worldwide energy supply" and "open access" to the world's oil. Underscored throughout the report was the necessity of finding ways to increase oil exports from Iraq and Iran, both then under U.S. economic sanctions.[9]

In 2001 the James Baker III Institute for Public Policy of Rice University and the Council on Foreign Relations cosponsored a study of *Strategic Energy Policy Challenges for the 21st Century*, chaired by energy analyst Edward L. Morse. Task force members included both oil optimists, such as Morse and Daniel Yergin of Cambridge Energy Research Associates, and oil pessimists such as peak oil proponent Simmons. The joint report of the Baker Institute and the Council on Foreign Relations emphasized the adequacy of world oil reserves for decades to come, but argued that world oil was facing "tight supply" due to "underinvestment" in new production capacity and "volatile states." Excess capacity had been "wiped out," falling to "negligible" amounts, partly due to oil producing countries devoting oil revenues to social projects rather than to investment in new production capacity.

In this situation, the joint report pointed out that Iraq had emerged as a key "swing producer" of oil, operating well below capacity, and in the previous year "turning its taps on and off when it has felt such action was in its strategic interests to do so." This presented a growing danger to the world capitalist economy, which included the "possibility that Saddam Hussein may remove Iraqi oil from the market for an extended period." Indeed, "Iraqi reserves," the *Strategic Energy Policy* report emphasized, "represent a major asset that can quickly add capacity to world oil markets and inject a more competitive tenor to oil trade." Investment in the enhancement of Iraqi oil production capacity was essential. The problem was what to do about Saddam Hussein.

Overall, the report of the Baker Institute and the Council on Foreign Relations emphasized that the stakes were exceedingly high, since there was a danger that oil price increases and supply shortages would make "the United States appear more similar to a poor developing country."

The answer was for the Western powers, led by the United States, to play a more direct role in the development of world oil resources. This would be coupled with the replacement of the current political economy of oil, dominated by national oil companies, which had arisen with the growth of "resource nationalism" in the third world, with one in which the multinational oil corporations, centered in the advanced capitalist economies, once again took charge of reserves and investments.[10]

These reports by national security analysts on strategic energy policy were followed in May 2001 by the White House release of its *National Energy Policy*, issued under the direction of Vice President Dick Cheney. It too emphasized the need for U.S. petroleum security, noting that total U.S. oil production had fallen 39 percent below its 1970 peak and that U.S. reliance on foreign oil imports could increase to almost two-thirds of its total gasoline and heating oil consumption by 2020. President Bush also warned in May 2001 that dependence on foreign crude oil put U.S. "national energy security" in the hands of "foreign nations, some of whom do not share our interests."

In terms of the long-term world oil supply outlook, the U.S. Department of Energy's *International Energy Outlook* in 2001 projected the need for a doubling of Persian Gulf oil production over 1999 levels by 2020 in order to meet expected world demand. This optimistic forecast could not possibly be fulfilled, however, without massive investment in an expansion of capacity in the Persian Gulf of a kind that key states, such as Iraq and Iran, and even Saudi Arabia, seemed unlikely to undertake. Iraqi crude oil production in 2001 was 31 percent less than in 1979, while Iran's had fallen by about 37 percent since 1976. Both nations were viewed as underproducing due to underinvestment and the effects of sanctions. The IEA estimated that Persian Gulf states would have to invest over half a trillion dollars on new equipment and technology for oil production capacity expansion by 2030 in order to meet projected oil production levels.[11]

U.S. national security and energy analysts, as well as energy corporations and the Bush administration, had thus arrived at the conclusion by spring 2001 that, while substantial oil reserves still existed, capacity was extremely tight, presaging a series of oil price shocks. Only a vast increase of oil production in the Persian Gulf as a whole could prevent an enormous gap emerging between oil production and demand over the next two decades. Behind all of this lay the specter of peak oil production.

Rather than try to solve the problem on the demand side by lessening consumption, the Bush administration turned, as had all other administrations before it, to the military as the ultimate guarantor. As Michael Klare wrote in his *Blood and Oil*:

> In the months before and after 9/11, the Bush administration fashioned a comprehensive strategy for American domination of the Persian Gulf and the procurement of ever-increasing quantities of petroleum. It is unlikely that this strategy was ever formalized in a single, all-encompassing White House document. Rather, the administration adopted a series of policies that together formed a blueprint for political, economic, and military action in the Gulf. This approach—I call it the strategy of maximum extraction—was aimed primarily at boosting the oil output of the major Gulf producers. But since the sought-after increases could be doomed by instability and conflict in the region, the strategy also entailed increased military intervention.[12]

Militarily, the issue was one of shoring up Saudi Arabia in the face of growing signs of instability, carrying out regime change in Iraq, and exerting maximum pressure on Iran. Key figures in the Bush administration such as Donald Rumsfeld and Paul Wolfowitz had been pushing for an invasion of Iraq even before the election. Once the September 2001 attacks occurred, the "War on Terrorism" led to the invasion first of Afghanistan, giving the United States a geopolitical doorway (and pipeline route) to Central Asia and the Caspian Sea Basin, followed by the invasion in 2003 of Iraq. From the standpoint of the geopolitics of oil, Saddam Hussein's removal and the occupation of Iraq was seen as enhancing the security of Middle East oil, presenting the possibility of a big boost in Iraqi oil production, and providing a staging ground for increased U.S. military, political, and economic dominance of the Gulf. U.S. strategic control of the Middle East and its oil was viewed as the key to establishing the basis of a "new American century."

As former Federal Reserve Board Chairman Alan Greenspan, the top U.S. economic official throughout this period, stated in his book *The Age of Turbulence* in 2007: "I am saddened that it is politically inconvenient to acknowledge what everyone knows: that the Iraq war is largely about oil." The U.S. invasion of Iraq, Greenspan claimed, needed to be seen against the background of previous Western military interventions aimed at securing the oil of the region, for example: "the reaction, to and reversal of, Mossadeq's nationalization of Anglo-Iranian oil in 1951 [resulting in the CIA's overthrow of Iranian Prime Minister Mossadeq and the installation of the Shah in 1953] and the aborted effort by Britain and France to reverse Nasser's takeover of the key Suez Canal link for oil flows to Europe in 1956." The U.S. intervention in Iraq and its increased military role in the Middle East was, for Greenspan—the leading spokesperson for financial capital in the 1990s and early 2000s—justified by the fact that "world growth over the next quarter century at rates commensurate with the past quarter century will require between one-fourth and two-fifths more oil than we use today." And this vast increase in oil production needed to come largely from the Persian Gulf, where two-thirds of the world's reserves and hence most of its capacity for increased extraction was located.[13]

Although the Bush administration criticized Greenspan's statement, the centrality of oil in the occupation of Iraq was not something that it could easily deny. In a September 13, 2007, prime time television speech, Bush declared that if the United States were to pull out of Iraq "extremists could control a key part of the global energy supply."[14]

PEAK OIL: A GLOBAL TURNING POINT?

Five years after the United States invaded Iraq the world oil supply problem was substantially worse. Estimates of the potential for increased Iraqi oil production made prior to the war had suggested that Iraq free of sanctions could potentially increase its crude oil production within a decade from its previous 1979 high of 3.5 million barrels a day (mb/d) to 6 or even 10 mb/d.[15] Instead, Iraq's average annual oil production in 2007 had fallen to 13 percent below its 2001 level, having declined from 2.4 to 2.1 mb/d. Oil production in the Persian Gulf as a whole increased by 2.4 mb/d on average between 2001 and 2005 and then dropped by 4 percent in 2005–07, along with the stagnation of world oil production as a whole.[16]

At the time U.S. troops reached Baghdad, peak oil was already a specter looming over the globe. Today, it is a factor in all establishment discussions of the world oil issue. Peak oil is not the same as *running out* of oil. Rather it simply means the *peaking* and subsequent terminal decline of oil production, as determined primarily by geological and technological factors. The extraction of oil from any given oil well typically takes the form of a symmetrical, bell-shaped curve with extraction steadily rising, e.g., by 2 percent a year, until a peak is reached when about half of the accessible oil has been extracted. Since oil production for an entire country is simply a product of the aggregation of individual wells, national oil production can be expected to take the form of a bell-shaped curve as well. Geologists have become adept at estimating the point at which a peak in national production will occur. These methods were pioneered in the 1950s by oil geologist M. King Hubbert, who achieved fame for successfully predicting the U.S. oil peak in 1970. The eventual peak in oil production is therefore sometimes known as "Hubbert's peak."

Peak oil is generally viewed in terms of the peaking of conventional crude oil supplies on which the main estimates of oil reserves are based.

There are also unconventional sources of oil that can be produced at much greater cost and with a much lower energy returned on energy invested (EROEI) ratio. These include heavy oil, petroleum derived from oil sand, and shale oil. As the price of oil rises some of these sources become more exploitable, but also at much greater cost—monetarily and to the environment. It is estimated that it takes an equivalent of two out of three barrels of oil produced to pay for the energy and other costs associated with extracting oil from the tar sands in Alberta. It requires one billion cubic feet of natural gas to generate one million barrels of synthetic oil from oil sands. Two tons of sand must be mined to get one barrel of oil. Oil sand mining also requires vast quantities of water, producing two and a half gallons of toxic liquid waste for every barrel of oil extracted. This liquid waste is stored in enormous and rapidly expanding "tailing ponds." The economic and environmental costs are thus prohibitive. Peak oil, therefore, inevitably signals the end of cheap oil.[17]

A key part of the argument of the peak oil hypothesis is the fact that discoveries of oil fields worldwide peaked in the 1960s, while the average size of new discoveries has also declined over time. Those who argue that peak oil is imminent insist that estimates of proven reserves are commonly exaggerated for political reasons, and that actual retrievable reserves may be considerably less. The conventional notion that there are forty years of crude oil production remaining at current rates of output is seen as misleading, since it exaggerates the reserves in the ground and downplays the fact that a growing economy at present requires that oil demand and production levels increase. Peak oil analysts, therefore, focus on production levels rather than reserves.

The peak oil crisis is more sharply defined than the more general crisis in energy, since not only is petroleum the most protean fuel, but it is also the preeminent liquid fuel in transportation, for which there is no easy substitute in the quantities needed. Therefore, more than two-thirds of U.S. oil demand is in the form of gasoline and petrodiesel consumption by cars and trucks. An imminent peak in conventional oil, thus, strikes at the lifeblood of the existing capitalist economy. It presents the possibility of a drastic economic dislocation and slowdown.[18]

The peak oil debate, which has often been fierce over the past decade, has now narrowed down to two basic positions. One of these is that of "early peakers" (usually seen as peak oil proponents proper). These analysts argue that peak oil will probably be reached by 2010–12, and may have already been reached in 2005–06. The alternative position, represented by "late peakers," is that the world oil peak will not be reached until 2020 or 2030.[19] Hence, there is a growing consensus that peak oil is or will soon be a reality. The chief question now is how soon, and whether it is already upon us.

An added consideration is whether world oil production will face a classic bell-shaped curve, culminating in a slender, rounded peak, to be followed quickly by a decline (within what can be viewed as a symmetrical curve)—or whether production will rise to a plateau and then stay there for a while, before declining. In fact, world oil supply appears already to have reached a plateau over the last three years at the level of 85 mb/d. This, therefore, has lent credence to the notion that this is the form the peak will initially take.

Chart 1 shows world oil production and supply from 1970 to 2007. "Oil" according to the IEA (and the EIA, which has adopted an almost identical approach) is defined to include "all liquid fuels and is accounted at the product level. Sources include natural gas liquids and condensates, refinery processing gains, and the production of conventional and unconventional oil." Conventional or crude oil is readily processed oil "produced from underground hydrocarbon reservoirs by means of production wells." Unconventional oil is derived from other processes, such as liquefied natural gas, oil sands, oil shales, coal-to-liquid, biofuels, "and/or [other fuel that] . . . needs additional processing to produce synthetic crude."[20] The lower line in Chart 1, labeled "crude oil production," refers simply to production of conventional oil. The higher line, labeled "world oil supply," also includes unconventional sources plus net refinery processing gains (losses). The "crude oil production" line shows a very slight dip in 2005–07, reflecting the fact that crude oil production fell from an average of 73.8 mb/d in 2005 to 73.3 mb/d in 2007. The "world oil supply" line, however, remains level at about 85 mb/d due to a compensating rise in unconventional sources over the same period, resulting in what appears to be a more definite plateau.

Explaining that a plateau is the most likely initial outcome at the world level, Richard Heinberg, a leading peak oil proponent, writes:

CHART 1: *World Oil Production and Supply*

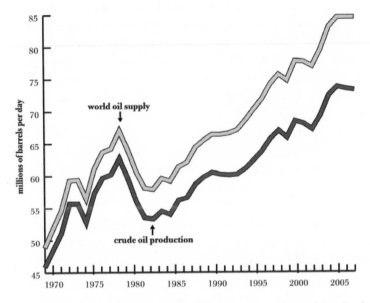

Source: Energy Information Administration, U.S. Department of Energy, *International Petroleum Monthly*, April 2008, http://www.eia.doe.gov/ipm/ supply.html, tables 1.4d and 4.4.

Why the plateau? Oil production is constrained by economic conditions (in an economic downturn, demand for oil falls off), as well as by political events such as war and revolutions. In addition, the shape of the production curve is modified by the increasing availability of unconventional petroleum sources (including heavy oil, natural gas plant liquids, and tar sands), as well as new extraction technologies. The combined effect of all of these factors is to cushion the peak and lengthen the decline curve.[21]

The notion that a partly geological-technical, partly political-economic, plateau is emerging has now become the dominant view in the industry. In November 2007, the *Wall Street Journal* reported:

A growing number of oil-industry chieftains are endorsing an idea long deemed fringe: The world is approaching a practical limit to the number of barrels of crude oil that can be pumped every day. . . . The near adherents [to the peak oil view]—who range from senior Western oil-company executives to current and former officials of the major world exporting countries—don't believe that the global oil tank is at the half-empty point. But they share the belief that a global production ceiling is coming for other reasons: restricted access to oil fields, spiraling costs, and increasingly complex oil-field geology. This will create a production plateau, not a peak, they contend, with oil output remaining relatively constant rather than rising or falling.

The *Wall Street Journal* article referred to the estimates of Cambridge Energy Research Associates, asserting that the peak will not be reached until 2030, and that it will manifest itself at first as an "undulating plateau." But the *Journal* article also took seriously the views of Simmons, who pointed out that, due to declining production in old fields, an increased average daily oil production equivalent to ten times current Alaskan production was needed "just to stay even." Indeed, "at the furthest out," he suggested, the crisis associated with the world peak in conventional oil production would be reached "in 2008 to 2012." Echoing many of the same worries, some oil executives have raised the specter of an oil supply ceiling of 100 million barrels (conventional and unconventional), with petroleum supply likely falling short of expected demand within a decade or less.[22]

Given the appearance of a world oil production plateau at present, and with oil supply seemingly stuck at the 85 mb/d level, it is not surprising that some analysts believe that peak oil has already been reached. Thus, Simmons and Texas oil billionaire T. Boone Pickens have both raised the question of whether the peak was reached in 2005, while the Energy Watch Group in Germany, which includes both scientists and members of the German parliament, contends that "world oil production . . . peaked in 2006."[23]

Establishment sources and the media have often characterized the peak oil problem as a "fringe issue." Yet over the past decade the question has been pursued systematically, and with increasing concern, within the highest echelons of capitalist society: within both states and corporations.[24] In February 2005, the U.S. Department of Energy released a major report that it had commissioned entitled *Peaking of World Oil Production: Impacts, Mitigation, and Risk Management.* The project leader was Robert L. Hirsch of Science Applications International Corporation. Hirsch had formerly occupied executive positions in the U.S. Atomic Energy Commission, Exxon, and ARCO. The Hirsch report concluded that peak oil was a little over two decades away or nearer. "Even the most optimistic forecasts," it stated, "suggest that world oil peaking will occur in less than 25 years." The main emphasis of the Hirsch report commissioned by the Department of Energy, however, was on the issue of the massive transformations that would be needed in the economy, and particularly transportation, in order to mitigate the harmful effects of the end of cheap oil. The enormous problem of converting virtually the entire stock of U.S. cars, trucks, and aircraft in just a quarter-century (at most) was viewed as presenting intractable difficulties.[25]

In October 2005, Hirsch wrote an analysis for *Bulletin of the Atlantic Council of the United States* on "The Inevitable Peaking of World Oil Production." He declared there that "previous energy transitions (wood to coal, coal to oil, etc.) were gradual and evolutionary; oil peaking will be abrupt and revolutionary. The world has never faced a problem like this. Without massive mitigation at least a decade before the fact, the problem will be pervasive and long lasting."[26]

Similarly, the U.S. Army released a major report of its own in September 2005 stating:

> The doubling of oil prices from 2003–2005 is not an anomaly, but a picture of the future. Oil production is approaching its peak; low growth in availability can be expected for the next 5 to 10 years. As worldwide petroleum production peaks, geopolitics and market economics will cause even more significant price increases and security risks. One can only speculate at the outcome from this scenario as world petroleum production declines.[27]

Indeed, by 2005 there was little doubt in ruling circles about the likelihood of serious oil shortages and that peak oil was on its way soon or sooner. In its 2005 *World Energy Outlook*, the IEA raised the issue of Simmons's claims in *Twilight in the Desert* that Saudi Arabia's supergiant Ghawar oil field, the largest in the world, "could," in the IEA's words, "be close to reaching its peak if it has not already done so." Likewise, the U.S. Department of Energy, which had initially rejected Simmons's assessment, backtracked between 2004 and 2006, degrading its projection of Saudi oil production in 2025 by 33 percent.[28]

In February 2007, the U.S. Government Accountability Office (GAO) released a seventy-five-page report on *Crude Oil* pointedly subtitled: *Uncertainty about Future Oil Supply Makes It Important to Develop a Strategy for Addressing a Peak and Decline in Oil Production.* It argued that almost all studies had shown that a world oil peak would occur sometime before 2040 and that U.S. federal agencies had not yet begun to address the issue of the national preparedness necessary to face this impending emergency. For the GAO, the threat of a major oil shortfall was worsened by the political risks primarily associated with four countries, accounting for almost one-third of world (conventional) reserves: Iran, Iraq, Nigeria, and Venezuela. The fact that Venezuela contained "almost 90 percent of the world's proven extra-heavy oil reserves" made it all the more noteworthy that it constituted a significant "political risk" from Washington's standpoint.[29]

In April 2008, Jeroen van der Veer, CEO of Royal Dutch Shell, pronounced that "we wouldn't be surprised if this [easy] oil would peak somewhere in the next ten years." Due to a combination of factors, including production shortfalls and a declining dollar, oil in May 2008 reached over $135 a barrel (it averaged $66 in 2006 and $72 in 2007). The same month Goldman Sachs shocked world capital markets by coming out with an assessment that oil prices could rise to as much as $200 a barrel in the next two years. Western oil interests were particularly distressed that the first production from Kazakhstan's Kashagan oil field (considered the largest oil deposit in the world outside the Middle East) was eight years behind schedule due in part to waters being frozen half the year. By May 2008 the IEA, according to analysts for the *New York Times,* was preparing to reduce its forecast of world oil production for 2030 from its earlier forecasts of 116 mb/d to no more than 100 mb/d.[30]

It was alarm about gasoline prices and national energy security (and no doubt the specter of a world oil peak) that induced the Bush administration in 2006 to take a more aggressive stance in promoting corn-based ethanol production as a fuel substitute. In 2007, 20 percent of U.S. corn production was devoted to ethanol to fuel automobiles. The price of grain spiked worldwide partly as a result. As environmentalist Lester R. Brown wrote in his *Plan B 3.0*: "Suddenly the world is facing a moral and political issue that has no precedent: Should we use grain to fuel cars or to feed people?. . . . The market says, Let's fuel the cars."[31]

THE NEW ENERGY IMPERIALISM

The response in U.S. national security circles to the apparent oil production plateau, the disappearance of surplus oil production capacity, and growing fears of peak oil was swift. In October 2005, the CSIS issued another report, this time on *Changing Risks in Global Oil Supply and Demand*, written by Anthony Cordesman (longtime national security analyst for the U.S. Department of Defense and now holder of the Arleigh A. Burke Chair in Strategy at CSIS) and Khalid R. Al-Rodhan (a strategic analyst specializing in Gulf issues). Cordesman and Al-Rodhan quoted the IEA's prediction, in its 2004 *World Energy Outlook*, that global oil production would not "peak before 2030 if the necessary investments are made." Rather, the immediate problem was "lagging investment" in the Middle East. Still, peak oil issues were not to be entirely discounted. Thus, Cordesman and Al-Rodhan noted that: "Some analysts have questioned the [Saudi] Kingdom's ability to meet sudden surges in demand because of its lack of spare production capacity, and others—like Matthew Simmons—have estimated that Saudi production may be moving towards a period of sustained decline."

"Stability in petroleum exporting regions," Cordesman and Al-Rodhan added, "is tenuous at best. Algeria, Iran, and Iraq all present immediate security problems, but recent experience has shown that exporting countries in Africa, the Caspian Sea, and South America are no more stable than the Gulf. There has been pipeline sabotage in Nigeria, labor strikes in Venezuela, alleged corruption in Russia, and civil unrest in Uzbekistan and other FSU [Former Soviet Union] states."[32]

Even more central than the CSIS study was a 2006 Council on Foreign Relations report, chaired by former CIA Director John Deutsch and James Schlesinger, entitled *National Security Consequences of U.S. Oil Dependency*. The Deutch and Schlesinger report zeroed in on inadequate oil production capacity, with OPEC no longer having the surplus capacity with which to keep prices under control. Production from existing conventional oil fields throughout the world was "declining, on average, about 5 percent per year (roughly 4.3 million barrels per day), and thus even sustaining current levels of consumption" would be enormously difficult. Moreover, "the depletion of conventional sources, especially those close to the major markets in the United States, Western Europe, and Asia, means that the production and transport of oil will become even more dependent on an infrastructure that is already vulnerable." Major energy suppliers, like Russia, Iran, and Venezuela, were using oil to pursue domestic and geopolitical goals, rather than reinvesting the oil proceeds. Saudi Arabia, Iraq, Iran, and West Africa were all centers of instability. China was trying to "lock up" oil supplies in Africa, the Caspian Sea, and elsewhere.

Although the Deutsch and Schlesinger report discussed some demand-side measures to reduce U.S. consumption and oil dependency, it stressed expanding the role of the U.S. military in securing oil supplies. Thus, the report declared that "the United States should expect and support a strong military posture [in the Persian Gulf in particular] that permits suitably rapid deployment to the region, if required. . . . Any nation (or subnational group) that contemplates violence on any scale must take into account the possibility of U.S. preemption, intervention, or retaliation."[33]

No less significant was an April 2007 "policy report" issued by the James A. Baker III Institute for Public Policy on "The Changing Role of National Oil Companies in International Energy Markets." Emphasizing that national oil companies now controlled 77 percent of the world's total reserves, whereas Western multinational oil companies controlled a mere 10 percent, it contended that this was the key issue in managing the current world oil supply problem. "If the United States were able to wish into existence a world that would favor its terms of trade and superpower status," the Baker Institute went so far as to declare,

all NOCs [national oil corporations] would be privatized, foreign
investors would be treated the same as local companies, and OPEC
would be disbanded, allowing free trade and competitive markets to
deliver energy that is needed worldwide at prices determined solely by
the market. But it is hard to imagine why major oil producing countries
would agree to that. . . . In light of this reality, the United States will have
to accept the existence of NOCs as a fact of life but should encourage
steps to make their activities more businesslike, transparent and—to the
extent possible—free of onerous government interference.

Above all, the U.S. imperial objective should be to "break up" wherever possible "the monopoly power of oil producers" and their use of
their oil resources to pursue national goals other than purely commercial
ones. The chief example of such state interference in oil production, the
Baker Institute report stated, was Venezuela under the leadership of
Hugo Chávez. Not only had the Bolivarian Revolution prioritized "the
government's national development policy" and "social and cultural
investment" over "commercial development strategy," it had also used oil
as an instrument of "foreign policy activism." This could be seen in its
geopolitically motivated agreements with Bolivia, Ecuador, Nicaragua,
and the Caribbean nations. Another case of the geostrategic wielding of
oil power was Iran, which had threatened that it "could block the vital oil
transitway, the Strait of Hormuz," if faced with a U.S. military attack. One
critical danger that the United States needed to guard against was a "hos-
tile" alliance between major oil producing and consuming states, such as
Russia, China, Iran, and the Central Asian states. Another key consideration in the geopolitics of tough oil, the Baker Institute underscored, was
the continuing political instability in Iraq. Despite Washington's attempts
to stabilize that country, political unrest and war continued, preventing oil
exploration in Iraq's western desert.[34]

The tightening oil situation has prompted rapid-on-the ground
growth of U.S. energy imperialism, beyond the continuing Iraq and
Afghan wars. The security of Saudi Arabia remains an overriding focus.
Washington's plans for a massive expansion of investment and production in Saudi Arabia, which according to the U.S. Department of Energy
needs to double its oil output by 2030, depends on the feudal kingdom

remaining in place. Meanwhile, there is rising social tension, emanating from the vastly unequal distribution of the country's oil revenues. Ninety percent of private sector jobs go to foreigners. The sexes are entirely segregated. The repressive structure of the society conceals massive popular resentment. Any destabilization of the society would likely prompt U.S. military intervention. As James Howard Kunstler has written in *The Long Emergency*, "a desperate superpower might feel it has no choice except to attempt to control the largest remaining oil fields on the planet at any cost"—particularly if faced by growing rivalry from other states.[35]

The United States has sought to counter the possibility of an energy alliance between Russia, China, Iran, and Central Asian oil states by expanding its military bases in Afghanistan and Central Asia, notably its Manas air base in Kyrgyzstan on the border of oil-rich Kazakhstan.

Threats of U.S. "preemptive" military intervention directed at Iran meanwhile have been continuous, based on its alleged attempts to acquire nuclear weapons through the aggressive pursuit of nuclear energy, and its "interference" in Iraq. Iran's pursuit of nuclear power, as a 2007 study published in the *Proceedings of the National Academy of Sciences* has confirmed, is due to an oil export decline rate of 10–12 percent, arising from the growth of domestic energy demand plus a high rate of oil field depletion and a lack of investment growth in expanded capacity. This led to Iran's recent inability to meet its OPEC oil export quota. The current trend points to the likelihood of Iranian petroleum exports falling to zero by 2014–15. From the standpoint of Western energy and national security analysts, Iran's government and its national oil corporation have adopted the monopolistic policy of underinvesting in oil, deliberating slowing its production in expectation of continually rising prices, thereby holding back on the lifeblood of the world economy.[36]

During the last few years, the U.S. military has dramatically increased its bases and operations in Africa, particularly in the Gulf of Guinea. The United States expects to get 20 percent of its oil imports from Africa by 2010, and 25 percent by 2015. The U.S. military set up a separate Africa Command in 2007 to govern all U.S. military operations in Africa (outside of Egypt). Washington sees itself in direct competition with Beijing over African oil—a competition that it perceives not simply in economic but also military-strategic terms.[37]

U.S. ruling interests also have increased their threats directed at Venezuela, Ecuador, Bolivia, and other Latin American states, accusing them of "resource nationalism" and presenting them as dangers to U.S. national security. Washington has made one attempt after another to unseat Venezuela's democratically elected president Hugo Chávez and to overthrow Venezuela's Bolivarian Revolution, with the clear object of regime change. This has included stepping up its massive military intervention in Colombia and backing the Colombian military and its intrusions into neighboring countries. In 2006 the U.S. Southern Command conducted an internal study, declaring that Venezuela, Bolivia, Ecuador, and conceivably even Mexico (which was then facing elections with a possible populist outcome) offered serious dangers to U.S. energy security. "Pending any favorable changes to the investment climate," it declared, "the prospects for long-term energy production in Venezuela, Ecuador and Mexico are currently at risk." The military threat was obvious.[38]

All of this is in accord with the history of capitalism, and the response of declining hegemons to global forces largely outside their control. The new energy imperialism of the United States is already leading to expanding wars, which could become truly global, as Washington attempts to safeguard the existing capitalist economy and to stave off its own hegemonic decline. As Simmons has warned: "If we don't create a solution to the enormous potential gap between our inherent demand for energy and the availability of energy we will have the nastiest and last war we'll ever fight. I mean a literal war."[39]

In January 2008, Carlos Pascual, vice president of the Brookings Institution and former director of the Bush administration's Office of Reconstruction and Stabilization, released an analysis of "The Geopolitics of Energy" that highlighted U.S. capitalism's *de facto* dependence on oil production in "Saudi Arabia, Russia, Iran, Iraq, Venezuela, Nigeria, and Kazakhstan"—all posing major security threats. "Due to commercial disputes, local instability, or ideology, Russia, Venezuela, Iran, Nigeria, and Iraq are not investing in new long-term production capacity." This, then, was then designated by Pascual as both an economic and a military problem for Washington.[40]

Especially disturbing, in this new phase of energy imperialism, is the lack of resistance from populations within central capitalist countries themselves. Thus, left-liberal publications in the wealthy nations often play on the prejudices of their readers (who are buffeted by rising gasoline prices), encouraging them to support oil imperialism designed to safeguard Western capitalism. David Litvin, writing on "Oil, Gas and Imperialism" in 2006 for the *Guardian* in London, claimed that "the inevitability of modern energy imperialism needs to be recognized." Threats from Russia, OPEC, Venezuela, and Bolivia were highlighted. The United States invaded Iraq, we were told, partly for "oil security." Clearly sympathizing with that form of energy imperialism that "involves consumer states launching political or military" interventions "to secure supplies," Litvin concluded: "Energy imperialism is here to stay, and efforts should [therefore] focus on making it a more benign force."[41]

Likewise, Joshua Kurlantzick, a contributing writer for *Mother Jones*, wrote a piece entitled "Put a Tyrant in Your Tank" for the May–June 2008 issue of that magazine. It attributed oil supply problems to national oil companies, and argued—referring to the Baker Institute report on "The Changing Role of National Oil Companies"— that oil would be better safeguarded if placed in the hands of multinational oil companies as of old. The latter, readers were told, "may cozy up to nasty regimes . . . but they are at least obligated to respond to public criticism." Kurlantzick presented repeated criticisms of Hugo Chávez in Venezuela for his "resource nationalism," going so far as to compare Venezuela to Burma and Russia, as "authoritarian and corrupt," citing a study from the neoconservative, largely U.S. government-funded, Freedom House. The *Mother Jones* article also gave credence to the 2006 internal study conducted by the Pentagon's Southern Command, pinpointing the national security dangers to the United States of resource nationalism in Venezuela, Bolivia, and Ecuador. Other petrostates that were subjected to sharp criticism were Iran, Russia, Kazakhstan, Nigeria, and Libya. Chinese state oil corporations were targeted for their aggressiveness in pursuing oil around the world and for their lack of environmental concerns. U.S. energy imperialism was thus seen as justified, even by the putatively progressive *Mother Jones*—with hope and confidence being placed mainly in Big Oil and the Pentagon.[42]

PLANETARY CONFLAGRATION?

The supreme irony of the peak oil crisis, of course, is that the world is rapidly proceeding down the path of climate change from the burning of fossil fuels, threatening within a matter of decades human civilization and life on the planet. Unless carbon dioxide emissions from the consumption of such fuels are drastically reduced, a global catastrophe awaits. For environmentalists peak oil is therefore not a tragedy in itself, since the crucial challenge facing humanity at present is weaning the world from excessive dependence on fossil fuels. The breaking of the solar energy budget that hydrocarbons allowed has generated a biospheric rift, which if not rapidly addressed will close off the future.[43]

Yet heavy levels of fossil fuel, and particularly petroleum, consumption are built into the structure of the present world capitalist economy. The immediate response of the system to the end of easy oil has been, therefore, to turn to a new energy imperialism—a strategy of maximum extraction by any means possible. It has as its object the placating of what Rachel Carson once called "the gods of profit and production."[44] This, however, presents the threat of multiple global conflagrations: global warming, peak oil, rapidly rising world hunger (resulting in part from growing biofuel production), and nuclear war—all in order to secure a system geared to growing inequality.

In the face of the immense perils now facing life on the planet, the world desperately needs to take a new direction—toward communal well-being and global justice: a socialism for the planet. The immense danger now facing the human species, it should be understood, is not due principally to the constraints of the natural environment, whether geological or climatic, but arises from a deranged social system wheeling out of control, and more specifically, U.S. imperialism. This is the challenge of our time.

CHAPTER FIVE

The Pentagon and Climate Change

Abrupt climate change has been a growing topic of concern for more than a decade for climate scientists, who fear that global warming could shut down the ocean conveyer that warms the North Atlantic, plunging Europe and parts of North America into Siberian-like conditions within a few decades or even years. But it was only with the appearance of a Pentagon report on the possible social effects—in terms of instability and war—of abrupt climate change that it riveted public attention. As the *Observer* put it, "climate change over the next 20 years could result in global catastrophe costing millions of lives in wars and natural disasters."[1] Indeed, widespread public alarm, particularly in Europe, was the predictable response to the release of the Pentagon's October 2003 report, *An Abrupt Climate Change Scenario and Its Implications for United States National Security*.[2] In an attempt to quiet these fears, Defense Department officials and the authors of the report quickly came forward to say that the entire exercise was speculative and "intentionally extreme"; that the whole thing had been misconstrued and overblown in certain press accounts.

Was this then simply a "hullabaloo" about nothing, as the *San Francisco Chronicle* suggested, or are there dangers associated with climate change that have not been sufficiently appreciated thus far? To answer this question it is necessary to approach the issue in stages, by first addressing global warming, then abrupt climate change and its inherent social dangers, and finally how the present system of production constitutes a barrier to any ready solution.

GLOBAL WARMING: HOW BAD IS IT?

A natural greenhouse effect is crucial to the earth's atmosphere. As carbon dioxide, methane, and other greenhouse gases accumulate in the atmosphere they trap heat that would otherwise radiate off into space. This natural greenhouse effect along with proximity to the sun serves to warm the earth-making it habitable to diverse species. But now, as a result of enhanced greenhouse gas emissions from human production, most notably the burning of fossil fuels, this same life-supporting greenhouse effect is pushing average global temperatures higher and higher. Carbon dioxide concentration in the atmosphere is now at its highest point in the last 420,000 years and likely in the last twenty million years. Rising sea levels, heat waves, crop failures, worsening floods and droughts, and more extreme weather conditions in general are all to be expected as a result of such increases in average global temperature.

Some of the warming to be experienced in coming decades is already locked-in. Greenhouse gases have atmospheric lifetimes of decades to centuries. Even if societies were to cease fossil fuel use and end all other forms of greenhouse gas emissions today, the accumulation of such gases in the atmosphere would likely generate significant further warming on the order of 0.5°C (0.9°F) during this century. While if we do nothing to limit such emissions global average surface temperature could conceivably rise as much as 5.8°C (10.4°F) between 1990 and 2100, exceeding the change in average temperature separating us from the last ice age. Few informed analysts now expect the increase in average global temperature to be kept below a 2°C (3.6°F) increase under business as usual. The main fear at present is that the rise in global temperature will be two or three times as large as that by the end of the century if human society is unable to act decisively.[3]

Global warming is expected to be a growing factor in coming decades in species extinction, the rate of which at present is higher than at any time since the disappearance of the dinosaurs sixty-five million years ago. In mountainous regions all around the earth plant and animal species are ascending higher and higher as warming occurs. But mountains only reach so far. Consequently, the species occupying the topmost ecological niches are now in the process of ascending "to heaven."[4] We do not know how many other species will share this fate during this century. But we do know that the earth's species in general will be massively affected, that biological diversity will continue to decrease, and that if we do nothing and average global temperatures rise to the upper levels that leading climate scientists think possible by the year 2100 it could prove catastrophic, seriously threatening ecosystems and destabilizing human society.

Still, the ruling economic and political interests and their attendant elites tell us not to be worried. Never mind the threats to other species. Human society, we are frequently told, is different. It can evolve rapidly by economic and technological means and, thus, adapt to global warming, which from its standpoint can be viewed as slow, "gradual" change. What is often projected for global society then is increased discomfort rather than massive social upheaval and dislocation. Orthodox economists generally caution that we should do nothing that might limit economic growth. Instead, they see the only answer as lying in a bigger economy, which will give us more means of addressing future contingencies.

ABRUPT CLIMATE CHANGE

Nevertheless, there is every reason to believe that placing so much faith in economic growth and technological change as answers to global warming is shortsighted and naive. Considerable uncertainty exists as to how far human society can actually support such "gradual" climate change—since human beings are themselves part of nature and dependent on the world around them in manifold ways. But the problem does not stop there. Scientists are now raising the even more alarming question of abrupt climate change, i.e., climate change of a scale and suddenness—shifting from a time-span of decades-to-centuries to one of years-to-decades—that would definitely have catastrophic effects for human society.

Abrupt climate change is usually seen as change arising from gradual causes that lead to the crossing of a threshold, triggering a sudden shift to a new state—with the shift determined by the climate system itself and occurring at a rate much faster than the initial cause.[5] Such shifts have occurred numerous times in history, one of the clearest being the abrupt cooling of the Younger Dryas (named after an arctic wildflower that thrived in the climate of the time), which began 12,700 years ago and lasted 1,300 years, interrupting the warming associated with the end of the last ice age. A lesser instance of abrupt climate change occurred 8,200 years ago and lasted around a century. In the worst of all current, plausible scenarios, such abrupt climate change could occur sometime over the next couple of decades—though this is still seen by scientists as highly unlikely.

Such abrupt climate change is believed to result from disruption of the thermohaline circulation, a global ocean conveyor that moves warm, saline tropical waters northward in the Atlantic with the Gulf Stream as its northern arm, and then loops south. ("Thermohaline" comes from the Greek words for heat, "thermos," and for salt, "halos.") The heat from this warmer water, when it reaches the North Atlantic, is released into the atmosphere, creating milder winters than would otherwise exist at those latitudes, and allowing the dense surface waters to cool and sink. This draws additional warmer, saline water from the south, helping to keep the conveyor going. Differences in the density of ocean waters associated with the saline content drive this ocean conveyor.

Abrupt climate change arises from a lessening or collapse of the thermohaline circulation due to increased river runoff, melting ice, and changes in precipitation—all of which serve to increase the amount of freshwater supplied to the North Atlantic. As the salinity of the ocean waters decreases a dramatic lessening or complete collapse of the North Atlantic conveyor circulation can occur. The current global warming is seen as potentially triggering this effect. According to the UN Intergovernmental Panel on Climate Change (IPCC), in *Climate Change 2001,* "beyond 2100, the thermohaline circulation could completely, and possibly irreversibly, shut-down in either hemisphere" if global warming is "large enough and applied long enough."[6] Two basic scenarios are worth considering: (1) If the ocean conveyor slows down or collapses during the next two decades, it could cool the North Atlantic region by as much as 5°C (9°F), creating winters of much greater severity. (2) If, however, the conveyor slows down in a century, the drop in temperature in the North Atlantic could temporarily compensate for the rise in surface temperature associated with the enhanced greenhouse effect— though once the thermohaline circulation recovered the "deferred" warming could be delivered within a decade. The second of these two scenarios is viewed as much more likely. Yet, recent scientific studies, including a major report in 2002 by the National Academy of Sciences, have stressed that the thermohaline circulation could possibly "decrease . . . very fast"—resulting in a sudden switch of climate early this century that although still thought unlikely cannot be ruled out altogether. Seeming to confirm these fears, a report in *Nature* in 2002 concluded that the North Atlantic has been freshening dramatically for forty years; while a report a year earlier suggested that the ocean conveyor may already be slowing down.[7]

Faced with the uncertain hazards of such a "low probability, high impact" event, scientists associated with the National Academy of Sciences study recommended that society take what steps it could, if not too costly, to protect itself against such an extreme outcome. "If a shutdown were to happen soon," Richard Alley, who chaired the scientific team releasing the National Academy of Sciences study, observed in *The Two-Mile Time Machine*, "it could produce a large event, perhaps almost as large as the Younger Dryas, dropping northern temperatures and spreading droughts far larger than the changes that have affected humans through recorded history, and perhaps speeding warming in the far south. The end of humanity? No. An uncomfortable time for humanity? Yes."[8]

These assessments and recommendations on abrupt climate change were offered with so much caution by climate scientists that they might easily have been ignored altogether by a society that in its upper echelons is devoted to the accumulation of capital and little else. That this did not happen is due to the fact that the issue was taken up and dramatized in the Pentagon report.

THE PENTAGON ELEVATES THE THREAT

The story behind the Pentagon report on abrupt climate change is almost as remarkable as the contents of the report itself. The National Academy study of this issue crossed the desk of Andrew Marshall, director of the Pentagon's Office of Net Assessment. Marshall, who has worked for every secretary of defense since James Schlesinger in the 1970s, is a legendary "wise man," known as "Yoda," at the Pentagon. When they need someone to think about big things, the Department of Defense turns to Marshall. His most famous achievement was the promotion of missile defense. It was Marshall who authorized the $100,000 grant for Peter Schwartz and Doug Randall of the Global Business Network to analyze abrupt climate change for the Pentagon. The intent was obviously to have economic futurologists visualize the possible effects of such abrupt climate change, since they would be in the best position to speculate on the economic and social fallout of such a catastrophic development, and thus upgrade it to a major Pentagon concern.

Schwartz was a surprising choice for such a task, since he was best known previously for his book *The Long Boom*. In the 1990s, he was a contributing writer to *Wired* magazine. Together with Peter Leyden, a senior editor of the magazine, and Joe Hyatt of the Stanford University Business School, he got caught up in the idea that the New Economy, rooted in today's digital high technology, pointed to a long economic boom stretching from 1980 to at least 2020. During this time, the economy would, they argued in the book, simply "grow more" based on the New Economy model pioneered by the United States, with global growth of "possibly even 6 percent."[9] The first version of this thesis, in their *Wired* article on the long boom, came out in July 1997 and created a stir. The article, together with the book that followed later, constituted the most extreme version of the great millennial celebration. According to Schwartz and his coauthors, who grossly misunderstood the main economic tendencies of the time, the U.S. economy was rocketing throughout the 1990s and was likely to accelerate further in the 2000s. All such New Economy mythology was put to an end, however, by the bursting of the speculative bubble and the dramatic stock market decline of 2000, followed by recession in 2001 and slow growth and employment stagnation ever since. Nevertheless, it was to Schwartz, the failed prophet of a long New Economy boom, to whom Marshall turned to dramatize the consequences of abrupt climate change.[10]

Schwartz and Randall's *An Abrupt Climate Change Scenario and Its Implications for United States National Security* begins by challenging the way in which climate change is usually approached:

> When most people think about climate change, they imagine gradual increases in temperature and only marginal changes in other climatic conditions, continuing indefinitely or even leveling off at some time in the future. The conventional wisdom is that modern civilization will either adapt to whatever weather conditions we face and that the pace of climate change will not overwhelm the adaptive capacity of society, or that our efforts such as those embodied in the Kyoto protocol will be sufficient to mitigate the impacts. The IPCC documents [that] the threat of gradual climate change and its impact to food supplies and other resources of importance to humans will not be so severe as to create security threats. Optimists assert that the benefits from technological innovation will be able to outpace the negative effects of climate change.
>
> Climatically, the gradual view of the future assumes that agriculture will continue to thrive and growing seasons will lengthen. Northern Europe, Russia, and North America will prosper agriculturally while southern Europe, Africa, and Central and South America will suffer from increased dryness, heat, water shortages, and reduced production. Overall, global food production under many typical climate scenarios increases.

Schwartz and Randall argue against such complacent views of global warming, insisting that they do not take sufficient account of the discontinuities that may arise as warming causes various thresholds to be crossed. More frequent droughts, for example, could have disastrous and cumulative effects. Still, the worst effects from such gradual warming are seen as applying mainly to the poorer countries of the global South rather than the richer countries of the global North—the main source of carbon dioxide emissions. All of this encourages a do-nothing or do-little attitude in the northern centers of world power.

Abrupt climate change alters this picture dramatically. Such change would create catastrophic conditions for human society; and rather than falling first and foremost on the global South the direct effects of a shutdown of the thermohaline conveyor would bear down on the global North—specifically those countries bordering the North Atlantic. Schwartz and Randall are clear that they are not actually predicting such abrupt climate change in the near future (though it is certain to occur in the long-term future). Rather, they offer a "plausible" if unlikely scenario "for which there is reasonable evidence," so as to "explore potential implications for United States national security." They model their scenario on the event of 8,200 years ago rather than on the much worse Younger Dryas. In their scenario, a "thermohaline circulation collapse" causes a drop in average surface temperature in northern Europe of up to 3.3°C (6°F) along with severe temperature drops throughout the North Atlantic, lasting about a century. Colder temperatures, wind, and dryness in the global North are accompanied by increased warmth and drought in much of the rest of the world.

The picture they paint is one of agricultural decline and extreme weather conditions, stretching energy resources, throughout the globe. Relatively well-off populations with ample natural resources and food producing capabilities, such as the United States and Australia, are seen as building "defensive fortresses" around themselves to keep massive waves of would-be immigrants out, while much of the world gyrates toward war:

> Violence and disruption stemming from the stresses created by abrupt changes in the climate pose a different type of threat to national security than we are accustomed to today. Military confrontation may be triggered by a desperate need for natural resources such as energy, food, and water rather than by conflicts over ideology, religion, or national honor. The shifting motivation for confrontation would alter which countries are most vulnerable and the existing warning signs for security threats.

As the world's carrying capacity declines under harsh climatic conditions, warfare becomes widespread—producing increased dangers of thermonuclear war.

For Schwartz and Randall the lesson is clear. Human society must "prepare for the inevitable effects of abrupt climate change—which will likely come [the only question is when] regardless of human activity." If the scenario that they depict is actually in the cards, it could already be too late to do anything to stop it. What can be done under these circumstances, they suggest, is to make sure that the necessary security measures are in place to stave off the most disastrous consequences resulting from social instability. Since this is a report commissioned by the Pentagon, the emphasis is on how to "create vulnerability metrics" to determine which countries are likely to be hit the hardest ecologically, economically, and socially and thus will be propelled in the direction of war. Such information will make it possible for the United States to act in its own security interest. The narrow objective is thus to safeguard Fortress America at all cost.

Although the ecological repercussions are supposed to hit the global North the hardest, the scenario provided by the Pentagon report with respect to instability and war follows conventional ideological paths, focusing mostly on the global South. The possibility that the United States itself might in such circumstances attempt to seize world oil supplies and other natural resources is not raised by the report. The U.S. response is depicted as entirely defensive, mainly concerned with holding off unwelcome waves of would-be immigrants, and trying to create an atmosphere of peace and stability in the world under much harsher global conditions.

Given the contents of this report, it is not surprising that it initially generated dismay and widespread fears when it was made public in February. At that point, the Pentagon quickly stepped in to quiet the alarm that the report had set off. Marshall himself released a statement that the Pentagon study "reflects the limits of scientific models and information when it comes to predicting the effects of abrupt global warming." Although backed up by "significant scientific evidence . . . much of what this study predicts," Marshall indicated, "is still speculation." Pentagon officials meanwhile declared that the abrupt climate change report, although commissioned by their legendary "Yoda," had not been passed on to Marshall's superiors in the Defense Department and the Bush administration.[11]

Yet, the real importance of *An Abrupt Climate Change Scenario* does not lie in its impact on the top brass in the Pentagon, much less their environmentally-challenged superiors then inhabiting the White House.

Instead, its historical significance derives from the more general contention made at the beginning of the report that "because of the potentially dire consequences, the risk of abrupt climate change, although uncertain and quite possibly small, should be elevated beyond a scientific debate to a U.S. national security concern." It is a small step from this view to one that insists that the nature of the threat demands that we begin to consider other, radical social alternatives to business-as-usual, which must be elevated to the forefront of public discussions.

ACCELERATED CLIMATE CHANGE

Here, it is crucial to recognize that abrupt climate change as currently modeled by scientists, though the most dramatic, is not the only non-gradual outcome possible as a result of global warming. Scientists are even more concerned, at present, about the potential for positive feedbacks that will greatly amplify global warming, increasing the rate of its advance and the speed with which it crosses various ecological thresholds. According to the IPCC in *Climate Change 2001*, "as the CO_2 concentration of the atmosphere increases, ocean and land will take up a decreasing fraction of anthropogenic CO_2 emissions. The net effect of land and ocean climate feedbacks as indicated by models is to further increase projected atmospheric CO_2 concentrations, by reducing both the ocean and land uptake of CO_2." The hydrological cycle (evaporation, precipitation, and runoff) could accelerate as a result of global warming, driving temperatures higher faster. Water vapor, the most potent natural greenhouse gas, could trap additional heat, increasing the rate at which average surface temperatures rise. The melting of highly reflective ice and snow could result in further absorption of sunlight, leading to additional global warming. The capacity of both forests and oceans to absorb carbon dioxide could decrease, creating a positive feedback loop that accelerates climate change. All of this is taken into account to some extent in the IPCC reports. But, given the level of uncertainty, the possibility of surprising developments under these circumstances is very great.

The grim reality is that the more threatening scenarios with respect to climate change are becoming increasingly plausible as the data keeps coming in. Carbon dioxide levels in the atmosphere increased at an accelerated level from 2003 to 2004. The increase of 3 parts per million was well above the 1.8 parts per million annual increase on average over the past decade, and three times the year-to-year increase experienced half a century ago. Although this may reflect mere annual variance, this kind of evidence is leading scientists to worry that positive feedbacks may already be at work, serving to accelerate the whole problem.[12]

CAPITALISM AND CARBON DIOXIDE

Both the capitalist economy and the world climate represent complex, dynamic systems. The uncertainty with respect to climate change and its economic effects has to do with the interaction of these two complex systems. To make matters worse, both the climate system and the human economy are subsets of the earth system and are inseparably interconnected in extremely complex ways with innumerable other biogeochemical processes. Many of these other biospheric processes are also being transformed by human action.

It is not uncommon for analyses of climate change to assume that the world economy is essentially healthy except for disturbances that could result from the climate. This, however, is in error and underestimates the economic vulnerability of populations and whole societies. At present, "half the world's population lives on less than two dollars per day, with most of those either chronically malnourished or continually concerned with where their next meal will come from. Many have no access to clean water (1 billion), electricity (2 billion), or sanitation (2.5 billion)."[13] Economic growth is slowing in ways that have deepened the economic crisis for human populations. At the same time, "nature's economy" is also in trouble, viewed in terms of the diversity of life on the planet. Economic and ecological vulnerabilities are everywhere.

For the Pentagon, the answer to all of these dangers would seem to be straightforward: arm to the teeth, prepare for greater threats than ever from thermonuclear war, and build an impregnable wall around the United States, closing the global masses out. All of this is depicted by Schwartz and Randall. Yet a more rational response to potential high-impact climate events would be to seek to reorganize society, and to move away from imperatives of accumulation, exploitation, and degradation of the natural environment—the "after me the deluge" system—that lies at the base of most of our global problems.

The truth is that addressing the global warming threat to any appreciable degree would require at the very least a chipping away at the base of the system. The scientific consensus on global warming suggests that what is needed is a 60–80 percent reduction in greenhouse gas emissions below 1990 levels, in the next few decades, in order to avoid catastrophic environmental effects by the end of this century—if not sooner. The threatening nature of such reductions for capitalist economies is apparent in the rather hopeless state, at present, of the Kyoto Protocol, which required the rich industrial countries to reduce their greenhouse gas emissions by an average of 5.2 percent below 1990 levels by 2008–2012. The United States, which had steadily increased its carbon dioxide emissions since 1990, despite its repeated promises to limit its emissions, pulled out of the Kyoto Protocol process in 2001 on the grounds that it was too costly. Yet the Kyoto Protocol was never meant to be anything but the first, small, and in itself totally inadequate step to curtail emissions. The really big cuts were to follow.

The Kyoto Protocol itself only generates bigger questions: Will the rich countries of the global North agree to cut their carbon emissions to the extent required? How can the poorer countries of the global South be brought into the climate accord? There would be little opportunity for most of these poor countries—still the victims of imperialism—to develop economically if they were forced to cut back sharply in their average level of per capita greenhouse gas emissions at this point. Since the atmosphere cannot support increasing levels of carbon dioxide and most of its capacity to do so without high levels of global warming has already been taken up by the rich countries of the center, countries in the periphery are likely to be severely constrained in their use of fossil fuels unless the countries in the center drastically reduce their levels of emissions—on the order of 80–90 percent.

Third world countries insist that the North has an ecological debt to the South, arising from a history of ecological imperialism, and that the only way to redress this and to create a just and sustainable climate regime is to base any solution on per capita emissions. Such a position is rooted in the recognition that the United States, to take the most notorious example, emits 5.6 metric tons of carbon dioxide per person per year (measured in carbon units), while the whole rest of the world outside of the G-7 countries (the United States, Canada, Germany, Britain, Japan, Italy and France) releases only 0.7 tons of carbon dioxide per person annually on average.[14] Inequality of this kind is a major barrier to a smooth climate transition and means that the necessary change must be revolutionary in nature. The only just and sustainable climate regime will be one in which there is a *contraction* of per capita carbon dioxide emissions to levels that are globally sustainable, together with a *convergence* of rich and poor countries around these low, globally sustainable emissions levels. Such safe per capita emissions levels would be less than a tenth of what the North currently emits per capita. One estimate claims that "based on the 1990 target for climate stabilization, everyone in the world would have a per capita allowance of carbon of around 0.4 tonnes, per year."[15]

Obviously, equalization of per capita emissions at low levels for all countries is not something that the United States and the other nations at the center of the system will readily accept. Yet third world countries that desperately need development cannot be expected to give up the right to equality in per capita emissions. Any attempt to impose the main burdens for global warming on underdeveloped countries, in accordance with past imperialistic practices, will thus inevitably fail. To the extent that the United States and other advanced capitalist nations promote such a strategy, they will only push the world into a state of barbarism, while catastrophically undermining the human relation to the biosphere.

EASTER ISLAND AND THE EARTH

For environmentalists the destruction of the ecology and civilization of Easter Island around 1400–1600 A.D. has long been both a mystery and metaphor for our times. We now know that the giant stone statues, the erection of which resulted in the destruction of the island's forests and with them a whole ecology and civilization, were the main symbols of the power and prestige of competing chiefs and their clans. As Jared

Diamond explains: "A chief's status depended on his statues: any chief who failed to cut trees to transport and erect statues would have found himself out of a job."[16] Due to such a narrow acquisitive logic—an early treadmill of production analogous to our own—the Easter Islanders drove their ecology and society to the point of extinction.

Are we headed for a similar disaster today—only on a planetary scale? To quote Diamond again:

> Thanks to globalization, international trade, jet planes, and the Internet, all countries on Earth today share resources and affect each other, just as did Easter's eleven clans. Polynesian Easter Island was as isolated in the Pacific Ocean as the Earth is today in space. When the Easter Islanders got into difficulties, there was nowhere to which they could flee, or to which they could turn for help; nor shall we modern Earthlings have recourse elsewhere if our troubles increase. Those are the reasons why people see the collapse of Easter Island society as a metaphor, a worst-case scenario, for what may lie ahead in our own future.

Easter Island society got into trouble because of a class system. With its island world increasingly under ecological strain, the chiefs and priests were overthrown by military leaders, and the society descended into the barbarism of civil war and then declined completely. Here too is a lesson for our time: we need to confront the class system and reorganize society in line with the needs of all of its inhabitants before barbarism descends upon us.

The Pentagon report itself takes on a different meaning here. It depicted abrupt climate change and a descent into internecine war. It was "intentionally extreme." But as the fate of Easter Island suggests, it may not have been extreme enough.

CHAPTER 6

The Jevons Paradox:
Environment and Technology under Capitalism

William Stanley Jevons (1835–1882) is best known as a British economist who was one of the pioneers of contemporary neoclassical economic analysis, with its subjective value theory rooted in marginal utility. His applied economics and theoretical insights marked new points of departure for later economists who would more fully shape the neoclassical tradition. But Jevons is also remembered as an early contributor to ecological economics and energetics, as a result of his pioneering work *The Coal Question* (1865), which raised fundamental issues regarding energy efficiency and the economy of fuel.[1]

Jevons's intellectual career bloomed for a mere twenty years, due to a late start and an early death. Likewise, his development as an economist included various detours that contributed to his economic theories. The well-to-do Jevons family was disrupted by the death of Jevons's mother in 1845 and the failure of his father's iron merchant business in 1848.[2] The economically vulnerable position of the family later contributed to Jevons's decision to leave University College at London, where he was studying chemistry and mathematics, to accept a position as an assistant assayer to the Royal Mint in Sydney, Australia, in 1853. In Australia, Jevons explored the colony, studying nature and meteorology. But his interests in studying and defining the operations of the human world led him to forgo the lucrative position in 1859, so that he could return to London to study philosophy, logic, political economy, mathematics, classics, and history. By 1862, Jevons had completed his BA and MA and was in the process of creating the synthesis of logic, mathematics, and philosophy that underlay his economic thought. He viewed economics as a mathematical science, dealing with quantities of time, consumption, production, and investment.[3] Jevons's laws of logic were so mechanically structured that he built a "logic machine," which is recognized as a forerunner of modern computers, to perform processes of reasoning.

Starting as a tutor at Owens College in Manchester in 1863, Jevons was promoted to Cobden Professor of Political Economy and professor of logic, mental, and moral philosophy by 1865 on the merits of his contributions to these fields of science.[4] Jevons's published works were on the laws of reasoning, changes in the value of gold, trade and price cycles, economic policy (free trade), and the role of the state. A type of Benthamite utilitarianism lay at the heart of his economic model, as presented in his 1871 *The Theory of Political Economy*. Labor for production was pain (disutility) and consumption was pleasure (utility). Equilibrium in prices was proportional to degrees of utility and costs of production.[5] Jevons assumed that individuals greedily operated to maximize satisfaction, thus laying the foundation for later theories of consumer behavior.

Jevons's obsessive drive to learn and write made him one of the leading thinkers of economics and logic, leading to his election by chancellors Gladstone and Lowe as a fellow of the Royal Society in 1872. But his health suffered under his relentless pace, leading to his resignation from Manchester in 1876. Jevons took a position at University College at London due to the lighter teaching duties, but he resigned in 1880 to pursue his studies and writings full-time. However, his health continued to decline, until the day he drowned while swimming on vacation in 1882.

In the 1860s, the House of Commons raised questions related to whether Britain's world supremacy in industrial production and economic competitiveness could be threatened in the long run by the exhaustion of coal reserves. At the time, no extensive study had been conducted on coal reserves and their impact on industrial consumption and economic growth. Edward Hull's *Coalfields of Great Britain*, published in 1861, only estimated the quantity of coal. Jevons seized the opportunity to study the topic, hoping it would bring him national recognition due to the popular concern over coal and British economic power. With his usual intensity, Jevons wrote in 1864, in a single summer, the book *The Coal Question: An Inquiry Concerning the Progress of the Nation, and the Probable Exhaustion of Our Coal-Mines*, which brought him national prominence and academic promotions. Jevons argued that British industrial growth had relied on cheap coal and that the increasing cost of coal, as deeper seams were mined, threatened economic stagnation. Substituting coal for corn, within the general Malthusian argument, he observed: "Our subsistence no longer depends upon our produce of corn. The momentous repeal of the Corn Laws throws us from corn upon coal."[6] Jevons argued that neither technology nor substitution of other energy sources for coal could alter this.

Jevons was stunningly wrong in his calculations. His chief mistake was to underestimate the importance of coal substitutes such as petroleum and hydroelectric power. Jevons's failure in this respect is somewhat ironic, given his treatment of an earlier substitution with respect to the history of the iron trade. Jevons draws attention to the use of timber, as charcoal, for the production of iron, preceding widespread use of coal in this process. Jevons noted, "The increase of the [iron] trade threatened to denude England of the forests which were considered an ornament to the country, as well as essential to its security, as providing the oak timber for our navy." When the woods were near exhaustion, production moved to Ireland, clearing (and depleting) their forests to produce iron for export to Britain. Jevons pointed out that "the substitution of coal for charcoal had become a necessity" to effectively compete due to the loss of wood to sustain growth and developments in the production process.[7] Thus, Jevons knew that coal had replaced timber use in this production, but he could not see any further substitution for coal. Jevons presented this history as if it were simply the natural development of productive systems, ignoring the social relationships that shaped these changes and the ecological ramifications of this process. In 1936, Keynes commented on Jevons's argument regarding coal consumption, stating that it was "overstrained and exaggerated." One might also add narrow in scope.[8]

But there is one aspect of Jevons's argument that continues to be considered one of the pioneering insights into ecological economics, and that is now known as the "Jevons Paradox."[9] Chapter 7 of *The Coal Question* was entitled "Of the Economy of Fuel." Here, Jevons argued that increased efficiency in using a natural resource, such as coal, only generated increased demand for that resource, not decreased demand as one might expect. This was because improvement in efficiency led to further economic expansion. "*It is wholly confusion of ideas,*" Jevons wrote,

> *to suppose that the economical use of fuel is equivalent to a diminished consumption. The very contrary is the truth.* As a rule, new modes of economy will lead to an increase of consumption according to a principle recognised in many parallel instances. . . . The same principles apply, with even greater force and distinctness, to the use of such a general agent as coal. It is the very economy of its use which leads to its extensive consumption. . . . Nor is it difficult to see how this paradox arises. . . . If the quantity of coal used in a blast-furnace, for instance, be diminished in comparison with the yield, the profits of the trade will increase, new capital will be attracted, the price of pig-iron will fall, but the demand for it [will] increase; and eventually the greater number of furnaces will more than make up for the diminished consumption of each. And if such is not always the result within a single branch, it must be remembered that the progress of any branch of manufacture excites a new activity in most other branches, and leads indirectly, if not directly, to increased inroads upon our seams of coal. . . . Civilisation, says Baron Liebig, is *the economy of power*, and our power is coal. It is the very economy of the use of coal that makes our industry what it is; and the more we render it efficient and economical, the more will our industry thrive, and our works of civilisation grow.[10]

Jevons went on to insist that the entire history of the steam engine was a history of successive economies in its use—and each time this led to economic expansion and increased aggregate demand for coal. "Every such improvement of the engine," he observed, "when effected, does but accelerate anew the consumption of coal. Every branch of manufacture receives a fresh impulse—hand labour is still further replaced by mechanical labour."[11]

The present-day significance of the Jevons paradox can be seen with respect to the automobile in the United States. The introduction of more energy-efficient automobiles in the United States, in the mid-1970s, did not decrease the demand for fuel because driving increased, and the number of cars on the road eventually doubled. Likewise, technological improvements in refrigeration merely resulted in more and larger refrigerators. This tendency is not confined to individual consumption but applies with even greater force within industry itself.

Although Jevons is credited for introducing his paradox, the main impetus behind the problem he raises is not analyzed in *The Coal Question*. As one of the early neoclassical economists, Jevons had abandoned the central emphasis on class and accumulation that distinguished the work of the classical economists. His economic analysis took the form of static equilibrium theory. Hence, it was ill equipped to deal with dynamic issues of accumulation and growth. Jevons, who saw capitalism more as a natural phenomenon than a socially constructed reality, could find no explanations for continuously increasing economic demand, other than to point to individual behavior and Malthusian demographics. The idea of class-based accumulation of capital, as the source of capitalism's unrelenting growth dynamic, was beyond his vision of things.

Although the Jevons paradox has great significance for the ecological problems of today (relating, for example, to attempts to decrease the rate of global warming through greater fuel efficiency), it would be a mistake to see his argument in *The Coal Question* as primarily ecological in character. Despite his importance to ecological economics, Jevons himself was not concerned with the ecological and social problems associated with the exhaustion of energy reserves in Great Britain or in the rest of the world. He even failed to address the air, land, and water pollution that accompanied coal production. The occupational illnesses and hazards confronting workers in the mines did not enter his analysis. Jevons's primary concern was how the rapid rate of coal consumption would affect the economic growth, competitiveness, and power of Great Britain within the global capitalist system. Jevons wanted to perpetuate British industry, even if it meant exhausting coal reserves.

Coal was the source of economic power for Great Britain, and Jevons feared that the (unlikely) development of an alternative energy source would destroy British industrial supremacy. Given British industrial development and trade relations, "food and raw materials are poured upon us from abroad, and our subsistence is gained by returning manufactures and articles of refinement of an equal value."[12]

The human relationship with nature, he believed, "consists in withdrawing and using our small fraction of energy in a happy mode and moment." "The resources of nature," he wrote, "are almost unbounded":

> Economy consists in discovering and picking out those almost infinitesimal portions that best serve our purpose. We disregard the abundant vegetation, and live upon the small grain of corn; we burn down the largest tree, that we may use its ashes; or we wash away ten thousand parts of rock, and sand, and gravel, that we may extract the particle of gold. Millions, too, live, and work, and die, in the accustomed grooves for the one Lee, or Savery, or Crompton, or Watt, who uses his minute personal contribution of labour to the best effect.[13]

Jevons simply assumes that this mass disruption and degradation of the earth is a natural process to be approached only from the standpoint of the pursuit of a growing economy. Although the shortage of coal generates questions in his analysis about whether growth can be sustained, the issue of ecological sustainability as such is never raised. Because the economy must remain in motion to accumulate wealth, Jevons disregarded natural forces of energy, such as water and wind, as unreliable sources of constant energy, limited to a particular time and space.[14] Coal offered capital a universal energy source to operate production without disruption of business patterns.

This disregard for nature can be contrasted with the views of Marx and Engels, Jevons's contemporaries who, although they have been compared unfavorably to Jevons in ecological terms, nonetheless argued against the abuse of nature—which Jevons did not.[15] Marx developed an overarching concept of the "metabolic rift" in the human relation to nature, which took into account the degradation of the earth and the conservation of energy.[16] Writing to Marx in 1882, Engels observed that "the working individual is not only a stabiliser of the *present* but also, and to a far greater extent, a squanderer of *past* solar heat. As to what we have done in the way of squandering our reserves of energy, our coal, ore, forests, etc., you are better informed than I am."[17]

In the *Dialectics of Nature*, Engels warned against the cutting of trees on hillsides, which later led to flooding, destruction of cultivated land, mudslides, and loss of soil. The Spanish planters in Cuba burned the forest for fertilizer, which allowed for a single year of profit, but the heavy rains washed away the soil because no trees covered the hillsides. In regard to the larger political economy and social relationship to nature, Engels commented: "The present mode of production is predominately concerned only about the immediate, the most tangible result; and then surprise is expressed that the more remote effects of actions directed to this end turn out to be quite different, are mostly quite the opposite in character; that the harmony of supply and demand is transformed into the very reverse opposite." He described the ecological destruction that took place under the capitalist system and called into question a system based on short-term profit and the accumulation of wealth. In regard to a sustainable, regulated interchange with nature, Engels stated, "a complete revolution in our hitherto existing mode of production and simultaneously a revolution in our whole contemporary social order" was needed.[18] These comments resonate with an awareness that overshadows the predicament that Jevons describes.

Jevons himself had no real answer to the paradox he raised. Britain could either use up its cheap source of fuel—the coal on which its industrialization rested—rapidly, or it could use it up more slowly. In the end, Jevons chose to use it up rapidly: "If we lavishly and boldly push forward in the creation of our riches, both material and intellectual, it is hard to over-estimate the pitch of beneficial influence to which we may attain in the present. *But the maintenance of such a position is physically impossible. We have to make the momentous choice between brief but true greatness and longer continued mediocrity.*"[19]

Expressed in these terms, the choice was clear: to pursue glory in the present and a drastically degraded position for future generations. Insofar as Jevons's paradox continues to apply to us today—and insofar as technology by itself, given certain patterns of production and accumulation, offers no way out of our environmental dilemmas, which increase with the scale of accumulation—we must either adopt Jevons's conclusion or pursue an alternative that Jevons never discussed and that doubtless never entered his mind: the transformation of the social relations of production in the direction of a society governed not by the search for profit but by people's genuine needs and the requirements of socio-ecological sustainability.

CHAPTER SEVEN

A Planetary Defeat: The Failure of Global Environmental Reform, 1992–2009

The first earth summit, held in Rio de Janeiro in 1992, generated considerable hope that the world would at long last address its global ecological problems and introduce a process of sustainable development. Yet, by the time of the second summit, held ten years later in Johannesburg, that dream had to a large extent faded. Today, with the twentieth anniversary of the Rio summit rapidly approaching, hopes of environmental reform are at such a low ebb that, in their desperation, environmentalists are increasingly turning to accumulation under capitalism, the main source of the problem, as the solution. This has to be understood as a great reversal for environmental reform, pointing to the need for ecological revolution.

FROM RIO TO JOHANNESBURG

By the time of the second Earth Summit, the 2002 World Summit on Sustainable Development in Johannesburg, it was clear to dedicated environmentalists, who were actively involved in the process, that the world sustainability movement had suffered a crushing defeat in the preceding decade. Johannesburg marked the almost complete failure of the Rio Earth Summit and its *Agenda 21* to produce meaningful results, highlighting the weaknesses of global environmental summitry. Among the obvious failures apparent to those who gathered in Johannesburg in 2002:

1. The U.S. refusal to ratify the Kyoto Protocol and the Convention on Biological Diversity—the two main conventions evolving out of Rio— raised serious questions about the capacity of capitalism to address the world environmental crisis. The United States, the hegemonic power of the capitalist system, had further signaled its rejection of global environmental reform by announcing that President Bush would not be attending the Johannesburg summit.

2. Both the rapid globalization of the neoliberal agenda in the 1990s and the emergence of a massive antiglobalization movement in Seattle in November 1999 highlighted the system's antagonism toward all attempts to promote economic and environmental justice.

3. The World Summit on Sustainable Development took place in a period of economic and financial crisis following the bursting of the New Economy or dot-com bubble that bode ill for those concerned with the issues of the environment and third world development. The capitalist world economy as a whole continued to experience global instability. Hardest hit were the countries of the global South, which—due to neoliberal globalization—were caught in worsening economic crises over which they had less and less control.

4. A virulent new wave of imperialism had arisen, as the United States had begun a world war on terrorism in response to the events of September 11, 2001. This took the form of U.S. military interventions not only in Afghanistan but also against Iraq (the threat of intervention rising sharply at the time of the Johannesburg summit itself), along with stepped-up U.S. military activities in locations throughout the third world. Under these circumstances, war trumped the environment.

5. South Africa, which near the end of the twentieth century had a emerged as a symbol of human freedom with the overthrow of apartheid, and which was chosen partly for that reason as the site of the second earth summit, had come to symbolize by the time of the Johannesburg summit something quite different: the rapacious growth of neoliberalism and the refusal to address major environmental and social crises.

THE UNDERMINING OF RIO

The inability of the 1992 Rio Earth Summit to set in motion processes that would lead to genuine sustainable development negatively affected perceptions of what was possible ten years later in Johannesburg. In the words of the sixteen environmentalists who contributed to *The Jo'burg Memo*, written for the World Summit on Sustainable Development and edited by Wolfgang Sachs:

> Rio 1992 reveals itself a vain promise. While governments at the Earth Summit had committed themselves in front of the eyes and ears of the world to curb environmental decline and social impoverishment, no reversal of these trends can be seen a decade down the line. On the contrary the world is sinking deeper into poverty and ecological decline, notwithstanding the increase of wealth in specific places. . . . Fifty years from now, when the Earth is likely to be hotter in temperature, poorer in diversity of living beings, and less hospitable to many people, Rio might be seen as the last exit missed on the road to decline.[1]

How can it be that the 1992 Rio Earth Summit, which was thought to mark a decisive change in the human relation to the environment, came to be seen as such a colossal failure? The answer is that it was undermined by global capital both from within and without.

A close examination of the Rio summit reveals that it was far from the earth-friendly phenomenon that it professed to be. The Convention on Biological Diversity was much more about deciding who was to have the right to exploit living nature than protecting the earth's biodiversity. (The

Convention was, nonetheless, opposed by the United States because it supported the South's rights to its genetic resources over the demands of the U.S. biotechnology industry.) The UN Framework for Climate Change, which later became the Kyoto Protocol, was resisted by the United States and other countries because of its attacks on the auto-petroleum economy. The Agreement on Forest Principles, which emerged out of Rio, never even mentioned the problem of deforestation, but was concerned much more with the sovereign right of each country to use and exploit its forests as it pleased. The forty chapters of *Agenda 21*, supposed to set the stage for twenty-first-century global environmentalism, presented economic growth under free market principles as the primary objective, within which a commitment to the environment was to be situated. "The market economy of the world" was seen as the place in which all ecological problems would be addressed. As Pratap Chatterjee and Matthias Finger observed in *The Earth Brokers*, the leading critique of the Rio Earth Summit: "The only mention of corporations in *Agenda 21* was to promote their role in sustainable development. No mention was made of corporations' role in the pollution of the planet."

These results stemmed, in part, from direct pressure exerted by capital. Important lobbying came from the Business Council for Sustainable Development, led by Swiss industrialist Stephan Schmidheiny. Membership on the Business Council included top officers of leading multinational corporations: Chevron Oil, Volkswagen, Mitsubishi, Nissan, Nippon Steel, S.C. Johnson and Son, Dow Chemical, Browning-Ferris Industries, ALCOA, DuPont, Royal/Dutch Shell, and others. Schmidheiny's 1992 book, *Changing Course*, which was written to influence the Rio summit, promoted the view that the market mechanism, if allowed to operate freely, was the only conceivable means of achieving sustainable development. The primary agents of such a transition to a more sustainable world were to be multinational corporations, which would supposedly extend principles of total quality management and full cost pricing to encompass environmental concerns. The Business Council for Sustainable Development played a role, through the corporations associated with it, in financing the 1992 Earth Summit, and was brought directly into the core planning of the summit.[2]

If the Rio summit was transformed from within into a vehicle that mainly served the interests of capital, other processes were also going on outside Rio that further weakened any attempts at global environmental reform. While the Rio summit was taking place, the Uruguay Round of the General Agreement on Tariffs and Trade (GATT) negotiations was proceeding. With the establishment of the World Trade Organization (WTO) in 1995, the leading capitalist states had created an international structure to promote neoliberal free market principles while making environmental reforms in individual countries much more difficult. Globalization of capitalism was to supplant local control, countries were to be encouraged to exploit their natural resources to the fullest, public goods were to be opened up to relentless privatization, and environmental regulations were to be geared to the lowest common denominator in order to not interfere with free trade. The WTO was meant to mark the total triumph of capitalism, limiting environment and development policies in the third world to those acceptable to the ruling interests of the wealthy capitalist states.

It was the promise of development in the periphery of the capitalist world economy that was invariably used as the justification for watering down and effectively eliminating meaningful global environmental change. As conceived by the centers of world capital, development could only be sustained by pursuing the neoliberal agenda of opening up whole countries and every single sphere of economic activity to market forces. Far from developing the global South, this strategy, however, only served to deepen the economic stagnation or decline of most third world countries and to reinforce a growing gap between rich and poor countries— along with accelerated destruction of the environment. Still, insofar as it served the economic interests of the rich countries, it was treated by the dominant powers as an unmitigated success.

A quick look at global trends in relation to the environment and development during this period shows just how disastrous unfettered global capitalism in the decade between Rio and Johannesburg proved to be. Carbon dioxide levels in the atmosphere continued to rise—to their highest level in 420,000 years. Carbon dioxide emissions (excluding other greenhouse gases) increased 9 percent globally between 1990 and 2000 and in the United States by double that rate. By the mid-1990s, about 40 percent of world population in some eighty countries were already suffering from serious water shortages. Habitat destruction, particularly of tropical forests, picked up, with as many as half of the world's terrestrial species projected to be threatened or endangered in the course of the century. Genetically modified crops posed, once again, the issue of the sorcerer's apprentice, as agribusiness continued to alter the bases of life and the human food supply in ways radically at variance with evolutionary processes.[3]

Where development itself was concerned, there were no appreciable gains in the relative position of the global South, which, taken as a whole, had fallen further behind the rich countries. Income inequality had increased both within countries and between countries. Fifty-two countries experienced negative growth over the 1990s. Between 1975 and 2000 per capita income in sub-Saharan Africa (in purchasing power parity terms) dropped from one-sixth to only one-fourteenth of that of the rich countries in the Organization for Economic Cooperation and Development. The income of the richest 10 percent of the U.S. population (around 25 million people) by 2002 equaled that of the poorest 43 percent of world population or some 2 billion people.[4]

THE JOHANNESBURG SUMMIT: GRASPING AT STRAWS

Given this generally dismal picture of past accomplishments, a tendency emerged by the time of the Johannesburg summit—even amongst those environmentalists who were sharply critical of global neoliberalism, multinational corporations, the IMF, the World Bank and the WTO—to seek out some sort of compromise in the face of defeat. Environmentalists were driven to such a state that they frequently sought salvation in the very institutions to which they attributed the present evils.

The Jo'burg Memo, perhaps the most important green document to emerge in relation to the World Summit on Sustainable Development, offered one example of this. The environmentalist authors of this memo were on the left in the sense of identifying with the antiglobalization movement. They argued that neoliberalism and particularly the WTO had crushed the global environmental reform program introduced at Rio.

They believed that the world needed to put the environment and social justice first. But their solutions for the World Summit on Sustainable Development constituted an attempt to find a middle ground in relation to neoliberal economic policies, without challenging the fundamentals of the neoliberal project, much less the logic of capital accumulation itself.

What had crushed the hopes engendered by Rio, according to *The Jo'burg Memo*, was "a fateful style of economics." What was needed, therefore, was a new *style* of economics, less opposed to sustainability. What would this new style of economics involve? Their more general proposals, in this respect, were derived from the work of U.S. environmentalist and green entrepreneur Paul Hawken. A contributor to the memo, Hawken argued in favor of what he called "natural capitalism"— or capitalism that fully incorporated nature into its system of value. As stated in *The Jo'burg Memo*, "as long as corporations' short and long term interests diverge from the public interest, no tinkering, reforms, regulations, or World Summits will change the status quo." The problem, then, became one of ensuring that corporations conformed to the public interest with respect to the environment. This could be achieved by turning environmental amenities, which were valueless from the standpoint of the market, into goods that had market value. An economic system was not fully "capitalist," the *Memo* stated, unless everything—including nature— was treated as capital. Moreover, the potential for "radical resource productivity"—the more efficient utilization of energy and materials through new technology—meant that there was no incompatibility between rapid and unlimited capitalist economic growth and environmental sustainability. Environmental reform needed, therefore, to tap into the "unrivaled effectiveness" of markets.

At an international level, according to *The Jo'burg Memo,* what was needed was a "global deal," particularly between the global North and the global South, that would make development sustainable while at the same time enhancing the developmental opportunities of the South.[5] Among the proposals was the notion that it was necessary to "frame the WTO sustainably." Thus, the WTO, which was concerned solely with the penetration of capital into every nook and cranny of the globe, was to be converted into a much broader institution concerned also with environmental sustainability. This was to be accomplished by launching, through the

WTO, a "Multilateral Agreement on Sustainable Investment" that would establish verifiable guidelines for the foreign direct investment of multinational corporations.

Nor did the reform plans stop with the WTO. "Both the IMF and the World Bank," the *Memo* stated, "need to be re-directed, democratized, and re-structured" to take into account environmental needs. The IMF would have to abandon its structural adjustment programs. Furthermore, a "balance of power" could be established between Bretton Woods institutions, namely, the IMF, the World Bank, and GATT, and the UN system. This would make possible an equilibrium between financial goals and more universal goals, such as those of the environment and social justice. One major step forward, it was suggested, would be the creation of a World Environment Organization within the UN system. Another key proposal of *The Jo'burg Memo* was the establishment of a convention on corporate accountability that would allow for legal redress in the face of corporate wrongdoing.

The International Forum on Globalization, a leading antiglobalization organization based in San Francisco and headed by John Cavanagh and Jerry Mander, introduced similar capital-centered proposals for change. In its *Intrinsic Consequences of Economic Globalization on the Environment*, prepared for the Johannesburg summit, the International Forum on Globalization recommended "reining in corporate power." In addition to the creation of an Organization for Corporate Accountability, which would monitor corporations and provide information on their business practices, they proposed cutting the staffs of the IMF and the World Bank and creating a separate International Finance Organization under the UN system. The main fault of the present world economy, readers were told, was its emphasis on the *globalization* of economic relations. Instead, a principle of *localization* was to be applied, wherever possible, in order to promote ecological well-being and sustainable development.

There is no doubt that the intention of these proposed reforms was to promote social and environmental justice. Yet such proposals sought to strike an accord with neoliberal institutions while leaving the underlying logic of the system intact. One thing should have been clear to those not blind to the harsh reality of twenty-first-century capitalism: the WTO and its sister institutions were simply unable to promote sustainability, since this would have contradicted their whole reason for existence. Their role was to facilitate the accumulation of global capital and to protect the big banks and financial centers up north. A "balance of power" strategy that set UN system institutions against Bretton Woods institutions was bound to come up short, since it was predicated on the vain illusion that real power was based in these institutions rather than in the vested interests they served.

Hence, the main lesson that ought to have been learned as a result of the failure of global environmental reform associated with the Rio summit, reinforced by the Johannesburg summit, was that there was no possibility for an effective movement for social justice and sustainability separate from the revolutionary struggle to create an alternative society. An approach that acknowledged the failure of global ecological reform, and at the same time adopted the position made famous by Margaret Thatcher, that "There Is No Alternative" to the present market-driven order, had little to offer in the way of real change. Its initiatives were limited to a few alterations or additions to international organizations, the mythical conversion of corporations into "public citizens," or the illusion that the earth's salvation lay in treating nature (and thus everything in existence) as capital.

THE REAL STRUGGLE

The truth is that the leading capitalist powers were not prepared to strike a deal at Rio or Johannesburg—nor have they been willing to do so at any time since—as that would have interfered with opportunities to make more and more profits. The main issue supposedly on the table at Johannesburg was that of free trade and development. The countries of the South were demanding that the North abide by its own principles by removing tariff and non-tariff barriers protecting northern industry, in precisely the same fashion as the North demanded that protectionist measures be removed in the South. Yet neither genuine free trade nor environmental sustainability was advanced by the earth summit talks. The rich countries at the center of the capitalist world system were not about to apply to themselves the very same rules they imposed on poor states in the periphery. Their goal was to continue to extract surplus from the periphery. Fiddling with their own trade barriers was not a means for achieving that end.

The way that the global struggle over sustainable development was being played out could be seen quite clearly in South Africa, which, during the preparations for the 2002 Johannesburg summit, had vowed to make it a true summit of the South. Tragically, the South African state came to symbolize the whole period of global neoliberalism and imperial expansion. By 2002, it was in a battle with its population over the privatization of water and basic services such as electricity. This was in sharp contrast to what was imagined only a decade earlier when the overthrow of apartheid made South Africa one of the foremost symbols of the advance of human freedom. Ten years after the anti-apartheid struggle shook the world, South Africa had become the principal, subimperialist force behind the neoliberal penetration of the African continent through the New Partnership for Africa's Development (NEPAD). It is with this subimperialist South Africa that the United States was increasingly willing to deal, since its goals were not incompatible with those of the American Empire. None of this, however, had anything to do with genuine sustainable development.

But there was also another South Africa. A militant mass movement arose in the same years in South Africa against neoliberalism, one that had its roots in the same townships that led the way in the fight against apartheid. This new anti-neoliberal, antiglobalization struggle was animated by a spirit of socialism and environmental justice in a way that belied the view that there was no alternative. If the Johannesburg earth summit, despite everything, still symbolized hope for the world, this had less to do with the summit process itself than with the mass social action that was taking place in the streets of Johannesburg, Durban, and throughout the world. In the end, there was one absolute certainty in an uncertain world—the global struggle for a just and sustainable future would continue.

DISASTER CAPITALISM
AND THE END OF ENVIRONMENTAL REFORMISM

Today, as the twentieth anniversary of the Rio summit rapidly approaches, the world ecological struggle is more polarized than ever. A considerable part of the environmental movement (including many formerly on the left) has gone over to strategies of "green capitalism" and "ecological modernism." Sustainable development has become increasingly identified with the promotion of accumulation within the system, and even with some kind of alliance with neoliberalism. Environmental reform is no longer seen mainly as the reformist creation of an environmental state on top of the capitalist economy (in a manner akin to the old welfare state), but is now frequently conceptualized, even more conservatively, as an investment-driven process that is simply the leading edge of the economy. This view has been popularized by the Breakthrough Institute and Thomas Friedman's market-driven model of a "green revolution."[6] The business of "sustainability," in this view, is simply a new frontier for accumulation, in which carbon trading is the model scheme.

In this tragic era, the threat to the planet and to living species has grown by leaps and bounds, with the annual rate of global carbon emissions so far during this decade more than three times the rate of the 1990s.[7] Tipping points that portend global ecological disaster are fast approaching. With the economic order also facing its worst crisis since the Great Depression, and with the outbreak of "preemptive wars," the world has fallen into what Naomi Klein has aptly called the age of "disaster capitalism."[8]

The result is that masses of people around the world—as was already evident in the grassroots struggles in South Africa at the beginning of the decade—are now struggling against disaster capitalism and for a radical ecological revolution. Such a revolution will not, in the manner of today's establishment environmentalism, seek to carry out technological change while keeping the whole accumulation system intact. Instead, it will seek to transform social relations themselves, and thus the human relation to the earth. Environmentalism is giving way to ecological revolution— which must necessarily be a social revolution, and on a scale never seen before in the history of human civilization.

As the first decade of the twenty-first century comes to a close, there are calls for a third earth summit in 2012. If support in the global command centers of the system for such a summit has been lukewarm so far, this may reflect the recognition that such a summit would no longer represent a movement for environmental reform, but for ecological revolution.

PART TWO

marx's ecology

CHAPTER EIGHT

Marx's Ecology in Historical Perspective

"For the early Marx the only nature relevant to the understanding of history is human nature . . . Marx wisely left nature (other than human nature) alone." These words are from George Lichtheim's influential book *Marxism: An Historical and Critical Study*, first published in 1961.[1] Although he was not a Marxist, Lichtheim's view here did not differ from the general outlook of Western Marxism at the time he was writing. Today, however, most socialists would regard this perspective as laughable. After decades of explorations of Marx's contributions to ecological discussions and publication of his scientific-technical notebooks, it is no longer a question of whether Marx addressed nature, and did so throughout his life, but whether he can be said to have developed an understanding of the nature-society dialectic that constitutes a crucial starting point for understanding the ecological crisis of capitalist society.[2]

Mounting evidence has conclusively demonstrated that Marx had profound insights into the environmental problem. Yet, while this is now widely acknowledged, numerous commentators, including some self-styled ecosocialists, still insist that these insights were relatively marginal to his work, that he never freed himself from "Prometheanism" (a term usually meant to refer to an extreme commitment to industrialization at any cost), and that he did not leave a significant ecological legacy that carried forward into later socialist thought or that had any relation to the subsequent development of ecology.[3] In a recent discussion in the journal *Capitalism, Nature, Socialism* a number of authors argued that Marx could not have contributed anything of fundamental relevance to the development of ecological thought, since he wrote in the nineteenth century, before the nuclear age and before the appearance of PCBs, CFCs and DDT—and because he never used the word "ecology" in his writings. Any discussion of his work in terms of ecology was, therefore, a case of taking 120 years of ecological thinking since Marx's death and laying it "at Marx's feet."[4]

My own view of the history of ecological thought and its relation to socialism, as articulated in my book *Marx's Ecology*, is different.[5] In this, as in other areas, I think we need to beware of falling into what E.P. Thompson called "the enormous condescension of posterity."[6] More specifically, we need to recognize that Marx and Engels, along with other early socialist thinkers, like Pierre-Joseph Proudhon (in *What Is Property?*) and William Morris, had the advantage of living in a time when the transition from feudalism to capitalism was still taking place or had occurred in recent memory. Hence, the questions that they raised about capitalist society and even about the relation between society and nature were often more fundamental than what characterizes social and ecological thought, even on the left, today. It is true that technology has changed, introducing massive new threats to the biosphere, undreamed of in earlier times. But, paradoxically, capitalism's antagonistic relation to the environment, which lies at the core of our current crisis, was in some ways more apparent to nineteenth and early twentieth century socialists than it is to the majority of today's green thinkers. This reflects the fact that it is not technology that is the primary issue, but rather the nature and logic of capitalism as a specific mode of production. Socialists have contributed in fundamental ways, at all stages, in the development of the modern ecological critique. Uncovering this unknown legacy is a vital part of the overall endeavor to develop an ecological materialist analysis capable of addressing the devastating environmental conditions that face us today.

METABOLISM IN LIEBIG AND MARX

I first became acutely aware of the singular depth of Marx's ecological insights through a study of the Liebig-Marx connection. In 1862, the great German chemist Justus von Liebig released the seventh edition of his pioneering scientific work, *Organic Chemistry in Its Application to Agriculture and Physiology* (first published in 1840 and commonly referred to as his *Agricultural Chemistry*). The 1862 edition contained a new, lengthy and, to the British, scandalous introduction. Building upon arguments that he had been developing in the late 1850s, Liebig declared the intensive, or "high farming," methods of British agriculture to be a "robbery system," opposed to rational agriculture.[7] They necessitated the transportation over long distances of food and fiber from the country to the city—with no provision for the recirculation of social nutrients, such as nitrogen, phosphorus and potassium, which ended up contributing to urban waste and pollution in the form of human and animal wastes. Whole countries were robbed in this way of the nutrients of their soil. For Liebig this was part of a larger British imperial policy of robbing the soil resources, including bones, of other countries. "Great Britain," he declared:

> . . . deprives all countries of the conditions of their fertility. It has raked up the battlefields of Leipsic, Waterloo and the Crimea; it has consumed the bones of many generations accumulated in the catacombs of Sicily; and now annually destroys the food for a future generation of three millions and a half of people. Like a vampire it hangs on the breast of Europe, and even the world, sucking its lifeblood without any real necessity or permanent gain for itself.[8]

The population in Britain was able to maintain healthy bones and greater physical proportions, he argued, by robbing the rest of Europe of their soil nutrients, including skeletal remains, which would otherwise have gone into nurturing their own soils, allowing their populations to reach the same physical stature as the English.

"Robbery," Liebig suggested, "improves the art of robbery." The degradation of the soil led to a greater concentration of agriculture among a small number of proprietors who adopted intensive methods. But none of this altered the long-term decline in soil productivity. England was able to maintain its industrialized capitalist agriculture by importing guano (bird droppings) from Peru as well as bones from Europe. Guano imports increased from 1,700 tons in 1841 to 220,000 tons only six years later.[9]

What was needed in order to keep this spoliation system going, Liebig declared, was the discovery of "beds of manure or guano . . . of about the extent of [the] English coalfields." But existing sources were drying up without additional sources being found. By the early 1860s, North America was importing more guano than all of Europe put together. "In the last ten years," he wrote, "British and American ships have searched through all the seas, and there is no small island, no coast, which has escaped their enquiries after guano. To live in the hope of the discovery of new beds of guano would be absolute folly."

In essence, rural areas and whole nations were exporting the fertility of their land: "Every country must become impoverished by the continual exportation of corn, and also by the needless waste of the accumulated products of the transformation of matter by the town populations."

All of this pointed to "the law of restitution" as the main principle of a rational agriculture. The minerals taken from the earth had to be returned to the earth. "The farmer" had to "restore to his land as much as he had taken from it," if not more.

The British agricultural establishment, needless to say, did not take kindly to Liebig's message, with its denunciation of British high farming. Liebig's British publisher, rather than immediately translating the 1862 German edition of his *Agricultural Chemistry*, as in the case of previous editions, destroyed the only copy in its possession. When this final edition of Liebig's great work was at last translated into English and published it was in an abridged form under a different title (*The Natural Laws of Husbandry*) and without Liebig's lengthy introduction. Hence, the English-speaking world was left in ignorance of the extent of Liebig's critique of industrialized capitalist agriculture.

Nevertheless, the importance of Liebig's critique did not escape the attention of one major figure residing in London at the time. Karl Marx, who was then completing the first volume of *Capital*, was deeply affected by Liebig's critique. In 1866 he wrote to Engels, "I had to plough through the new agricultural chemistry in Germany, in particular Liebig and Schönbein, which is more important for this matter than all of the economists put together." Indeed, "to have developed from the point of view of natural science the negative, i.e., destructive side of modern agriculture," Marx noted in volume one of *Capital*, "is one of Liebig's immortal merits."[10]

Marx's two main discussions of modern agriculture both end with an analysis of "the destructive side of modern agriculture." In these passages, Marx makes a number of crucial points: (1) capitalism has created an "irreparable rift" in the "metabolic interaction" between human beings and the earth, the everlasting nature-imposed condition of production; (2) this demanded the "systematic restoration" of that necessary metabolic relation as "a regulative law of social production"; (3) nevertheless, the growth under capitalism of large-scale agriculture and long-distance trade only intensifies and extends the metabolic rift; (4) the wastage of soil nutrients is mirrored in the pollution and waste in the towns—"In London," he wrote, "they can find no better use for the excretion of four and a half million human beings than to contaminate the Thames with it at heavy expense"; (5) large-scale industry and large-scale mechanized agriculture work together in this destructive process, with "industry and commerce supplying agriculture with the means of exhausting the soil"; (6) all of this is an expression of the antagonistic relation between town and country under capitalism; (7) a rational agriculture, which needs either small independent farmers producing on their own, or the action of the associated producers, is impossible under modern capitalist conditions; and (8) existing conditions demand a rational regulation of the metabolic relation between human beings and the earth, pointing beyond capitalist society to socialism and communism.[11]

Marx's concept of the metabolic rift was the core element of this ecological critique. The human labor process itself was defined in *Capital* as "the universal condition for the metabolic interaction between man and nature, the everlasting nature-imposed condition of human existence."[12] It followed that the rift in this metabolism meant nothing less than the undermining of the "everlasting nature-imposed condition of human existence." Further, there was the question of the sustainability of the earth—i.e., the extent to which it is to be passed on to future generations in a condition equal or better than in the present. As Marx wrote:

From the standpoint of a higher socio-economic formation, the private property of particular individuals in the earth will appear just as absurd as the private property of one man in other men. Even an entire society, a nation, or all simultaneously existing societies taken together, are not owners of the earth. They are simply its possessors, its beneficiaries, and have to bequeath it in an improved state to succeeding generations, as *boni patres familias* [good heads of the household].[13]

The issue of sustainability, for Marx, went beyond what capitalist society, with its constant intensification and enlargement of the metabolic rift between human beings and the earth, could address. Capitalism, he observed, "creates the material conditions for a new and higher synthesis, a union of agriculture and industry on the basis of the forms that have developed during the period of their antagonistic isolation." Yet, in order to achieve this "higher synthesis," he argued, it would be necessary for the associated producers in the new society to "govern the human metabolism with nature in a rational way"—a requirement that raised fundamental and continuing challenges for post-revolutionary society.[14]

In analyzing the metabolic rift, Marx and Engels did not stop with the soil nutrient cycle, or the town-country relation. They addressed at various points in their work such issues as deforestation, desertification, climate change, the elimination of deer from the forests, the commodification of species, pollution, industrial wastes, toxic contamination, recycling, the exhaustion of coal mines, disease, overpopulation, and the evolution (and co-evolution) of species.[15]

MARX AND THE MATERIALIST CONCEPTION OF NATURE

After having the power and coherence of Marx's analysis of the metabolic rift impressed on me in this way, I began to wonder how deeply embedded such ecological conceptions were in Marx's thought as a whole. What was there in Marx's background that could explain how he was able to incorporate natural scientific observations into his analysis so effectively? How did this relate to the concept of the alienation of nature, which along with the alienation of labor was such a pronounced feature of his early work? Most of all, I began to wonder whether the secret to Marx's ecology was to be found in his materialism. Could it be that this materialism was not adequately viewed simply in terms of a materialist conception of *human* history, but also had to be seen in terms of *natural* history and the dialectical relation between the two? Or to put it somewhat differently, was Marx's materialist conception of history inseparable from what Engels had termed the "materialist conception of nature"?[16] Had Marx employed his dialectical method in the analysis of both?

The search for an answer to these questions took me on a long intellectual journey through Marx's works, and the historical-intellectual context in which they were written, which eventually became *Marx's Ecology*. Let me mention just a few highlights of the story I uncovered—since I do not have the space to explore it all in detail here, and because part of my purpose here is to add additional strands to the story. My account differs from most present-day accounts of Marx's development in that it highlights the formative significance of Marx's doctoral thesis on Epicurus, the greatest of the ancient materialists, and goes on to situate Marx and Engels's lifelong engagement with developments in the natural sciences. This includes Marx and Engels's opposition to the natural theology tradition, particularly as manifested by Malthus, their treatment of Liebig's work on nutrient cycling and its relation to the metabolic rift, and finally their creative encounter with Darwin, co-evolution, and what has been called "the revolution in ethnological time" following the discovery of the first prehistoric human remains.[17]

In most interpretations of Marx's development his early thought is seen as largely a response to Hegel, mediated by Feuerbach. Without denying Hegel's significance, I argue that Marx's formative phase is much more complex than is usually pictured. Along with German idealism Marx was struggling early on with ancient materialist natural philosophy and its relation to the seventeenth century scientific revolution, and the eighteenth century Enlightenment. In all of this, Epicurus loomed very large. For Kant, "Epicurus can be called the foremost philosopher of sensibility," just as Plato was the foremost philosopher "of the intellectual." Epicurus, Hegel claimed, was "the inventor of empiric natural science." For Marx himself, Epicurus was the "the greatest figure of the Greek Enlightenment."[18]

Epicurus represented, for Marx, most importantly, a non-reductionist, nondeterministic materialism, and had articulated a philosophy of human freedom. In Epicurus could be found a materialist conception of nature that rejected all teleology and all religious conceptions of natural and social existence. In studying Epicurus's natural philosophy, Marx was addressing a view that had had a powerful influence on the development of European science and modern naturalist-materialist philosophies, and one that had at the same time profoundly influenced the development of European social thought. In the Epicurean materialist worldview knowledge of the world started with the senses. The two primary theses of Epicurus's natural philosophy make up what we today call the principle of conservation: nothing comes from nothing, and nothing being destroyed is reduced to nothing. For Epicureans there was no scale of nature, no set of sharp, unbridgeable gaps between human beings and other animals. Knowledge of Epicurus provides a way of understanding Marx's deep materialism in the area of natural philosophy. His study of ancient and early modern materialism brought Marx inside the struggle over the scientific understanding of the natural world in ways that influenced all of his thought and was deeply ecological in its significance, since it focused on evolution and emergence, and made nature not God the starting point. Moreover, Marx's dialectical encounter with Hegel has to be understood in terms of the struggle that he was carrying on simultaneously regarding the nature of materialist philosophy and science.

Darwin had similar roots in natural philosophy, linked to the anti-teleological tradition extending back to Epicurus, which had found its modern exponent in Bacon. We now know, as a result of the publication of Darwin's notebooks, that the reason that he waited so long—twenty years—before making public his theory on species transmutation was due to the fact that his theory had strong materialist roots, and thus raised the issue of heresy in Victorian England. Darwin's view went against all teleological explanations, such as those of the natural theology tradition. He presented an account of the evolution of species that was dependent on no supernatural forces, no miraculous agencies of any kind, but simply on nature's own workings.

Marx and Engels greeted Darwin's theory immediately as "the death of teleology," and Marx described it as "the basis in natural history for our view."[19] Not only did they study Darwin intensely, they were also drawn into the debates concerning human evolution that followed immediately on Darwin's work, as a result of the discovery of the first prehistoric human remains. Neanderthal remains had been found in France in 1856. But it was the discovery of prehistoric remains, which were quickly accepted as such in England in Brixham Cave in 1859, the same year that Darwin published his *The Origin of Species*, that generated the revolution in ethnological time, erasing forever within science the biblical chronology for human history and prehistory. Suddenly it became clear that the human species (or hominid species) had existed in all probability for a million years or longer, not simply a few thousand. (Today, it is believed that hominid species have existed for around 7 million years.)

Many major works, mostly by Darwinians, emerged in just a few years to address this new reality, and Marx and Engels studied them with great intensity. Among these were Charles Lyell's *Geological Evidences of the Antiquity of Man* (1863), Thomas Huxley's *Evidence as to Man's Place in Nature* (1863), John Lubbock's *Prehistoric Times* (1865), Darwin's *Descent of Man* (1871), along with a host of other works in the ethnological realm, including Lewis Henry Morgan's *Ancient Society* (1881).

Out of Marx and Engels's studies came a thesis on the role of labor in human evolution that was to prove fundamental. Inspired by the ancient Greek meaning for organ (*organon*), or tool, which expressed the idea that organs were essentially the "grown-on" tools of animals, Marx referred to such organs as "natural technology," which could be compared in certain respects to human technology. A similar approach was evident in Darwin, and Marx was thus able to use Darwin's comparison of the development of specialized organs in plants and animals to that of specialized tools (in chapter 5 of *The Origin of Species* on "Laws of Variation") to help explain his own conception of the development of natural and human technology. The evolution of natural technology, Marx argued, rooting his analysis in *The Origin of Species*, was a reflection of the fact that animals and plants were able to pass on through inheritance organs that had been developed through natural selection in a process that might be called "'accumulation' through inheritance." Indeed, the driving force of evolution for Darwin, in Marx's interpretation, was "the gradually accumulated [naturally selected] inventions of living things."[20]

In this conception, human beings were to be distinguished from animals in that they more effectively utilized tools, which became extensions of their bodies. Tools, and through them the wider realm of nature, as Marx said early on in his *Economic and Philosophic Manuscripts*, became the "inorganic body of man." Or as he was to observe in *Capital*, "thus nature becomes one of the organs of his [man's] activity, which he annexes to his own bodily organs, adding stature to himself in spite of the Bible."[21]

Engels was to develop this argument further in his pathbreaking work, "The Part Played by Labour in the Transition from Ape to Man" (written in 1876 and published posthumously in 1896). According to Engels's analysis—which derived from his materialist philosophy, but which was also influenced by views voiced by Ernst Haeckel a few years before—when the primates, who constituted the ancestors of human beings, descended from the trees, erect posture developed first (prior to the evolution of the human brain), freeing the hands for tool-making. In this way

> . . . *the hand became free* and could henceforth attain ever greater dexterity and skill, and the greater flexibility thus acquired was inherited and increased from generation to generation. Thus the hand is not only the organ of labour, *it is also the product of labour.*[22]

As a result early humans (hominids) were able to alter their relation to their local environment, radically improving their adaptability. Those who were most ingenious in making and using tools were most likely to survive, which means that the evolutionary process exerted selective pressures toward the enlargement of the brain and the development of language (necessary for the social processes of labor and tool-making), leading eventually to the rise of modern humans. Thus, the human brain, like the hand, in Engels's view, evolved through a complex, interactive set of relations, now referred to by evolutionary biologists as "gene-culture co-evolution." All scientific explanations of the evolution of the human brain, Stephen Jay Gould has argued, have thus far been theories of gene-culture co-evolution, and "the best 19th century case for gene-culture co-evolution was made by Frederick Engels."[23]

All of this points to the fact that Marx and Engels had a profound grasp of ecological and evolutionary problems, as manifested in the natural science of their day, and were able to make important contributions to our understanding of how society and nature interact. If orthodoxy in Marxism, as Lukács taught, relates primarily to method, then we can attribute these insights to a very powerful method, but one which, insofar as it encompasses *both* a materialist conception of natural history and of human (i.e., social) history, has not been fully investigated by subsequent commentators. Behind Marx and Engels's insights in this area lay an uncompromising materialism, which embraced such concepts as emergence and contingency, and which was dialectical to the core.

MARXIST ECOLOGICAL MATERIALISM AFTER MARX

Engels's *Dialectics of Nature* is known to incorporate numerous ecological insights. But it is frequently contended that Marxism, after Marx and Engels, either missed out on the development of ecological thought altogether or was anti-ecological and that there were no important Marxian contributions to the study of nature after Engels until the Frankfurt School and Alfred Schmidt's *The Concept of Nature in Marx*, first published in 1962.[24] This position, however, is wrong. There were in fact numerous penetrating Marxist contributions to the analysis of the nature-society relation, and socialists played a very large role in the development of ecology, particularly in its formative stages. The influence of Marx and Engels's ideas in this respect was not confined to the nineteenth century.

But it is not just a question of the direct inheritance of certain propositions with respect to nature-ecology. Marx and Engels employed a materialist conception of nature, which was fundamental to the major revolutions in science of their day (as evident in Darwin's theory), and which they combined with a dialectic of emergence and contingency. A very large part of this was reflected in both socialist and scientific thought in the immediately succeeding generations. Among the socialists (some of them leading natural scientists) who incorporated naturalistic and ecological conceptions into their thinking, after Marx and up through the 1940s, we can include such figures as William Morris, Henry Salt, August

Bebel, Karl Kautsky, Rosa Luxemburg, V. I. Lenin, Nikolai Bukharin, V. I. Vernadsky, N. I. Vavilov, Alexander Oparin, Christopher Caudwell, Hyman Levy, Lancelot Hogben, J. D. Bernal, Benjamin Farrington, J. B. S. Haldane, and Joseph Needham—and in the more Fabian tradition, but not unconnected to Marx and Marxism, E. Ray Lankester and Arthur Tansley. Bukharin employed Marx's concept of the metabolism of nature and society in his writings, and explicitly situated human beings in the biosphere. "If human beings," he wrote

> are both products of nature and part of it; if they have a biological basis when their social existence is excluded from account (it cannot be abolished!); if they are themselves natural magnitudes and products of nature, and if they live within nature (however much they might be divided off from it by particular social and historical conditions of life and by the so called "artistic environment"), then what is surprising in the fact that human beings share in the rhythm of nature and its cycles?[25]

Kautsky in his *The Agrarian Question*, following Liebig and Marx, addressed the problem of the soil nutrient cycle, raised the question of the fertilizer treadmill, and even referred to the dangers of the intensive application of pesticides—all in 1899! Luxemburg addressed ecological problems in her letters, discussing the disappearance of songbirds through the destruction of their habitat. Lenin promoted both conservation and ecology in the Soviet Union, and demonstrated an awareness of the degradation of soil fertility and the breaking of the soil nutrient cycle under capitalist agriculture—the Liebig-Marx problem.

The Soviet Union in the 1920s had the most developed ecological science in the world. Vernadsky had introduced the concept of the biosphere in a dialectical framework of analysis that reaches down to the most advanced ecology of our day. Vavilov used the historical materialist method to map out the centers of the origin of agriculture and the banks of germplasm throughout the globe, now known as the Vavilov areas. Oparin, simultaneously with Haldane in Britain, developed the first influential modern materialist explanation for the origin of life on earth based on Vernadsky's biosphere concept—a theory that was to have an important impact on Rachel Carson's concept of ecology.[26]

Yet this early Marxist ecological thought, or rather the traditions that sustained it, largely died out. Ecology within Marxism suffered something of a double death. In the East in the 1930s, Stalinism literally purged the more ecological elements within the Soviet leadership and scientific community—not arbitrarily so, since it was in these circles that some of the resistance to primitive socialist accumulation was to be found. Bukharin was executed. Vavilov died of malnutrition in a prison cell in 1943. At the same time in the West, Marxism took an often extreme, avidly anti-positivistic form. The dialectic was seen as inapplicable to nature—a view often associated with Lukács, though we now know that Lukács's position was somewhat more complex.[27] This affected most of Western Marxism, which tended to see Marxism increasingly in terms of a human history severed for the most part from nature. Nature was relegated to the province of natural science, which was seen as properly positivistic within its own realm. In Lukács, Gramsci, and Korsch, marking the Western Marxist revolt of the 1920s, nature was increasingly conspicuous in its absence. Nature entered into the Frankfurt School's critique of the Enlightenment, but the nature under consideration was almost always human nature (reflecting the concern with psychology), and rarely so-called "external nature." There was no materialist conception of nature. Hence, genuine ecological insights were rare.

If an unbroken continuity is to be found, nonetheless, in the development of socialist nature-science discussions and ecological thought, its path has to be traced primarily in Britain, where a continuous commitment to a materialist dialectic in the analysis of natural history was maintained. A strong tradition in Britain linked science, Darwin, Marx, and dialectics. Although some of the negative features of this tradition, which has been referred to as a "Baconian strand in Marxism," are well known, its more positive ecological insights have never been fully grasped.[28] Any account of the ecology of British Marxism in this period has to highlight Caudwell, who—though he died at the age of twenty-nine behind a machine-gun on a hill in Spain fighting for the Republic in the Spanish Civil War—left an indelible intellectual legacy. His *Heredity and Development*, perhaps the most important of his science-related works, was suppressed by the Communist Party in Britain due to the Lysenkoist controversy (he was anti-Lysenkoist) and so was not published until 1986.[29] But it contains an impressive attempt to develop an ecological dialectic. Haldane, Levy, Hogben, Needham, Bernal, and Farrington—as previously noted—all developed ecological notions (though Bernal's legacy is the most contradictory in this respect). All indicated profound respect not only for Marx and Darwin but also for Epicurus, who was seen as the original source of the materialist conception of nature. The influence of these thinkers carries down to the present day, in the work of later biological and ecological scientists, such as Steven Rose in Britain, and Richard Lewontin, Richard Levins, and Stephen Jay Gould in the United States.

MATERIALISM AND THE RISE OF THE ECOSYSTEM CONCEPT

In order to grasp more fully the complex relation between materialist ecology and historical materialism from the late nineteenth to the early twentieth century, I want to focus here on two figures who are less well known to historical materialists, more Fabian than Marxist, but clearly socialists in the broader sense—namely, E. Ray Lankester and Arthur Tansley. Lankester taught at University College, London, and Tansley was his student there. Lankester was Huxley's protégé and was considered the greatest Darwinian scientist of his generation. When he was a boy Darwin had carried him on his shoulders. Lankester was also a young friend of Karl Marx and a socialist, though not himself a Marxist. He was a frequent guest at Marx's household in the last few years of Marx's life. Marx and his daughter Eleanor also visited Lankester at his residence in London. Marx and Lankester had in common, above all, their materialism. Marx was interested in Lankester's research into degeneration—the notion that evolution did not necessarily simply go forward—and made an attempt to get Lankester's work published in Russian. Lankester wrote to Marx that he was absorbing "your great work on Capital . . . with the greatest pleasure and profit." Lankester was to become one of the most ecologically concerned thinkers of his time. He wrote some of the most powerful essays that have ever been written on species extinction due to human causes, and discussed the pollution of London and other ecological issues with an urgency that was not found again until the late twentieth century.[30]

Arthur Tansley was the foremost plant ecologist in Britain of his generation, one of the greatest ecologists of all time, and the originator of the concept of ecosystem. He was to become the first president of the British Ecological Society. Tansley was deeply influenced by Lankester, along with the botanist Francis Wall Oliver, in his years at University College, London. Like Lankester, Tansley was a Fabian-style socialist and an uncompromising materialist. And like Lankester, who wrote a scathing criticism of Henri Bergson's concept of vitalism or *élan vital*, Tansley directly challenged attempts to conceive evolutionary ecology in anti-materialist, teleological terms.[31]

In the 1920s and 1930s a major split occurred in ecology. In the United States, Frederic Clements and others developed the important concept of ecological succession (the notion of successive stages in the development of plant "communities" in a particular region culminating in a "climax" or mature stage linked to certain dominant species). But in a much more controversial move, Clements and his followers extended this analysis to a concept of super-organism meant to account for the process of succession. This ecological approach inspired other innovations in ecological theory in Edinburgh and South Africa.

South African ecological thinkers, led by Jan Christian Smuts, introduced a concept of "holism" in the ecological realm, most notably in Smuts's book *Holism and Evolution* (1926), which was to lead to modern conceptions of deep ecology. Smuts, who was usually referred to as General Smuts because of his military role in the Boer War (he fought on the side of the Boers), was one of the principal figures in the construction of the apartheid system. How much Smuts himself contributed directly to the development of apartheid may be disputed. But he was a strong advocate of the territorial segregation of the races and what he called "the grand white racial aristocracy." He is perhaps best remembered worldwide as the South African general who arrested Gandhi. Smuts was South African Minister of Defense from 1910 to 1919, and Prime Minister and Minister of Native Affairs from 1919 to 1924. He was sometimes seen as a figure soaked in blood. When the Native Labour Union demanded political power and freedom of speech, Smuts crushed it with violence, killing 68 people in Port

Elizabeth alone. When black Jews refused to work on Passover, Smuts sent in the police, and 200 were killed on his orders. When certain black tribal populations in Bondelwaart refused to pay their dog tax, Smuts sent in planes and bombed them into submission. Not surprisingly, Smuts's ecological holism was also a form of ecological racism, since it was a holism that contained natural-ecological divisions along racial lines.

The legendary opponent of Smuts's holistic philosophy, in the great "Nature of Life" debate that took place at the British Association for the Advancement of Science meetings in South Africa in 1929, was the British Marxist biologist Lancelot Hogben (who had a position at the University of Cape Town at that time). Hogben not only debated Smuts— opposing his materialism to Smuts's holism, and attacking Smuts for his racist eugenics—but also reportedly hid black rebels fleeing the racist state in a secret compartment in his basement. Another major opponent of Smuts was the British Marxist mathematician Hyman Levy, who, in his *The Universe of Science*, developed a critique of Smuts's holism along similar lines to those of Hogben.[32]

In 1935 Tansley found himself increasingly at odds with anti-materialist conceptions of ecology that were then gaining influence, and entered the lists against ecological idealism. Tansley wrote an article for the journal *Ecology* entitled "The Use and Abuse of Vegetational Concepts and Terms" that declared war on Clements, Smuts, and Smuts's leading follower in South African ecology, John Phillips. In one fell swoop, Tansley attacked the teleological notions that ecological succession was always progressive and developmental, always leading to a climax; that vegetation could be seen as constituting a super-organism; that there was such a thing as a biotic "community" (with members), encompassing both plants and animals; that "organismic philosophy," which saw the whole universe as an organism, was a useful way to understand ecological relations; and that holism could be seen as both cause and effect of everything in nature. Smuts's holistic view, Tansley claimed, was "at least partly motivated by an imagined future 'whole' to be realised in an ideal human society whose reflected glamour falls on less exalted wholes, illuminating with a false light the image of the 'complex organism.'" This was quite possibly a polite way of referring to the system of racial stratification that was built into Smutsian holistic ecology.

In combating this type of mystical holism and super-organicism, and introducing the concept of ecosystem in response, Tansley turned to the systems theory utilized in Levy's *The Universe of Science*, and at the same time referred to materialist conceptions of dynamic equilibrium in natural systems going back to Lucretius (Epicurus's Roman follower and author of the great philosophical poem *The Nature of Things*). "The fundamental conception" represented by his new ecosystem concept, Tansley argued, was that of:

> . . . the whole system (in the sense of physics), including not only the organism complex, but also the whole complex of physical factors forming what we call the environment of the biome—the habitat factors in the widest sense. Though the organisms may claim our primary interest, when we are trying to think fundamentally, we cannot separate them from their special environment, with which they form one physical system . . . These ecosystems, as we may call them, are of the most various kinds and sizes. They form one category of the multitudinous physical systems of the universe, which range from the universe as a whole down to the atom.

Following Levy, Tansley emphasized a dialectical conception:

> The systems we isolate mentally are not only included as part of larger ones, but they also overlap, interlock, and interact with one another. The isolation is partly artificial, but it is the only possible way in which we can proceed.

Rather than seeing ecology in terms of natural, teleological order, Tansley stressed disruptions to that order, referring to "the destructive human activities of the modern world," and presenting human beings as an "exceptionally powerful biotic factor, which increasingly upsets the equilibrium of pre-existing ecosystems and eventually destroys them, at the same time forming new ones of very different nature." "Ecology," he argued, "must be applied to conditions brought about by human activity," and for this purpose the ecosystem concept, which situated life within its larger material environment, and penetrated "beneath the forms of the 'natural' entities," was the most practical form for analysis. Tansley's ecosystem concept was, paradoxically, more genuinely holistic and more dialectical than the super-organicism and "holism" that preceded it, because it brought both the organic and inorganic world within a more complex materialist synthesis.[33]

THE DIALECTICS OF ALIENATION OF NATURE AND SOCIETY

At this point, you may think that I have deviated from my path in addressing Tansley so extensively. But an analysis that is materialist and at the same time dialectical is bound to provide a more powerful set of insights into both ecology and society, natural history and human history. The Marxian materialist perspective was bound to such an approach. Figures like Bukharin, Vernadsky, Vavilov, Oparin, Caudwell, Haldane, Hogben, Needham and Levy—but also Lankester and Tansley—shared, albeit with considerable variance among them, both a materialist conception of nature and history and a commitment to dialectical readings of human and natural relations. The fact that these thinkers to varying degrees also sometimes lapsed into mechanism should warn us to approach their work cautiously, but it should not blind us to their genuine insights.

Some environmental commentators of course continue to claim that Marx believed one-sidedly in the struggle of human beings against nature, and was thus anthropocentric and unecological, and that Marxism as a whole carried forth this original ecological sin. But the evidence, as I have suggested, strongly contradicts this. In *The German Ideology*, Marx assailed Bruno Bauer for referring to "the antitheses in nature and history as though they were two separate things." In fact, "the celebrated 'unity of man with nature,'" Marx argued, "has always existed in industry . . . and so has the 'struggle' of man with nature." A materialist approach would deny neither reality—neither unity nor struggle in the human relation to nature. Instead, it would concentrate on "the sensuous world," as Marx said, "as consisting of the total living sensuous *activity* of those living in it."[34] From this standpoint, human beings make their own environments, though not under conditions entirely of their choosing, but based on conditions handed down from the earth and from earlier generations, in the course of history both natural and human.

CHAPTER NINE

Marx's Theory of Metabolic Rift: Classical Foundations for Environmental Sociology

This chapter addresses a paradox: on the one hand, environmental sociology, as currently developed, is closely associated with the thesis that the classical sociological tradition is devoid of systematic insights into environmental problems; on the other hand, evidence of crucial classical contributions in this area, particularly in Marx, but also in Weber, Durkheim, and others, is too abundant to be convincingly denied. The nature of this paradox, its origins, and the means of transcending it are illustrated primarily through an analysis of Marx's theory of metabolic rift, which, it is contended, offers important classical foundations for environmental sociology.

CLASSICAL BARRIERS TO ENVIRONMENTAL SOCIOLOGY

In recent decades, we have witnessed a significant transformation in social thought as various disciplines have sought to incorporate ecological awareness into their core paradigms in response to the challenge raised by environmentalism and by what is now widely perceived as a global ecological crisis. This transformation has involved a twofold process of rejecting much of previous thought as ecologically unsound, together with an attempt to build on the past, where possible. This can be seen as occurring with unequal degrees of success in the various disciplines. Geography, with its long history of focusing on the development of the natural landscape and on biogeography, was the social science that adapted most easily to growing environmental concerns.[1] Anthropology, with a tradition of investigating cultural survival and its relation to ecological conditions, also adjusted quickly to a period of greater environmental awareness.[2] In other social science disciplines, significant progress in incorporating ecological ideas has been made, yet with less discernible effect on the core understandings of these fields. Economics, which was able to draw on the theoretical foundations provided by A. C. Pigou's 1920 work, *Economics of Welfare*, has seen the rapid development of a distinctive, if limited, approach to environmental issues focusing on the internalization of "externalities"— making "environmental economics . . . one of the fastest-growing academic sub-disciplines throughout the industrial world."[3] As a relatively atheoretical field, political science has had little difficulty in incorporating environmental issues into its analysis of public policy, its focus on pluralist interest groups, its social contract theory, and more recently its emphasis on rational choice theory. However, the pragmatic character of most political science in the United States, together with the lack of a strong Green political party and the absence of a clear connection between identification with environmental causes and voting behavior, has kept the politics of the environment on the margins of the discipline.[4]

In sociology too, dramatic progress has been made, as seen by the rapid growth of the subfield of environmental sociology in the 1970s and again, after a period of quiescence, in the late 1980s and 1990s.[5] Nevertheless, sociology is perhaps unique within the social sciences in its degree of resistance to environmental issues. An early barrier erected between society and nature, sociology and biology—dividing the classical sociologies of Marx, Weber, and Durkheim from the biological and naturalistic concerns that played a central role in the preclassical sociology of the social Darwinists—has hindered the incorporation of environmental sociology within the mainstream of the discipline, according to an interpretation repeatedly voiced by prominent environmental sociologists over the last two and a half decades.[6]

Hence, until recently "there has . . . been general agreement among environmental sociologists that the classical sociological tradition has been inhospitable to the nurturing of ecologically informed sociological theory."[7] "From an environmental-sociological point of view," Frederick Buttel has argued, "the classical tradition can be said to be 'radically sociological,' in that in their quest to liberate social thought and sociology from reductionisms, prejudices, power relations, and magic, the classical theorists (and, arguably more so, the 20th century interpreters of the classical tradition) wound up exaggerating the autonomy of social processes from the natural world."[8] Likewise, Ted Benton has observed that "the conceptual structure or 'disciplinary matrix' by which sociology came to define itself, especially in relation to potentially competing disciplines such as biology and psychology, effectively excluded or forced to the margins of the discipline questions about the relations between society and its 'natural' or 'material' substrate."[9] "Sociology," according to one prominent environmental sociologist, "was constructed as if nature didn't matter."[10] Such marginalization of the physical environment was made possible, in part, through the enormous economic and technological successes of the industrial revolution, which have long given the impression that human society is independent of its natural environment. This is seen as offering an explanation for the fact that "sociological work on resource scarcity never appeared in the discipline's top journals" in the United States.[11]

Modern sociology in its classical period, according to the prevailing outlook within environmental sociology, was consolidated around a humanistic worldview that emphasized human distinctiveness in relation to nature. This has been referred to by some as the old "human exemptionalist paradigm" in contrast to the "new environmental paradigm," which rejects the anthropocentrism supposedly characteristic of the former view.[12] With respect to Durkheim, for example, it has been argued that the social constituted a distinct reality, relatively autonomous from the physical individual and from psychological and biological pressures. "The thrust of Durkheim's and Weber's methodological arguments," according to Goldblatt, was to cordon off sociology from biology and nature, rejecting "all forms of biological determinism"; while Marx's treatment of such issues, though considerable, was largely confined to the "marginal" realm of agricultural economics.[13]

In the language of contemporary environmentalism, then, sociology is a discipline that is "anthropocentric" in orientation, allowing little room for consideration of society's relation to nature, much less the thorough-going "ecocentrism" proposed by many environmentalists. It is rooted in a "socio-cultural determinism" that effectively excludes ecological issues. For Riley Dunlap and William Catton, sociology needs to shed "the 'blinders' imposed by [human] exceptionalism" and to acknowledge "the ecosystem dependence of all human societies."[14]

One result of this problem of theoretical dissonance is that environmental sociology, despite important innovations, has continued to have only a marginal role within the discipline as a whole. Although an environmental sociology section of the American Sociological Association was launched in 1976, it did not have the paradigm-shifting effect on sociology that leading figures in the section expected. Neither was sociology as a whole much affected by the rise of environmental sociology, nor did environmental issues gain much notice within the profession. As one leading practitioner of environmental sociology observed in 1987, "the discipline at large has handily withstood the challenges to its theoretical assumptions posed by environmental sociologists."[15]

Where the core sociological discipline has been most ready to acknowledge environmental issues is in the area of environmental move-ments. There the literature has rapidly expanded in recent years through the growth of the environmental justice movement, concerned with the impact of environmental degradation on distinct sociological groupings, conceived in terms of race, class, gender, and international hierarchy. But this literature owes much more to social movement theory than to the environmentalist challenge to traditional sociological conceptions.

One way in which environmental sociologists have sought to address this problem of what are generally perceived as barriers within classical sociology to any consideration of the physical environment is by reaching out to the preclassical social Darwinist tradition: thinkers such as Malthus and Sumner.[16] Recently, however, there has been a great deal of research within environmental sociology directed not at circumventing the main classical sociological theorists but at unearthing alternative foundations within the classical literature, neglected in later interpretations. For exam-ple, an impressive attempt has been made by Raymond Murphy to establish a neo-Weberian sociology by applying Weber's critique of rationalization to the ecological realm and developing an "ecology of social action."[17] Timo Järvikoski has argued that we should reject the view that Durkheim simply neglected nature, choosing to address instead Durkheim's social constructionism with respect to nature, while examining how society fit within the hierarchical conception of nature that he generally envisioned.[18] Others have stressed Durkheim's use of biological analogies and the demographic basis that he gave to his social morphology of the division of labor and urbanism, which seemed to foreshadow the urban oriented human ecology of Robert Park and other Chicago sociologists.[19] The most dramatic growth of literature in relation to classical sociology, however, has centered on Marx's ecological contributions, which were more extensive than in the other classical theorists, and which have spawned a vast and many-sided international debate, encompassing all stages of Marx's work.[20]

Significantly, this growing literature on the relation of classical sociological theorists to environmental analysis has caused some of the original critics of classical sociology within environmental sociology to soften their criticisms. Buttel, one of the founders of the subdiscipline, has gone so far as to suggest that, despite all of their deficiencies in this respect, "a meaningful environmental sociology can be fashioned from the works of the three classical theorists."[21] We now know, for example, that Weber, writing as early as 1909 in his critique of Wilhelm Ostwald's social energetics, demonstrated some concern over the continued availability of scarce natural resources and anticipated the ecological economist Georgescu-Roegen in arguing that the entropy law applied to materials as well as energy.[22] Durkheim's analysis of the implications of Darwinian evolutionary theory—as we shall see below—pointed toward a complex, coevolutionary perspective. Nevertheless, the widespread impression of rigid classical barriers to environmental sociology continues to exert its influence on most environmental sociologists, leaving them somewhat in the state of the mythical centaur, with the head of one creature and the body of another, unable fully to reconcile their theoretical commitment to classical sociology with their environmental sociology, which demands that an emphasis be placed on the relations between society and the natural environment.

The following will focus on addressing the seemingly paradoxical relation of classical sociological theory and environmental sociology by centering on the work of Marx, while referring only tangentially to the cases of Weber and Durkheim. It will be argued that neglected but crucial elements within Marx's social theory offer firm foundations for the development of a strong environmental sociology. In contrast to most treatments of Marx's ecological writings, emphasis will be placed not on his early philosophical works but rather on his later political economy. It is in the latter that Marx provided his systematic treatment of such issues as soil fertility, organic recycling, and sustainability in response to the investigations of the great German chemist Justus von Liebig—and in which we find the larger conceptual framework, emphasizing the metabolic rift between human production and its natural conditions.[23]

It may seem ironic, given Marx's peculiar dual status as an insider founder and outsider critic of classical sociology (not to mention his reputation in some quarters as an enemy of nature), to turn to him in order to help rescue sociology from the embarrassing dilemma of having paid insufficient attention to the relation between nature and human society. Yet the discovery or rediscovery of previously neglected features of Marx's vast intellectual corpus has served in the past to revitalize sociology in relation to such critical issues as alienation, the labor process, and, more recently, globalization. The irony may seem less, in fact, when one considers that there already exists "a vast neo-Marxist literature in environmental sociology, and [that] there are few other areas of sociology today that remain so strongly influenced by Marxism."[24]

In constructing this argument around Marx, an attempt will be made to comment more broadly on the paradox of the existence—as we are now discovering—of a rich body of material on environmental issues within classical sociological theory, on the one hand, and the widespread perception that the classical tradition excluded any serious consideration of these issues, and itself constitutes a barrier inhibiting the development of environmental sociology, on the other. Here two hypotheses will be advanced arising out of the treatment of Marx. First, the apparent blindness of classical sociological theory to ecological issues is partly a manifestation of the way classical sociology was appropriated in the late 20th century. This can be viewed as *the appropriation problem*. Second, environmental sociology's critique of classical traditions has itself often been rooted in an overly restrictive conception of what constitutes environmental theorizing, reducing it to a narrow "dark green" perspective (as exemplified by the deep ecology tradition).[25] This can be thought of as *the definitional problem.*

THE DEBATE ON MARX AND THE ENVIRONMENT

It is a sign of the growing influence of environmental issues that in recent years numerous thinkers, from Plato to Gandhi, have had their work reevaluated in relation to ecological analysis. Yet, it is in relation to Marx's work that the largest and most controversial body of literature can be found, far overshadowing the debate over all other thinkers. This literature (insofar as it takes environmental issues seriously) has fallen into four camps: (1) those who contend that Marx's thought was anti-ecological from beginning to end and indistinguishable from Soviet practice;[26] (2) those who claim that Marx provided illuminating insights into ecology but ultimately succumbed to "Prometheanism" (pro-technological, anti-ecological views)—a corollary being that he believed that environmental problems would be eliminated as a result of the "abundance" that would characterize postcapitalist society;[27] (3) those who argue that Marx provided an analysis of ecological degradation within agriculture, which remained, however, segregated off from his core social analysis[28]; and (4) those who insist that Marx developed a systematic approach to nature and to environmental degradation (particularly in relation to the fertility of the soil) that was intricately bound to the rest of his thought and raised the question of ecological sustainability.[29]

Some of the sharpest criticisms of Marx from an environmentalist standpoint have come from leading sociologists (both non-Marxist and Marxist), particularly in Britain. Giddens has contended that Marx, although demonstrating considerable ecological sensitivity in his earliest writings, later adopted a "Promethean attitude" toward nature. Marx's "concern with transforming the exploitative human social relations expressed in class systems does not extend," Giddens writes, "to the exploitation of nature."[30] Similarly, Redclift has observed that for Marx the environment served "an enabling function but all value was derived from labor power. It was impossible to conceive of a 'natural' limit to the material productive forces of society. The barriers that existed to the full realization of resource potential were imposed by property relations and legal obligations rather than resource endowments."[31] More recently, Redclift and Woodgate have added that "while Marx considered our relations with the environment as essentially social, he also regarded them as ubiquitous and unchanging, common to each phase of social existence. Hence, for Marx, the relationship between people and nature cannot provide a source of change in society. . . . Such a perspective does not fully acknowledge the role of technology, and its effects on the environment."[32] Finally, Alec Nove has contended that Marx believed that "the problem of production had been 'solved' " by capitalism and that the future society of associated producers therefore would not have "to take seriously the problem of the allocation of scarce resources," which meant that there was no need for an "ecologically conscious" socialism.[33]

Marx thus stands accused of wearing *blinders* in relation to the following: (1) the exploitation of nature; (2) nature's role in the creation of value; (3) the existence of distinct natural limits; (4) nature's changing character and the impact of this on human society; (5) the role of technology in environmental degradation; and (6) the inability of mere economic abundance to solve environmental problems. If these criticisms were valid, Marx's work could be expected to offer no significant insights into problems of ecological crisis and, indeed, would itself constitute a major obstacle to the understanding of environmental problems.

In contrast, an attempt will be made to demonstrate here, in the context of a systematic reconstruction of Marx's theory of metabolic rift, that these ecological blinders are not in fact present in Marx's thought—and that each of the problems listed above was addressed to some extent in his theory. Of more significance, it will be contended that Marx provided a powerful analysis of the main ecological crisis of his day—the problem of soil fertility within capitalist agriculture—as well as commenting on the other major ecological crises of his time (the loss of forests, the pollution of the cities, and the Malthusian specter of overpopulation). In doing so, he raised fundamental issues about the antagonism of town and country, the necessity of ecological sustainability, and what he called the "metabolic" relation between human beings and nature. In his theory of metabolic rift and his response to Darwinian evolutionary theory, Marx went a considerable way toward a historical-environmental-materialism that took into account the coevolution of nature and human society.

MARX AND THE SECOND AGRICULTURAL REVOLUTION: THE METABOLIC RIFT

The Concept of the Second Agricultural Revolution

Although it is still common for historians to refer to a single agricultural revolution that took place in Britain in the seventeenth and eighteenth centuries and that laid the foundation for the industrial revolution that followed, agricultural historians commonly refer to a second and even a third agricultural revolution. The first agricultural revolution was a gradual process occurring over several centuries, associated with the enclosures and the growing centrality of market relations; technical changes included improved techniques of crop rotation, manuring, drainage, and livestock management. In contrast, the second agricultural revolution occurred over a shorter period, between 1830 and 1880, and was characterized by the growth of a fertilizer industry and a revolution in soil chemistry, associated in particular with the work of the great German agricultural chemist Justus von Liebig.[34] The third agricultural revolution was to occur still later, in the twentieth century, and involved the replacement of animal traction with machine traction on the farm and the eventual concentration of animals in massive feedlots, together with the genetic alteration of plants (resulting in narrower monocultures) and the more intensive use of chemical inputs—such as fertilizers and pesticides.

Marx's critique of capitalist agriculture and his main contributions to ecological thought have to be understood in relation to the second agricultural revolution occurring in his time. For Marx, writing in *Capital* in the 1860s, there was a gulf separating the treatment of agricultural productivity and soil fertility in the work of classical economists like Malthus and Ricardo, and the understanding of these problems in his own day. In Marx's words, "The actual causes of the exhaustion of the land . . . were unknown to any of the economists who wrote about differential rent, on account of the state of agricultural chemistry in their time."[35]

The source of the differential fertility from which rent was derived was, in the work of Malthus and Ricardo in the opening decades of the nineteenth century, attributed almost entirely to the natural or absolute productivity of the soil—with agricultural improvement (or degradation) playing only a marginal role. As Ricardo observed, rent could be defined as "that portion of the produce of the earth, which is paid to the landlord for the use of the original and indestructible powers of the soil."[36] These thinkers argued—with the presumed backing of natural law—that lands that were naturally the most fertile were the first to be brought into production and that rising rent on these lands and decreasing agricultural productivity overall were the result of lands of more and more marginal fertility being brought into cultivation, in response to increasing demographic pressures. Further, while some agricultural improvement was possible, it was quite limited, since the increases in productivity to be derived from successive applications of capital and labor to any given plot of land were said to be of diminishing character, thereby helping to account for the slowdown in growth of productivity in agriculture. All of this pointed to the Malthusian dilemma of a tendency of population to outgrow food supply—a tendency only countered as a result of vice and misery that served to lower fecundity and increase mortality, as Malthus emphasized in his original essay on population, or through possible moral restraint, as he was to add in later editions of that work.

Classical Marxism, in contrast, relied from the beginning on the fact that rapid historical improvement in soil fertility was possible, though not inevitable, given existing social relations. In his "Outlines of a Critique of Political Economy," published in 1844, a young Friedrich Engels was to point to revolutions in science and particularly soil chemistry—singling out the discoveries of such figures as Humphry Davy and Liebig—as constituting the main reason why Malthus and Ricardo would be proven wrong about the possibilities for rapidly improving the fertility of the soil and thereby promoting a favorable relation between the growth of food and the growth of population. Engels went on to observe that: "To make earth an object of huckstering—the earth which is our one and all, the first condition of our existence—was the last step toward making oneself an object of huckstering."[37] Three years later in *The Poverty of Philosophy*, Marx wrote that at "every moment the modern application of chemistry is changing the nature of the soil, and geological knowledge is just now, in our days, beginning to revolutionize all the old estimates of relative fertility. . . . Fertility is not so natural a quality as might be thought; it is closely bound up with the social relations of the time."[38]

This emphasis on historical changes in soil fertility in the direction of agricultural improvement was to be a continuing theme in Marx's thought, though it eventually came to be coupled with an understanding of how capitalist agriculture could undermine the conditions of soil fertility, resulting in soil degradation rather than improvement. Thus, in his later writings, increasing emphasis came to be placed on the exploitation of the earth in the sense of the failure to sustain the conditions of its reproduction.

Liebig and the Depletion of the Soil

During 1830–70, the depletion of soil fertility through the loss of soil nutrients was the overriding environmental concern of capitalist society in both Europe and North America, comparable only to concerns over the growing pollution of the cities, deforestation of whole continents, and the Malthusian fears of overpopulation.[39] In the 1820s and 1830s in Britain, and shortly afterward in the other developing capitalist economies of Europe and North America, widespread concerns about "soil exhaustion" led to a phenomenal increase in the demand for fertilizer. The value of bone imports to Britain increased from £14,400 in 1823 to £254,600 in 1837. The first boat carrying Peruvian guano (accumulated dung of sea birds) unloaded its cargo in Liverpool in 1835; by 1841, 1,700 tons were imported, and by 1847, 220,000. European farmers in this period raided Napoleonic battlefields such as Waterloo and Austerlitz, so desperate were they for bones to spread over their fields.[40]

The second agricultural revolution, associated with the rise of modern soil science, was closely correlated with this demand for increased soil fertility to support capitalist agriculture. In 1837, the British Association for the Advancement of Science commissioned Liebig to write a work on the relationship between agriculture and chemistry. The following year saw the founding of the Royal Agricultural Society of England, viewed by economic historians as a leading organization in the British high-farming movement—a movement of wealthy landowners to improve farm management. In 1840, Liebig published his *Organic Chemistry in Its Applications to Agriculture and Physiology,* which provided the first convincing explanation of the role of soil nutrients, such as nitrogen, phosphorus, and potassium, in the growth of plants. One of the figures most influenced by Liebig's ideas was the wealthy English landowner and agronomist J. B. Lawes. In 1842, Lawes invented a means of making phosphate soluble, enabling him to introduce the first artificial fertilizer, and in 1843, he built a factory for the production of his new "superphosphates." With the repeal of the Corn Laws in 1846, Liebig's organic chemistry was seen by the large agricultural interests in England as the key to obtaining larger crop yields.[41]

In the 1840s, this scientific revolution in soil chemistry, together with the rise of a fertilizer industry, promised to generate a faster rate of agricultural improvement—impressing many contemporary observers, including Marx and Engels, who up to the 1860s believed that progress in agriculture might soon outpace the development of industry in general. Still, capital's ability to take advantage of these scientific breakthroughs in soil chemistry was limited by development of the division of labor inherent to the system, specifically the growing antagonism between town and country. By the 1860s, when he wrote *Capital,* Marx had become convinced of the contradictory and unsustainable nature of capitalist agriculture, due to two historical developments in his time: (1) the widening sense of crisis in agriculture in both Europe and North America associated with the depletion of the natural fertility of the soil, which was in no way alleviated, but rather given added impetus by the breakthroughs in soil science; and (2) a shift in Liebig's own work in the late 1850s and early 1860s toward an ecological critique of capitalist development.

The discoveries by Liebig and other soil scientists, while holding out hope to farmers, also intensified in some ways the sense of crisis within capitalist agriculture, making farmers more acutely aware of the depletion of soil minerals and the paucity of fertilizers. The contradiction was experienced with particular severity in the United States—especially among farmers in New York and in the plantation economy of the Southeast. Blocked from ready access to guano (which was high in both nitrogen and phosphates) by the British monopoly of Peruvian guano supplies, U.S. capitalists spread across the globe looking for alternative supplies. Nevertheless, the quantity and quality of natural fertilizer obtained in this way fell far short of U.S. needs.[42]

Peruvian guano was largely exhausted in the 1860s and had to be replaced by Chilean nitrates. Potassium salts discovered in Europe gave ample access to that mineral, and phosphates became more readily available through both natural and artificial supplies. Yet prior to the development of a process for producing synthetic nitrogen fertilizer in 1913, fertilizer nitrogen continued to be in chronically short supply. It was in this context that Liebig was to state that what was needed to overcome this barrier was the discovery of "deposits of manure or guano . . . in volumes approximating to those of the English coalfields."[43]

The second agricultural revolution, associated with the application of scientific chemistry to agriculture, was therefore at the same time a period of intense contradictions. The decline in the natural fertility of the soil due to the disruption of the soil nutrient cycle, the expanding scientific knowledge of the need for specific soil nutrients, and the simultaneous limitations in the supply of both natural and synthetic fertilizers, all served to generate serious concerns about present and future soil fertility under capitalist agriculture.

In upstate New York, increased competition from farmers to the west, in the decades following the opening of the Erie Canal in 1825, intensified the concern over the "worn-out soil." In 1850, the Scottish soil chemist, James F. W. Johnston, whom Marx was to call "the English Liebig," visited the United States. In his *Notes on North America*, Johnston recorded the depleted condition of the soil in upstate New York, comparing it unfavorably to the more fertile, less exhausted farmlands to the west.[44] These issues were taken up by the U.S. economist Henry Carey, who in the late 1840s and 1850s laid stress on the fact that long-distance trade, which he associated with the separation of town from country and of agricultural producers from consumers, was the major factor in the net loss of nutrients to the soil and in the growing soil fertility crisis. "As the whole energies of the country," Carey wrote of the United States in his *Principles of Social Science,* "are given to the enlargement of the trader's power, it is no matter of surprise that its people are everywhere seen employed in 'robbing the earth of its capital stock.'"[45]

Carey's views were to have an important impact on Liebig. In his 1859 *Letters on Modern Agriculture*, Liebig argued that the "empirical agriculture" of the trader gave rise to a "spoliation system" in which the "conditions of reproduction" of the soil were undermined. "A field from which something is permanently taken away," he wrote, "cannot possibly increase or even continue equal in its productive power." Indeed, "every system of farming based on the spoliation of the land leads to poverty." "Rational agriculture, in contrast to the spoliation system of farming, is based on the principle of restitution; by giving back to the fields the conditions of their fertility, the farmer insures the permanence of the latter." For Liebig, English "high farming" was "not the open system of robbery of the American farmer . . . but is a more refined species of spoliation which at first glance does not look like robbery." Echoing Carey, Liebig observed that there were hundreds, sometimes thousands, of miles in the United States between the centers of grain production and their markets. The constituent elements of the soil were, thus, shipped to locations far removed from their points of origin, making the reproduction of soil fertility that much more difficult.[46]

The problem of the pollution of the cities with human and animal wastes was also tied to the depletion of the soil. In Liebig's words: "If it were practicable to collect, with the least loss, all the solid and fluid excrements of the inhabitants of the town, and return to each farmer the portion arising from produce originally supplied by him to the town, the productiveness of the land might be maintained almost unimpaired for ages to come, and the existing store of mineral elements in every fertile field would be amply sufficient for the wants of increasing populations."[47] In his influential *Letters on the Subject of the Utilisation of the Municipal Sewage*, Liebig argued—basing his analysis on the condition of the Thames—that organic recycling that would return the nutrients contained in sewage to the soil was an indispensable part of a rational urban-agricultural system.[48]

Marx and the Metabolic Rift

When working on *Capital* in the early 1860s, Marx was deeply affected by Liebig's analysis. In 1866, he wrote to Engels that in developing his critique of capitalist ground rent, "I had to plough through the new agricultural chemistry in Germany, in particular Liebig and Schönbein, which is more important for this matter than all the economists put together."[49] Indeed, "to have developed from the point of view of natural science the negative, i.e., destructive side of modern agriculture," Marx was to note in *Capital*, "is one of Liebig's immortal merits."[50] Far from having ecological blinders with regard to the exploitation of the earth, Marx, under the influence of Liebig's work of the late 1850s and early 1860s, was to develop a systematic critique of capitalist "exploitation" (in the sense of robbery, i.e., failing to maintain the means of reproduction) of the soil.

Marx concluded both of his two main discussions of capitalist agriculture with an explanation of how large-scale industry and large-scale agriculture combined to impoverish the soil and the worker. Much of the resulting critique was distilled in a remarkable passage at the end of Marx's treatment of "The Genesis of Capitalist Ground Rent" in *Capital*, volume 3, where he wrote:

> Large landed property reduces the agricultural population to an ever decreasing minimum and confronts it with an ever growing industrial population crammed together in large towns; in this way it produces conditions that provoke an irreparable rift in the interdependent process of the social metabolism, a metabolism prescribed by the natural laws of life itself. The result of this is a squandering of the vitality of the soil, which is carried by trade far beyond the bounds of a single country. (Liebig.). . . . Large-scale industry and industrially pursued large-scale agriculture have the same effect. If they are originally distinguished by the fact that the former lays waste and ruins the labour-power and thus the natural power of man, whereas the latter does the same to the natural power of the soil, they link up in the later course of development, since the industrial system applied to agriculture also enervates the workers there, while industry and trade for their part provide agriculture with the means of exhausting the soil.[51]

Marx provided a similar and no less important distillation of his critique in this area in his discussion of "Large-scale Industry and Agriculture" in volume 1 of *Capital*:

> Capitalist production collects the population together in great centres, and causes the urban population to achieve an ever-growing preponderance. This has two results. On the one hand it concentrates the historical motive force of society; on the other hand, it disturbs the metabolic interaction between man and the earth, i.e., it prevents the return to the soil of its constituent elements consumed by man in the form of food and clothing; hence it hinders the operation of the eternal natural condition for the lasting fertility of the soil. . . . But by destroying the circumstances surrounding that metabolism . . . it compels its systematic restoration as a regulative law of social production, and in a form adequate to the full development of the human race. . . . All progress in capitalist agriculture is a progress in the art, not only of robbing the worker, but of robbing the soil; all progress in increasing the fertility of the soil for a given time is a progress toward ruining the more long-lasting sources of that fertility. . . . Capitalist production, therefore, only develops the techniques and the degree of combination of the social process of production by simultaneously undermining the original sources of all wealth—the soil and the worker.[52]

In both of these passages from Marx's *Capital*—the first concluding his discussion of capitalist ground rent in volume 3 and the second concluding his discussion of large-scale agriculture in volume 1—the central theoretical construct is that of a "rift" in the "metabolic interaction between man and the earth," or in the "social metabolism prescribed by the natural laws of life," through the removal from the soil of its constituent elements, requiring its "systematic restoration." This contradiction is associated with the growth simultaneously of large-scale industry and large-scale agriculture under capitalism, with the former providing agriculture with the means of the intensive exploitation of the soil. Following Liebig, Marx argued that long-distance trade in food and clothing made the problem of the alienation of the constituent elements of the soil that much more of an "irreparable rift." As he indicated elsewhere in

Capital, the fact that "the blind desire for profit" had "exhausted the soil" of England could be seen daily in the conditions that "forced the manuring of English fields with guano" imported from Peru.[53] Central to Marx's argument was the notion that capitalist large-scale agriculture prevents any truly rational application of the new science of soil management. Despite all of its scientific and technological development in the area of agriculture, capitalism was unable to maintain those conditions necessary for the recycling of the constituent elements of the soil.

The key to Marx's entire theoretical approach in this area is the concept of social-ecological metabolism (*Stoffwechsel*), which was rooted in his understanding of the labor process. Defining the labor process in general (as opposed to its historically specific manifestations), Marx employed the concept of metabolism to describe the human relation to nature through labor:

> Labour is, first of all, a process between man and nature, a process by which man, through his own actions, mediates, regulates and controls the metabolism between himself and nature. He confronts the materials of nature as a force of nature. He sets in motion the natural forces which belong to his own body, his arms, legs, head, and hands, in order to appropriate the materials of nature in a form adapted to his own needs. Through this movement he acts upon external nature and changes it, and in this way he simultaneously changes his own nature. . . . It [the labor process] is the universal condition for the metabolic interaction [*Stoffwechsel*] between man and nature, the everlasting nature-imposed condition of human existence.[54]

Only a few years before this, Marx had written in his *Economic Manuscript of 1861–63* that "actual labour is the appropriation of nature for the satisfaction of human needs, the activity through which the metabolism between man and nature is mediated." It followed that the actual activity of labor was never independent of nature's own wealth creating potential, "since material wealth, the world of use-values, exclusively consists of natural materials modified by labour."[55]

Much of this discussion of the metabolic relation between human beings and nature reflected Marx's early, more directly philosophical attempts to account for the complex interdependence between human beings and nature. In the *Economic and Philosophical Manuscripts* of 1844, Marx had explained that: "Man *lives* from nature, i.e., nature is his *body*, and he must maintain a continuing dialogue with it if he is not to die. To say that man's physical and mental life is linked to nature simply means that nature is linked to itself, for man is a part of nature."[56] But the later introduction of the concept of metabolism gave Marx a more solid—and scientific—way in which to depict the complex, dynamic interchange between human beings and nature, resulting from human labor. The material exchanges and regulatory action associated with the concept of metabolism encompassed both "nature-imposed conditions" and the capacity of human beings to affect this process. According to Tim Hayward, Marx's concept of socio-ecological metabolism "captures fundamental aspects of humans' existence as both natural and physical beings: these include the energetic and material exchanges which occur between human beings and their natural environment. . . . This metabolism is regulated from the side of nature by natural laws governing the various physical processes involved, and from the side of society by institutionalized norms governing the division of labor and distribution of wealth, etc."[57]

Given the fundamental way in which Marx conceived of the concept of metabolism—as constituting the complex, interdependent process linking human society to nature—it should not surprise us that this concept enters into Marx's vision of a future society of associated producers: "Freedom, in this sphere [the realm of natural necessity]," he wrote in *Capital*, "can consist only in this, that socialized man, the associated producers, govern the human metabolism with nature in a rational way, bringing it under their own collective control rather than being dominated by it as a blind power; accomplishing it with the least expenditure of energy and in conditions most worthy and appropriate for their human nature."[58]

Just as the introduction of the concept of "metabolism" allowed Marx to provide a firmer, scientific grounding for his ideas, so the central position that this concept came to occupy in his theory encouraged him to draw out some of its larger implications. The term "metabolism" (*Stoffwechsel*) was introduced as early as 1815 and was adopted by

German physiologists in the 1830s and 1840s to refer to material exchanges within the body related to respiration.[59] But the term was given a somewhat wider application (and therefore greater currency) in 1842 by Liebig in his *Animal Chemistry*, the great work that followed his earlier work on the soil, where he introduced the notion of metabolic process (in the context of tissue degradation). It was subsequently generalized still further and emerged as one of the key concepts, applicable both at the cellular level and in the analysis of entire organisms, in the development of biochemistry.[60]

Within biological and ecological analysis, the concept of metabolism, beginning in the 1840s and extending down to the present day, has been used as a central category in the systems-theory approach to the relation of organisms to their environments. It refers to a complex process of metabolic exchange, whereby an organism (or a given cell) draws upon materials and energy from its environment and converts these by way of various metabolic reactions into the building blocks of proteins and other compounds necessary for growth. The concept of metabolism is also used to refer to the regulatory processes that govern this complex interchange between organisms and their environment.[61] Leading system ecologists like Odum employ "metabolism" to refer to all biological levels, beginning with the single cell and ending with the ecosystem.[62]

Recently, the notion of metabolism has become what Fischer-Kowalski has called "a rising conceptual star" within social-ecological thought, as a result of the emergence of cross-disciplinary research in "industrial metabolism." For some thinkers, it offers a way out of one of the core dilemmas of environmental sociology raised by Dunlap and Catton and Schnaiberg, which requires a way of envisioning the complex interaction between society and nature.[63] Further, the concept of metabolism has long been employed to analyze the material interchange between city and country, in a manner similar to the way in which Liebig and Marx used the concept.[64] Within this rapidly growing body of literature on social-ecological metabolism, it is now well recognized that "within the nineteenth-century foundations of social theory, it was Marx and Engels who applied the term 'metabolism' to society."[65]

Indeed, environmental sociologists and others exploring the concept of "industrial metabolism" today argue that just as the materials that birds use to build their nests can be seen as material flows associated with the metabolism of birds, so similar material flows can be seen as part of the human metabolism. Fischer-Kowalski has thus suggested "considering as part of the metabolism of a social system *those material and energetic laws that sustain the material compartments of the system.*"[66] The tough question, however, is how such a human metabolism with nature is regulated on the side of society. For Marx, the answer was human labor and its development within historical social formations.

MARX AND SUSTAINABILITY

An essential aspect of the concept of metabolism is the notion that it constitutes the basis on which life is sustained and growth and reproduction become possible. Contrary to those who believe that he wore an ecological blinder that prevented him from perceiving natural limits to production, Marx employed the concept of metabolic rift to capture the material estrangement of human beings in capitalist society from the natural conditions of their existence. To argue that large-scale capitalist agriculture created such a metabolic rift between human beings and the soil was to argue that basic conditions of sustainability had been violated. "Capitalist production," Marx wrote, "turns toward the land only after its influence has exhausted it and after it has devastated its natural qualities."[67] Moreover, this could be seen as related not only to the soil but to the antagonism between town and country. For Marx, like Liebig, the failure to recycle nutrients to the soil had its counterpart in the pollution of the cities and the irrationality of modern sewage systems. In *Capital*, he observed: "In London . . . they can do nothing better with the excrement produced by 4 1/2 million people than pollute the Thames with it, at monstrous expense."[68] Engels was no less explicit on this point. In addressing the need to transcend the antagonism between town and country, he referred, following Liebig, to the fact that "in London alone a greater quantity of manure than is produced by the whole kingdom of Saxony is poured away every day into the sea with an expenditure of enormous sums" and to the consequent need to reestablish an "intimate connection between industrial and agricultural production" along with "as uniform a distribution as possible of the population over the whole country."[69] For Marx, the "excrement produced by man's natural metabolism," along with the waste of industrial production and consumption, needed to be recycled back into production, as part of a complete metabolic cycle.[70]

The antagonistic division between town and country, and the metabolic rift that it entailed, was also evident at a more global level: whole colonies saw their land, resources, *and soil* robbed to support the industrialization of the colonizing countries. "For a century and a half," Marx wrote, "England has indirectly exported the soil of Ireland, without even allowing its cultivators the means for replacing the constituents of the exhausted soil."[71]

Marx's view of capitalist agriculture and of the necessity of recycling the nutrients of the soil (including the organic wastes of the city) thus led him to a wider concept of ecological sustainability—a notion that he thought of very limited practical relevance to capitalist society, which was incapable of such consistent rational action, but essential for a future society of associated producers. "The way that the cultivation of particular crops depends on fluctuations in market prices and the constant change in cultivation with these prices—the entire spirit of capitalist production, which is oriented towards the most immediate monetary profits—stands in contradiction to agriculture, which has to concern itself with the whole gamut of permanent conditions of life required by the chain of successive generations."[72]

In emphasizing the need to maintain the earth for "successive generations," Marx captured the essence of the contemporary notion of sustainable development, defined most famously by the Brundtland Commission as "development which meets the needs of the present without compromising the ability of future generations to meet their needs."[73] For Marx, the "conscious and rational treatment of the land as permanent communal property" is "the inalienable condition for the existence and reproduction of the chain of human generations."[74] Indeed, in a remarkable, and deservedly famous, passage in *Capital*, Marx wrote: "From the standpoint of a higher socio-economic formation, the private property of particular individuals in the earth will appear just as absurd as the private property of one man in other men. Even an entire society, a nation, or all simultaneously existing societies taken together, are not owners of the earth, they are simply its possessors, its beneficiaries, and have to bequeath it in an improved state to succeeding generations, as *boni patres familias* [good heads of the household]."[75]

This took on greater significance near the end of Marx's life, when, as a result of his investigations into the revolutionary potential of the archaic Russian commune (the Mir), he argued that it would be possible to develop an agricultural system "organized on a vast scale and managed by cooperative labor" through the introduction of "modern agronomic methods." The value of such a system, he argued, would be that it would be "in a position to incorporate all the positive acquisitions devised by the capitalist system" without falling prey to the purely exploitative relation to the soil—that is, the robbery, that characterized the latter.[76] Marx's absorption in the literature of the Russian populists at the end of his life, and his growing conviction that the revolution would emerge first within Russia—where economic, and more specifically agricultural, abundance could not be assumed—forced him to focus on agricultural underdevelopment and the ecological requirements of a more rational agricultural system.[77]

Marx and Engels did not restrict their discussions of environmental degradation to the robbing of the soil; they also acknowledged other aspects of this problem, including the depletion of coal reserves, the destruction of forests, and so on. As Engels observed in a letter to Marx, "the working individual is not only a stabaliser of *present* but also, and to a far greater extent, a squanderer of *past,* solar heat. As to what we have done in the way of squandering our reserves of energy, our coal, ore, forests, etc., you are better informed than I am."[78] Marx referred to the "devastating" effects of "deforestation" and saw this as a long-term result of an exploitative relation to nature (not simply confined to capitalism): "The development of civilization and industry in general," Marx wrote, "has always shown itself so active in the destruction of forests that everything that has been done for their conservation and production is completely insignificant in comparison."[79] He lamented the fact that the forests in England were not "true forests" since "the deer in the parks of the great are demure domestic cattle, as fat as London aldermen"; while in Scotland, the so-called deer-forests that were established for the benefit of huntsmen (at the expense of rural laborers) contained deer but no trees.[80] Under the influence of Darwin, Marx and Engels repudiated the age-old view that human beings were at the center of the natural universe. Engels expressed "a withering contempt for the idealistic exaltation of man over the other animals."[81]

Some critics attribute to Marx an ecological blinder associated with an overly optimistic faith in the cornucopian conditions supposedly made possible by the forces of production under capitalism. In this view, he relied so much on the assumption of abundance in his conception of a future society that ecological factors such as the scarcity of natural resources were simply nonexistent. Yet whatever Marx may have thought in his more "utopian" conceptions, it is clear from his discussions of both capitalism and of the transition to socialism that he was far from believing, as Nove contends, "that the problem of production" had already been "solved" under capitalism or that natural resources were "inexhaustible."[82] Rather, capitalism, as he emphasized again and again, was beset with a chronic problem of production in agriculture, which ultimately had to do with an unsustainable form of production in relation to natural conditions. Agriculture, Marx observed, "when it progresses spontaneously and is not *consciously controlled* . . . leaves deserts behind it."[83] Within industry too, Marx was concerned about the enormous waste generated and emphasized the "reduction" and "re-use" of waste—particularly in a section of *Capital* entitled "Utilization of the Refuse of Production."[84] Moreover, he gave every indication that these problems would continue to beset any society attempting to construct socialism (or communism). Hence, although some critics, such as McLaughlin, assert that Marx envisioned "a general material abundance as the substratum of communism," and therefore saw "no basis for recognizing any interest in the liberation of nature from human domination," overwhelming evidence to the contrary, much of it referred to above, suggests that Marx was deeply concerned with issues of ecological limits and sustainability.[85]

Moreover, there is simply no indication anywhere in Marx's writings that he believed that a sustainable relation to the earth would come automatically with the transition to socialism. Rather, he emphasized the need for planning in this area, including such measures as the elimination of the antagonism between town and country through the more even dispersal of the population and the restoration and improvement of the soil through the recycling of soil nutrients.[86] All of this demanded a radical transformation in the human relation to the earth via changed production relations. Capitalism, Marx wrote, "creates the material conditions for a new and higher synthesis, a union of agriculture and industry on the basis of the forms that have developed during the period of their antagonistic isolation."[87] But in order to achieve this "higher synthesis" in a society of freely associated producers, he argued, it would be necessary for the associated producers to "govern the human metabolism with nature in a rational way"—a requirement that raised fundamental challenges for post-capitalist society.[88]

Another ecological blinder commonly attributed to Marx is that he denied the role of nature in the creation of wealth by developing a "labor theory of value" that saw all value as derived from labor, and by referring to nature as a "free gift" to capital, lacking any intrinsic value of its own.[89] Yet this criticism is based on a misunderstanding of Marx's political economy. Marx did not invent the idea that the earth was a "gift" of nature to capital. Malthus and Ricardo advanced this notion as a key proposition in their economic works.[90] It was taken up later, in the twentieth century, by the great neoclassical economist Alfred Marshall and persisted in neoclassical economics textbooks into the 1980s. Thus, in the 10th edition of a widely used introductory economics textbook, we discover the following: "Land refers to all natural resources—all 'free gifts of nature'—which are usable in the production process." And further on we read: "Land has no production cost; it is a 'free and nonre-producible gift of nature.'"[91] Marx was aware of the social-ecological contradictions embedded in such views, and in his *Economic Manuscript of 1861–63* he attacked Malthus repeatedly for falling back on the "physiocratic" notion that the environment was "a gift of nature to man," while ignoring how this was connected to the definite set of social relations brought into being by capital.[92]

To be sure, Marx agreed with liberal economics that under the law of value of capitalism nature was accorded no value. "The earth . . . is active as an agent of production in the production of a use-value, a material product, say wheat," he wrote. "But it has nothing to do with producing the *value of the wheat*."[93] The value of the wheat, as in the case of any commodity under capitalism, was derived from labor. For Marx, however, this merely reflected the narrow, limited conception of wealth embodied in capitalist commodity relations and in a system built around exchange-value. Genuine wealth consisted of use-values—the characteristic of production in general, transcending its capitalist form. Hence, nature, which contributed to the production of use-values, was just as much a source of wealth as labor. "What Lucretius says," Marx wrote in *Capital*, "is self-evident: '*nil posse creari de nihilo*,' out of nothing, nothing can be created . . . Labour-power itself is, above all else, the material of nature transposed into a human organism."[94]

It follows that "labour," as Marx stated at the beginning of *Capital*, "is not the only source of material wealth, that is, of the use-values it produces. As William Petty says, labour is the father of material wealth, and the earth is its mother."[95] In the *Critique of the Gotha Programme*, Marx criticized those socialists who had attributed what he called "*supernatural creative power* to labour" by viewing it as the sole source of wealth and disregarding the role of nature.[96] Under communism, he argued, wealth would need to be conceived in far more universal terms, as consisting of those material use-values that constituted the basis for the full development of human creative powers, "the development of the rich individuality which is all sided in its production as in its consumption"—expanding the wealth of connections allowed for by nature, while at the same time reflecting the developing human metabolism with nature.[97]

Marx, therefore, set himself in opposition to all those who thought the contribution of nature to the production of wealth could be disregarded, or that nature could be completely subordinated to human ends regardless of their character. Commenting in the *Grundrisse* on Bacon's great maxim that "nature is only overcome by obeying her"—on the basis of which Bacon also proposed to "subjugate" nature—Marx replied that for capitalism the theoretical discovery of nature's "autonomous laws appears merely as a ruse so as to subjugate it under human needs, whether as an object of consumption or a means of production."[98]

For Engels, too, it was clear that to construct a society built on the vain hope of the total conquest of external nature was sheer folly. As he wrote in the *Dialectics of Nature*: "Let us not, however, flatter ourselves overmuch on account of our human conquest of nature. For each such conquest takes revenge on us. . . . At every step we are reminded that we by no means rule over nature like a conqueror over a foreign people, like someone standing outside nature—but that we, with flesh, blood, and brain, belong to nature, and exist in its midst, and that all our mastery of it consists in the fact that we have the advantage of all other beings of being able to know and correctly apply its laws."[99]

For Marx, "the human metabolism with nature" was a highly dynamic relationship, reflecting changes in the ways human beings mediate between nature and society through production. Engels and Marx read *The Origin of Species* soon after it appeared in 1859, and were enthusiastic supporters of Darwin's theory of natural selection. Marx called Darwin's book an "epoch-making work," and in January 1861, Marx wrote a letter to the German socialist Ferdinand Lasalle stating that Darwin had dealt the "death blow" to "'teleology' in the natural sciences."[100] Marx expressed no reservations about Darwin's fundamental theory itself—not even with regard to Darwin's application of the Malthusian "struggle for existence" to the world of plants and animals—yet he was sharply critical of all attempts by social Darwinists to carry this analysis beyond its proper domain and to apply it to human history. Unfortunately, some critics have viewed his cautionary notes in this respect as criticisms of Darwin himself.[101]

Darwin's evolutionary theory led Marx and Engels to what would now be called a "cautious constructionism."[102] For Marx, human evolution, that is, human history, was distinct from evolution, as it occurred among plants and animals. Marx maintained that the natural evolution of the physical organs of the latter, that is, "the history of natural technology," had its counterpart in human history in the conscious development of the "productive organs of man in society" (technology), which helped establish the conditions for the human mediation between nature and society via production.[103] Marx was of course aware that the Greek word organ (*organon*) also meant tool, and that organs were initially viewed as "grown-on" tools of animals—an approach that was utilized by Darwin himself, who compared the development of specialized organs to the development of specialized tools.[104]

Engels was later to add to this an analysis of "The Part Played by Labour in the Transition from Ape to Man."[105] According to this theory (verified in the twentieth century by the discovery of *Australopithecus*), erect posture developed first, prior to the evolution of the human brain, freeing the hands for tools. In this way, the human (hominid) relation to the local environment was radically changed, altering the basis of natural selection. Those hominids that were most successful at tool making were best able to adapt, which meant that the evolutionary process exerted selective pressures toward the development of the brain, eventually leading to the rise of modern humans. The human brain, according to Engels, evolved then through a complex, interactive process, now referred to as "gene-culture evolution." As biologist and paleontologist Stephen Jay Gould has observed, all scientific explanations of the evolution of the human brain thus far have taken the form of gene-culture coevolution, and "the best nineteenth-century case for gene-culture coevolution was made by Friedrich Engels."[106] The analysis of Marx and Engels thus pointed to coevolution, neither reducing society to nature, nor nature to society, but exploring their interactions.[107] Indeed, the view that "nature exclusively reacts on man, and natural conditions everywhere exclusively determined his historical development," Engels observed, "is . . . one-sided and forgets that man also reacts on nature, changing it and creating new conditions of existence for himself."[108]

The key to the metabolic relation of human beings to nature then is technology, but technology as conditioned by both social relations and natural conditions. Contrary to those who argue that Marx wore an ecological blinder when it came to envisioning the limitations of technology in surmounting ecological problems, he explicitly argued in his critique of capitalist agriculture that while capitalism served to promote "technical development in agriculture," it also brought into being social relations that were "incompatible" with a sustainable agriculture. The solution, thus, lay less in the application of a given technology than in the transformation of social relations. Moreover, even if the most advanced technical means available were in the hands of the associated producers, nature, for Marx, sets certain limits. The reproduction of "plant and animal products," for example, is conditioned by "certain organic laws involving naturally determined periods of time."[109] Marx reiterated the Italian political economist Pietro Verri's statement that human production was not properly an act of creation but merely "a reordering of matter" and was thus dependent on what the earth provided.[110] The human interaction with nature always had to take the form of a metabolic cycle that needed to be sustained for the sake of successive generations. Technological improvements were a necessary but insufficient means for the "improvement" in the human relation to the earth. For Marx, human beings transformed their relation to nature, but not exactly as they pleased; they did so in accordance with conditions inherited from the past and as a result of a complex process of historical development that reflected a changing relation to a natural world, which was itself dynamic in character. Redclift and Woodgate are, therefore, wrong when they say that Marx wore blinders in relation to the coevolution of nature and society, viewing the human relation to nature as an "unchanging" one.[111] Engels began his *Dialectics of Nature* with a dramatic description of the historic defeat of eighteenth-century conceptions of nature, in which the natural world existed only in space and not in time, and "in which all change, all development of nature was denied."[112]

BEYOND THE APPROPRIATION AND DEFINITIONAL PROBLEMS

The foregoing suggests that Marx's analysis provides a multilayered and multivalent basis for linking sociology, and in particular the classical tradition of sociology, with environmental issues. Yet, if this is so, why has this concern with ecological issues not found a strong echo in the Marxist tradition throughout its development, and why has our understanding of Marx so often excluded these issues? Why has environmental sociology, which is concerned directly with these questions, been so slow to acknowledge Marx's importance in this respect? The first question relates to what we referred to at the beginning of this article as "the appropriation problem," the second to what was labeled "the definitional problem."

The Appropriation Problem

Marx's reputation as an ecological thinker was no doubt affected by the fact that, as Massimo Quaini has pointed out, he "denounced the spoliation of nature before a modern bourgeois ecological conscience was born."[113] Nevertheless, Marx's ecological critique was fairly well-known and had a direct impact on Marxism in the decades immediately following his death. It came to be discarded only later on, particularly within Soviet ideology, as the expansion of production at virtually any cost became the overriding goal of the Communist movement. The influence of Marx's critique in this respect can be seen in the writings of such leading Marxist thinkers as Kautsky, Lenin, and Bukharin.

Karl Kautsky's great work, *The Agrarian Question*, published in 1899, contained a section on "The Exploitation of the Countryside by the Town" in which he held that the net external flow of value from countryside to town "corresponds to a constantly mounting loss of nutrients in the form of corn, meat, milk, and so forth which the farmer has to sell to pay taxes, debt-interest, and rent. . . . Although such a flow does not signify an exploitation of agriculture in terms of the law of value [of the capitalist economy], it does nevertheless lead . . . to its material exploitation, to the impoverishment of the land of its nutrients."[114] Arguing at a time when the fertilizer industry was further developed than in Marx's day, Kautsky discussed the fertilizer treadmill resulting from the metabolic rift:

> Supplementary fertilisers . . . allow the reduction in soil fertility to be avoided, but the necessity of using them in larger and larger amounts simply adds a further burden to agriculture—not one unavoidably imposed by nature, but a direct result of current social organization. By overcoming the antithesis between town and country . . . the materials removed from the soil would be able to flow back in full. Supplementary fertilisers would then, at most, have the task of enriching the soil, not staving off its impoverishment. Advances in cultivation would signify an increase in the amount of soluble nutrients in the soil without the need to add artificial fertilisers.[115]

Some of the same concerns were evident in Lenin's work. In *The Agrarian Question and the "Critics of Marx,"* written in 1901, he observed that "The possibility of substituting artificial for natural manures and the fact that this is already being done (*partly*) do not in the least refute the irrationality of wasting natural fertilisers and thereby polluting the rivers and the air in suburban and factory districts. Even at the present time there are sewage farms in the vicinity of large cities which utilise city refuse with enormous benefit to agriculture; but by this system only an infinitesimal part of the refuse is utilised."[116]

It was Nikolai Bukharin, however, who developed the most systematic approach to ecological issues in a chapter on "The Equilibrium between Society and Nature" in his important work of the 1920s, *Historical Materialism*. Stephen Cohen has characterized Bukharin's position as one of "'naturalistic' materialism," because of its emphasis on the interaction between society and nature.[117] As Bukharin wrote:

> This material process of "metabolism" between society and nature is the fundamental relation between environment and system, between "external conditions" and human society. . . . The metabolism between man and nature consists, as we have seen, in the transfer of material energy from external nature to society. . . . Thus, the interrelation between society and nature is a process of social reproduction. In this process, society applies its human labor energy and obtains a certain quantity of energy from nature ("nature's material," in the words of Marx). The *balance* between expenditures and receipts is here obviously the decisive element for the growth of society. If what is obtained exceeds the loss by labor, important consequences obviously follow for society, which vary with the amount of this excess.[118]

For Bukharin, technology was the chief mediating force in this metabolic relationship between nature and society. The human metabolism with nature was thus an "unstable equilibrium," one which could be progressive or regressive from the standpoint of human society. "The productivity of labor," he wrote, "is a precise measure of the 'balance' between society and nature." An increase in social productivity was seen as a progressive development; conversely, if the productivity of labor decreased—here Bukharin cited "the exhaustion of the soil" as a possible cause of such a decline—the relationship was a regressive one. Such a decline in social productivity resulting from an ill-adapted metabolic relation between society and nature could, he argued, lead to society being "barbarianized."[119]

Thus, the whole "process of social production," Bukharin wrote, "is an adaptation of human society to external nature." "Nothing could be more incorrect than to regard nature from the teleological point of view: man, the lord of creation, with nature created for his use, and all things adapted to human needs."[120] Instead, human beings were engaged in a constant, active struggle to adapt. "Man, as an animal form, as well as human society, are products of nature, part of this great, endless whole. Man can never escape from nature, and even when he 'controls' nature, he is merely making use of the laws of *nature* for his own ends." "No system, including that of human society," Bukharin insisted, "can exist in empty space; it is surrounded by an 'environment,' on which all its conditions ultimately depend. If human society is not adapted to its environment, it is not meant for this world." "For the tree in the forest, the environment means all the other trees, the brook, the earth, the ferns, the grass, the bushes, together with all their properties. Man's environment is society, in the midst of which he lives; the environment of human society is external nature."[121] Indeed, human beings, as Bukharin emphasized in 1931, need to be conceived as "living and working in the biosphere."[122]

Other early Soviet thinkers connected to Bukharin demonstrated a similar concern for ecological issues. Komrov quoted at length from the long passage on the illusion of the conquest of nature in Engels's *Dialectics of Nature* and went on to observe that "The private owner or employer, however necessary it may be to make the changing of the world comply with the laws of Nature, cannot do so since he aims at profit and only profit. By creating crisis upon crisis in industry he lays waste natural wealth in agriculture, leaving behind a barren soil and in mountain districts bare rocks and stony slopes." Similarly, Uranovsky placed heavy emphasis, in a discussion of Marxism and science, on Marx's research into Liebig and "the theory of the exhaustion of the soil." [123]

Burkharin's ecological work and that of those associated with him was a product of the early Soviet era. The tragedy of the Soviet relation to the environment, which was eventually to take a form that has been characterized as "ecocide,"[124] has tended to obscure the enormous dynamism of early Soviet ecology in the 1920s and the role that Lenin personally played in promoting conservation. In his writings and pronouncements, Lenin insisted that human labor could never substitute for the forces of nature and that a "rational exploitation" of the environment, or the scientific management of natural resources, was essential. As the principal leader of the young Soviet state, he argued for "preservation of the monuments of nature" and appointed the dedicated environmentalist Anatolii Vasil'evich Lunacharskii as head of the People's Commissariat of Education (Enlightenment), which was put in charge of conservation matters for all of Soviet Russia. Lenin had considerable respect for V. I. Vernadsky, the founder of the science of geochemistry (or biogeochemistry) and the author of *The Biosphere.* It was in response to the urging of Vernadsky and the mineralogist E. A. Fersman that Lenin in 1919 established, in the southern Urals, the first nature preserve in the USSR—and, indeed, the first reserve established anywhere by a government exclusively aimed at the scientific study of nature. Under Lenin's protection, the Soviet conservation movement prospered, particularly during the New Economic Policy period (1921–1928). But with the early death of Lenin and the triumph of Stalinism in the late 1920s, conservationists were attacked for being "bourgeois." Worse still, with the rise of Trofim Denisovich Lysenko, as an arbiter of biological science, "scientific" attacks were launched first on ecology and then genetics. By the late 1930s, the conservation movement in the Soviet Union had been completely decimated.[125]

The disconnection of Soviet thought from ecological issues, from the 1930s on, was severe and affected Marxism in the West as well, which, between the 1930s and the 1970s, tended to ignore ecological issues. Yet there was a revival of interest in this area in Marxism, as well, with the renewal of environmentalism following the publication of Rachel Carson's *Silent Spring* in 1962. To be sure, when Western Marxism had first emerged as a distinct tradition in the 1920s and 1930s, one of the major influences was the Frankfurt School, which developed an ecological critique.[126] But this critique was largely philosophical, and while it recognized the ecological insights in Marx's *Economic and Philosophical Manuscripts,* it lost sight of the ecological argument embedded in *Capital.* Hence, it generally concluded that classical Marxism (beginning with the later Marx) supported a "Promethean" philosophy of the straightforward domination of nature. Not until the 1960s and 1970s did a more complex interpretation begin to emerge in the writings of the thinkers influenced by the Frankfurt tradition.[127] And it was not until the late 1980s and 1990s that scholars began to resurrect Marx's argument on soil fertility and organic recycling.[128] Much of the renewed emphasis on Marx's (and Liebig's) treatment of soil fertility and its ecological implications has come from agronomists and ecologists concerned directly with the debates around the evolution of soil science and the struggles over agribusiness versus organic agriculture.[129]

It is scarcely surprising, then, that interpretations of Marx within sociology, and environmental sociology in particular, have been affected by an "appropriation problem." Sociologists in general tend to have little knowledge of volume 3 of Marx's *Capital,* where his critique of capitalist agriculture (and of the undermining of soil fertility) is most fully developed, and while these issues were well-known to the generations of Marxist thinkers who immediately followed Marx, they largely vanished within Marxist thought in the 1930s. Even today, treatments of Marx's relation to ecology that purport to be comprehensive focus on his early writings, largely ignoring *Capital.*[130] This appropriation problem had important ramifications. It left the appearance that there were no explicit linkages between human society and the natural world within classical Marxism, thus facilitating the notion that there was an unbridgeable gulf between classical sociology and environmental sociology.

Analogous appropriation problems might be raised with respect to the other classical theorists. Martinez-Alier has argued that Weber's important essay on Ostwald's social energetics has also been neglected; indeed, it has yet to be translated into English. This has left the false impression that Weber had nothing to say in this area.[131] Durkheim discussed the sociological origins of the classification of nature within what he called the "first philosophy of nature," and related this to modern scientific evolutionism. He also commented in profound ways about Darwinian evolutionary theory, the indestructibility of matter, the conservation of energy, and so on.[132] The systematic character of his more naturalistic thinking has never been properly addressed, and works like *Pragmatism and Sociology,* in which he presents some of his more complex views in this regard, have generally been ignored. Nevertheless, it is clear that his analysis pointed toward a complex, coevolutionary perspective. "Sociology," he wrote, "introduces a relativism that rests on the relation between the physical environment on the one hand and man on the other. The physical environment presents a relative fixity. It undergoes evolution, of course; but reality never ceases to be what it was in order to give way to a reality of a new kind, or to one constituting new elements. . . . The organic world does not abolish the physical world and the social world has not been formed in contradistinction to the organic world, but together with it."[133]

The Definitional Problem

Along with the appropriation problem, which deals with how received sociology has been affected by the selective appropriation of the classical tradition, there is also the definitional problem, which stands for the fact that sociology's—specifically environmental sociology's—failure to address the classical inheritance in this regard is at least partly due to overly narrow, preconceived definitions as to what constitutes genuinely environmental thought.

Here, a major role was assumed by the contrast, drawn by Catton and Dunlap, between the "human exemptionalist paradigm" and the "new environmental paradigm." All of the competing perspectives in sociology, such as "functionalism, symbolic interactionism, ethnomethodology, conflict theory, Marxism, and so forth" were seen as sharing a common trait of belonging to a "human exceptionalist paradigm" (later renamed "human exemptionalist paradigm"), and thus the "apparent diversity" of these theories was "not as important as the fundamental anthropocentrism underlying *all* of them." The human exemptionalist paradigm was depicted as embracing the following assumptions: (1) the existence of culture makes human beings unique among the creatures of the earth; (2) culture evolves much more rapidly than biology; (3) most human characteristics are culturally based and hence can be socially altered; and (4) a process of cultural accumulation means that human progress can be cumulative and without limit. The habits of mind produced by this human exemptionalist paradigm, Catton and Dunlap argued, led to an overly optimistic faith in human progress, a failure to acknowledge ecological scarcity, and a tendency to neglect fundamental physical laws such as the entropy law.[134]

For Catton and Dunlap, this "human exemptionalist paradigm," which encompassed nearly all of existing sociology, could be contrasted to what they termed the "new environmental paradigm" emerging from environmental sociology, which was based on the following assumptions: (1) human beings are one of many species that are interdependently connected within the biotic community; (2) the biotic community consists of an intricate web of nature, with complex linkages of cause and effect; and (3) the world itself is finite, there are natural (physical and biological) limits to social and economic progress.[135] In contrast to the "anthropocentrism" that characterized the human exemptionalist paradigm, the new environmental paradigm represented a shift toward what is now called an "ecocentric" point of view in which human beings are seen as part of nature, interconnected with other species and subject to the natural limits of the biosphere.

Ironically, the chief problem with this contrast between the human exemptionalist paradigm and the new environmental paradigm is that, even while emphasizing environmental factors, it tended to perpetuate a dualistic view of society versus the physical environment, anthropocentrism versus ecocentrism, and thus easily fell into the fallacy of the excluded middle (or a false dichotomy). There is a tendency in this view to see any theory that emphasizes socioeconomic progress or cultural accumulation as thereby "anthropocentric" and opposed to an "ecocentric" perspective, which seeks to decenter the human world and human interests. Nevertheless, logic suggests that there is no reason for such a stark opposition, since there are numerous ways in which sociology can embrace a concern for ecological sustainability without abandoning its emphasis on the development of human culture and production. Moreover, extreme ecocentrism runs the risk of losing sight of the sociological construction of much of the "natural world." Although classical sociology may have been anthropocentric to some extent in its focus on socioeconomic advance and its relative neglect of external nature, it was not necessarily anti-ecological (in the sense of ignoring natural limits) insofar as it acknowledged ecological sustainability as a requirement of social progress. The current preoccupation with sustainable development and coevolutionary theories within environmental discussions suggests that there have always been complex views that attempted to transcend the dualisms of humanity versus nature, anthropocentrism versus ecocentrism, socioeconomic progress versus natural limits.

Marx in particular has been criticized for being "anthropocentric" rather than "ecocentric" in orientation and, hence, outside of the framework of green theory.[136] Yet this kind of dualistic conception would have made little sense from his more dialectical perspective, which emphasized the quality (and sustainability) of the *interaction* between society and its natural conditions. It is the commitment to ecological sustainability, not the abstract notion of "ecocentrism," which most clearly defines whether a theory is part of ecological discourse. Moreover, a comprehensive *sociology* of the environment must by definition be coevolutionary in perspective, taking into account changes in both society and nature and their mutual interaction.

CONCLUSION:

THE ELEMENTS OF ENVIRONMENTAL SOCIOLOGY

The burden of argument in this chapter has been to demonstrate, using the case of Marx, that it is wrong to contend that classical sociology "was constructed as if nature didn't matter."[137] A central claim, backed up by logic and evidence, has been that each of the six ecological blinders commonly attributed to Marx—namely, his alleged inability to perceive (1) the exploitation of nature; (2) nature's role in the creation of wealth; (3) the existence of natural limits; (4) nature's changing character; (5) the role of technology in environmental degradation; and (6) the incapacity of mere economic abundance to solve environmental problems—are in fact wrongly (or misleadingly) attributed to him. The point of course is not that Marx provided definitive treatments of all of these problems but rather that he was sufficiently cognizant of these issues to elude the main traps and to work the vitally important notion of the "human metabolism with nature" into his overall theoretical framework. Hence, his work constitutes a possible starting point for a comprehensive sociology of the environment. No doubt some will still insist, despite the argument presented above, that Marx did not place sufficient *emphasis* on natural conditions, or that his approach was too anthropocentric, more along the lines of utilitarian-conservationism than genuine green radicalism. Some will still say that he in fact never entirely renounced economic development, despite his insistence on a sustainable relation to the earth. But the evidence regarding his concern with ecological issues—particularly the crisis of the soil as it was perceived in the mid-nineteenth century—is too extensive, and too much a part of his overall critique of capitalism, to be simply disregarded. Marx certainly argued *as if nature mattered,* and his sociology thus takes on a whole new dimension when viewed from this standpoint.

Just as Marx translated his early theory of the alienation of labor into more material terms through his later analysis of exploitation and the degradation of work, so he translated his early notion of the alienation of nature (part of the Feuerbachian naturalism that pervaded his *Economic and Philosophical Manuscripts*) into more material terms through his later concept of a metabolic rift. Without the latter concept, it is impossible to understand Marx's developed analysis of the antagonism of town and country, his critique of capitalist agriculture, or his calls for the "restoration" of the necessary metabolic relation between humanity and the earth, that is, his basic notion of sustainability. Marx's response to Liebig's critique of capitalist agriculture was coupled, moreover, with a sophisticated response to Darwin's evolutionary theory. What emerges from this is a historical materialism that is ultimately connected to natural history; one that rejects the crude, one-sided traditions of mechanical materialism, vitalism, and social Darwinism that existed in Marx's day.

Yet, at the same time, Marx avoided falling into the trap sometimes attributed to Engels's later "dialectical materialism," of drawing too heavily on both Hegel's *Logic* and his *Philosophy of Nature*—abstractly superimposing a despiritualized Hegelian dialectic (i.e., conceived in purely logical terms, divorced from Hegel's self-mediating spirit) on top of what was otherwise a mechanical view of the universe. Instead, Marx provides, as we have seen, a cautious constructionism, fully in tune with his own practical materialism, which always emphasized the role of human praxis, while remaining sensitive to natural conditions, evolutionary change, and the metabolic interaction of humanity and the earth.

Marx's main contribution in this area was methodological. He saw "the economic formation of society" as part of a process of "natural history" and struggled within his critique of political economy to take account of both natural conditions and the human transformation of nature.[138] In the process, he applied a dialectical mode of analysis not to external nature itself (recognizing that the dialectic had little meaning aside from the self-mediating role of human beings as the agents of history) but rather to the *interaction* between nature and humanity, emphasizing the alienation of nature in existing forms of reproduction and the contradictory, nonsustainable character of the metabolic rift between nature and society that capitalism in particular had generated. Moreover, Marx conceived this metabolic rift not simply in abstract terms but in terms of the concrete crisis represented by the degradation of the soil and by the problem of human and animal "wastes" that engulfed the cities. Both were equal indications, in his analysis, of the metabolic rift between humanity and the soil, reflected in the antagonism of town and country.

The way in which Marx's analysis prefigured some of the most advanced ecological analysis of the late twentieth century—particularly in relation to issues of the soil and the ecology of cities—is nothing less than startling. Much of the recent work on the ecology of the soil has focused on successive, historical breaks in nutrient cycling.[139] The first such break, associated with the second agricultural revolution, is often conceived in essentially the same terms in which it was originally discussed by Liebig and Marx, and is seen as related to the physical removal of human beings from the land. This resulted in the failure to recycle human organic wastes back to the land, as well as the associated break in the metabolic cycle and the net loss to the soil arising from the transfer of organic products (food and fiber) over hundreds and thousands of miles.

It was these developments that made the creation of a fertilizer industry necessary. A subsequent break occurred with the third agricultural revolution (the rise of agribusiness), which was associated in its early stages with the removal of large animals from farms, the creation of centralized feedlots, and the replacement of animal traction with farm machinery. No longer was it necessary to grow legumes, which had the beneficial effect of naturally fixing nitrogen in the soil, in order to feed ruminant animals. Hence, the dependence on fertilizer nitrogen increased, with all sorts of negative environmental consequences, including the contamination of ground water, the "death" of lakes, and so on.

These "modernizing" trends, and other related processes, are now seen as related to the distorted pattern of development that has characterized capitalism (and other social systems such as the Soviet Union that replicated this pattern of development, sometimes in even more distorted fashion), taking the form of a more and more extreme metabolic rift between city and country—between what is now a mechanized humanity and a mechanized nature. Similarly, the ecological problem of the city is increasingly viewed in terms of its metabolic relationship to its external environment (focusing on the flows of organic nutrients and energy) and the ecological distortions that this entails.[140]

The fact that Marx was able to conceive a sociological approach that pointed to these developments when they were still in their very early stages represents one of the great triumphs of classical sociological analysis. It stands as an indication of how sociology could be extended into the ecological realm. It reinforces the view that ecological analysis, devoid of sociological insight, is incapable of dealing with the contemporary crisis of the earth—a crisis which has its source and its meaning ultimately in society itself.

It is not just Marxist sociology that is in a position to draw on Marx's insights in this respect, which are sociological as much as they are Marxist. Moreover, other paradigms within classical sociology have much more to contribute to the analysis of the natural environmental context of human social development than is commonly supposed. There is no doubt that Weber and Durkheim were both concerned in their own ways with the metabolic interaction between nature and society. Although systematic investigations into the work of Weber and Durkheim in this respect still have to be undertaken, it is not to be doubted that embedded in their sociologies are important insights into ecological problems. When Weber wrote, at the end of *The Protestant Ethic and the Spirit of Capitalism*, of a civilization characterized by "mechanized petrification" that might continue along the same course—that of formal or instrumental rationality—"until the last ton of fossilized coal" was burnt, he was suggesting the possibility of a wider social and environmental critique of this civilization.[141] Likewise, Durkheim's discussions of Darwinian theory and its implications for social analysis pointed the way toward a sociological understanding of the coevolution of nature and society. In the cases of Weber and Durkheim—as in Marx—we may surmise that an appropriation problem, coupled with a definitional problem, has hindered the appreciation of the way in which their sociologies took natural conditions into account.

Today, even among leading environmental sociologists, who have criticized the classical traditions of sociology for failing to take into account
the physical environment, there is a dawning recognition that these classical traditions have proven themselves to be resilient in the face of challenges from environmental sociology and are open to reinterpretation and
reformulation along lines that give greater weight to ecological factors.
Dunlap points to the emergence, in recent years, of "'greener' versions of
Marxist, Weberian, and symbolic interactionist theories."[142] Ironically, it
is coming to be recognized that the problem of "human exemptionalism,"
that is, the neglect of the physical environment, may have been less characteristic of classical sociology than it was of the sociology that predomi-
nated after the Second World War—during a period when the faith in
technology and the human "conquest" of nature reached heights never
before attained, only to lead to disillusionment and crisis beginning with
the 1960s. Developing an environmental sociology as an integral part of
sociology as a whole thus requires that we reach back into past theories in
order to develop the intellectual means for a thoroughgoing analysis of
the present. For environmental sociology the crucial issue, today, is to
abandon the "strong constructionism" of most contemporary sociological theory, which tends to view the environment as simply a product of
human beings, and to move toward a more "cautious constructionism"
that recognizes that there is a complex metabolic relation between human
beings and society.[143] Surprisingly, this is turning out to be an area in
which the classical sociology of the mid-nineteenth and early twentieth
centuries still has much to teach us as we enter the twenty-first century—
a century that is bound to constitute a turning point for good or ill in the
human relation to the environment.

CHAPTER TEN

Capitalism and Ecology: The Nature of the Contradiction

The social relation of capital is a contradictory one. The contradictions that characterize it, though stemming from capitalism's internal laws of motion, extend out to phenomena that are usually conceived as external to the system, threatening the integrity of the entire biosphere and everything within it. How to understand capitalism's ecological contradictions has, therefore, become a subject of heated debate among socialists. Two crucial questions have emerged in this debate. First, must ecological crisis be seen through the prism of economic crisis under capitalism? And second, to what extent is there an ecological flaw at the heart of capitalist society?

What is at issue here, I believe, can be best understood if we turn to Marx. One of the key elements in Marx's ecological analysis is his theory of metabolic rift.[1] Marx employed the concept of a rift in the metabolic relation between human beings and the earth to capture the material estrangement of human beings within capitalist society from the natural conditions that formed the basis for their existence. One way in which this manifested itself was in the extreme separation of town and country under capitalism, which grew out of the separation of the mass of the population from the soil.

Nineteenth century agricultural chemists, most notably Justus von Liebig, had discovered that the loss of soil nutrients—such as nitrogen, phosphorus, and potassium—through the exportation of food and fiber to the city, was disrupting the soil nutrient cycle and undermining capitalist agriculture, while burying cities in waste. Rather than constituting a rational form of production, British high farming (the most advanced capitalist agriculture of the day) could be best described, according to Liebig, as a "robbery system" because of its effects on the soil. The historical answer of the system to this declining soil productivity was, initially, importation of vast quantities of bones from the Continent and guano (bird droppings) from Peru, and, later, the development of synthetic fertilizers. Synthetic fertilizers, however, created further problems. Thus, there arose an ever widening and more complex metabolic rift, leading to the severe disarticulations in the nature-society relation that characterize contemporary agriculture and industry.

Marx recognized that this metabolic rift represented a problem of sustainability. In an oft-quoted passage, he remarked that capitalism sapped the vitality of the everlasting sources of wealth—the soil and the worker. Nor was the problem confined simply to the soil. Marx developed an account of sustainability—the conservation and if need be "restoration" of the earth so that it could be passed on in an equal or "improved" state to the succeeding chain of human generations—that directly addressed such issues as soil nutrient recycling, pollution, sanitary conditions, deforestation, floods, desertification, climate change, recycling of industrial wastes, diversity of species, the commodification of species, and other issues. His closely related studies of evolutionary theory led him toward notions of coevolution. His conflict with Malthus forced him to consider the historical (rather than natural) sources of "overpopulation" (a term Marx used while Malthus did not). Marx's analysis of primitive accumulation pointed to the separation of workers from the land as the formative contradiction of capitalism. His critique of political economy highlighted the commodification of all of life and the dominant role played by accumulation without end, rooted in exchange-value as opposed to use-value. Quoting Thomas Müntzer, the revolutionary leader of the sixteenth century German Peasants War, Marx observed: "it [is] intolerable that 'all creatures have been made into property, the fish in the water, the birds in the air, the plants on the earth—all living things must also become free.'"[2]

Nevertheless, it has become the fashion in certain ecosocialist circles to stress not so much the wealth of ecological insights that Marx provided, as to focus on what are characterized as major shortcomings of his analysis that prevented him from developing a full-fledged ecological Marxism. Writing in *Capitalism, Nature, Socialism*, a leading journal of ecosocialism, Alan Rudy contended that a "limitation to Marx's ecology is that Marx did not theorize the 'metabolic rift' as an important moment in the crisis tendencies of capitalism." This point was enunciated more fully by James O'Connor, the founding editor of that journal, who has argued that, while Marx recognized the existence of "ecologically destructive methods" within agriculture, "he never considered the possibility" that ecological degradation "might threaten economic crisis of a particular type, namely, underproduction of capital," due to the impairment of the natural conditions of production. Hence Marx, O'Connor stated, failed to "put two and two together" so as to develop a theory of how increasing ecological costs contributed to decreasing profitability and an accumulation crisis. His analysis, thus, fell short of the conceptual framework that O'Connor has labeled "ecological Marxism."[3]

O'Connor's own theoretical contributions attempted to do what Marx failed to do here—demonstrating how capital's impairment of the conditions of production created a specific form of economic crisis for capitalism, or what O'Connor called "the second contradiction of capitalism." Capitalism, he argued, has always been beset by a "first contradiction," or economic crisis tendency, associated with a rising rate of surplus value and the resulting barriers to the realization of surplus value or profits through the sale of goods and services, due to inequalities in income and wealth. This first contradiction represented an economic crisis that manifested itself on the demand side (that is, on the side of the realization of profits).

Yet, in focusing exclusively on this first contradiction, O'Connor insisted, socialist critics of capitalism neglected the "second contradiction" associated with the undermining of capitalism's conditions of production. O'Connor derived from Marx's analysis three types of "conditions of production": (1) the personal conditions of production associated with the reproduction of human labor-power; (2) the external-natural conditions of production (forests, oil fields, water supplies, bird species, and so forth); and (3) the general-communal conditions of production (i.e., the built environment, for example, cities, including their urban infrastructure). What gave all of these elements the status of conditions of production was that they were not produced (or fully produced) by capitalism but were rather "fictitious commodities," to use Karl Polanyi's term. Capitalism did not directly produce human beings or even the capacity to labor—however much it might wish to treat labor-power as a commodity virtually like any other. Nor did it produce external nature. The built environment, for its part, emerged in a way that was dictated by spatial and temporal factors not directly subject to the law of value.

Capital in this conception was thus dependent for its production on the use and transformation of natural *conditions* of production that to some extent represented natural scarcities and that the economic system was incapable of preserving intact and in relatively costless form. Degradation of these conditions of production generated rising costs for capitalism, squeezing profits on the cost (or supply) side: thus, the "second contradiction" of capitalism. Following O'Connor, Joel Kovel's book *The Enemy of Nature* referred to ecological crisis arising from capital's degradation of its own conditions of production on an ever-increasing scale as an "iron necessity." For Kovel, "this degradation will have a contradictory effect on profitability itself . . . either directly, by so fouling the natural ground of production that it breaks down, or indirectly," through the reinternalization of "the costs that had been expelled into the environment."[4]

O'Connor identified what he called "ecological Marxist theory" entirely with this "second contradiction," while he saw the first contradiction as related to "traditional Marxism." Both the first and second contradictions took the form of economic crisis tendencies, and both exist simultaneously. But the argument suggested that the "second contradiction," and hence supply-side economic contradictions, rooted in increasing costs, were increasingly dominant. Capitalism was therefore caught up in an economic crisis tendency associated with the *underproduction* of capital, resulting from its damaging of its own conditions of production: a form of economic crisis that, in O'Connor's terms, had more to do with *external* or natural barriers than with the *internal* or class antagonisms of the system.

An important part of this argument was the way it was tied to the growth of contemporary radical social movements. The first contradiction was associated in O'Connor's conception with the class-based labor movement, and while this could still be said to exist, it was visibly on the wane in comparison to new social movements arising from the "second contradiction." O'Connor contended that there were three general types of new social movements, each of which had its counterpart in the undermining of a different condition of production. Movements, such as feminism, which are concerned with the politics of the body, were engendered by the undermining of the personal conditions of production. The environmental movement proper had its source in the undermining of the external-natural conditions of production. And urban movements had their origin in the undermining of the general-communal conditions of production.

The power of the "second contradiction" thesis, and the reason for its influence on socialist (and nonsocialist) thought, should now be obvious. It provided a single logical argument that linked ecological scarcity, economic crisis, and the growth of new movements for social change. Nevertheless, there were difficulties with this approach that limited its proper field of application.

One way of understanding how designation of the "second contradiction" of capitalism as *the* defining thesis of ecological Marxism had tended to divide socialist analysts in the ecological realm can be seen in a 2001 exchange in *Capitalism, Nature, Socialism,* that was given the title *"Marx's Ecology* or Ecological Marxism." The term *"Marx's Ecology"* in this case referred ostensibly to the title of a book I had written, but the nature of the argument presented by the critics was that Marx's own contributions to ecology, as described there, were deficient precisely because they did not lead to "ecological Marxism" as defined by O'Connor's "second contradiction." Specifically, the point was made that Marx did not explain how ecological crisis generated a crisis of accumulation for capitalism, and hence his analysis was incomplete, unsystematic, and undeveloped. Thus, as Alan Rudy put it: Marx's "analysis of the role of ecological crisis in crises of capitalism" remained "underdeveloped."[5]

But is it reasonable to contend that a Marxist approach to ecological problems is one that must lead directly to a theory of economic crisis under capitalism? Should the extent to which a socialist ecological analysis is perceived as a developed view be determined by the degree in which it feeds into a specific theory of economic crisis?

A certain economism and functionalism, arguably, creeps in when the problem is framed in this way. The whole thrust of the "second contradiction" conception was that once ecological damage was translated into an economic crisis for capitalism, a feedback mechanism was set into play. This occurred both directly through capital's attempt to hold down the growing costs of production associated with the undermining of its conditions of production, and indirectly through attempts by social movements to force the system to internalize the externalities. In the latter case, movements sought to force business to pay the social and environmental costs of production that it had dumped on nature and the public, thereby pushing capital in the direction of more ecologically sustainable production. The obvious presumption was that an economic crisis stemming from ecological causes constituted an opportunity for the left, a bandwagon to jump on so to speak—and one, moreover, that allowed it to build an alliance between a class-based labor movement and the new social movements.

It is my contention, however, that there is no such convenient feedback mechanism—at least for capitalism as a whole. As the German Greens have said, the system will recognize that money cannot be eaten only when the last tree has been cut—and not before.[6] We should not underestimate capitalism's capacity to accumulate in the midst of the most blatant ecological destruction, to profit from environmental degradation (for example through the growth of the waste management industry), and to continue to destroy the earth to the point of no return—both for human society and for most of the world's living species. In other words, the dangers of a deepening ecological problem are *all the more serious* because the system does not have an internal (or external) regulatory mechanism that causes it to reorganize. There is no ecological counterpart to the business cycle.[7]

Indeed, there is no reason to believe that the damage inflicted on the environment is most serious where it principally affects the conditions of production, which by definition involve elements of the natural-physical environment that have been substantially incorporated into the system. The Amazon forest may have provided hardwood timber and other resources for capital, but most of it has, until recently, been outside of what can be called the conditions of production of capitalism. The 50 percent of all species that are believed to reside in the tropical forests and are currently threatened with extinction in a matter of decades, are not only for the most part not incorporated into the global accumulation process, most of them remain undocumented, still unknown to science. If we take the case of the ozone layer, which has been thinned enormously, imperiling the very existence of life on earth, it would clearly be a mistake to try to squeeze this into an analysis of the conditions of production—as if it were simply a precondition of the economy and not a precondition of life as we know it.

All of this suggests that an argument focusing on conditions of production and the "second contradiction" of capitalism tends to downplay the full dimensions of the ecological crisis and even of capitalism's impact on the environment in the process of trying to force everything into the locked box of a specific economic crisis theory. Capitalism's tendency to displace environmental problems—the fact that it uses the whole biosphere as a giant trash can and, at the same time is able to run from one ecosystem to another, operating, as Marx said, under the principle of "after me the deluge"—means that the earth remains in large part a "free gift to capital." Nor is there any prospect that this will change fundamentally, since capitalism is in many ways a system of unpaid costs.

One can find an illustration of this by referring to the Bush Administration's *Climate Action Report, 2002* on global warming, issued by the Environmental Protection Agency (EPA).[8] The EPA acknowledged the dangers to life and living conditions represented by global warming, but emphasized that, in the United States, the environmental damage would be most visible in the melting of snow in the mountains and the like. Where the conditions of production of agriculture were concerned, global warming, it was suggested, might even increase overall agricultural productivity. This lack of a clear connection between environmental damage and damage to the economic conditions of production was used (via standard cost-benefit analysis) to justify a policy of *adapting* to global warming as it developed, rather than taking measures to decrease the extent of global warming—since these would increase the costs of production.

It follows that there is no natural feedback mechanism that automatically turns environmental destruction into increasing costs for capital itself—however much it may be a cost for nature and society. And if social movements seek to contain the damage by "regulating" capitalism, there is no surety that this will seriously squeeze profit margins on the cost side, forcing capital to reform—or that this will not, in fact, provide entirely new ways to profit from environmental destruction. Hence, there is every reason to doubt the inevitability of economic crises in the near future emanating primarily from such causes.

There are also empirical problems, I believe, with this theory of ecologically induced economic crisis. Logically, it is true, rising raw material costs and other costs associated with natural scarcity could undermine profit margins and generate economic crisis. This factor played a role in nineteenth century accumulation crises, as reflected in the classical theory of the tendency of the rate of profit to fall. It is always important to capital that such costs, associated with natural scarcity, are kept down. Yet there is little evidence that such costs constitute serious, insuperable barriers to accumulation for the system as a whole today. As Marx indicated in his time, the exhaustion of coal mines may eventually increase the cost of coal, but in the meantime production is often boosted by falling energy costs.[9] In 2007–2009, crude oil prices rose spectacularly in response to fears of insufficient supply and then fell rapidly as a result of economic decline. Peak oil is now a consideration. But at no time has the world price of oil reflected the long-term ecological costs associated with oil depletion, carbon emissions, and other factors.

Nor has pollution abatement put an unbearable burden on capital. Government estimates that rely on surveys of business executives indicate that business is concerned about increasing environmental costs, but this type of evidence is not a very convincing basis for arguing that environmental costs are actually squeezing profit margins in the aggregate—and should be taken no more seriously than the unceasing complaints of business executives with regard to wage costs squeezing profits. Indeed, I would argue—but of course cannot develop the argument here for lack of space—that the main economic crisis tendency of capitalism is still a rising rate of exploitation and, hence, widening profit margins and an inability to realize surplus value—what O'Connor calls the first contradiction.

A further difficulty with the "second contradiction" of capitalism conception—as a way of defining ecological Marxism—is that it forces a rigidly dualistic, mechanistic economic perspective on us that once entered into is difficult to escape from. There are two contradictions of capitalism (both economic crisis tendencies), one *internal* and emanating principally from class struggle, the other *external* and emanating principally from the undermining of the conditions of production. These in turn create two forms of social movements—traditional class-based movements emanating from the first contradiction, and new social movements, emanating from the "second contradiction." Naturally, this suggests an alliance between the two types of movements based on the combined force of the two contradictions.

Since the "second contradiction" is now conceived as dominant (displacing the first contradiction) and the new social movements consequently more vital, the class-based movement tends to take a subordinate role in this analysis and strategy. Ecological Marxism, understood in this way, is clearly an approach that sees the labor-based class struggle playing second fiddle. In this way, it arguably divides the movement artificially (adding a further theoretical layer to existing divisions), reducing the field of hope. As Kovel, representing this perspective, has put it in *The Enemy of Nature*, "there is no privileged agent of ecosocialist transformation"—class revolt is not necessarily the key.[10]

My purpose here is not to deny the significance of the "second contradiction" theory altogether, or to gainsay the fact that it has illuminated important aspects of the problem of ecology under capitalism. There are certainly localized crises that can be viewed usefully in this way. Nor would I want to deny O'Connor's formidable contribution to ecological socialism. Rather the intent is to argue that there is a danger that if we delimit the environmental problem in this way we will develop a Marxist analysis of ecological problems that is too economistic, too narrow, too functionalist, and too prone to economic dualism—and of course too undialectical—to allow us to explore the full scale of the biospheric contradiction that capitalism presents.

Here, it makes sense to return once again to Marx. If one were to seek an example in the nineteenth century of the undermining of the conditions of production in the manner suggested by O'Connor's "second contradiction" theory, one could not find a better instance of this than the crisis of agriculture induced by the robbing of the soil of its nutrients. This crisis of the soil was widely perceived in Europe and the United States from the 1840s on, and was resolved only haphazardly, at first, through the raiding of European battlefields and catacombs for bones to spread on the soil and, then, through the massive importation of guano from Peru; to be followed soon after by the development of the first synthetic fertilizers, which were already coming into use in Marx's day, leading to the eventual development of nitrogen-based fertilizer by the time of the First World War. It might therefore have been possible for Marx to have emphasized the increasing ecological costs and the barriers to accumulation that this crisis of the soil (as a condition of production) generated. But Marx's own emphasis instead was on the metabolic rift, the larger structural ecological problem that this crisis of the soil reflected, which was in his terms irreparable under capitalism—despite the fact that technology, as in the case of synthetic fertilizer, might provide a temporary remedy.

Marx did not focus primarily on how the ecological problems that he discerned contributed to economic crisis, nor did he discuss their direct influence on the revolutionary overthrow of capitalism, which he saw as imminent.[11] Instead, in this sphere he was primarily—and increasingly—concerned with questions of sustainability, and the rational regulation of the metabolism of human society and nature (through the organization of human labor). It was for him a central issue in the building of communist society, which would demand a new relation to nature.

Indeed, it was precisely because Marx and Engels placed so much emphasis on the dissolution of the antagonistic relation between town and country as a key to overcoming the alienation of humanity from nature that they tended to see the ecological problem in terms that transcended both the narrow horizons of bourgeois society and the immediate objectives of the proletarian movement. Careful to avoid falling into the trap of the utopian socialists of proposing blueprints for a future society that went too far beyond the existing movement, they nonetheless emphasized—like Fourier and some of the other utopian socialists—the need for the movement to address the alienation of nature in the attempt to create a sustainable society.

Today, ecological crisis looms much larger in our vision of anticapitalist revolt—to a degree that Marx did not and could not have anticipated. But our overall vision of the ecological features of a socialist revolution is scarcely more radical than what Marx himself envisioned, with his idea of the dissolution of the antagonistic relation of town and country and an attempt to overcome the metabolic rift through sustainable production based on a communal society of freely associated producers. When William Morris developed his ideas for the reorganization of relations between town and country, in *News from Nowhere*, he was very close to the spirit of Marx, who had influenced his ideas.

We have no more reason today than Marx did in his day to restrict our analysis of ecological contradictions to what can be incorporated into some specific theory of economic crisis. Economic crisis theory, though important, can be overemphasized, even fetishized. An example of this can be found in the fact that for many years Marxist political economists of various persuasions engaged in elaborate attempts to explain the imperialistic tendencies of capitalism—that is, the drive of the center of the system to exploit the periphery—by pointing to various specific theories of economic crisis. Yet the problem of all such perspectives was that they frequently missed the point: imperialism is not the product of this or that economic crisis (nor does its significance lie in how it, in turn, bears on economic crisis phenomena); rather it is just as basic to the system, as it has historically evolved, as the search for profits itself. In other words, imperialism is a necessary product of capitalism as a globalizing force, and to the extent that Marx himself dealt with imperialism it was, of course, mainly in this sense. Economic crisis can complicate things in certain instances. But attempts to see the whole reality of imperialism through the prism of economic crisis only obscures its essential nature.

In the case of ecological degradation, we are dealing with a first order, not a second order, problem of capitalism (and not just of capitalism). Ecological degradation, like imperialism, is as basic to capitalism as the pursuit of profits itself (which depend to a large extent upon it). Nor should the environmental problem be seen largely through the economic prism in the sense that it derives its significance from the extent to which it generates economic crisis for capitalism. As Rosa Luxemburg pointed out, song birds were dying out not because they were directly part of capitalism, or its conditions of production, but simply because their habitat was destroyed in the process of the system's relentless expansion. Luxemburg, rightly, did not connect this phenomenon directly to economic crisis, but this did not stop her from raging against the destruction of what she called "these defenseless little creatures."[12]

There is no doubt that Luxemburg believed that the economy could be organized under socialism so as to lessen such destruction. But her reasons for advocating change were not in this case economic, though they were consistent with materialism. The ultimate strength of Marxist analysis has never resided chiefly in its economic crisis theory, nor even in its analysis of class struggle as such, but lies much deeper in its materialist conception of history, both human and natural—understood, as this only truly can be, as a dialectical and endlessly contingent process. This means overcoming, in a nonreductive way, the split between natural-physical science and social science that has been one of the main alienated intellectual products of bourgeois society.

Here, I want to refer, by way of conclusion, to the legacy of Stephen Jay Gould, one of the greatest evolutionary thinkers since Darwin. Gould was a Marxist, who learned his Marxism—as he said in his crowning work, *The Structure of Evolutionary Theory*—"at his daddy's knee."[13] He was also a materialist, a self-consciously dialectical thinker, a critic of reification and reductionism, a theorist of evolution, an analyst of ecological problems, an exponent of the enormous contingency of natural and human existence, and a defender of human freedom. His work had nothing to do with the theme of the "second contradiction" of capitalism. Yet that did not prevent him in my view from being, by any meaningful definition, an ecological Marxist.

CHAPTER ELEVEN

The Communist Manifesto
and the Environment

The rise of environmental issues to the forefront of contemporary political life, over the last few decades, has sparked a searching reexamination of the entire history of social thought. In a context set by a widening ecological crisis that now seems to engulf the entire planet, all of the great traditions of modern thought—liberalism, socialism, anarchism, feminism—have sought to reexamine their intellectual forerunners, dropping some ideas and picking up others in an effort to "green" their understandings of society. As a result, an impressive array of thinkers from Plato to Gandhi—have all had their work scrutinized in relation to ecological analysis.

It is in connection with the work of Marx, however, that one finds by far the most voluminous and controversial body of literature in this regard. This, of course, is to be expected since Marx remains the preeminent critic of capitalist society. The extent to which his general critique (and that of the various traditions to which he gave rise) can be integrated with an ecological critique of machine capitalism is therefore of great importance. Indeed, much more is involved here than a mere question of "political correctness" (understood in green terms). The overriding question is rather whether Marx's critique of political economy plays an essential part in the reconstruction of social theory in an age of planetary crisis. Further, how far does he offer insights that are crucial to our understanding of the contemporary ecological malaise?

The participants in this debate have fallen into three camps: (1) those who argue that Marx's thinking was anti-ecological to its core, and directly reflected in Soviet environmental depredations; (2) those who contend that Marx provided "illuminating asides" on ecology in his work, even if he chose in the end to adopt a "Promethean" (pro-technological, anti-ecological) viewpoint; and (3) those who insist that Marx had a deep awareness of ecological degradation (particularly with respect to questions of the earth or soil), and that he approached these issues systematically, to the point that they entered into his basic conceptions of both capitalism and communism, and led him toward a notion of sustainability as a key ingredient of any future society.[1]

Most of the debate about Marx's relation to environmental thought has focused on the early philosophical critique of capitalism in his *Economic and Philosophic Manuscripts of 1844* and on his later economic critique embodied in *Capital* in the 1860s—since in both of these works he had a great deal to say about human interactions with nature. Nevertheless, the *Communist Manifesto* has often been invoked as presenting a view that was anti-ecological—some would say the very definition of anti-ecological modernism.

Indeed, the *Manifesto* is customarily viewed as a work that is, at best, oblivious to environmental concerns, at worst, "productivist"—even "Promethean"—in character, steeped in notions of progress and the subjection of nature that are deeply antithetical to nature. This is important because the *Manifesto* is generally viewed as lying at the heart of the Marxian system and whatever flaws are to be found in the overall analysis are seen as having their roots there. Yet the question of the relation of the *Manifesto* to the environment is one that has never been addressed systematically. In our time, this is no longer adequate, and it is necessary to ask: To what extent is the *Manifesto*—arguably the most influential political pamphlet of all time—compatible with ecological values, as we understand them today? Moreover, how is the *Manifesto* to be situated within the rest of Marx and Engels's thought in this respect?

THE SEARCH FOR A SMOKING GUN

One might suppose that compelling textual evidence that Marx and Engels were anti-environmentalist in orientation would not be hard to find. They wrote at a time when most thinkers embraced a mechanistic worldview in which nature and human beings were seen as diametrically opposed to one another. Indeed, much of the European view of science from the sixteenth and seventeenth centuries on was governed by the notion that science had allowed humanity to escape nature's dominance and to become dominant in turn; and Marx and Engels certainly referred frequently—as did nearly all nineteenth century (and most twentieth century) thinkers—to the "mastery," "domination," "conquest," and "subjection" of nature.

But they did so almost invariably in contexts which refrained from making nature the enemy. Rather, they saw the domination of nature as a phase of historical development—part and parcel of the whole self-alienation of human society that also meant its alienation from nature—which would necessarily have to be transcended under communism. There are innumerable passages, strewn throughout their writings, where Marx and Engels demonstrate enormous sensitivity to environmental issues. For example, the twenty-three-year-old Engels, in his first work on political economy, written in 1843, noted: "To make the earth an object of huckstering—the earth which is our one and all, the first condition of our existence—was the last step toward making oneself an object of huckstering."[2] For his part, Marx observed in 1844, in his *Economic and Philosophical Manuscripts,* that "man lives from nature, i.e., nature is his *body,* and he must maintain a continuing dialogue with it if he is not to die." In this same work, Marx complained that under the alienated existence of capitalism "Even the need for fresh air ceases to be a need for the worker. Man reverts once more to living in a cave, but the cave is now polluted by the mephitic and pestilential breath of civilization."[3]

In his more mature works, from the 1860s on, Marx became increasingly concerned about signs of ecological crisis, particularly with respect to the degradation of the soil, which induced him to envision future communist society to a very large extent in terms of sustainability. Writing in volume 1 of *Capital,* Marx argued that "the destruction" under capitalist agriculture "of the eternal natural condition of the lasting fertility of the soil"—of the basic elements of "the metabolic interaction between man and the earth"—through the disruption of the soil nutrient cycle, compelled "its systematic restoration as a regulative law of social production, and in a form adequate to the full development of the human race."[4] So dialectical (in the sense of many-sided) was this kind of analysis that William Leiss concluded in his pioneering study, *The Domination of Nature,* that taken together, the writings of Marx and Engels, "represent the most profound insight into the complex issues surrounding the mastery of nature to be found anywhere in nineteenth-century thought or *a fortiori* in the contributions of earlier periods."[5]

Still, none of this has kept critics from attempting to find a "smoking gun" to demonstrate beyond all doubt that Marx and Engels adopted a one-sided, exploitative view of nature. But in order to do so, green critics have had to go to quite extraordinary lengths. In attempting to demonstrate (against all the evidence to the contrary) that the early Marx was insensitive to nature, the social ecologist John Clark lays stress on the fact that Marx, while frequently referring to nature as "man's body," also referred to it as an "inorganic" bodily link. He ends his critique by stating that "Marx's Promethean and Oedipal 'man' is a being who is not at home in nature, who does not see the Earth as the 'household' of ecology. He is an indomitable spirit who must subjugate nature in his quest for self-realization." As evidence to back up this charge, Clark is only able to offer some stanzas from Marx's youthful and not very remarkable poetry. At the age of nineteen, Marx composed these lines, dedicated to his future wife Jenny von Westphalen, in his "Book of Love, Part II":

> I am caught in endless strife,
> Endless ferment, endless dream;
> I cannot conform to Life.
> Will not travel with the stream.[6]

For Clark, this is definitive proof that "for such a being [Marx], the forces of nature, whether in the form of his own unmastered internal nature or the menacing powers of external nature must be subdued."[7] One cannot but wonder how many youthful poets Clark might not condemn based on like evidence. Who has never wanted to go "against the stream"?

Other green critics have pointed, with more *prima facie* justice, to a passage by Engels in *Anti-Dühring* on the growing mastery of nature that will ensue once human beings have transcended social alienation:

> The conditions of existence forming man's environment, which up to now have dominated man, at this point pass under the dominion and control of man, who now for the first time becomes the real conscious master of Nature, because and in so far as he has become master of his own social organization. The laws of his own social activity, which have hitherto confronted him as external, dominating laws of Nature, will then be applied by man with complete understanding, and hence will be dominated by man. . . . It is humanity's leap from the realm of necessity into the realm of freedom.[8]

Ted Benton criticizes Engels on the grounds that such a view "presupposes control over nature" and hence "an underlying antagonism between human purposes and nature: either we control nature, or it controls us!"[9] In other words, Engels is said to have adopted an extreme anthropocentric rather than ecocentric perspective. But is Engels's argument here really vulnerable to such criticism? Despite the use of such terms as "master of Nature" the intent of this passage ought to be quite clear. It is that a revolution in social organization is necessary to allow human beings to avoid being simply prey to natural forces (or forces that purport to be "natural," as capitalist economic forces are represented in bourgeois political economy). In fact, what is being celebrated here is not human mastery of nature so much as the human mastery of the making of history, which gives humanity the capacity to reorganize its relation to nature, under conditions of human freedom and the full development of human needs and potentials. There is nothing here to suggest an underlying antagonism toward nature in Engels's notion of the realm of freedom. Communism, Engels observed elsewhere, was a society in which people would "not only feel, but also know, their *unity* with nature."[10]

The same response may be given to criticism of Marx's closely related discussion of the "realm of necessity" and "the realm of freedom" in volume 3 of *Capital*. "The true realm of freedom, the development of human powers as an end in itself," commences where the realm of necessity ends, "though it can only flourish with this realm of necessity as its basis. The reduction of the working day is the basic prerequisite."[11] The full development of human freedom and the human relation to nature, for Marx, therefore requires the transcendence of a bourgeois order which makes labor—the means by which the metabolic relationship between human beings and nature is expressed—simply a matter of bare, material necessity for the workers, even as the accumulated wealth and the combined powers of society grow. As Paul Burkett writes: "The expansion of free time and collective-democratic control over the social use of the conditions of production in Marx's communism" establishes the fundamental basis for sustainability in social and ecological relationships because it creates "conditions conducive to noninstrumental valuation of nature (i.e., to the further development of ecological needs and capabilities among the society of producers)."[12]

In the most revolutionary phase of human development, Engels along with Marx always insisted, the object would be to transform the human relationship to nature in ways that went beyond the childish notion of having "conquered" nature. "At every step," Engels wrote near the end of his life, "we are reminded that we by no means rule over nature like a conqueror over a foreign people, like someone standing outside nature—but that we, with flesh, blood, and brain, belong to nature, and exist in its midst, and that all our mastery of it consists in the fact that we have the advantage over all other beings of being able to know and correctly apply its laws." One of the basic principles in relating to nature was in fact reciprocity, leading Engels to argue that one could view as a natural necessity the "demand . . . that man shall give back to the land what he receives from it."[13]

It is true that Marx and Engels mainly focused on human needs rather than on those of nature and, thus, can be accused of being "anthropocentric" rather than "ecocentric." But this is, from Marx and Engels's own standpoint, a false dualism. Nature and society, in their perspective, cannot be viewed as diametrically opposed categories, but evolve in relation to each other as part of a dynamic process of "metabolic" interaction. This was similar in its broad outlines to what is now called the "coevolutionary" perspective, in which it is argued that nature and human society each coevolve in a complex process of mutual dependence. The complexity of the interaction between nature and society envisioned by coevolutionary theory leaves little room for such ideas as "anthropocentric" and "ecocentric" since even in defending nature we are often defending something that was reshaped by human beings.[14]

RURAL SOCIETY AND AGRICULTURE

The difficulty of finding anything that would even today be considered a strongly anti-ecological statement in the work of Marx and Engels has meant that critics have often been compelled to quote the reference to "the idiocy of rural life" in Part I of the *Manifesto* as their main textual "evidence" (frequently their only such evidence) of the alleged anti-environmental orientation of the founders of historical materialism. For example, Victor Ferkiss states: "Marx's attitude toward nature can in large measure be inferred from his numerous remarks about such things as 'the idiocy of rural life.' He was a notorious critic and indeed an enemy of the peasantry. . . . Such an attitude is hardly compatible with idealization of unspoiled nature." The deep ecologist Gary Snyder adopts a similar view, claiming that within the U.S. today we are seeing "an alliance of Capitalist Materialists and Marxist Idealists in an attack on the rural world that Marx reputedly found idiotic and boring."[15]

There is a host of questions raised by these statements. What did Marx and Engels mean by "the idiocy of rural life"? Is this to be regarded as an anti-ecological statement? Was Marx really "an enemy of the peasantry"? In order to be an environmentalist is it necessary to idealize unspoiled nature? Was Marx a one-sided advocate of urbanism in opposition to rural existence, as some critics like Ferkiss and Snyder have suggested? Such questions are best addressed not in the abstract but through an examination of the *Manifesto* itself, along with Marx's other writings. The reference to "the idiocy of rural life" in the standard Samuel Moore translation of the *Manifesto* comes in the midst of the paean in Part I of the *Manifesto* to the bourgeoisie's revolutionary historical role:

The bourgeoisie has subjected the country to the rule of the towns. It has created enormous cities, has greatly increased the urban population as compared with the rural, and has thus rescued a considerable part of the population from the idiocy of rural life. Just as it has made the country dependent on the towns, so it has made barbarian and semi-barbarian countries dependent on the civilized ones, nations of peasants on nations of bourgeois, the East on the West.[16]

This is a very compressed statement, which needs sorting out. In the first place, Marx had a classical education and we may presume knew that the meaning of "idiot" in classical Athens, derived from "Idiotes," a citizen who, unlike those who took the trouble to participate in the assembly, was cut off from public life and who viewed it from the parochial, privatized standpoint. Pre-capitalist Europe—tribal, feudal—made peasants necessarily "idiotic" in this sense. It has long been recognized therefore that "idiocy of rural life" was a mistranslation, and should have been rendered "isolation of rural life." New English translations of *The Communist Manifesto* have in fact been provided correcting this and other mistranslations.[17]

Indeed, while primitive accumulation only made the isolation of the rural worker more severe, there seems no reason to doubt that Marx thought the long-run effect of capitalism was to "rescue" people from this by driving them into cities and new forms of association with each other. Like nearly all nineteenth century European intellectuals, Marx and Engels saw the forces of enlightenment and civilization in their time as emanating principally from the towns. But their recognition of the way in which the bourgeoisie had made the "country dependent on the towns" should not be seen as uncritical support for this social arrangement, since the best that could be said for it from their point of view (at least at this stage in their thought) was that it was a necessary part of the whole bourgeois revolution, inseparable from the general achievements of the latter.

Marx and Engels viewed the dependence of the country on the towns as a product, in part, of the enormous "agglomerations of population" that emerged within cities during the bourgeois era—an issue that they discussed in the paragraph immediately following the above quotation. Hence included in their vision of revolutionary change, as depicted in Part II of the *Communist Manifesto* (which was devoted to the historically specific demands of proletarians and communists), was an insistence on the need to carry out "a gradual abolition of the distinction between town and country, by a more equable distribution of population over the country." Indeed, throughout their writings—and with increasing emphasis in the later works such as Engels's *The Housing Question*—Marx and Engels insisted on the need for the abolition of the antagonism between town and country, whereby the latter became dependent on the former. They saw this antagonism as one of the chief contradictions of capitalism and a principal means through which a double exploitation of the urban proletariat and the rural worker (in England no longer a peasant) was carried out. "The abolition of the antithesis between town and country," Engels wrote in *The Housing Question*, "is no more and no less utopian than the abolition of the antithesis between capitalists and wage-workers."[18]

This sense of the contradiction between town and country was not a mere slogan inherited from the utopian socialists but was seen as taking the form of a rupture in the necessary "metabolic" relation between human beings and nature. Thus, in *Capital* Marx was to contend that agglomerating the population in large urban centers capitalism both: (1) "prevents the return to the soil of its constituent elements consumed by man in the form of food and clothing; hence it hinders the operation of the eternal natural condition for the lasting fertility of the soil"; and (2) "destroys at the same time the physical health of the urban worker, and the intellectual life of the rural."

It was the combined action of the emigration of all culture to the city, the dispersal of a shrinking rural labor force over a wider countryside, and the annihilation of traditional connections both to the soil and to human community that Marx saw as the source of the isolation of rural life within bourgeois civilization. Thus, he took seriously (though not without offering some criticism) David Urquhart's observation that society was increasingly divided into "clownish boors" and "emasculated dwarfs" as a result of the extreme division between rural and urban existence, which deprived one part of the working population of material sustenance, the other of intellectual sustenance. The point was not that nature was to be despised but rather that the antagonism between town and country was one of the chief manifestations of the alienated nature of bourgeois civilization.[19]

In their reference to the "idiocy [i.e., isolation] of rural life," Marx and Engels, who already saw capitalism as evolving largely along the lines of England, were not referring only to the peasantry, since one of the things that most distinguished the English political economy was the thoroughness with which the expropriation of peasant lands had taken place, leaving behind a landless rural proletariat (as well as landed proprietors and tenant farmers). Nevertheless, it is worth noting—in the face of Ferkiss's criticisms—that Marx's view of the peasantry was always complex—because historically nuanced. It is true that he saw the French peasantry as a class playing a reactionary role by the time of Napoleon III's Second Empire, yet he also distinguished the revolutionary from the conservative peasantry. The former he described in heroic terms, as "the peasant that strikes out beyond the condition of his social existence, the smallholding." The revolutionary peasant, for Marx, was characterized by "enlightenment" and represented the future, the "modern Cevennes." Marx and Engels were also strong admirers of the seventeenth century German peasant revolutionary Thomas Müntzer.[20]

In *Anti-Dühring*, Engels argued that large landholders have almost invariably been more destructive in their relation to the land than peasants and free agricultural laborers. The Roman Republic in Pliny's day replaced tillage with stock raising and thereby brought "Italy to ruin (*latifundia Italiam perdidere*)"; in North America "the big landlords of the South with their slaves and their improvident robbery of the land, exhausted the soil until it could only grow firs"—thereby representing a much more destructive relation to the earth (as well as to society) than the labor of free farmers.[21]

Moreover, the whole question of peasant societies (and peasants within capitalist societies) should not be confused with the issue of pristine nature—as Ferkiss seems to do. Peasant agriculture is nonindustrial in character and "closer to the earth," but it is already well down the road of the human transformation of nature, including human nature. If one looks back far enough there were subsistence economies—i.e., not defined by market relations—but one should be careful not to idealize them. Long before primitive accumulation generated capitalist social forms, genuine communal agriculture had been largely eliminated under noncapitalist modes of production in most of Europe. In some of these societies the majority of human beings were, as Raymond Williams observes, "working animals, tied by forced tribute, forced labour, or 'bought and sold like beasts'; 'protected' by law and custom only as animals and streams are protected, to yield more labour, more food, more blood."[22]

For Marx and Engels, nature was intertwined with human history. On these grounds they sharply attacked those conservative romantics of their day who sought to root themselves and society in a conception of unspoiled nature—as an adequate basis for a revolt against capitalism. Hence, in criticizing idealizations of a rural order emanating from feudal times, they were not thereby rejecting "unspoiled nature"—though they carefully avoided any idealization of pristine nature. Indeed, Marx thought it important to remark in volume 1 of *Capital* that "Everyone knows that there are no true forests in England. The deer in the parks of the great are demure domestic cattle, as fat as London aldermen." While in Scotland the so-called deer forests that were being established for the benefit of the huntsmen (at the expense of rural laborers), contained deer but no trees. "The development of civilization and industry in general," Marx wrote in volume 2 of *Capital*, "has always shown itself so active in the destruction of forests that everything that has been done for their conservation and production is completely insignificant in comparison."[23]

SUSTAINABILITY AND THE EARTH

In the *Communist Manifesto*, Marx and Engels included in their ten-point program for revolutionary change not only the "abolition of property in land and application of all rents of land to public purposes," and the "gradual abolition of the distinction between town and country, by a more equable distribution of population over the country," but also "the bringing into cultivation of waste lands, and the improvement of soil generally in accordance with a common plan."[24] At this point in the development of their thought, they adopted what might be thought of as an early conservationist approach in relation to such issues as the "improvement of soil." They had been influenced early on (as early as 1843 in the case of

Engels) by the pioneering research of the great German soil chemist Justus von Liebig. From Liebig, whom they considered to be the greatest representative of bourgeois science in the area of agriculture, as well as from other figures like the Scottish political economist James Anderson, Marx and Engels learned of the necessity of returning to the soil the nutrients that had been taken from it. Their insistence on the "improvement of [the] soil generally in accordance with a common plan" is then to be understood in this sense.[25]

Marx saw the bourgeoisie engaging in the utmost exploitation of the earth or soil on the same basis as every other element of commerce. For the bourgeoisie, he wrote in 1852, "the soil is to be a marketable commodity, and the exploitation of the soil is to be carried on according to the common commercial laws. There are to be manufacturers of food as well as manufacturers of twist and cottons, but no longer any lords of the land."[26]

Beginning in the 1860s, when he was completing *Capital*, Marx was influenced by the widespread concern that emerged in Europe and North America over the crisis of the earth or soil, resulting from the forms of exploitation applied by capitalist agriculture—a crisis that was given definitive expression in the work of such thinkers as Liebig, the Scottish agricultural chemist James F.W. Johnston, and the U.S. economist Henry Carey. By 1859, Liebig was arguing that the "empirical agriculture" of the trader had given rise to a "spoliation system" in which the "conditions of reproduction" of the soil were violated. Soil nutrients (such as nitrogen, phosphorus, and potassium) were "carried away in produce year after year, rotation after rotation." Both the open system of exploitation of American farming and the so-called high farming of European agriculture were forms of "robbery." "Rational agriculture," in contrast, would give "back to the fields the conditions of their fertility."[27]

Marx's concern over the condition of agriculture and the crisis of the soil led him toward a much more sophisticated understanding of environmental problems. In the 1860s and onward, he focused on the issues of ecological degradation (disruption of the soil nutrient cycle), restoration, and sustainability—all of which were linked in his analysis to changing social relations. "Large landed property," he wrote at the end of his critique of capitalist ground rent in volume 3 of *Capital*:

reduces the agricultural population to an ever decreasing minimum and confronts it with an ever growing industrial population crammed together in large towns; in this way it produces conditions that provoke an irreparable rift in the interdependent process of the social metabolism, a metabolism prescribed by the natural laws of life itself. The result of this is a squandering of the vitality of the soil, which is carried by trade far beyond the bounds of a single country.[28]

Sustainable development has been defined in our time by the Brundtland Commission as "development which meets the needs of the present without compromising the ability of future generations to meet their need."[29] It was the need for sustainability in precisely this sense that Marx came to emphasize as a result of his research into the crisis of the earth or soil under capitalism, and which became an integral part of his conception of a future communist society. As he himself put it, "the way that the cultivation of particular crops depends on fluctuations in market prices and the constant changes in cultivation with these price fluctuations—the entire spirit of capitalist production, which is oriented towards the most immediate monetary profits— stands in contradiction to agriculture, which has to concern itself with the whole gamut of permanent conditions of life required by the chain of successive generation."[30]

Indeed, for Marx, who understood that transcending the ecological contradictions of capitalist agriculture was an absolute necessity for communist society, the question of sustainability was central to the future development of humanity. "A conscious and rational treatment of the land as permanent communal property," he wrote, was "the inalienable condition for the existence and reproduction of the chain of human generations. . . ."[31] In this sense, ecological sustainability could be viewed as a nature-imposed necessity for human production. The implications of this, as understood by Marx, were truly global in scope:

From the standpoint of a higher socio-economic formation, the private property of particular individuals in the earth will appear just as absurd as the private property of one man in other men. Even an entire society, a nation, or all simultaneously existing societies taken together, are not owners of the earth. They are simply its possessors, its beneficiaries, and have to bequeath it in an improved state to succeeding generations, as *boni patres familias* [good heads of the household].[32]

Devising a sustainable alternative to the destructive ecological tendencies of capitalist society was, thus, not merely a technical problem for Marx, but one that required a far-reaching transformation of society. The basic change needed was a shift to a society controlled by the associated producers, characterized by the expansion of free time and collective-democratic organization, and hence by a non-instrumentalist approach to nature and human society. Among the revolutionary changes necessary to bring this about was an end to "the monopolized earth" of private property. "Private property," Marx contended, referring to James Johnston's analysis of the impoverishment of the soil in the mid-nineteenth century, "places insuperable barriers on all sides to a genuinely rational agriculture."[33]

WAS MARX "PROMETHEAN"?

In his *Contemporary Critique of Historical Materialism*, Anthony Giddens contends that those passages in Marx's writings which suggest that "nature is more than a medium through which human history unfolds" are mostly confined to his "early writings" and that overall a "Promethean attitude," in which the technology of production is praised while nature is treated simply in instrumental terms, "is preeminent" in Marx's work. Indeed, for Giddens, Marx is to be sharply criticized because "his concern with transforming the exploitative human social relations expressed in class systems does not extend to the exploitation of nature."[34] The foregoing discussion, however, has shown that Giddens's condemnation of Marx on the first and third counts (abandoning his ecological insights after his "early writings," and failing to acknowledge the exploitation of the earth) are both contradicted by a mass of evidence. Marx referred again and again to the exploitation of the earth or soil and he did so in his later writings even more than his earlier works. Indeed, as Massimo Quaini noted, Marx "denounced the spoliation of nature before a modern bourgeois ecological conscience was born."[35]

But what of the other charge that Giddens levels at Marx, that of advocating a "Promethean" (in the sense of productivist or instrumentalist) attitude to nature? This same broad criticism—so broad and all-encompassing that it is usually thought unnecessary to provide any evidence to support it—has been voiced not only by Giddens but by numerous others, including such varied thinkers as Ted Benton, Kate Soper, Robyn Eckersley, John Clark and Victor Ferkiss.[36]

If what is meant by this charge of "Prometheanism" is that Marx, in line with the Enlightenment tradition, placed considerable faith in rationality, science, technology, and human progress, and that he often celebrated the growing human mastery over natural forces, there is no denying this to be the case. Here, we only have to turn to the *Communist Manifesto* itself where Marx wrote his panegyric to the bourgeoisie:

> The bourgeoisie, during its rule of scarce one hundred years, has created more massive and more colossal productive forces than have all preceding generations together. Subjection of Nature's forces to man, machinery, application of chemistry to industry and agriculture, steam-navigation, railways, electric telegraphs, clearing of whole continents for cultivation, canalization of rivers, whole populations conjured out of the ground. What earlier century had even a presentiment that such productive forces slumbered in the lap of social labour?[37]

It would be a mistake, however, to conclude from this that Marx and Engels suspended all critical judgment where science, technology and the idea of progress were concerned. Marx and Engels were well aware of the fact that science and technology could be misused and distorted by bourgeois civilization, a form of society, which, they note in the *Communist Manifesto*, "is like the sorcerer, who is no longer able to control the powers of the nether world whom he has called up by his spells."[38] The whole giant apparatus of modern relations of production, exchange, and property, backed up by science and technology, that constituted the creative power of capitalist society, was, Marx and Engels argued, vulnerable to its own achievements, leading to economic crises and the rise of the modern working class or proletariat as the gravedigger of the system. Moreover, as Marx and Engels were to emphasize again and again, the same productive forces resulting from the coupling of capitalist market society with modern science and technology resulted in the exploitation not only of human beings but also of the earth itself, in the sense of violating the conditions of its sustainability.

Robyn Eckersley, in her influential book *Environmentalism and Political Theory*, has written that "Marx fully endorsed the . . . technical accomplishments of the capitalist forces of production and . . . thoroughly absorbed the Victorian faith in scientific and technological progress as the means by which humans could outsmart and conquer nature."[39] Yet, in his "Speech at the Anniversary of The People's Paper," delivered in April 1856, Marx observed that

> In our days, everything seems pregnant with its contrary. Machinery, gifted with the wonderful power of shortening and fructifying human labour, we behold starving and overworking it. The new-fangled sources of wealth, by some strange weird spell, are turned into sources of want. The victories of art seem bought by the loss of character. At the same pace that mankind masters nature, man seems to become enslaved to other men or to his own infamy. Even the pure light of science seems unable to shine but on the dark background of ignorance. All our invention and progress seem to result in endowing material forces with intellectual life, and in stultifying human life into a material force. This antagonism between modern industry and science on the one hand, modern misery and dissolution on the other hand; this antagonism between the productive powers and the social relations of our epoch is a fact, palpable, overwhelming, and not to be controverted.[40]

Despite the faith that they generally placed in "the pure light of science," Marx and Engels exhibited a complex view of science, technology, and human progress, as can be seen in their analysis of the exploitation of the soil. With the introduction of machinery and large scale industry into agriculture under capitalist conditions, Marx argued, "a conscious, technological application of science replaces the previous highly irrational and slothfully traditional way of working." But it is precisely this science and technology in capitalist hands, Marx goes on to observe, that "disturbs the metabolic interaction between man and the earth," by being turned into a force for the exploitation of both the worker and the soil.[41]

REVOLUTIONARY IMPERATIVES

As Joseph Schumpeter emphasized, one of the most original and profound insights of the *Communist Manifesto* was Marx and Engels's perception of the technological dynamism of capitalism, which, to an extent never before seen in world history, demanded the "constant revolutionizing of production" in order to survive.[42] It was this understanding of the inner dynamism of production under capitalism that led Marx, in fact, to his most comprehensive assessment of the impact of capitalism on nature and on everything that appeared external to itself. Thus, in the *Grundrisse* Marx wrote:

> Just as production founded on capital creates universal industriousness on one side . . . so does it create on the other side a system of general exploitation of the natural and human qualities, a system of general utility, utilising science itself just as much as all the physical and mental qualities, while there appears nothing *higher in itself*, nothing legitimate for itself, outside this circle of social production and exchange. Thus capital creates the bourgeois society, and the universal appropriation of nature as well as of the social bond itself by the members of society. Hence the great civilizing influence of capital; its production of a stage of society in comparison to which all earlier ones appear as mere *local developments* of humanity and as *nature-idolatry*. For the first time, nature becomes purely an object for humankind, purely a matter of utility; ceases to be recognized as a power for itself; and the theoretical discovery of its autonomous laws appears merely as a ruse so as to subjugate it under human needs, whether as an object of consumption or as a means of production. In accord with this tendency, capital drives beyond national barriers and prejudices as much as beyond nature worship, as well as all traditional, confined, complacent, encrusted satisfactions of present needs, and reproductions of old ways of

life. It is destructive towards all of this, and constantly revolutionizes it, tearing down all the barriers which hem in the development of the forces of production, the expansion of needs, the all-sided development of production, and the exploitation and exchange of natural and mental forces.

But from the fact that capital posits every such limit as a barrier and hence gets *ideally* beyond it, it does not by any means follow that it has *really* overcome it, and, since every such barrier contradicts its character, its production moves in contradictions which are constantly overcome but just as constantly posited.[43]

The drive to unlimited accumulation, the incessant revolutionizing of the means of production, the subjugation of all that was external to itself to its own commodity logic—all of this, Marx argued, was part of the juggernaut of capital. Capital sees nature purely as an object, as an external barrier to be overcome.[44] Commenting on Bacon's famed maxim that "nature is only overcome by obeying her"—on the basis of which Bacon also proposed to "subjugate" nature—Marx, as we have seen, replies that for capitalism the discovery of nature's autonomous laws "appears merely as a ruse so as to subjugate it under human need."[45] He thus decried the one-sided, instrumental, exploitative relation to nature associated with contemporary social relations. Despite its clever "ruse," capital is never able to transcend the barrier of natural conditions, which continually reassert themselves with the result that "production moves in contradictions which are constantly overcome but just as constantly posited." No other thinker in Marx's time, and perhaps no other thinker up to our own day, has so brilliantly captured the full complexity of the relationship between nature and modern society.

Much of the criticism that has been leveled at Marx and Engels in the area of ecology stems, in fact, from a post-materialist or postmodernist ecology which is no longer so influential today, displaced by the growth of materialist ecology. The social ecology of the 1960s, 1970s and early 1980s was often built around the "post-materialist thesis" that environmental issues arose only in conditions of affluence. Emphasis on the limits of growth, which were viewed as positing an absolute conflict between economic growth and the environment, often contributed to a neglect of the political economy of environmental degradation. Instead, the principal focus was on cultural factors, frequently abstracted from material conditions—such as the question of anthropocentric versus ecocentric culture. Over the past decade, however, we have witnessed growing concern about the future of the biosphere, with the rise of such problems as global warming, the destruction of the ozone layer, and the worldwide extinction of species to the forefront of the ecological discussion. Among analysts of social ecology, attention has shifted to issues of sustainable development, environmental injustice (or the intersection of environmental degradation with class, race, gender, and nation-state divisions), and coevolution.[46]

In this changing context, it is not surprising that Marx's approach to the question of the natural conditions underlying human society—emphasizing as it did sustainability, the connection between the exploitation of the earth and other forms of exploitation, and the interdependent, "metabolic" character of the evolving human-nature interaction—should now be exciting new interest. In all of these respects, Marx was well ahead of contemporary environmental thought.

Nevertheless, Marx's approach to environmental issues was inadequate in one very important respect, most evident in the *Communist Manifesto*. The *Manifesto* was first and foremost a revolutionary document, but ecological contradictions, though perceived by Marx and Engels even at this early stage in their analysis, play little or no role in the anticipated revolution against capitalism. Marx and Engels clearly thought that the duration of capitalism would be much shorter than earlier modes of production, brought to a relatively rapid end by the intensity of its contradictions and by the actions of the proletariat—the gravedigger of the system. As a result, they tended to view the ecological problems that they perceived as having more bearing on the future of communist than capitalist society.[47] This is why ecological considerations enter much more explicitly into their program for communism in the *Manifesto* than into their assessment of the conditions leading to the demise of capitalism.

Today, it is obvious that this approach is inadequate. The ecological contradictions of capitalism have developed to the point that they will inevitably play a large role in the demise of the system—with ecology now constituting a major source of antisystemic resistance to capitalism. Our whole notion of the revolt against capitalism has to be reshaped accordingly. Marx's conception of a sustainable society, in which the earth would be bequeathed "in an improved state to succeeding generations," in the context of a reconstituted social order organized around the collective realization of human needs, is perhaps the most complete vision of a feasible utopia—judged in social and ecological terms—that has yet been developed. It therefore constitutes the essential starting point for the articulation of a truly revolutionary social ecology. Today, we must give a much fuller meaning than originally intended to the famous lines of *The International*:

> The earth shall rise on new foundations,
> We have been naught, we shall be all.[48]

CHAPTER TWELVE

Ecological Imperialism:
The Curse of Capitalism

In the spring of 2003, the United States, backed by Britain, invaded Iraq, a country with the second largest oil reserves in the world. The United States is now working to expand Iraqi oil production, while securing for itself an increasingly dominant position in the control of this crucial resource as part of its larger economic and geopolitical strategy. Earlier, the same U.S. administration that invaded Iraq had pulled out of the Kyoto Protocol process, designed to limit the growth in the emissions of carbon dioxide and other greenhouse gases responsible for global warming—a phenomenon threatening the living world as we know it. It is no wonder, then, that there has been a growth of concern about ecological imperialism, which in the eyes of many has become as significant as the more familiar political, economic, and cultural forms of imperialism to which it is related.

In 1986, Alfred Crosby published a work entitled *Ecological Imperialism: The Biological Expansion of Europe, 900–1900*, which described the destruction wrought on indigenous environments—most often inadvertently—by the European colonization of much of the rest of the world.[1] Old World flora and fauna introduced into New World environments experienced demographic explosions with adverse effects on native species. As the subtitle of Crosby's book suggested, his historical analysis dealt mainly with "biological expansion" and, thus, had no direct concern with imperialism as a political-economic phenomenon. It did not consider how ecology might relate to the domination of the periphery of the capitalist world economy by the center, or to rivalry between different capitalist powers. Like the infectious diseases that killed tens of millions of indigenous peoples following Columbus's landing in the Americas, ecological imperialism in this view worked as a purely biological force, following "encounters" between regions of the earth that had previously been separated geographically. Social relations of production were largely absent from this historical account.

The ecological problem under capitalism is a complex one. An analysis at the level of the entire globe is required. Ecological degradation at this universal level is related to the divisions within the world capitalist system, arising from the fact that a single world economy is nonetheless divided into numerous nation-states, competing with each other both directly and via their corporations. It is also divided hierarchically into center and periphery, with nations occupying fundamentally different positions in the international division of labor, and in a world-system of dominance and dependency.

All of this makes the analysis of ecological imperialism complicated enough, but understanding has also been impeded by the underdevelopment of an ecological materialist analysis of capitalism within Marxist theory as a whole.[2] Nevertheless, it has long been apparent—and was stipulated in Marx's own work—that transfers in economic values are accompanied in complex ways by real "material-ecological" flows that transform relations between city and country, and between global metropolis and periphery.[3] Control of such flows is a vital part of competition between rival industrial and financial centers. Ecological imperialism, thus, presents itself most obviously in the following ways: (1) the pillage of the resources of some countries by others and the transformation of whole ecosystems upon which states and nations depend; (2) massive movements of population and labor that are interconnected with the extraction and transfer of resources; (3) the exploitation of ecological vulnerabilities of societies to promote imperialist control; (4) the dumping of ecological wastes in ways that widen the chasm between center and periphery; and (4) overall, the creation of a global "metabolic rift" that characterizes the relation of capitalism to the environment, and at the same time limits capitalist development.

THE METABOLIC RIFT

The main ecological contradictions of capitalism, associated with ecological imperialism, were already evident to a considerable extent in the writings of Marx. The accumulation of capital is in some respects a self-propelling process; the surplus accumulated in one stage becomes the investment fund for the next. One of the crucial questions in classical political economy, therefore, was where the original capital had come from that set off the dynamic accumulation that characterized the late eighteenth and nineteenth century. This raised the issue of prior, primary or "primitive" accumulation.

Taking Britain as the classical case, Marx saw primitive accumulation as having three aspects. First, the removal of peasants from the land by land enclosures and the abrogation of customary, common rights, so they no longer had direct access to or control over the material means of production. Second, the creation by this means of a pauperized pool of landless laborers, who became wage laborers under capitalism, and who flocked to the towns where they emerged as an industrial proletariat. Third, an enormous concentration and centralization of wealth as the means of production (initially through the control of the land) came to be monopolized by fewer and fewer individuals, and as the surplus thus made available flowed to the industrial centers. Newly proletarianized workers were available to be exploited, while "Lazarus layers" of the unemployed kept down wages, making production more profitable.

The whole process of primitive accumulation—involving, as Marx put it, "the forcible expropriation of the people from the soil," and the "sweeping" of them, as Malthus expressed it, into the towns—had deep ecological implications.[4] Already land under feudal property had been converted into "the inorganic body of its lord." Under capitalism, with the further alienation of the land (and nature), the domination of human beings by other human beings was extended. "Land, like man," Marx noted, was reduced "to the level of a venal object."[5]

Marx's concept of a "metabolic rift" was developed in the context of the alarm raised by agricultural chemists and agronomists in Germany, Britain, France and the United States about the loss of soil nutrients—such as nitrogen, phosphorus, and potassium—through the export of food and fiber to the cities. Rather than being returned to the soil, as in traditional agricultural production, these essential nutrients were being shipped hundreds or even thousands of miles away and ended up as waste polluting the cities. The most advanced form of capitalist agricultural production at the time, British "high farming," was, the German chemist Justus von Liebig contended, nothing but a "robbery system," due to its effects on the soil.[6]

Marx, who was a careful student of Liebig and other soil chemists, saw this antagonism between human beings and the earth as an important problem. Capitalism had, as he put it, created an "irreparable rift" in the "metabolic interaction" between human beings and the earth; a "systematic restoration" of that necessary metabolic interaction as a "regulative law of social production" was needed, but the growth under capitalism of large-scale industrial agriculture and long-distance trade intensified and extended the metabolic rift (and still does). Moreover the wastage of soil nutrients had its counterpart in pollution and waste in the towns.[7]

Marx treated both primitive accumulation and the metabolic rift as embodying global implications fundamental to the understanding of the development of capitalism as a world system. As he famously put it:

> The discovery of gold and silver in America, the extirpation, enslavement and entombment in mines of the indigenous population of that continent, the beginnings of the conquest and plunder of India, and the conversion of Africa into a preserve for the commercial hunting of black-skins, are all things which characterize the dawn of the era of capitalist production. These idyllic proceedings are the chief moments of primitive accumulation.[8]

The genocide inflicted on the indigenous populations went hand in hand with the seizure of wealth in the New World. "The treasures captured outside Europe by undisguised looting, enslavement, and murder

flowed back to the mother country and were turned into capital there."
Great fortunes were built on robbing the periphery of its natural wealth
and exploiting ecological resources. In India "the monopolies of salt,
opium, betel, and other commodities were inexhaustible mines of
wealth."[9] In his famous 1848 speech on free trade Marx observed: "You
believe perhaps, gentlemen, that the production of coffee and sugar is the
natural destiny of the West Indies. Two centuries ago, nature, which does
not trouble herself about commerce, had planted neither sugar-cane nor
coffee trees there."[10]

The creation of such monocultures for the export of cash crops to
Europe—and the enslaved or semi-enslaved laboring populations that
worked them—were products of the development of the capitalist world
economy, with its open plunder of the periphery for the benefit of the center. Monoculture plantations constituted, in the words of Eduardo
Galeano in his *Open Veins of Latin America*,

> a sieve for the draining-off of natural wealth. . . . Each region, once inte-
> grated into the world market, experiences a dynamic cycle; then decay
> sets in with the competition of substitute products, the exhaustion of the
> soil, or the development of other areas where conditions are better. The
> initial productive drive fades with the passing years into a culture of
> poverty, subsistence economy, and lethargy. . . . The more a product is
> desired by the world market, the greater the misery it brings to the Latin
> American peoples whose sacrifice creates it.[11]

But tropical monoculture was not the only mode of ecological imperialism in the nineteenth century. British "high farming"—or early industrialized agriculture—robbed the soil of England of its nutrients, and
then sought to compensate for this by robbing other countries of the
means to replace them. Marx was again well aware of this. Following
Liebig, he noted that British agriculture, in effect, imported the soil of
some countries by shipping soil nutrients and natural fertilizers from
these countries back to Britain. British agriculture had become dependent on imported guano.

This illustrated precisely the "rift" in the natural metabolism that
Marx identified, as Jason Moore notes:

With the transition to capitalism, a new division of labor between town and country took shape—on a world scale and within regions—whereby the products of the countryside (especially, but not only in the peripheries) flowed into the cities, which were under no obligation to return the waste products to the point of production. Nutrients were pumped out of one ecosystem in the periphery and transferred to another in the core. In essence, the land was progressively mined until its relative exhaustion fettered profitability. At this point, economic contraction forced capital to seek out and develop new ways of exploiting territories hitherto beyond the reach of the law of value.[12]

FROM THE CURSE OF NITRATES TO THE CURSE OF OIL

British cotton textiles, as Galeano noted, were exchanged for the hides of Rio de la Plata, the copper of Chile, the sugar of Cuba, and the coffee of Brazil—but also for the guano and nitrates of Peru.[13] In 1840, the same year that Liebig first pointed to the issue of the loss of soil nutrients, a French scientist, Alexandre Cochet, discovered that valuable quantities of nitrate of soda could be extracted from guano and nitrates (saltpeter), both of which were abundant in Peru. In 1841, shortly after Cochet's laboratory results were published, an international guano rush began, as European (especially British) and U.S. agriculturists sought the precious fertilizer to compensate for the soil nutrients that they were losing. In the early 1850s, a British officer reported witnessing the simultaneous loading of guano on ships from the following countries from a single island off the coast of Peru: forty-four United States ships, forty English, five French, two Dutch, one Italian, one Belgian, one Norwegian, one Swedish, one Russian, one Armenian and three Peruvian. Loading the guano into ships required digging into deep mounds of excrement that covered rocky islands. Acrid dust penetrated the eyes, the nose, and the mouth of a worker, and the stench was appalling. After slavery was abolished in 1854, tens of thousands of Chinese coolies were contracted through Macao and Hong Kong. By 1875, some eighty thousand were working under conditions of virtual slavery in the desert and islands of Peru.[14]

In 1853, a process was discovered for efficiently mining the nitrate fields in the Tarapacá desert province of Peru, and soon afterwards rich deposits were also found in the adjacent Bolivian province of Atacama. By the 1860s, these nitrate fields had become even more important as a source of fertilizer than guano, the availability of which had begun to diminish. Nitrates were in high demand not only for fertilizers, but also for the recently invented TNT and other explosives, crucial to the expanding war industries of the industrial capitalist states.[15] By 1875, British investments primarily in the nitrate industry in Peru totaled £1,000,000.

The Peruvian ruling class grew enormously wealthy as a result of the guano trade and the mining of nitrates. This wealth did not, however, flow significantly into economic development, apart from the building of railways. For the rest of the population the nitrate resource soon proved to be a curse. Peru became heavily indebted, in a classic pattern, primarily to British investors, with its guano exports mortgaged well into the future. In 1875, attempting to get out of its debt trap, Peru imposed a state monopoly in its nitrate zones in Tarapacá, expropriating the holdings of private investors (many of whom were foreign, particularly British) and offering them government certificates of payment. Subsequently, the Peruvian government also sought to regulate the output of guano and nitrates so that they would not compete against each other.

This led to the War of the Pacific (also sometimes called the Nitrate War), which broke out four years after the Peruvian expropriation of the nitrate industry, when Bolivia, breaking a previous treaty, attempted to raise taxes on exports by Chilean intermediaries of nitrates from its Atacama province. Chile, backed by British investors, declared war not only on Bolivia but also on Peru, with which the former was allied. With its more modern, British-built navy and French-trained army, Chile was soon able to seize Bolivia's Atacama province and Peru's Tarapacá—never to leave. Before the war Chile had almost no nitrate fields and no guano deposits. By the end of the war in 1883, it had seized all of the nitrate zones in Bolivia and Peru and most of Peru's coastal guano deposits, though not its guano islands.[16] Before the war, the British controlled 13 percent of Peru's Tarapacá nitrate industry; immediately after the war—given Chile's possession of the region—the British share rose to 34 percent, and by 1890 it was 70 percent.[17] As the former U.S. Secretary of State James G.

Blaine told a congressional committee investigating the U.S. diplomatic role during the war, the war was about guano and nitrates: "Nothing else. . . . It is an English war on Peru, with Chili as the instrument. . . . Chili would never have gone into this war one inch but for her backing by English capital, and there was never anything played out so boldly in the world as when they came to divide the loot and the spoils."[18]

Having lost all of its nitrates and much of its guano, its two principal resources for export, the Peruvian economy collapsed after the war. As the great Peruvian Marxist José Carlos Mariátegui noted, defeat in the War of the Pacific increased Peruvian dependence on British capital. "Very soon [after the war] the capitalist group that had formed during the period of guano and nitrates resumed its activity and returned to power. . . . The Grace Contract [which they negotiated] ratified British domination in Peru by delivering the state railways to the English bankers who until then had financed the republic and its extravagances."[19] Now that the Peruvian government no longer had the same wealth of resources to exploit, it had no other way to pay off the foreign debts with which it was still encumbered except by handing its railroads over to British investors who had themselves clandestinely backed Chile in its seizing of much of Peru's territory and its most valuable natural resources. According to Bruce Farcau, the guano and nitrate deposits in Peru turned out, "like the Midas touch," to be "a curse disguised as a blessing," first in creating a debt-laden economy, and then giving rise to a war and the loss of these resources.[20]

As a result of its seizure of the nitrate territories in the War of the Pacific, Chile was to take on the curse of nitrates in the decades that followed. Europe still needed guano and nitrates in vast quantities to maintain its agricultural productivity and sought to control this trade imperialistically for the benefit of its own capitalists, exploiting these ecological resources to their limit while siphoning off the bulk of the economic wealth they generated. In 1888, the Chilean President José Manuel Balmaceda, who had carried out modernizing reforms including extensive public works and support for education, announced that the nitrate areas of Chile would have to be nationalized through the formation of Chilean enterprises, and blocked the sale of state-owned nitrate fields to the British. Three years later, a civil war broke out, with British and other foreign investors supporting the opponents of Balmaceda with money and armaments. The press in London characterized Balmaceda (in tones very recognizable today) as a "dictator of the worst stripe." When the defeated Balmaceda committed suicide in 1891, the British ambassador wrote to the Foreign Office: "The British community makes no secret of its satisfaction over the fall of Balmaceda, whose victory, it is thought, would have implied serious harm to British commercial interests." State control of industries and economic infrastructure in Chile quickly receded after the civil war, as the British extended their investments.

By the early 1890s, Chile was delivering three-quarters of all its exports to Britain while obtaining almost half of its imports from the same country, creating a trade dependence on Britain greater than that of India at that time. When the First World War broke out in Europe, two-thirds of Chile's national income was derived from nitrate exports primarily to Britain and Germany. The British monopoly of the nitrate trade through its control of the Chilean economy had put Germany at a serious disadvantage in its competition with Britain, since nitrates were necessary for explosives as well as fertilizer. Like Britain, Germany had worked to have Balmaceda ousted, but Chile remained largely under British control, creating a problem for Germany. Just prior to the First World War, however, the German chemist and nationalist Fritz Haber devised a process for producing nitrates by fixing nitrogen from the air. The result within a few years was to destroy almost completely the value of Chilean nitrates, creating a severe crisis for the Chilean economy.[21]

But the curse of nitrates (and nitrogen) did not end there; it was transferred to the world at large, including the rich countries themselves. Nitrogen fertilizers, used on an ever-increasing scale (currently around one hundred million tons annually) to maintain agricultural productivity, now pollute more and more of the world's groundwater, lakes, and rivers through fertilizer runoff, giving rise to one of the major ecological problems facing the world today.[22]

Outside of Latin America, the history of the curse of nitrates is now forgotten. But the modern history of the curse of oil, with its all too close parallels with that earlier history, is still very much ongoing. As the *New York Times* noted in its June 7, 2003, issue, in an article entitled "Striking It Poor: Oil as a Curse," "scholarly studies for more than a decade have consistently warned of what is known as the resource curse: that developing countries whose economies depend on exporting oil, gas or extracted materials are likely to be poor, authoritarian, corrupt and rocked by civil war." The mainstream argument attributes this persistent "curse" to bad governments in poor countries, which supposedly lack the capacity to utilize the enormous and potentially corrupting economic benefits provided by such resources in a productive manner.

The root explanation of the "curse of oil," however, like that of nitrates, is to be found in ecological imperialism. As Michael Perelman has cogently stated:

> The origins of the curse of oil do not lie in the physical properties of petroleum but rather in the social structure of the world. . . . A rich natural resource base makes a poor country, especially a relatively powerless one, an inviting target—both politically and militarily—for dominant nations. In the case of oil, the powerful nations will not risk letting such a valuable resource fall under the control of an independent government, especially one that might pursue policies that do not coincide with the economic interests of the great transnational corporations. So, governments that display excessive independence soon find themselves overthrown, even if their successors will foster an environment of corruption and political instability.[23]

Nowadays, the curse of oil has also come back to haunt the rich countries too—their environments and their economies—in the form of global warming, or what might be called a planetary rift in the human relation to the global commons—the atmosphere and oceans. This planetary ecological rift, arising from the workings of the capitalist system and its necessary companion imperialism, while varied in its outcomes in specific regions, has led to ecological degradation on a scale that threatens to undermine all existing ecosystems and species—including the human species.

THE ECOLOGICAL DEBT

The mobilization of opposition to ecological imperialism is now increasingly taking place via the concept of "ecological debt." Acción Ecológica, an Ecuador based organization that is leading the ecological debt campaign, defines ecological debt broadly as "the debt accumulated by Northern, industrial countries toward Third World countries on account of resource plundering, environmental damages, and the free occupation of environmental space to deposit wastes, such as greenhouse gases, from the industrial countries."[24] Accounting for ecological debt radically alters the question "Who Owes Whom?"

Fundamental to this position is an analysis of the social interactions between nature and society, as organized by ecological imperialism. The history of pillage and super-exploitation of peoples is seen as part of a larger ecological debt. Capital remains a central focus, since it is the production and consumption patterns of the central capitalist countries that are held responsible for the deteriorating ecological conditions of the planet.[25] A wide range of activities contribute, third world critics contend, to the ecological debt: the extraction of natural resources; unequal terms of trade; degradation of land and soil for export crops; other unrecognized environmental damage and pollution caused by extractive and productive processes; appropriation of ancestral knowledge; loss of biodiversity; contamination of the atmosphere and oceans; the introduction of toxic chemicals and dangerous weapons; and the dumping of hazardous waste in the periphery.[26]

Within the discussion of ecological debt there are two major dimensions: (1) the social-ecological destruction and exploitation that takes place within nations under the influence of ecological imperialism; and (2) the imperialist appropriation of global commons and the unequal use (exploitation) of the absorption capacity of these commons.

In his *Hungry Planet*, first published in 1965, Georg Borgstrom introduced the concept of "ghost acres" to illustrate Britain's dependence on food and raw materials from colonial (or neo-colonial) hinterlands in order to sustain the production, consumption, and trade operations of that nation. The growth of capital has increased the demands placed on the world as a whole. The "ecological footprint" of the core nations continues to expand, as they deplete their own historic stocks of material and energy, as well as those of other nations.[27] Debt cycles and military interventions maintain global inequalities, as the South continues to subsidize the North in terms of labor, commodities and natural resources.

Extraction of raw materials for commodity production is organized around meeting the demands of the countries of the North, where approximately 25 percent of the world's population lives but which consumes 75 percent of global resources.[28] For hundreds of years, the center has depended on cheap primary materials and labor from the periphery. The volume of material and economic value that flows out of the South increases (the volume of exports from Latin America increased by 245 percent between 1980 and 1995),[29] yet the financial debt of these nations continues to grow, exacerbated by arbitrary increases in interest rates. At the same time, monopoly capital, dominating the world market, is able to overvalue the North's industrial, high-value commodity exports, further unbalancing international trade.[30]

Imperialist forces impose socio-ecological regimes of production on the world, deepening the antagonistic division between town and country, as well as between the North and South. Agro-ecosystems (including both labor and nature) are restructured and "rationally and systematically reshaped in order to intensify, not merely the production of food and fiber, but the accumulation of personal wealth" by comprador bourgeoisies and monopoly capital.[31] As Josué de Castro noted in a classic 1952 study: "It was to the advantage of economic imperialism and international commerce, both controlled by profit-seeking minorities, that the production, distribution and consumption of food products be regarded as purely business matters rather than as phenomena of the highest importance to society as a whole."[32]

At the planetary level, ecological imperialism has resulted in the appropriation of the global commons (i.e., the atmosphere and oceans) and the carbon absorption capacity of the biosphere, primarily to the benefit of a relatively small number of countries at the center of the capitalist world economy.[33] The North rose to wealth and power in part through high fossil-fuel consumption, which is now culminating in a climate crisis due to the dumping of ecological wastes into the atmosphere. Climate change is already occurring due to the increased concentrations of carbon dioxide and other minor greenhouse gases, warming the earth 0.7°C during the last hundred years.

The ecological debt approach to the question of ecological imperialism, while addressing the larger problem in its full dimensions, nonetheless focuses tactically on the carbon debt as its most concrete, empirical basis—taking advantage of the urgent global necessity of addressing this problem. The nations of the North that cause a disproportionate amount of the emissions due to industries, automobiles, and lifestyles, are largely responsible for climate change, as the "fossil-fuel economy creates waste emissions faster than natural systems can absorb them."[34] The Intergovernmental Panel on Climate Change (IPCC) now expects an increase in temperature of 1.5–6.0° C during this century. "A temperature rise of 4°C would create an earth that was warmer than at any time in the last 40 million years," potentially undermining the ability of human civilization to survive.[35] The extreme weather patterns (hurricanes, floods, droughts, and so forth) in recent decades, which disproportionately affect the nations of the South, may be partly the result of greenhouse gases accumulating in the atmosphere. Global warming leading to a rise in sea levels threatens many islands, as well as some densely populated, low-lying countries such as Bangladesh, with floods that would submerge them.

Given that no one owns the atmosphere or oceans, calculating the carbon debt is an attempt to measure how unsustainable the production and consumption of a given economy is, relative to all the others. Simply stated, if a nation uses fossil fuel above a set rate, then it is accumulating a carbon debt, making a disproportionate use of environmental space in the commons for the disposal of its carbon waste.

In determining how to calculate this set rate of emissions, several things must be considered. In the year 1996, already, approximately seven billion metric tons of carbon were released into the atmosphere, more than 50 percent of it by the United States and Europe—a massively disproportionate share. Second, current carbon emissions exceed the amount that the environment can absorb. The IPCC has estimated that at least a 60 percent reduction in carbon emissions from 1990 levels (down to 2,800 million metric tons) is necessary to stabilize or reduce the risk of further climate change.

For all these reasons it follows that the rich industrialized nations, whose output alone already exceeds the world's total allowable amount, must—from a moral standpoint—bear the brunt of the necessary reduction in emissions. As Agarwal and Narain suggested in 1991, any just and reasonable approach for determining how much carbon a nation can emit into the global commons, without accumulating a carbon debt, must be based on emissions per head of population.[36] Andrew Simms and his colleagues calculated that "based on the 1990 target for climate stabilization, everyone in the world would have a per capita allowance of carbon of around 0.4 tonnes, per year."[37] But as time passes and the release and accumulation of gases continue, that allowance decreases. Before long the per capita allowance of carbon will only be 0.2 tons, per year. Inaction creates an ever more difficult position for the future. In fact, if current trends continue, global warming could spiral out of control, seriously threatening the sustainability of life on earth. An "ecological discontinuity" can occur with few, if any, immediate warning signs.[38]

When the North's current excess of carbon emissions (beyond what is sustainable per capita for the entire world) was translated into dollar terms—based on "the historically close correlation between the basic measure of economic activity, Gross Domestic Product (GDP) and carbon dioxide emissions"—the ecological debt owed by the North to the South in terms of carbon emissions alone was found in the 1990s to be an estimated $13 trillion per year.[39] The annual ecological debt of the North owed to the South, without even looking at the cumulative impact, was thus calculated to be at least three times the financial debt that the South "owed" to the North. Paying it at that time, analyses showed, would have canceled out the loans that imprisoned third world nations, and would also have allowed them to adopt more fuel-efficient technologies.

But payment of ecological debt and new technologies cannot solve the carbon rift, if capitalist production in the South takes place in the same way that it has in the North. Ecological debt proponents, therefore, advocate a process of contraction and convergence. In this scenario, the rich nations of the North would reduce their carbon (and other greenhouse gas) emissions to an appropriate level to meet the IPCC recommendations, while the poor nations of the South would be allowed to increase their emissions gradually in the interest of social and economic development. The nations of the world would thus converge toward "equal, and low, per capita allotments."[40] Variations in allotments may exist, given differences in climate, but per capita emissions for the world as a whole would be within acceptable standards.

Assessing ecological degradation and conditions of international inequality, as these relate to global warming, is, of course, only the beginning in trying to estimate the ecological debt owed to the South. The ocean, another global commons, has long been used for the dumping of toxins and hazardous waste, and its ability to serve as a sink for carbon is decreasing. Furthermore, the depletion of the ocean fish stock threatens to disrupt metabolic relationships within the ocean ecosystem. The full extent of the damage caused by ecological imperialism is, indeed, unaccounted for, especially if we consider the historical pillage carried out over several centuries throughout the global periphery as a result of the economic expansion of the core capitalist states.

The ecological debt movement, today, fights for the restoration and renewal of nature on a global basis. And as ecological sustainability is impossible without social and economic balance, ecological debt activists are increasingly confronting the forces of capitalist expansion, calling into question the legitimacy of the global order. The concentration of wealth is explicitly linked to the impoverishment and exploitation of people and nature throughout the world. A system of incessant accumulation on an ever-increasing scale—and of consumption without bounds—is recognized as one bent on suicide. Stopping the destruction caused by ecological imperialism is seen as the only solution to this global problem. A transformation of the social-ecological relationships of production is needed. If the global commons is the sink where wastes are absorbed, the sink is clogged and overflowing. To challenge ecological imperialism, Acción Ecológica insists that "it's time to shut off the tap" to prevent the "unjust flow of energy, natural resources, food, cheap labour, and financial resources from the South to the North."[41]

THE STRUGGLE AGAINST ECOLOGICAL IMPERIALISM TODAY

The problem with the ecological debt campaign is, clearly, that given the current balance of world forces it cannot hope to succeed. This is indicated by the level of resistance on the part of capital marked by the U.S. withdrawal from the Kyoto Protocol process under the Bush administration, and by the declaration of victory by the Global Climate Coalition (representing many of the leading global monopolistic corporations) with the effective collapse of the protocol. As they stated on their web page:

> The Global Climate Coalition has been deactivated. The industry voice on climate change has served its purpose by contributing to a new national approach to global warming. The Bush administration will soon announce a climate policy that is expected to rely on the development of new technologies to reduce greenhouse emissions, a concept strongly supported by the GCC. The coalition also opposed Senate ratification of the Kyoto Protocol that would assign such stringent targets for lowering greenhouse gas emissions that economic growth in the US would be severely hampered and energy prices for consumers would skyrocket. The GCC also opposed the treaty because it does not require the largest developing countries to make cuts in their emissions. At this point, both Congress and the Administration agree that the US should not accept the mandatory cuts in emissions required by the protocol.[42]

If global warming is a problem, the Bush administration contended, it did not constitute an immediate threat to the United States; hence, actions to address the problem that would carry high economic costs should be avoided. Better to depend on futuristic "carbon-sequestration" or "geo-engineering" technologies and similar means. For many island or low-lying nations, watching sea levels rise as the arctic glaciers melt, such a stance is a particularly extreme case of ecological imperialism. While the poor nations of the periphery are expected to continue to pay financial debts to banks of the rich nations of the center, the enormous ecological debt incurred by the latter is not even being acknowledged—and the entire planetary problem is growing worse by the year. The struggle is, therefore, likely to intensify.

The ecological debt struggle, organized around the degradation of the global commons—particularly the warming of the atmosphere—brought on disproportionately by the rich countries, has certainly given a new practical meaning to the concept of ecological imperialism. This age-old fight has now become associated with an organized form of resistance centered on the need to set the ecological debt of the rich countries against the financial debts of the poor countries. This immediate struggle, moreover, brings the larger ecological curse of capitalism more and more clearly into view. The economic development of capitalism has always carried with it social and ecological degradation as its other side: the degradation of work, as Marx argued, is accompanied by the degradation of the earth. Further, ecological imperialism has meant that the worst forms of ecological destruction in terms of pillage of resources, the disruption of sustainable relations to the earth, and the dumping of wastes— all fall on the periphery more than the center. This relation has not changed at all over the centuries as witnessed by the wars over guano and nitrates of the late nineteenth century and the wars over oil (and the geopolitical power to be obtained through control of oil) of the late twentieth and early twenty-first century.

It is in the nature of this process that it continually worsens. Capital in the late twentieth century and the twenty-first century is running up against ecological barriers at a biospheric level that cannot be overcome, as was the case previously, through the "spatial fix" of geographical expansion and exploitation. Ecological imperialism—the growth of the center of the system at unsustainable rates, through the more thorough-going ecological degradation of the periphery—is now generating a planetary-scale set of ecological contradictions, imperiling the entire biosphere. Only a revolutionary social solution that addresses the rift in ecological relations on a planetary scale and their relation to global structures of imperialism and inequality offers any genuine hope that these contradictions can be transcended. More than ever, the world needs what the early socialist thinkers, including Marx, called for: the rational organization of the human metabolism with nature by freely associated producers. The fundamental curse to be exorcised is capitalism itself.

PART THREE

ecology and revolution

CHAPTER THIRTEEN

Envisioning Ecological Revolution

The goal of ecological revolution, as I shall present it here, has as its initial premise that we are in the midst of a global environmental crisis of such enormity that the web of life of the entire planet is threatened and with it the future of civilization.

This is no longer a very controversial proposition. To be sure, there are different perceptions about the extent of the challenge that this raises. At one extreme, there are those who believe that since these are human problems arising from human causes they are easily solvable. All we need is ingenuity and the will to act. At the other extreme, there are those who believe that the world ecology is deteriorating on a scale and with a rapidity beyond our means to control, giving rise to the gloomiest forebodings.

Although often seen as polar opposites, these views nonetheless share a common basis. As Paul Sweezy observed, they each reflect "the belief that *if present trends continue to operate*, it is only a matter of time until the human species irredeemably fouls its own nest."[1]

WARNING BELLS

The more we learn about current environmental trends, the more the unsustainability of our present course is brought home to us. Among the warning signs:

- There is now a virtual certainty that the critical threshold of a 2° C (3.6° F) increase in average world temperature above the preindustrial level will soon be crossed due to the buildup of greenhouse gases in the atmosphere. Scientists believe that climate change at this level will have portentous implications for the world's ecosystems. The question is no longer whether significant climate change will occur but how great it will be.[2]

- There are growing worries in the scientific community that the estimates of the rate of global warming provided by the United Nations Intergovernmental Panel on Climate Change (IPCC), which in its worst case scenario projected increases in average global temperature of up to 5.8° C (10.4° F) by 2100, may prove to be too low. For example, results from the world's largest climate modeling experiment, based in Oxford University in Britain, indicate that global warming could increase almost twice as fast as the IPCC has estimated.[3]

- Experiments at the International Rice Institute and elsewhere have led scientists to conclude that with each 1°C (1.8°F) increase in temperature, rice, wheat, and corn yields could drop 10 percent.

- It is now increasingly believed that the world is approaching peak crude oil production. The world economy is, therefore, confronting more constrained oil supplies, despite a rapidly increasing demand. All of this points to a growing world energy crisis and mounting resource wars.[4]

- The planet is facing global water shortages due to the drawing down of irreplaceable aquifers, which make up the bulk of the world's fresh water supplies. This poses a threat to global agriculture, which has become a bubble economy based on the unsustainable exploitation of groundwater. One in four people in the world today do not have access to safe water.[5]

- Two thirds of the world's major fish stocks are currently being fished at or above their capacity. Over the last half-century 90 percent of large predatory fish in the world's oceans have been eliminated.[6]

- The species extinction rate is the highest in sixty-five million years with the prospect of cascading extinctions, as the last remnants of intact ecosystems are removed. Already the extinction rate is in some cases (as in the case of bird species) one hundred times the "benchmark" or "natural" rate. Scientists have pinpointed twenty-five hot spots on land that account for 44 percent of all vascular plant species and 35 percent of all species in four vertebrate groups, while taking up only 1.4 percent of the world's land surface. All of these hot spots are now threatened with rapid annihilation due to human causes. According to Stephen Pimm and Clinton Jenkins, writing in *Scientific American*: "Substantial tracts of intact wilderness remain: humid tropical forests such as the Amazon and Congo, drier woodlands of Africa, and coniferous forests of Canada and Russia. If deforestation in these wilderness forests continues at current rates, the combined extinction rate in them and in the hot [spots around the world] will soon be 1,000 times higher than the benchmark one in a million."[7]

- According to a study published by the National Academy of Sciences in 2002, the world economy exceeded the earth's regenerative capacity in 1980 and by 1999 had gone beyond it by as much as 20 percent. This means, according to the study's authors, that "it would require 1.2 earths, or one earth for 1.2 years, to regenerate what humanity used in 1999."[8]

- The question of the ecological collapse of past civilizations from Easter Island to the Mayans is now increasingly seen as extending to today's world capitalist system. This view, long held by environmentalists, has been popularized by Jared Diamond in his book *Collapse*.[9]

These and other warning bells indicate that the present human relation to the environment is no longer supportable. The most developed capitalist countries have the largest per capita ecological footprints, demonstrating that the entire course of world capitalist development at present represents a dead end.

The main response of the ruling capitalist class, when confronted with the growing environmental challenge, is to fiddle while Rome burns. To the extent that it has a strategy, it is to rely on revolutionizing the forces of production, i.e., on technical change, while keeping the existing system of social relations intact. It was Karl Marx who first pointed in *The Communist Manifesto* to "the constant revolutionizing of production" as a distinguishing feature of capitalist society. Today's vested interests are counting on this built-in process of revolutionary technological change coupled with the proverbial magic of the market to solve the environmental problem when and where this becomes necessary.

In stark contrast, many environmentalists now believe that technological revolution alone will be insufficient to solve the problem and that a more far-reaching social revolution aimed at transforming the present mode of production is required.

GREAT TRANSITION SCENARIOS

Historically, addressing this question of the ecological transformation of society means that we need to ascertain: (1) where the world capitalist system is heading at present; (2) the extent to which it can alter its course by technological or other means in response to today's converging ecological and social crises; and (3) the historical alternatives to the existing system. The most ambitious attempt thus far to carry out such a broad assessment has come from the Global Scenario Group, a project launched in 1995 by the Stockholm Environmental Institute to examine the transition to global sustainability. The Global Scenario Group has issued three reports—*Branch Points* (1997), *Bending the Curve* (1998), and their culminating study, *Great Transition* (2002). In what follows, I will focus on the last of these reports, the *Great Transition*.[10]

As its name suggests, the Global Scenario Group employs alternative scenarios to explore possible paths that society caught in a crisis of ecological sustainability might take. Their culminating report presents three classes of scenarios: Conventional Worlds, Barbarization, and Great Transitions. Each of these contains two variants. Conventional Worlds consists of Market Forces and Policy Reform. Barbarization manifests itself in the forms of Breakdown and Fortress World. Great Transitions is broken down into Eco-communalism and the New Sustainability Paradigm. Each scenario is associated with different thinkers: Market Forces with Adam Smith; Policy Reform with John Maynard Keynes and the authors of the 1987 Brundtland Commission report; Breakdown with Thomas Malthus; Fortress World with Thomas Hobbes; Eco-communalism with William Morris, Mahatma Gandhi, and E. F. Schumacher; and the New Sustainability Paradigm with John Stuart Mill.[11]

Within the Conventional Worlds scenarios, Market Forces stands for naked capitalism or neoliberalism. It represents, in the words of the *Great Transition* report, "the firestorm of capitalist expansion."[12] Market Forces is an unfettered capitalist world order geared to the accumulation of capital and rapid economic growth without regard to social or ecological costs. The principal problem raised by this scenario is its rapacious relation to humanity and the earth.

The drive to amass capital that is central to a Market Forces regime is best captured by Marx's general formula of capital (though not referred to in the *Great Transition* report itself). In a society of simple commodity production (an abstract conception referring to pre-capitalist economic formations in which money and the market play a subsidiary role), the circuit of commodities and money exists in a form, C–M–C, in which distinct commodities or use-values constitute the end points of the economic process. A commodity (C) embodying a definite use-value is sold for money (M) which is used to purchase a different commodity (C). Each such circuit is completed with the consumption of a use-value.

In the case of capitalism, or generalized commodity production, however, the circuit of money and commodities begins and ends with money, or M–C–M. Moreover, since money is merely a quantitative relationship such an exchange would have no meaning if the same amount of money was acquired at the end of the process as exchanged in the beginning, so the general formula for capital, in reality, takes the form of M–C–M´, where M´ equals M + △m or surplus-value. What stands out, when contrasted with simple commodity production, is that there is no real end to the process, since the object is not final use but the accumulation of surplus-value or capital. M–C–M´ in one year, therefore, results in the △m being reinvested, leading to M–C–M´´ in the next year and M–C–M´´´ the year after that, *ad infinitum*. In other words, capital by its nature is self-expanding value.[13]

The motor force behind this drive to accumulation is competition. The competitive struggle ensures that each capital or firm must grow and, hence, must reinvest its "earnings" in order to survive.

Such a system tends toward exponential growth punctuated by crises or temporary interruptions in the accumulation process. The pressures placed on the natural environment are immense and will lessen only with the weakening and cessation of capitalism itself. During the last half-century the world economy has grown more than seven-fold while the biosphere's capacity to support such expansion has, if anything, diminished due to human ecological depredations.[14]

The main assumption of those who advocate a Market Forces solution to the environmental problem is that it will lead to increasing efficiency in the consumption of environmental inputs by means of technological revolution and continual market adjustments. Use of energy, water, and other natural resources will decrease per unit of economic output. This is often referred to as "dematerialization." However, the central implication of this argument is false. Dematerialization, to the extent that it can be said to exist, has been shown to be a much weaker tendency than M–C–M´. As the *Global Transition* report puts it, "The 'growth effect' outpaces the 'efficiency effect.'"[15]

This can be understood concretely in terms of what has been called the Jevons Paradox, named after William Stanley Jevons, who published *The Coal Question* in 1865. Jevons, one of the founders of neoclassical economics, explained that improvements in steam engines that decreased the use of coal per unit of output also served to increase the scale of production as more and bigger factories were built. Hence, increased efficiency in the use of coal had the paradoxical effect of expanding aggregate coal consumption.[16]

The perils of the Market Forces model are clearly visible in the environmental depredations during the two centuries since the advent of industrial capitalism, and especially in the last half-century. "Rather than abating" under a Market Forces regime, the *Great Transition* report declares, "the unsustainable process of environmental degradation that we observe in today's world would [continue to] intensify. The danger of crossing critical thresholds in global systems would increase, triggering events that would radically transform the planet's climate and ecosystems." Although it is "the tacit ideology" of most international institutions, Market Forces leads inexorably to ecological and social disaster and even collapse. The continuation of "'business-as-usual' is a utopian fantasy."[17]

A far more rational basis for hope, the report contends, is found in the Policy Reform scenario. "The essence of the scenario is the emergence of the political will for gradually bending the curve of development toward a comprehensive set of sustainability targets," including peace, human rights, economic development, and environmental quality.[18] This is essentially the Global Keynesian strategy advocated by the Brundtland Commission Report in the late 1980s—an expansion of the welfare state, now conceived as an environmental welfare state, to the entire world. It represents the promise of what environmental sociologists call "ecological modernization."

The Policy Reform approach is prefigured in various international agreements such as the Kyoto Protocol on global warming and the environmental reform measures advanced by the Earth Summits in Rio in 1992 and Johannesburg in 2002. Policy Reform would seek to decrease world inequality and poverty through foreign aid programs emanating from the rich countries and international institutions. It would promote environmental best practices through state-induced market incentives. Yet, despite the potential for limited ecological modernization, the realities of capitalism, the *Great Transition* report contends, would collide with Policy Reform. This is because Policy Reform remains a Conventional Worlds scenario—one in which the underlying values, lifestyles, and structures of the capitalist system endure. "The logic of sustainability and the logic of the global market are in tension. The correlation between the accumulation of wealth and the concentration of power erodes the political basis for a transition." Under these circumstances the "lure of the God of Mammon and the Almighty dollar" will prevail.[19]

The failure of both of the Conventional Worlds scenarios to alleviate the problem of ecological decline means that Barbarization threatens: either Breakdown or the Fortress World. Breakdown is self-explanatory and to be avoided at all costs. The Fortress World emerges when "powerful regional and international actors comprehend the perilous forces leading to Breakdown" and are able to guard their own interests sufficiently to create "protected enclaves."[20] Fortress World is a planetary apartheid system, gated and maintained by force, in which the gap between global rich and global poor constantly widens and the differential access to environmental resources and amenities increases sharply. It consists of "bubbles of privilege amidst oceans of misery.... The elite[s] have halted barbarism at their gates and enforced a kind of environmental management and uneasy stability."[21] The general state of the planetary environment, however, would continue to deteriorate in this scenario leading either to a complete ecological Breakdown or to the achievement through revolutionary struggle of a more egalitarian society, such as Eco-communalism.

This description of the Fortress World is remarkably similar to the scenario released in the 2003 Pentagon report, *Abrupt Climate Change and Its Implications for United States National Security*.[22] The Pentagon report envisioned a possible shutdown due to global warming of the thermohaline circulation warming the North Atlantic, throwing Europe and North America into Siberia-like conditions. Under such unlikely but plausible circumstances, relatively well-off populations, including those in the United States, are pictured as building "defensive fortresses" around themselves to keep masses of would-be immigrants out. Military confrontations over scarce resources intensify.

Arguably naked capitalism and resource wars are already propelling the world in this direction at present, though without a cause as immediately earth-shaking as abrupt climate change. With the advent of the "War on Terror," unleashed by the United States against one country after another since September 11, 2001, an "Empire of Barbarism" is making its presence felt.[23]

Still, from the standpoint of the Global Scenario Group, the Barbarization scenarios are there simply to warn us of the worst possible dangers of ecological and social decline. A Great Transition, it is argued, is necessary if Barbarization is to be avoided.

Theoretically, there are two Great Transitions scenarios envisioned by the Global Scenario Group: Eco-communalism and the New Sustainability Paradigm. Yet Eco-communalism is never discussed in any detail, on the grounds that for this kind of transformation to come about it would be necessary for world society first to pass through Barbarization. The Global Scenario Group authors see the social revolution of Eco-communalism as lying on the other side of Jack London's *Iron Heel*. The discussion of Great Transition is thus confined to the New Sustainability Paradigm.

The essence of the New Sustainability Paradigm is that of a radical ecological transformation that goes against unbridled "capitalist hegemony" but stops short of full social revolution. It is to be carried out primarily through changes in values and lifestyles rather than the transformation of social structures. Advances in environmental technology and policy that began with the Policy Reform scenario, but that were unable to propel sufficient environmental change due to the dominance of acquisitive norms, are here supplemented by a "lifestyle wedge."[24]

In the explicitly utopian scenario of the New Sustainability Paradigm, the United Nations is transformed into the "World Union," a true global federation. Globalization has become "civilized." The world market is fully integrated and harnessed for equality and sustainability not just wealth generation. The War on Terrorism has resulted in the defeat of the terrorists. Civil society, represented by non-governmental organizations (NGOs), plays a leading role in society at both the national and global levels. Voting is electronic. Poverty is eradicated. Typical inequality has decreased drastically. Dematerialization is real, as is the "polluter pays" principle. Advertising is nowhere to be seen. There has been a transition to a solar economy. The long commute from where people live to where they work is a thing of the past; instead, there are "integrated settlements" that place home, work, retail shops, and leisure outlets in close proximity to each other. The giant corporations have become forward-looking societal organizations, rather than simply private entities. They are no longer concerned exclusively with the economic bottom line, but have revised this to incorporate environmental sustainability and social ecology as ends irrespective of profit.

Four agents of change are said to have combined to bring all of this about: (1) giant transnational corporations; (2) intergovernmental organizations such as the United Nations, World Bank, International Monetary Fund, and World Trade Organization; (3) civil society acting through NGOs; and (4) a globally aware, environmentally-conscious, democratically organized world population.[25]

Underpinning this economically is the notion of a stationary state, as depicted by Mill in his 1848 work, *Principles of Political Economy*, and advanced today by the ecological economist Herman Daly and Whiteheadian process philosopher John Cobb. Most classical economists—including Adam Smith, David Ricardo, Thomas Malthus, and Karl Marx—saw the specter of a stationary state as presaging the demise of the bourgeois political economy. In contrast, Mill, who Marx (in the afterword to the second German edition of *Capital*) accused of a "shallow syncretism," saw the stationary state as somehow compatible with existing productive relations, requiring only changes in distribution.[26] In the New Sustainability Paradigm scenario, which takes Mill's view of the stationary state as its inspiration, the basic institutions of capitalism remain intact, as do the fundamental relations of power, but a shift in lifestyle and consumer orientation mean that the economy is no longer geared to economic growth and the enlargement of profits, but to efficiency, equity, and qualitative improvements in life. A capitalist society formerly driven to expanded reproduction through investment of surplus product (or surplus-value) has been replaced with a system of simple reproduction (Mill's stationary state), in which the surplus is consumed rather than invested. The vision is one of a cultural revolution supplementing technological revolution, and radically changing the ecological and social landscape of capitalist society, without fundamentally altering the productive, property, and power relations that define the system.

In my view, there are both logical and historical problems with this projection. It combines the weakest elements of utopian thinking (weaving a future out of mere hopes and wishes) with a "practical" desire to avoid a sharp break with the existing system.[27] The failure of the Global

Scenario Group to address its own scenario of Eco-communalism is part and parcel of this perspective, which seeks to elude the question of the more thoroughgoing social transformation that a genuine Great Transition would require.

The result is a vision of the future that is contradictory to an extreme. Private corporations are institutions with one and only one purpose: the pursuit of profit. The idea of turning them to entirely different and opposing social ends is reminiscent of the long-abandoned notions of the "soulful corporation" that emerged for a short time in the 1950s and then vanished in the harsh light of reality. Many changes associated with the New Sustainability Paradigm would require a class revolution to bring about. Yet this is excluded from the scenario itself. Instead, the Global Scenario Group authors engage in a kind of magical thinking—denying that fundamental changes in the relations of production must accompany (and sometimes even precede) changes in values. No less than in the case of the Policy Reform Scenario—as pointed out in *The Great Transition* report itself—the "God of Mammon" will inevitably overwhelm a value-based Great Transition that seeks to escape the challenge of the revolutionary transformation of the whole society.

AN ECOLOGICAL-SOCIAL REVOLUTION

Put simply, my argument is that a global ecological revolution worthy of the name can only occur as part of a larger social—and I would insist, socialist—revolution. Such a revolution, were it to generate the conditions of equality, sustainability, and human freedom worthy of a genuine Great Transition, would necessarily draw its major impetus from the struggles of working populations and communities at the bottom of the global capitalist hierarchy. It would demand, as Marx insisted, that the associated producers rationally regulate the human metabolic relation with nature. It would see wealth and human development in radically different terms than capitalist society.

In conceiving such a social and ecological revolution, we can derive inspiration, as Marx did, from the ancient Epicurean concept of "natural wealth." As Epicurus observed in his *Principal Doctrines*: "Natural wealth is both limited and easily obtainable; the riches of idle fancies go on forever." It is the unnatural, unlimited character of such alienated wealth that is the problem. Similarly, in what has become known as the *Vatican Sayings*, Epicurus stated: "Poverty, when measured by the natural purpose of life, is great wealth; but unlimited wealth is great poverty."[28] Free human development, arising in a climate of natural limitation and sustainability, is the true basis of wealth, of a rich, many-sided existence; the unbounded pursuit of wealth is the primary source of human impoverishment and suffering. Needless to say, such a concern with natural well-being, as opposed to artificial needs and stimulants, is the antithesis of capitalist society and the precondition of a sustainable human community.

A Great Transition, therefore, must have the characteristics implied by the Global Scenario Group's neglected scenario: Eco-communalism. It must take its inspiration from William Morris, one of the most original and ecological followers of Karl Marx, from Gandhi, and from other radical, revolutionary and materialist figures, including Marx himself, stretching as far back as Epicurus. The goal must be the creation of sustainable communities geared to the development of human needs and powers, removed from the all-consuming drive to accumulate wealth (capital).

As Marx wrote, the new system "starts with the self-government of the communities."[29] The creation of an ecological civilization requires a social revolution, one that, as Roy Morrison explains, needs to be organized democratically from below: "community by community ... region by region." It must put the provision of basic human needs—clean air, unpolluted water, safe food, adequate sanitation, social transport, and universal health care and education, all of which require a sustainable relation to the earth—ahead of all other needs and wants. "An ecological dialectic" along these lines, Morrison insists, "rejects not struggle but the endless slaughter of industrial negation" in the interest of unlimited profits.[30] Such a revolutionary turn in human affairs may seem improbable. But the continuation of the present capitalist system for any length of time will prove impossible—if human civilization and the web of life as we know it are to be sustained.

CHAPTER FOURTEEN

Ecology and the Transition from Capitalism to Socialism

The transition from capitalism to socialism is the most difficult problem of socialist theory and practice. To add to this the question of ecology might, therefore, be seen as unnecessarily complicating an already intractable issue. I shall argue here, in the closing chapter of this book, however, that the human relation to nature lies at the heart of the transition to socialism. An ecological perspective is pivotal to our understanding of capitalism's limits, the failures of the early socialist experiments, and the overall struggle for egalitarian and sustainable human development.

My argument has three parts. First, it is crucial to understand the intimate connection between classical Marxism and ecological analysis. Far from being an anomaly for socialism, as we are often led to believe, ecology was an essential component of the socialist project from its inception—notwithstanding the numerous later shortcomings of Soviet-type societies in this respect. Second, the global ecological crisis that now confronts us is deeply rooted in the "world-alienating" logic of capital accumulation, traceable to the historical origins of capitalism as a system. Third, the transition from capitalism to socialism is a struggle for sustainable human development in which societies on the periphery of the capitalist world system have been leading the way.

CLASSICAL MARXISM AND ECOLOGY

Research carried out over the last two decades has demonstrated that there was a powerful ecological perspective in classical Marxism. Just as a transformation of the human relation to the earth was, in Marx's view, an essential presupposition for the transition from feudalism to capitalism, so the rational regulation of the metabolic relation to nature was understood as an essential presupposition for the transition from capitalism to socialism.[1] Marx and Engels wrote extensively about ecological problems arising from capitalism and class society in general, and the need to transcend these under socialism. This included discussions of the nineteenth-century soil crisis, which led Marx to develop his theory of a metabolic rift between nature and society. Basing his analysis on the work of the German chemist Justus von Liebig, he pointed to the fact that soil nutrients (nitrogen, phosphorus, and potassium) were removed from the soil and shipped hundreds and thousands of miles to the cities where they ended up polluting the water and the air and contributing to the poor health of the workers. This break in the necessary metabolic cycle between nature and society demanded for Marx nothing less than the "restoration" of ecological sustainability for the sake of "successive generations."[2]

In line with this, Marx and Engels raised the main ecological problems of human society: the division of town and country, soil depletion, industrial pollution, urban maldevelopment, the decline in health and crippling of workers, bad nutrition, toxicity, enclosures, rural poverty and isolation, deforestation, human-generated floods, desertification, water shortages, regional climate change, the exhaustion of natural resources (including coal), conservation of energy, entropy, the need to recycle the waste products of industry, the interconnection between species and their environments, historically conditioned problems of overpopulation, the causes of famine, and the issue of the rational employment of science and technology.

This ecological understanding arose from a deep materialist conception of nature that was an essential part of Marx's underlying vision. "Man," he wrote, "*lives* from nature, i.e., nature is his *body*, and he must maintain a continuing dialogue with it if he is not to die. To say that man's physical and mental life is linked to nature simply means that nature is linked to itself, for man is a part of nature."[3] Not only did Marx declare, in direct opposition to capitalism, that no individual owned the earth, he also argued that no nation or people owned the earth; that it belonged to successive generations and should be cared for in accordance with the principle of good household management.[4]

Other early Marxists followed suit, although not always consistently, in incorporating ecological concerns into their analyses and embodying a general materialist and dialectical conception of nature. William Morris, August Bebel, Karl Kautsky, Rosa Luxemburg, and Nikolai Bukharin all drew on ecological insights from Marx. The Ukrainian socialist Sergei Podolinsky's early attempt at developing an ecological economics was inspired to a considerable extent by the work of Marx and Engels. Lenin stressed the importance of recycling soil nutrients and supported both conservation and pioneering experiments in community ecology (the study of the interaction of populations within a specific natural environment). This led to the development in the Soviet Union in the 1920s and early 1930s of probably the most advanced conception of ecological energetics or trophic dynamics (the basis of modern ecosystem analysis) in the world at the time. The same revolutionary-scientific climate produced V. I. Vernadsky's theory of the biosphere, A. I. Oparin's theory of the origin of life, and N. I. Vavilov's discovery of the world centers of germplasm (the genetic sources of the world's crop plants). In the West, and in Britain in particular, leading scientists influenced by Marxism in the 1930s, such as J. B. S. Haldane, J. D. Bernal, Hyman Levy, Lancelot Hogben, and Joseph Needham, pioneered in exploring the dialectics of nature. It is even possible to argue that ecological science had its genesis almost entirely in the work of thinkers on the left (socialist, social democratic, and anarchist).[5]

Obviously, not all major figures or all developments in the socialist tradition can be seen as ecological. Soviet Marxism succumbed to an extreme version of the productivism that characterized early twentieth-century modernity in general, leading to its own version of ecocide. With the rise of the Stalinist system the pioneering ecological developments in the Soviet Union were largely crushed (and some of the early ecologically oriented Marxists such as Bukharin and Vavilov were killed).

Simultaneously, a deep antipathy to natural science, emerging out of an extreme negation of positivism, led to the abandonment of attempts to theorize the dialectics of nature in Western Marxism, seriously weakening its link to ecology—though the question of the domination of nature was raised by the Frankfurt School as part of its critique of science. If today socialism and ecology are once again understood as dialectically interconnected, it is due both to the evolution of the ecological contradictions of capitalism and the development of socialism's own self-critique.

CAPITALISM'S WORLD ALIENATION

The key to understanding capitalism's relation to the environment is to examine its historical beginnings, i.e., the transition from feudalism to capitalism. This transition was enormously complex, occurring over centuries, and obviously cannot be fully addressed here. I shall focus on just a few factors. The bourgeoisie arose within the interstices of the feudal economy. As its name suggests, the bourgeoisie had its point of origin as a class primarily in the urban centers and mercantile trade. What was necessary, however, in order for bourgeois society to emerge fully *as a system*, was the revolutionary transformation of the feudal mode of production and its replacement by capitalist relations of production. Since feudalism was predominantly an agrarian system, this meant, of course, transformation of agrarian relations, i.e., the relation of workers to the land as a means of production.

Capitalism, therefore, required for its development a new relation to nature, one that severed the direct connection of labor to the means of production, i.e., the earth, along with the dissolution of all customary rights in relation to the commons. The classical location of the industrial revolution was Britain, where the removal of the workers from the land by means of expropriation took the form of the enclosure movement from the fifteenth to the eighteenth centuries. Under colonialism and imperialism, an even more brutal transformation occurred on the outskirts or the external areas of the capitalist world economy. There all preexisting human productive relations to nature were torn asunder in what Marx called the "extirpation, enslavement, and entombment in mines of the indigenous population"—the most violent expropriation in all of human history.[6]

The result was proletarianization within the center of the system, as masses of workers were thrown out of work and moved to the city. There, they were met by the capital being amassed through organized robbery, giving rise to what Marx called "modern industry." Simultaneously, various forms of servitude and what we now call precarious work were imposed on the periphery, where social reproduction was always secondary to the most rapacious imperialist exploitation. The surplus forcibly extracted from the periphery fed industrialization at the center of the world economy.[7]

What made this new system work was the incessant accumulation of capital in one cycle after another, with each new phase of accumulation taking the last as its starting point. This meant ever more divided, more alienated human beings, together with a more globally destructive metabolism between humanity and nature. As Joseph Needham observed, the "conquest of Nature" under capitalism turned into "the conquest of man"; the "technological instruments utilized in the dominance of Nature" produced "a qualitative transformation in the mechanisms of social domination."[8]

There is no doubt that this dialectic of domination and destruction is now spiraling out of control on a planetary scale. Economically, overall inequality between the center and periphery nations of the world system is increasing together with the intensification of class inequality within each capitalist state. Ecologically, a process of runaway global warming is transforming the world's climate and the life-support systems of the entire earth.[9]

In addressing this planetary environmental problem, it is useful to turn to Hannah Arendt's concept of "world alienation," introduced fifty years ago in *The Human Condition*. "World alienation" for Arendt began with the "alienation from the earth" at the time of Columbus, Galileo, and Luther. Galileo trained his telescope on the heavens, thereby converting human beings into creatures of the cosmos, no longer simply earthly beings. Science seized on cosmic principles in order to obtain the "Archimedean point" with which to move the world, but at the cost of immeasurable world alienation. Human beings no longer apprehended the world immediately through the direct evidence of their five senses. The original unity of the human relation to the world exemplified by the Greek *polis* was lost.

Arendt noted that Marx was acutely aware of this world alienation from his earliest writings, pointing out that the world was "denatured" as all natural objects—the wood of the wood-user and the wood-seller— were converted into private property and the universal commodity form. Original or primitive accumulation, the alienation of human beings from the land, as Marx described it, became a crucial manifestation of world alienation. However, Marx, in Arendt's view, chose to stress human self-alienation rooted in labor rather than world alienation. In contrast, "world alienation, and not [primarily] self-alienation as Marx thought," she concluded, "has been the hallmark of the modern age."

"The process of wealth accumulation, as we know it," Arendt went on to observe, depended on expanding world alienation. It "is possible only if the world and the very worldliness of man are sacrificed." This process of the accumulation of wealth in the modern age "enormously increased [the] human power of destruction," so "that we are able to destroy all organic life on earth and shall probably be able one day to destroy even the earth itself." Indeed, "under modern conditions," she explained, "not destruction but conservation spells ruin because the very durability of conserved objects is the greatest impediment to the turnover process, whose constant gain in speed is the only constancy left wherever it has taken hold."[10]

Arendt had no final answers to the dire problem she raised. Despite tying world alienation to a system of destruction rooted in wealth accumulation, she identified it with the development of science, technology, and modernity rather than capitalism as such. World alienation in her view was the triumph of *homo faber* and *animal laborans*. In this tragic conception, her readers were called upon to look back to the lost unity of the Greek *polis*, rather than, as in Marx, toward a new society based on the restoration of the human metabolism with nature at a higher level of development. In the end, world alienation for Arendt was a Greek tragedy raised to a planetary scale.

There is no doubt that the concrete manifestations of this world alienation are evident everywhere today. The latest scientific data indicate that global emissions of carbon dioxide from fossil fuels experienced a "sharp acceleration . . . in the early 2000s" with the growth rate reaching levels "greater than for the most fossil-fuel intensive of the Intergovernmental Panel on Climate Change emissions scenarios developed in the late 1990s." Further, "the mean global atmospheric CO_2 concentration" has been increasing "at a progressively faster rate each decade." The most rapid acceleration in emissions has been in a handful of emergent indus-trializing countries such as China, but "no region" in the world is current-ly "decarbonizing its energy supply." All ecosystems on earth are in decline, water shortages are on the rise, and energy resources are becom-ing more than ever the subject of global monopolies enforced by war.

The "man-made fingerprint of global warming" has been detected "on 10 different aspects of Earth's environment: surface temperatures, humidity, water vapor over the oceans, barometric pressure, total pre-cipitation, wildfires, change in species of plants and animals, water run-off, temperatures in the upper atmosphere, and heat content in the world's oceans." The cost now descending on the world if it doesn't radically change course is a *regression* of civilization and life itself beyond comprehension: an economy and ecology of destruction that will finally reach its limits.[11]

SOCIALISM AND SUSTAINABLE HUMAN DEVELOPMENT

How are we to meet this challenge, arguably the greatest that human civ-ilization has ever faced? A genuine answer to the ecological question, transcending Arendt's tragic understanding of world alienation, requires a revolutionary conception of sustainable human development—one that addresses both human self-estrangement (the alienation of labor) and world alienation (the alienation of nature). It was Ernesto "Che" Guevara who most famously argued, in his "Man and Socialism in Cuba," that the crucial issue in the building of socialism was not economic development but human development. This needs to be extended by recognizing, in line with Marx, that the real question is one of sustainable human devel-opment, explicitly addressing the human metabolism with nature through human labor.[12]

Too often, the transition to socialism has been approached mechanistically as the mere expansion of the means of production, rather than in terms of the development of human social relations and needs. In the system that emerged in the Soviet Union, the indispensable tool of planning was misdirected to production for production's sake, losing sight of genuine human needs, and eventually gave rise to a new class structure. The detailed division of labor, introduced by capitalism, was retained under this system and extended in the interest of higher productivity. In this type of society, as Che critically observed, "the period of the building of socialism . . . is characterized by the extinction of the individual for the sake of the state."[13]

The revolutionary character of Latin American socialism, today, derives its strength from an acute recognition of the negative (as well as some positive) lessons of the Soviet experience, partly through an understanding of the problem raised by Che: the need to develop socialist humanity. Further, the Bolivarian vision proclaimed by Chávez has its own deep roots of inspiration, drawing on an older pre-Marxian socialism. Thus, it was Simon Bolívar's teacher Simón Rodríguez who wrote in 1847: "The division of labour in the production of goods only serves to brutalize the workforce. If to produce cheap and excellent nail scissors, we have to reduce the workers to machines, we would do better to cut our finger nails with our teeth." Indeed, what we most admire today with regard to Bolívar's own principles is his uncompromising insistence that equality is "the law of laws."[14]

The same commitment to the egalitarian, universal development of humanity was fundamental to Marx. The evolution of the society of associated producers was to be synonymous with the positive transcendence of human alienation. The goal was a many-sided human development. Just as "all history is nothing but a continuous transformation of human nature," so "the *cultivation* of the five senses is the work of all previous history." Socialism, thus, appears as the "complete emancipation of the senses," of human sensuous capacities, and their wide-ranging development. "Communism, as fully developed naturalism," Marx wrote, "equals humanism, and as fully developed humanism equals naturalism."[15]

The contrast between this revolutionary, humanistic-naturalistic vision and today's dominant mechanical-exploitative reality could not be starker.

We find ourselves in a period of imperialist development that is potentially the most dangerous in all of history.[16] There are two ways in which life on the planet as we know it can be destroyed—either instantaneously through global nuclear holocaust, or in a matter of a few generations by climate change and other manifestations of environmental destruction. Nuclear weapons continue to proliferate in an atmosphere of global insecurity promoted by the world's greatest power. War is currently being waged in the Middle East over geopolitical control of the world's oil, while carbon emissions from fossil fuels and other forms of industrial production are generating global warming. Biofuels offered up today as a major alternative to pending world oil shortages are destined only to enlarge world hunger.[17] Water resources are being monopolized by global corporations. Human needs are everywhere being denied: either in the form of extreme deprivation for a majority of the population of the world, or, in the richer countries, in the form of the most intensive self-estrangement conceivable, extending beyond production to a managed consumption, enforcing lifelong dependence on alienating wage labor. More and more, life is debased in a welter of artificial wants dissociated from genuine needs.

All of this is altering the ways in which we think about the transition from capitalism to socialism. Socialism has always been understood as a society aimed at reversing the relations of exploitation of capitalism and removing the manifold social evils to which these relations have given rise. This requires the abolition of private property in the means of production, a high degree of equality in all things, replacement of the blind forces of the market by planning by the associated producers in accordance with genuine social needs, and the elimination to whatever extent possible of invidious distinctions associated with the division of town and country, mental and manual labor, racial divisions, and gender divisions. Yet the root problem of socialism goes much deeper. The transition to socialism is possible only through a revolutionizing practice that *revolutionizes human beings themselves*.[18] The only way to accomplish this is by altering our human metabolism with nature, along with our human-social relations, transcending both the alienation of nature and of humanity. Marx, like Hegel, was fond of quoting Terence's famous statement: "Nothing human is alien to me." Now it is clear that we must deepen and extend this to: *Nothing of this earth is alien to me*.[19]

Mainstream environmentalists seek to solve ecological problems almost exclusively through three mechanical strategies: (1) technological bullets; (2) extending the market to all aspects of nature; and (3) creating what are intended as mere islands of preservation in a world of almost universal exploitation and destruction of natural habitats. In contrast, a minority of critical human ecologists have come to understand the need to change our fundamental social relations. Some of the best, most concerned ecologists, searching for concrete models of change have therefore come to focus on those states (or regions) that are both ecological and socialistic (in the sense of relying to a considerable extent on social planning rather than market forces) in orientation. Thus, Cuba, Curitiba and Porto Alegre in Brazil, and Kerala in India are singled out as the leading lights of ecological transformation by some of the most committed environmentalists, such as Bill McKibben, best known as the author of *The End of Nature*.[20] More recently, Venezuela has been using its surplus from oil to transform its society in the direction of sustainable human development, thereby laying the foundation for a greening of its production. Although there are contradictions to what has been called Venezuelan "petro-socialism," the fact that an oil-generated surplus is being dedicated to genuine social transformation rather than feeding into the proverbial "curse of oil" makes Venezuela unique.[21]

Of course, there are powerful environmental movements within the center of the system as well to which we might look for hope. But severed from strong socialist movements and a revolutionary situation, they have been constrained much more by a perceived need to adapt to the dominant accumulation system, thereby drastically undermining the ecological struggle. Hence, revolutionary strategies and movements with regard to ecology and society are world-historical forces at present largely in the periphery, in the weak links and breakaways from the capitalist system.

I can only point to a few essential aspects of this radical process of ecological change as manifested in areas of the global South. In Cuba, the goal of human development that Che advanced is taking on a new form through what is widely regarded as "the greening of Cuba." This is evident in the emergence of the most revolutionary experiment in agroecology on earth, and the related changes in health, science, and education. As McKibben states, "Cubans have created what may be the world's largest working model of a semisustainable agriculture, one that relies far less than the rest of the world does on oil, on chemicals, on shipping vast quantities of food back and forth. . . . Cuba has thousands of *organopóni-cos*—urban gardens—more than two hundred in the Havana area alone." Indeed, according to the World Wildlife Fund's *Living Planet Report,* "Cuba alone" in the entire world has achieved a high level of human development, with a human development index greater than 0.8, while also having a per capita ecological footprint below the world's average.[22]

This ecological transformation is deeply rooted in the Cuban revolution rather than, as frequently said, simply a forced response in the Special Period following the fall of the Soviet Union. Already in the 1970s, Carlos Rafael Rodriguez, one of the founders of Cuban ecology, had introduced arguments for "integral development, laying the ground-work"—as ecologist Richard Levins points out—for "harmonious development of the economy and social relations with nature." This was followed by the gradual flowering of ecological thought in Cuba in the 1980s. The Special Period, Levins explains, simply allowed the "ecologists by conviction," who had emerged through the internal development of Cuban science and society, to recruit the "ecologists by necessity," turning many of them, too, into ecologists by conviction.[23]

Venezuela, under Chávez, has not only advanced revolutionary new social relations with the growth of Bolivarian circles, community councils, and increased worker control of factories, but has introduced some crucial initiatives with regard to what István Mészáros has called a new "socialist time accountancy" in the production and exchange of goods. In the new Bolivarian Alternative for the Americas (ALBA), the emphasis is on *communal exchange*, the exchange of activities rather than exchange-values.[24] Instead of allowing the market to establish the priorities of the entire economy, planning is being introduced to redistribute resources and capacities to those most in need and to the majority of the populace. The goal here is to address the most pressing individual and collective requirements of the society, related in the first place to physiological needs, and hence raising directly the question of the human relation to nature. This is the absolute precondition of the creation of a sustainable society. In the countryside, preliminary attempts have also been made to green Venezuelan agriculture.[25]

In Bolivia, the rise of a socialist current (though embattled at present), embedded in the needs of indigenous peoples and struggling for control of basic resources such as water and hydrocarbons, offers hope of another kind of development. Evo Morales, the socialist president of Bolivia, has emerged as one of the world's most eloquent defenders of the global environment and indigenous rights. The cities of Curitiba and Porto Alegre in Brazil point to the possibility of more radical forms of management of urban space and transportation. Curitiba, in McKibben's words, "is as much an example for the sprawling, decaying cities of the first world as for the crowded, booming cities of the Third World." Kerala, in India, has taught us that a poor state or region, if animated by genuine socialist planning, can go a long way toward unleashing human potentials in education, health care, and basic environmental conditions. In Kerala, McKibben observes, "the Left has embarked on a series of 'new democratic initiatives' that come as close as anything on the planet to actually incarnating 'sustainable development.' "[26]

To be sure, these are mainly islands of hope at present. They constitute fragile new experiments in social relations and in the human metabolism with nature. They are still subject to the class and imperial war imposed from above by the larger system. The planet as a whole remains firmly in the grip of capital and its world alienation. Everywhere we see manifestations of a metabolic rift, now extended to the biospheric level.

It follows that there is little real prospect for the needed global ecological revolution, unless these attempts to revolutionize social relations in the struggle for a just and sustainable society, now emerging in the periphery, are somehow mirrored in movements for ecological and social revolution in the advanced capitalist world. It is only through fundamental change at the center of the system, from which the pressures on the planet principally emanate, that there is any genuine possibility of avoiding ultimate ecological destruction.

Calls for a Green New Deal to be carried out by the Obama administration reflect, if nothing else, a growing constituency for major ecological change. This, however, will only be substantively realized to the extent that there is a major revolt from below in support of social and ecological transformation, pointing beyond the existing system.

For some, this vision of far-reaching ecological transformation may seem to be an impossible goal. Nevertheless, it is important to recognize that there is now an *ecology* as well as a political economy of revolutionary change. The emergence in our time of sustainable human development, in various revolutionary interstices within the global periphery, could mark the beginning of a universal revolt against both world alienation and human self-estrangement. Such a revolt, if consistent, could have only one objective: the creation of a society of associated producers rationally regulating their metabolic relation to nature, and doing so not only in accordance with their own needs but also those of future generations and life as a whole. Today, the transition to socialism and the transition to an ecological society are one.

Notes

PREFACE

1. Barry Commoner, *Making Peace with the Planet* (New York: The New Press, 1992), ix.
2. "Resources for a Journey of Hope" is the title of the last chapter of Raymond Williams's *The Year 2000* (New York: Pantheon, 1983). See also Ernst Bloch, *The Principle of Hope*, vol. 3 (Cambridge, Massachusetts: MIT Press, 1986); Bertolt Brecht, *Tales from the Calendar* (London: Lion and Unicorn Press, 1979), 26; Michael A. Lebowitz, *Build It Now, Socialism for the Twenty-First Century* (New York: Monthly Review Press, 2006).
3. See Michelle A. M. Lueck, "Hope for a Cause as Cause for Hope: The Need for Hope in Environmental Sociology," *American Sociologist* 38 (2007): 250–61.

INTRODUCTION

1. Niles Eldredge, *Life in the Balance: Humanity and the Biodiversity Crisis* (Princeton: Princeton University Press, 1998), xi.
2. Carolyn Merchant, *Ecological Revolutions* (Chapel Hill: University of North Carolina Press, 1989), 2–3.
3. Proponents of a green industrial revolution usually use the eighteenth century industrial revolution in Britain as their model, simply suggesting that a new green one will counter the old brown industrial revolution. For examples of this, see Andres R. Edwards, *The Sustainability Revolution* (Gabriola Island, B.C.: New Society Publishers, 2005); Thomas Friedman, *Hot, Flat and Crowded: Why We Need a Green Revolution—And How it Can Renew America* (New York: Farrar, Straus and Giroux, 2008), 173; and Lester Brown et. al., *State of the World, 1992* (New York: W. W. Norton, 1992).
4. On "possessive individualism" as characterizing the bourgeois order see C. B.

Macpherson, *The Political Theory of Possessive Individualism* (Oxford: Oxford University Press, 1962).

5.   Lewis Mumford, *Technics and Human Development* (New York: Harcourt Brace Jovanovich, 1967).

6.   Compare Karl Marx, *Contribution to a Critique of Political Economy* (Moscow: Progress Publishers, 1970), 21.

7.   Mark Lynas, *Six Degrees: Our Future on a Hotter Planet* (Washington, D.C.: National Geographic, 2008), 263.

8.   David Christian, *Maps of Time* (Berkeley: University of California Press, 2004), 479–81.

9.   Richard York, "Ecological Paradoxes: William Stanley Jevons and the Paperless Office," *Human Ecology Review*, 13, no. 2 (2006): 143–47.

10. Rudolf Bahro, *Avoiding Social and Ecological Disaster* (Bath: Gateway Books, 1994), 42.

11. Friedman, *Hot, Flat and Crowded*, 5, 53, 172–73 186–87, 199, 318.

12. Newt Gingrich, *A Contract with the Earth* (New York: Penguin, 2007).

13. Ted Nordhaus and Michael Shellenberger, *Break Through* (Boston: Houghton Mifflin, 2007), 15, 165-68, 223-24, 261, 270-73; and "Saving the World Ain't Cheap," *New Republic*, January 29, 2008.

14. Arthur P. J. Mol and David Sonnenfeld, "Ecological Modernization Theory in Debate," in *Ecological Modernization Around the World* (London: Frank Cass, 2000), 22–24; Charles Leadbeater, *The Weightless Society* (New York: Texere, 2000). For a critique see Richard York and Eugene A. Rosa, "Key Challenges to Ecological Modernization Theory," *Organization & Environment*, 16, no. 3 (September 2000): 273–88. For empirical evidence against "dematerialization" see World Resources Institute, *The Weight of Nations: Material Outflows from Industrial Economies* (Washington, D.C.: 2000). The Jevons Paradox is described in chapter 6 below.

15. Kenneth A. Gould, David N. Pellow, and Allan Schnaiberg, *The Treadmill of Production* (Boulder: Paradigm Publishers, 2008), 80-81, 123.

16. Friedman, *Hot, Flat, and Crowded*, 14, 190. The problem of economic growth and entropy was classically described in Nicholas Georgescu-Roegen, *The Entropy Law and the Economic Process* (Cambridge, Massachusetts: Harvard University Press, 1971).

17. Karl Marx and Frederick Engels, *Selected Correspondence* (Moscow: Progress Publishers, 1975), 33 (Marx to Annenkov, December 28, 1846).

18. Daniel M. Berman and John T. O'Connor, *Who Owns the Sun?* (White River Junction, Vermont: Chelsea Green Publishing, 1996).

19. Umbra Fisk, "If by Clean You Mean Filthy," *Grist*, July 23, 2008, http://www.grist.org.

20. Running quoted in John S. Adams, "Clean Coal: Why Is Nobody Buying It?," *The Missoula Independent*, August 9, 2007, http://www.truthout.org/article/clean-coal-why-is-nobody-buying-it; Peter Montague, "Carbon Sequestration," *Rachel's Democracy and Health News*, no. 932, November 8, 2007, http://www.precaution.org.

21. James Hansen, "Coal-Fired Power Stations are Death Factories. Close Them," *The Observer* (London), February 15, 2009.

22. István Mészáros, *Beyond Capital* (New York: Monthly Review Press, 1995), 877.

23. On monopoly-finance capital see John Bellamy Foster and Fred Magdoff, *The Great Financial Crisis* (New York: Monthly Review Press, 2009).

24. John Maynard Keynes, *Essays in Persuasion* (New York: Harcourt Brace Jovanovich, 1932), 372.

25. See Thorstein Veblen, *Absentee Ownership and Business Enterprise in Recent Times* (New York: Augustus M. Kelley, 1923), 300; Paul A. Baran and Paul M. Sweezy, *Monopoly Capital* (New York: Monthly Review Press, 1966), 132-33.

26. K. William Kapp, *The Social Costs of Private Enterprise* (Cambridge, Massachusetts: Harvard University Press, 1971), 231.

27. John Kenneth Galbraith, *The Economics of Innocent Fraud* (Boston: Houghton Mifflin, 2004).

28 David Hume, *A Treatise of Human Nature* (London: Penguin, 1969), 463.

29. See "Ecology: Moment of Truth" in this book; John Bellamy Foster, *Ecology Against Capitalism* (New York: Monthly Review Press, 2002), 63-65.

30. See John Browne, "The Ethics of Climate Change," *Scientific American* 298, no. 6 (June 2008): 97-100.

31. Stephen H. Schneider, *Laboratory Earth* (New York: Basic Books, 1997), 129-35; William D. Nordhaus, "An Optimal Transition Path for Controlling Greenhouse Gases," *Science* 258 (November 20, 1992): 1318; Stephen Schneider, "Pondering Greenhouse Policy," *Science* 259 (March 5, 1993): 1381.

32. William Nordhaus, *A Question of Balance: Weighing the Options on Global Warming Policies* (New Haven: Yale University Press, 2008), 13-14; Simon Dietz and Nicholas Stern, "On the Timing of Greenhouse Gas Emissions Reductions: A Final Rejoinder to the Symposium on 'The Economics of Climate Change: The Stern Review and Its Critics,'" *Review of Environmental Economics and Policy*, posted online December 4, 2008; Lynas, *Six Degrees*, 241.

33. James and Anniek Hansen, "Dear Barack and Michelle: An Open Letter to the President and the First Lady from the Nation's Top Climate Scientist," *Gristmill*, January 2, 2009, http://www.grist.org; Nicholas Stern, *The Economics of Climate Change* (New York: Cambridge University Press, 2007), 16.

34. Hansen and Hansen, "Dear Barack and Michelle"; James Hansen, "Carbon Tax and 100% Dividend—No Alligator Shoes!," http://www.columbia.edu/~jeh1/mailings/2008/20080604_TaxAndDividend.pdf; Nordhaus, *A Question of Balance*, 12-13.

35. Robert M. Solow, "The Economics of Resources or the Resources of Economics," *American Economic Review* 64, no. 2 (May 1974): 11; "Climate Warming Gases Rising Faster than Expected," *Guardian*, February 15, 2009.

36. Schneider, *Laboratory*, 135.

37. Freeman Dyson, "The Question of Global Warming," *New York Review of Books*, June 12, 2008, 43-45.

38.   John P. Holdren, "The Energy Innovation Imperative," *Innovations* 1, no. 2 (Spring 2006): 3–23; and "The Science and Economics of Sustainability," (keynote address, Global Katoomba Meeting XII, Washington, D.C., June 9–10, 2008), http://www.katoombagroup.org/documents/events/event20/John Holdren.pdf.

39.   E. P. Thompson, *Beyond the Cold War* (New York: Pantheon, 1982), 41–80; Bahro, *Avoiding Social and Ecological Disaster*, 19. On capitalism's "production of destruction" see István Mészáros, *The Challenge and Burden of Historical Time* (New York: Monthly Review Press, 2008), 96–100.

40.   Mumford, *The Condition of Man*, 348, 412.

41.   Roy Morrison, *Ecological Democracy* (Boston: South End Press, 1995), 165. David Korten has promoted a radical notion of "ecological revolution" that takes its cue from opposition to globalization and global corporations, rather than focusing on either technological change, as in the dominant approach, or the transformation of the social relations of production of capitalism, as in this analysis. A shift toward local empowerment, and the end of imperialism, is crucial to an ecological revolution. The emphasis in the present argument, however, is on the changes in the entire set of social relations of production, and the human agency (mass-democratic change) required for such an ecological and social revolution. Such changes would not only alter the global/local relation, but more fundamentally the division of labor in industry, the division between town and country, and the division of nature. It is not merely a question of a local economy, but the creation of communal relations of production. See David Korten, *When Corporations Rule the World* (Bloomfield, Connecticut: Kumarian Press, 2001), 233–48; and *The Great Turning* (Bloomfield, Connecticut: Kumarian Press, 2006), 281–301.

42.   Mumford, *The Condition of Man*, 411.

43.   John Stuart Mill, *Principles of Political Economy* (New York: Longmans, Green, and Co., 1904), 453–55; and *The Autobiography of John Stuart Mill* (New York: Columbia University Press, 1924), 161–64. Mumford, *The Condition of Man*, 411. The influence of socialism on Mills's thought at this time was of the utopian variety, derived from Robert Owen and Saint-Simon. It tended to avoid the issue of class struggle and revolution, falling into what Marx called a "shallow syncretism," which attempted to "reconcile the irreconcilables." Karl Marx, *Capital*, vol. 1 (London: Penguin, 1976), 98.

44.   *Mumford, The Condition of Man*, 411–12.

45.   Mumford, *The Condition of Man*, vi, 369, 399, 406–08, 415–18. Percy Bysshe Shelley and Mary Wollstonecraft Shelley, *Essays, Letters from Abroad, Translations and Fragments* (London: Edward Moxon, 1840), 46. Mumford here saw Shelley's comment as demanding Marx's fully developed individual, as presented in his conception of socialism in *Capital*.

46.   Mumford, *Condition of Man*, 419–23.

47.   Herman E. Daly and John B. Cobb, *For the Common Good* (Boston: Beacon Press, 1989), 168–72; Phillippe Buonarroti, *Babeuf's Conspiracy for Equality* (New York: Augustus M. Kelley, 1836), 364–74.

48. Karl Marx, *Critique of the Gotha Programme* (New York: International
     Publishers, 1938), 10. Pierre Bourdieu goes so far as to defend the "non-eco-
     nomic economy" that rejects the "economics of calculation" and the "exact
     equivalents" that characterize capitalism. See Pierre Bourdieu, *Practical
     Reason* (Stanford: Stanford University Press, 1998), 93, 104–05. Mészáros sees
     socialism as inseparable from the development of "communal exchange" based
     on the exchange of use-values/material processes. See Mészáros, *Beyond
     Capital*, 758–63.
49. Leopold, *A Sand County Almanac* (New York: Oxford University Press, 1949),
     viii–ix, 203–4, 214, 224–25; Foster, *Ecology Against Capitalism*, 86–87.
50. Karl Marx, *Capital*, 283; and *Capital*, vol. 3 (London: Penguin, 1981), 949,
     959.
51. Michael Lebowitz, "The Path to Human Development," *Monthly Review* 60,
     no. 9 (February 2009): 20–22; Marx, *Capital*, vol. 3, 911; Paul Burkett,
     "Marx's Vision of Sustainable Human Development," *Monthly Review* 57, no.
     5 (October 2005): 34-62.
52. On the Soviet Union and the environment see John Bellamy Foster, *The
     Vulnerable Planet* (New York: Monthly Review Press, 1999), 96–101. For a
     Marxist critique of Soviet planning and emphasis on incorporating ecological
     planning under socialism see Fred Magdoff and Harry Magdoff, "Approaching
     Socialism," *Monthly Review* 57, no. 3 (July-August 2005): 19–61.
53. Paul M. Sweezy, "Capitalism and the Environment," *Monthly Review* 41, no. 2
     (June 1989): 6. A similar position was hinted at by Mumford who, in comment-
     ing on Mill's notion of a stationary state, wrote: "the unfortunately misleading
     name that he [Mill] chose for this chapter [of his *Principles of Political
     Economy*], 'The Stationary State,' failed to emphasize the dynamic nature of any
     organic equilibrium, which must allow for contraction as well as growth."
     Mumford, *The Condition of Man*, viii.
54. Evo Morales, "Save the Planet from Capitalism," *Links: International Journal
     for Socialist Renewal*, November 28, 2008, http://links.org.au/node/769.

CHAPTER ONE: THE ECOLOGY OF DESTRUCTION

This chapter was adapted for this book from an article by the same title that
appeared in *Monthly Review* 58, no. 9 (February 2007), 1–14. It was based on
talks delivered in the state of Santa Catarina in Brazil on November 21–23,
2006, at the Regional University of Blumenau and the Federal University of
Santa Catarina in Florianópolis. These presentations were part of the third
annual Bolivarian Days Conference organized by the Institute of Latin
American Studies in Brazil.

1.   The late Italian filmmaker Gillo Pontecorvo (1919-2006) was a Marxist and
     anti-imperialist, most famous as the director of the classic film of revolutionary
     insurgency, *The Battle of Algiers* (1966). *Burn!* was made in response to
     Vietnam and intended as an allegory on the war—but one that extended to a cri-
     tique of capitalism itself.

2.   Joseph Schumpeter, *Capitalism, Socialism, and Democracy* (New York: Harper and Row, 1942), 81–86.

3.   István Mészáros, *Socialism or Barbarism* (New York: Monthly Review Press, 2001), 61.

4.   A more detailed analysis of the two earth summits is provided in chapter 7.

5.   Paul M. Sweezy, "The Triumph of Financial Capital," *Monthly Review*, 46, no. 2 (June 1994): 1–11; John Bellamy Foster, "Monopoly-Finance Capital," *Monthly Review* 58, no. 7 (December 2006): 14.

6.   Bill McKibben, "The Debate Is Over," *Rolling Stone*, November 17, 2005, 79–82.

7.   The quasi-religious Gaia hypothesis, which claimed that life on earth always keeps the surface conditions of the planet favorable to the ensemble of organisms, conflicted with Darwinian evolution, and has now been abandoned in its original form by Lovelock himself. It helped inspire, however, the development by numerous scientists of a more holistic earth system science that seeks to understand the earth as a single self-regulating system, in which the biosphere and the geosphere constitute one dialectical unity. Lovelock now adheres to what he calls the "Gaia theory," which conforms to the basic tenets of earth system science, but nonetheless clings teleologically to the idea that the "goal" of the continual reproduction of conditions favorable to the ensemble of life is somehow an "emergent" property of the living earth system. The "revenge of Gaia" is a revenge on civilization, which is threatened as Gaia suddenly flips to a new equilibrium in response to human-induced climate change. See James Lovelock, *The Revenge of Gaia* (New York: Basic Books, 2006), 23–25, 147, 162.

8.   Lovelock, *Revenge of Gaia*, 34–35; John Atcheson, "Ticking Time Bomb," *Baltimore Sun*, December 15, 2004.

9.   Lovelock, *Revenge of Gaia*, 55–59, 147; Bill McKibben, "How Close to Catastrophe?," *New York Review of Books*, November 16, 2006, 23–25.

10. Jim Hansen, "The Threat to the Planet," *New York Review of Books*, July 13, 2006, 12–16; Goddard Institute for Space Studies, "NASA Study Finds World Warmth Edging Ancient Levels," September 25, 2006, http://www.giss.nasa.gov.

11. John Bellamy Foster, *The Vulnerable Planet* (New York: Monthly Review Press, 1994), 11.

12. Karl Marx, *Capital*, vol. 1 (London: Penguin, 1976), 742. The treadmill of production theory emerged in the work of Allan Schnaiberg. See Schnaiberg, *The Environment: From Surplus to Scarcity* (New York: Oxford University Press, 1980); John Bellamy Foster, "The Treadmill of Accumulation," *Organization & Environment* 18, no. 1 (March 2005): 7–18.

13. The second contradiction theory originated with Marxian political economist James O'Connor. See O'Connor, *Natural Causes* (New York: Guilford, 1998).

14. Marx's theory of metabolic rift is discussed in detail in John Bellamy Foster, *Marx's Ecology: Materialism and Nature* (New York: Monthly Review Press, 2000) and part two of this book. See also Paul Burkett, *Marxism and Ecological*

Economics (Boston: Brill, 2006), 204–07, 292–93.

15. Jimmy M. Skaggs, *The Great Guano Rush* (New York: St. Martin's Press, 1994).

16. Brett Clark and Richard York, "Carbon Metabolism: Global Capitalism, Climate Change, and the Biospheric Rift," *Theory and Society* 34, no. 4 (2005): 391–428; Rebecca Clausen and Brett Clark, "The Metabolic Rift and Marine Ecology: An Analysis of the Oceanic Crisis within Capitalist Production," *Organization & Environment* 18: no. 4 (2005), 422–44.

17. Marx, *Capital*, vol. 1, 283, 290, 636–39, 860; Marx, *Capital*, vol. 3 (London: Penguin, 1981), 911, 959.

18. Karl Marx, *The Poverty of Philosophy* (New York: International Publishers, 1973), 223.

19. The analysis of capital as a system of "socio-metabolic reproduction" is developed in István Mészáros, *Beyond Capital* (New York: Monthly Review Press, 1995), 39–71.

20. Karl Marx and Frederick Engels, *Collected Works*, vol. 25 (New York: International Publishers, 1975), 460–61.

CHAPTER TWO: ECOLOGY: THE MOMENT OF TRUTH

This chapter was adapted and revised for this book from an article, coauthored with Brett Clark and Richard York, that appeared under the title "Ecology: The Moment of Truth—An Introduction," in *Monthly Review* 60, no. 3 (July-August 2008): 1-11.

1.   John Bellamy Foster, *The Vulnerable Planet* (New York: Monthly Review Press, 1994), 12. The four decades projection was based on work by the Worldwatch Institute. See Lester R. Brown et. al., "World Without End," *Natural History* (May 1990): 89; and *State of the World 1992* (London: Earthscan, 1992), 3–8.

2.   James Hansen, "Tipping Point," in E. Fearn and K. H. Redford ed., *The State of the Wild 2008* (Washington, D.C.: Island Press, 2008), 7–15, http://pubs.giss.nasa.gov/docs/2008/2008_Hansen_1.pdf. See also James Hansen, "The Threat to the Planet," *New York Review of Books*, July 13, 2006. The argument on tipping points with respect to climate change is best understood in the context of a series of biospheric rifts generated by the system of economic accumulation. On this see Brett Clark and Richard York, "Carbon Metabolism and Global Capitalism: Climate Change and the Biospheric Rift," *Theory and Society* 34, no. 4 (2005): 391–428.

3.   Percentages of bird, mammal, and fish species "vulnerable or in immediate danger of extinction" are "now measured in double digits." Lester R. Brown, *Plan B 3.0* (New York: W.W. Norton, 2008), 102. The share of threatened species in 2007 was 12 percent of the world's bird species; 20 percent of the world's mammal species; and 39 percent of the world's fish species evaluated. See International Union for the Conservation of Nature (IUCN), *IUCN Red List of Threatened Species*, Table 1, "Numbers of Threatened Species by Major Groups of Organisms," http://www.iucnredlist.org/info/stats. Additionally, climate change is having significant effects on plant diversity. "Recent studies pre-

dict that climate change could result in the extinction of up to half the world's plant species by the end of the century." See Belinda Hawkins, Suzanne Sharrock, and Kay Havens, *Plants and Climate Change* (Richmond, UK: Botanic Gardens Conservation International, 2008), 9.

4.   David Spratt and Philip Sutton, *Climate Code Red* (Fitzroy, Australia: Friends of the Earth, 2008), 4, http://www.climatecodered.net; Brown, *Plan B 3.0*, 3; James Hansen et al., "Climate Change and Trace Gases," *Philosophical Transactions of the Royal Society* 365 (2007): 1925–54; James Lovelock, *The Revenge of Gaia* (New York: Basic Books, 2006), 34; Minqi Li, "Climate Change, Limits to Growth, and the Imperative for Socialism," *Monthly Review* 60, no. 3 (July-August 2008): 51–67; "Arctic Summers Ice-Free 'by 2013,'" *BBC News*, December 12, 2007.

5.   Hansen, "Tipping Point," 7–8.

6.   Brown, *Plan B 3.0*, 4–5. Brown, correctly depicts the seriousness of the ecological problem, but, as a mainstream environmentalist, he insists that all can easily be made well without materially altering society by a clever combination of technological fixes and the magic of the market. See Li, "Climate Change, the Limits to Growth, and the Imperative for Socialism."

7.   Nicholas Stern, *The Economics of Climate Change: The Stern Review* (Cambridge: Cambridge University Press, 2007).

8.   The *Stern Review* has been criticized by more conservative mainstream economists, including William Nordhaus, for its ethical choices, which, it is claimed, place too much emphasis on the future as opposed to present-day values by adopting a much lower discount rate on future costs and benefits as compared to other, more standard economic treatments such as that of Nordhaus. This then gives greater urgency to today's environmental problem. Nordhaus discounts the future at 6 percent a year; Stern by less than a quarter of that at 1.4 percent. This means that for Stern having a trillion dollars a century from now is worth $247 billion today, while for Nordhaus it is only worth $2.5 billion. Nordhaus calls the *Stern Review* a "radical revision of the economics of climate change" and criticizes it for imposing "excessively large emissions reductions in the short run." John Browne, "The Ethics of Climate Change," *Scientific American* 298, no. 6 (June 2008): 97–100; William Nordhaus, *A Question of Balance* (New Haven: Yale University Press, 2008), 18, 190.

9.   James Hansen, et. al., "Target Atmospheric CO_2: Where Should Humanity Aim?," abstract of article submitted to *Science*, http://pubs.giss.nasa.gov/abstracts/submitted/Hansen_etal.html (accessed in May 2008). Even before this, Hansen and his colleagues at NASA's Goddard Institute argued that due to positive feedbacks and climatic tipping points global average temperature increases had to be kept to less than 1°C below 2000 levels. This meant that atmospheric CO_2 needed to be kept to 450 ppm or below. See Pushker A. Kharecha and James E. Hansen, "Implications of 'Peak Oil' for Atmospheric CO_2 and Climate," *Global Biogeochemistry* (2008, in press), http://pubs.giss. nasa.gov/abstracts/inpress/Kharecha_Hansen.html.

10. Stern, *The Economics of Climate Change*, 4–5, 11–16, 95, 193, 220–34, 637, 649–51; "Evidence of Human-Caused Global Warming Is Now 'Unequivocal,'" *Science Daily*, http://www.sciencedaily.com; Browne, "The Ethics of Climate Change," 100; Spratt and Sutton, *Climate Code Red*, 30; Editors, "Climate Fatigue," *Scientific American* 298, no. 6 (June 2008): 39; Ted Trainer, "A Short Critique of the *Stern Review*," *Real-World Economics Review*, 45 (2008): 51–67, http://www.paecon.net/PAEReview/issue45/Trainer45.pdf. Despite the *Stern Review*'s presentation of France's nuclear switch as a greenhouse gas success story there are strong environmental reasons for not proceeding along this path. See Robert Furber, James C. Warf, and Sheldon C. Plotkin, "The Future of Nuclear Power," *Monthly Review* 59, no. 9 (February 2008): 38–48.

11. Paul M. Sweezy, "Capitalism and the Environment," *Monthly Review* 41, no. 2 (June 1989): 1–10.

12. Michael Shellenberger and Ted Nordhaus, "The Death of Environmentalism," Environmental Grantmakers Association, October 2004, http://thebreakthrough.org/PDF/Death_of_Environmentalism.pdf.

13. James Gustave Speth, *The Bridge at the End of the World: Capitalism, the Environment, and Crossing from Crisis to Sustainability* (New Haven: Yale University Press, 2008), xi, 48–63, 107, 194–98; Samuel Bowles and Richard Edwards, *Understanding Capitalism* (New York: Oxford University Press, 1985), 119, 148–52. On the Global Scenario Group see chapter 13 below. On ecological sustainability, classical socialism, and Marx's critique of capitalism's metabolic rift with nature see John Bellamy Foster, *Marx's Ecology* (New York: Monthly Review Press, 2000).

14. William Morris, "Why Not?" in Morris, *Political Writings* (Bristol: Thoemmes Press, 1994), 24–27.

CHAPTER THREE: RACHEL CARSON'S ECOLOGICAL CRITIQUE

This chapter has been adapted for this book from an article with the same title, coauthored with Brett Clark, that appeared in *Monthly Review* 59, no. 9 (February 2008): 1–17.

1. Rachel Carson, *Lost Woods* (Boston: Beacon Press, 1998), 210; *Silent Spring* (Boston: Houghton Mifflin, 1994), 13; Mark Hamilton Lytle, *The Gentle Subversive* (New York: Oxford University Press, 2007).

2. Lytle, *The Gentle Subversive*, 184; Carson, *Silent Spring*, 277–97; Appendix IV, "Recommendations of the President's Scientific Advisory Committee on the Use of Pesticides," in Robert L. Rudd, *Pesticides and the Living Landscape* (Madison: University of Wisconsin Press, 1964), 297.

3. Data on pesticide active ingredients noted here refers simply to "conventional pesticides" (herbicides and insecticides) and excludes wood preservatives (fungicides) and other ingredients on the EPA's expanded list. Carson, *Silent Spring*, 8; Shirley A. Briggs, "Thirty-Five Years with Silent Spring," *Organization & Environment*, 10:1 (March 1997): 73–84; Al Gore,

"Introduction," in Carson, *Silent Spring*, xv–xxvi; Carson, *Lost Woods*, 218, 244; Dan Fagin and Marianne Lavelle, *Toxic Deception* (Monroe, Maine: Common Courage Press, 1999); Theo Colborn et. al., *Our Stolen Future* (New York: Dutton, 1996); "Sperm in the News," *Rachel's Environment and Health Weekly*, January 18, 1996; Audubon, "Reduce All Pesticides but Eliminate Those Used on the Lawn," http://www.audubon.org/bird/at_home/Reduce PesticideUse.html.

4.   Carson quoted in Paul Brooks, *The House of Life* (Boston: Houghton Mifflin, 1989), 301–02; Carson, *Silent Spring*, 211; Carson, *Lost Woods*, 106–109.

5.   Carson, *Silent Spring*, 36–37. On the mutagenic effects of organochlorines, including some pesticides, see Joe Thornton, *Pandora's Poison* (Cambridge, Massachusetts: MIT Press, 2000), 84–85.

6.   Loren R. Graham, *Science and Philosophy in the Soviet Union* (New York: Alfred A. Knopf, 1972), 451–53; H. J. Muller, "Lenin's Doctrines in Relation to Genetics" (1934) in Graham, 463; Elof Axel Carlson, *Genes, Radiation, and Society* (Ithaca: Cornell University Press, 1981). Muller was a controversial figure in another respect, because of his lifelong advocacy of "progressive eugenics." His overall humanistic commitments, however, were evident. In 1963 he received the "humanist of the year award" from the American Humanist Association.

7.   H. J. Muller, "Silent Spring" (review), *New York Herald Tribune*, September 23, 1962.

8.   Barry Commoner, *Science and Survival* (New York: Viking, 1966); Joel B. Hagen, *An Entangled Bank* (New Brunswick, NJ: Rutgers University Press, 1992), 100–107, 115–18; Richard Rhodes, *Dark Sun* (New York: Simon and Schuster, 1995), 541–42; Tokue Shibata, "The H-Bomb Terror in Japan," *Monthly Review* 4, no. 2 (June 1954): 72–76; Eugene P. Odum, *Fundamentals of Ecology* (Philadelphia: Saunders, 1959), 467; Carson, *Lost Woods*, 108–109, 237–38; "U.S. Nuclear Testing Program in the Marshall Islands," http://www.nuclearclaimstribunal.com; Helen Caldicott, *Nuclear Power Is Not the Answer* (New York: New Press, 2006), 64, 73.

9.   Virginia Brodine, *Green Shoots and Red Roots* (New York: International Publishers, 2007), 3–10; Carson, *Lost Woods*, 232, 240. Briggs was editor of the CNI/CEI's publication *Nuclear Information* (later *Science and Citizen*) from 1962 to 1969.

10. A. G. Tansley, "The Use and Abuse of Vegetational Concepts and Terms," *Ecology* 16, no. 3 (July 1935): 299, 303–104. In developing his ecosystem concept, Tansley was influenced by the dialectical systems analysis presented by the British Marxist mathematician Hyman Levy in *The Universe of Science* (New York: The Century Co., 1933).

11. Charles Elton, *The Ecology of Invasions by Animals and Plants* (London: Methuen and Co., 1958), 137–42; Carson, *Lost Woods*, 190; *Silent Spring*, 155.

12. Robert L. Rudd, "The Irresponsible Poisoners," *The Nation*, May 30, 1959, 496–97; "Pesticides: The *Real* Peril," *The Nation*, November 28, 1959, 399–401; *Pesticides and the Living Landscape*, 154–55, 284–91; Frank

Graham Jr., *Since Silent Spring* (Boston: Houghton Mifflin, 1970), 167–69; Linda Lear, *Rachel Carson* (New York: Henry Holt, 1997), 331–32; Murray Bookchin (under the pseudonym of Lewis Herber), *Our Synthetic Environment* (New York: Knopf, 1962), 55–61; Carson, *Lost Woods,*, 244–45.

13. Robert M. Hazen, *Genesis* (Washington D.C.: John Henry Press, 2005), 85–90; J. D. Bernal, *The Origin of Life* (New York: World Publishing Co., 1967); Rachel Carson, *The Sea Around Us* (New York: Oxford University Press, 1989), 7; Carson, *Lost Woods*, 230–31.

14. Mary McCay, *Rachel Carson* (New York: Twayne Publishers, 1993), 23–24, 42–43, 109.

15. Carson, *Lost Woods*, xi.

16. Brooks quoted in Shirley A. Briggs, "Rachel Carson," in Gino J. Marco et. al., ed., *Silent Spring Revisited* (Washington, D.C.: American Chemical Society, 1987), 6; Lear, *Rachel Carson*, 334.

17. Carson, *Lost Woods*, 162, 194–95, 218, 220–21; Carson, *Silent Spring*, 9; Carson quote in Lytle, 178–79.

18. Carson, *Silent Spring*, 1–3; *Lost Woods*, 89.

19. U.S. Department of Agriculture, *Pesticide Data Program, Annual Summary, Calendar Year 2006* (December 2007), x, http://www.ams.usda.gov.

20. "Methyl Bromide Still Finds Its Way into U.S. Fields," *San Francisco Chronicle*, November 24, 2007; "Everyday Items, Complex Chemistry," *New York Times*, December 22, 2007.

21. Rachel Carson, *The Sense of Wonder* (New York: Harper and Row, 1965), 43.

CHAPTER FOUR: PEAK OIL AND ENERGY IMPERIALISM

This chapter is adapted and revised for this book from an article with the same title that appeared in *Monthly Review* 60, no. 3 (July-August 2008): 12–33.

1. Influential mainstream political analyst (and former Nixon White House strategist) Kevin Philips has recently argued that oil in the Middle East and elsewhere has emerged as perhaps the single most important strategic (non-monetary) factor in "the Global Crisis of American Capitalism," and is closely tied up with the world's need to shift to a "new energy regime." See Phillips, *Bad Money: Reckless Finance, Failed Politics, and the Global Crisis of American Capitalism* (New York: Viking, 2008), 124–27. Indeed, the struggle to control world oil can be seen as the centerpiece of the new geopolitics of U.S. empire, designed at the same time to combat the decline of U.S. hegemony. See John Bellamy Foster, "A Warning to Africa: The New U.S. Imperial Grand Strategy," *Monthly Review* 58, no. 2 (June 2006): 1–12.

2. Michael T. Klare, *Blood and Oil* (New York: Henry Holt, 2004), 82.

3. Colin J. Campbell and Jean H. Laherrère, "The End of Cheap Oil," *Scientific American* (March 1998): 78–83; International Energy Agency, *World Energy Outlook, 1998* (Paris: OECD, 1998), 94–103.

4. Matthew R. Simmons, "Has Technology Created $10 Oil?," *Middle East Insight* (May–June 1999), 37, 39.

5.   Matthew R. Simmons, "An Oil Man Reconsiders the Future of Black Gold,"
     Good Magazine, February 11, 2008, http://www.goodmagazine.com/section/
     Features/the_accidental_environmentalist/. The insert in brackets in the quote
     is in original.

6.   Matthew R. Simmons, *Twilight in the Desert: The Coming Saudi Oil Shock and
     the World Economy* (Hoboken, New Jersey: John Wiley and Sons, 2005).

7.   John Wood and Gary Long, "Long Term World Oil Supply (A Resource
     Base/Production Path Analysis)," Energy Information Administration, U.S.
     Department of Energy, July 28, 2000, http://www.eia.doe.gov/pub/oil_gas/
     petroleum/presentations/2000/long_ term_supply/.

8.   See Klare, *Blood and Oil*, 13-14.

9.   Sam Nunn and James R. Schlesinger, co-chairs, *The Geopolitics of Energy
     into the 21st Century*, 3 volumes (Washington, D.C.: Center for Strategic and
     International Studies, November 2000), vol. 1, xvi–xxiii; vol. 2, 30–31; vol.
     3, 19.

10. Edward L. Morse, chair, *Strategic Energy Policy Challenges for the 21st
     Century*, cosponsored by the James A. Baker III Institute for Public Policy of
     Rice University and the Council on Foreign Relations (Washington, D.C:
     Council on Foreign Relations Press, April 2001), http://www.cfr.org/
     content/publications/attachments/Energy%20TaskForce.pdf, 3–17, 29, 43–47,
     84–85, 98; see also Edward L. Morse, "A New Political Economy of Oil?,"
     Journal of International Affairs 53, no. 1 (Fall 1999): 1–29.

11. White House, *National Energy Policy* (Cheney report), May 2001,
     http://www.whitehouse.gov/energy/National-Energy-Policy.pdf, 1–13, 8–4.;
     Department of Energy, Energy Information Administration, *International
     Economic Outlook*, 2001, http://www.eia.doe.gov/oiaf/archive/ieo01/pdf/
     0484(2001).pdf, 240; *International Petroleum Outlook*, April 2008, tables
     4.1b and 4.1d; Klare, *Blood and Oil*, 15, 79-81.

12. Klare, *Blood and Oil*, 82-83.

13. Alan Greenspan, *The Age of Turbulence* (London: Penguin, 2007), 462-63.

14. James A. Baker Institute for Public Policy, "The Changing Role of National Oil
     Companies in International Markets," *Baker Institute Policy Report*, no. 35,
     April 2007, 1, 10–12, 17–19, http://www.bakerinstitute.org/publications/BI_
     PolicyReport_35.pdf.

15. Fareed Muhamedi and Raad Alkadiri, "Washington Makes Its Case for War,"
     Middle East Report, no. 224 (Autumn 2002): 5; John Bellamy Foster, *Naked
     Imperialism* (New York: Monthly Review Press, 2006), 92.

16. U.S. Department of Energy, Energy Information Administration, *International
     Petroleum Monthly*, April 2008, tables 4.1b and 4.1d.

17. Richard Heinberg, *The Party's Over* (Garbiola Island, B.C: New Society
     Publishers, 2005), 127–28; Michael Klare, *Rising Powers, Shrinking Planet*
     (New York: Henry Holt, 2008), 41; Greenpeace, "Stop the Tar Sands/Water
     Pollution," http://www.greenpeace.org/canada/en/campaigns/tarsands/threats/
     water-pollution.

18. Energy Watch Group, *Crude Oil: The Supply Outlook*, October 2007, 33–34,

http://www.energywatchgroup.org/filadmin/global/pdf/EWG_Oilreport_10-2007.pdf.

19. The distinction between "early" and "late" peakers is to be found in Richard Heinberg, *The Oil Depletion Protocol* (Gabriola Island, B.C: New Society Publishers, 2006), 17–23. For some representative works from the "early peaker" perspective see Kenneth S. Deffeyes, *Hubbert's Peak* (Princeton: Princeton University Press, 2001); David Goodstein, *Out of Gas* (New York: W. W. Norton, 2004); and Heinberg, *The Party's Over*. Cambridge Energy Research Associates is the leading independent representative of the "late peaker" view. See http://www.cera.com/aspx/cda/public1/home/home.aspx.

20. International Energy Agency, *World Energy Outlook, 1998*, 83–84. The increased prominence of unconventional oil has recently led to increasing references to "liquids," as opposed to "oil" as such, in Department of Energy reports. See Michael T. Klare, "Beyond the Age of Petroleum," *The Nation*, October 25, 2007.

21. Richard Heinberg, *Power Down* (Gabriola Island, B.C.: New Society Publishers, 2004), 35; James Howard Kunstler, *The Long Emergency* (New York: Atlantic Monthly Press, 2005), 67–68. In an important paper on the implications of peak oil for global warming, Pushker Kharecha and James Hansen of NASA's Goddard Institute for Space Studies and the Columbia University Earth Institute provide a graph (in one scenario) of a plateau in oil-based CO_2 emissions, stretching from approximately 2016 to 2036. Pushker A. Kharecha and James E. Hansen, "Implications of 'Peak Oil' for Atmospheric CO_2 and Climate," *Global Biogeochemistry* (2008, in press), figure 3, http://pubs.giss.nasa.gov/abstracts/inpress/Kharecha_Hansen.html.

22. "Oil Officials See Limit Looming on Production," *Wall Street Journal*, November 11, 2007; Klare, *Beyond the Age of Petroleum*.

23. Phillips, *Bad Money*, 130–31, 153; Energy Watch Group, *Crude Oil: The Supply Outlook*, October 2007, 71.

24. Phillips sees this discrepancy between the analysis at the top and public statements in Washington as due in large part to a desire to keep from the public the view that the U.S. system is itself peaking. See Phillips, *Bad Money*, 127.

25. Robert L. Hirsch, project leader, *Peaking of World Oil Production: Impacts, Mitigation, and Risk Management*, U.S. Department of Energy, February 2005, 13, 23–25, http://www.netl.doe.gov/publications/others/pdf/Oil_Peaking_NETL.pdf. A different and more official position was issued by the EIA in 2004–2005 in the form of a presentation on "When Will World Oil Production Peak?" by EIA administrator Guy Caruso at the 10th Annual Oil and Gas Conference, Kuala Lumpur, Malaysia, June 13, 2005. The central scenario, however, estimated the world oil peak occurring in 2044, a figure too out of line with all other studies to be considered credible. See http://www.eia.doe.gov/neic/speeches/Caruso061305.pdf.

26. Robert L. Hirsh, "The Inevitable Peaking of World Oil Production," *Bulletin of the Atlantic Council of the United States* 16, no. 2 (October 2005): 8.

27. Daniel F. Fournier and Eileen T. Westervelt, U.S Army Engineer Research and

Development Center, U.S. Army Corps of Engineers, *Energy Trends and Their Implications for U.S. Army Installations*, September 2005, vii, http://www.globalpolicy.org/empire/challenges/overstretch/2005/09energytrends.pdf.

28. International Energy Agency, *World Energy Outlook, 2005* (Paris: OECD, 2005), 510–12; Simmons, *Twilight in the Desert*, 170–79; Klare, *Rising Powers, Shrinking Planet*, 38.

29. United States Government Accountability Office, *Crude Oil: Uncertainty about Future Oil Supply Makes It Important to Develop a Strategy for Addressing a Peak and Decline in Oil Production*, February 28, 2007, 4, 20–22, 35–38.

30. Bloomberg.com, "Goldman's Murti Says Oil 'Likely' to Reach a $150–$200 (Update 5)," May 6, 2008; "The Cassandra of Oil Prices," *New York Times*, May 21, 2008; Klare, *Rising Powers, Shrinking Planet*, 121–22; Jeroen van der Veer (interview), "Royal Dutch Shell CEO on the End of 'Easy Oil,'" http://www.cfr.org/publication/15923/end_of_easy_oil.html?breadcrumb=%2F; "Not Enough Oil Is Lament of BP, Exxon on Spending (Update 1)," Bloomberg.com, May 19, 2008; Mike Nizza, "Market Faces a Disturbing Oil Forecast," *The Lede* (*New York Times* blog), May 22, 2008, http://thelede.blogs.nytimes.com/2008/05/22/market-faces-a-disturbing-oil-forecast.

31. Lester R. Brown, *Plan B 3.0* (New York: W. W. Norton, 2008), 41; Fred Magdoff, "The World Food Crisis," *Monthly Review* 60, no. 1 (May 2008): 1–15; and "The Political Economy and Ecology of Biofuels," *Monthly Review* 60, no. 3 (July-August 2008).

32. Anthony H. Cordesman and Khalid R. Al-Rodhan, *The Changing Risks in Global Oil Supply and Demand*, Center for Strategic and International Studies, October 3, 2005 (first working draft), 8, 13–19, 55–59, 79, 83.

33. John Deutsch and James R. Schlesinger, chairs, *National Security Consequences of U.S. Oil Dependence*, Council on Foreign Relations, 2006, 3, 16–30, 48–56, http://www.cfr.org/publication/11683/.

34. Baker Institute, "The Changing Role of National Oil Companies in International Oil Markets," 1, 10–12, 17–19.

35. Kunstler, *The Long Emergency*, 76–84; Baker Institute, "Changing Role of National Oil Companies," 12.

36. Roger Stern, "The Iranian Petroleum Crisis and the United States National Security," *Proceedings of the National Academy of Sciences* 104, no. 1 (January 2, 2007): 377–82.

37. Foster, "A Warning to Africa"; Michael Watts, "The Empire of Oil: Capitalist Dispossession and the New Scramble for Africa," *Monthly Review* 58, no. 4 (September 2006): 1–17; Klare, *Rising Powers, Shrinking Planet*, 146–76.

38. "U.S. Military Sees Oil Nationalism Spectre," *Financial Times*, June 26, 2006; Council on Foreign Relations, "The Return of Resource Nationalism," August 13, 2007, http://www.cfr.org/publication/13989/return_of_resource_nationalism.html; Eva Golinger, *Bush vs. Chávez* (New York: Monthly Review Press, 2008).

39. Simmons, "An Oil Man Reconsiders the Future of Black Gold."

40. Carlos Pascual, "The Geopolitics of Energy," *Brookings Institution*, January

2008, 3–4, http://www.cfr.org/publication/15342/brookings.html.

41.   Daniel Litvin, *The Guardian* (UK), "Oil, Gas and Imperialism," January 4, 2006.

42.   Joshua Kurlantzick, "Put a Tyrant in Your Tank," *Mother Jones*, May–June 2008, 38–42, 88–89.

43.   See Richard Heinberg's excellent chapter on "Bridging Peak Oil and Climate Change Activism" in his *Peak Everything* (Gabriola Island, B. C.: New Society Publishers, 2008), 141–57. On the concept of a biospheric rift see Brett Clark and Richard York, "Carbon Metabolism: Global Capitalism, Climate Change, and the Biospheric Rift," *Theory & Society* 34, no. 4 (2005): 391–428. In their paper on peak oil and global warming, Kharecha and Hansen present a baseline atmospheric carbon stabilization scenario in which oil-based CO_2 emissions peak by 2016, due principally to the "peaking" of world oil production (mediated by economic and social as well as geological factors). If such a peak were to occur, they argue, it would facilitate the stabilization of atmospheric carbon at (or below) what scientists increasingly consider to be the maximum safe level of 450 parts per million (associated with a rise in global average temperature of around 2°C above pre-industrial). But stabilization of atmospheric CO_2 at this level would also require that CO_2 emissions from coal-fired power plants peak by 2025 and that coal-fired plants without sequestration be phased out completely "before mid-century." Pusher and Kharecha, "Implications of 'Peak Oil' for Atmospheric CO_2 and Climate."

44.   Rachel Carson, *Lost Woods* (Boston: Beacon Press, 1998), 210.

CHAPTER FIVE: THE PENTAGON AND CLIMATE CHANGE

This chapter has been adapted and revised for this book from an article with the same title in *Monthly Review* 56, no. 1 (May 2004): 1–13.

1.   *The Observer* (London), February 22, 200

2.   Peter Schwartz and Doug Randall, *An Abrupt Climate Change Scenario and Its Implications for United States National Security*, October 2003, http://www.grist.org/pdf/AbruptClimateChange2003.pdf.

3.   Thomas R. Karl and Kevin E. Trenberth, "Modern Global Climate Change," *Science* 302:1721; Intergovernmental Panel on Climate Change, *Climate Change 2001* (Cambridge: Cambridge University Press, 2001), 7, 13; Tom Athanasiou and Paul Baer, *Dead Heat* (New York: Seven Stories, 2002), 43–47.

4.   "All Downhill from Here?," *Science* 303 (March 12, 2004).

5.   National Research Council, *Abrupt Climate Change: Inevitable Surprises* (Washington, D.C.: National Academy Press, 2002), 14.

6.   United Nations Intergovernmental Panel on Climate Change, *Climate Change, 2001: Synthesis Report* (Cambridge: Cambridge University Press, 2001), 16.

7.   Robert B. Gagosian, "Abrupt Climate Change: Should We Be Worried?," World Economic Forum, Davos, Switzerland, January 27, 2003, http://www.whoi.edu; National Research Council, Abrupt Climate Change, 115–16B. Dickson et. al., "Rapid Freshening in the Deep Atlantic Ocean over the Past Four Decades," *Nature*, 416 (April 25, 2002); B. Hansen, et. al.,

"Decreasing Overflow from the Nordic Seas into the Atlantic Ocean through the Faroe Bank Channel since 1950," *Nature*, 411 (June 21, 2001).

8.   Richard B. Alley, *The Two-Mile Time Machine* (Princeton: Princeton University Press, 2000), 184.

9.   Peter Schwartz, Peter Leyden, and Joel Hyatt, *The Long Boom: A Vision for the Coming Age of Prosperity* (Cambridge, Massachusetts: Perseus Publishers, 2000), 266.

10.   There were, no doubt, rational motives to assigning the task of writing such a report to Schwartz, who had shown that he had all the necessary dramatic skills of the professional futurologist. Given his past history, and his absolute faith in the system, he could not be viewed as a prophet of doom and gloom or as an enemy of business. Further, a paragraph of *The Long Boom* (p. 153) had actually pointed to the possibility of a shutdown of the thermohaline circulation and the coming of "another Ice Age"—though this was introduced in a generally Pollyannaish view of the ecological crisis in which the "long boom" itself provided all the answers.

11.   *San Francisco Chronicle,* February 25, 2004; *New York Times,* February 29, 2004.

12.   *New York Times,* March 21, 2004.

13.   Fred Magdoff, "A Precarious Existence," *Monthly Review* 55, no. 9 (February 2004).

14.   John Bellamy Foster, *Ecology Against Capitalism* (New York: Monthly Review Press, 2002), 18. See also chapter 12 below.

15.   Andrew Sims, Aubrey Meyer, and Nick Robbins, "Who Owes Who?: Climate Change, Debt, Equity and Survival"; Athanasiou and Baer, *Dead Heat*, 63-97.

16.   Jared Diamond, "Twilight at Easter," *New York Review of Books*, March 25, 2004, 6-10.

CHAPTER SIX: THE JEVONS PARADOX:
ENVIRONMENT AND TECHNOLOGY UNDER CAPITALISM

This chapter is adapted and revised for this book from an earlier article, coauthored with Brett Clark, entitled "William Stanley Jevons and *The Coal Question*: An Introduction to Jevons's 'Of the Economy of Fuel,'" *Organization and Environment* 14, no. 1 (March 2001): 93-98.

1.   William Stanley Jevons, *The Coal Question: An Inquiry concerning the Progress of the Nation, and the Probable Exhaustion of Our Coal-Mines* (London: Macmillan, 1906); Juan Martinez-Allier, *Ecological Economics* (Oxford: Basil Blackwell, 1987).

2.   R. D. C. Black, "W. S. Jevons, 1835-82," in D. P. O'Brien and J. R. Presley, ed., *The Pioneers of Modern Economics in Britain* (Totowa, NJ: Barnes & Noble, 1981), 2-4.

3.   R.D.C. Black, "Jevons, William Stanley," in J. Eatwell, M. Milgate, and P. Newman, eds., *The New Palgrave Dictionary of Economics* (London: Macmillan, 1987), 1009.

4.   Black, "W. S. Jevons," 4-6.

5.   William Stanley Jevons, *The Theory of Political Economy*, ed. R.D.C. Black (London: Penguin, 1970), 203–05.

6.   Jevons, *The Coal Question*, 194–95.

7.   Jevons, *The Coal Question*, 373–79.

8.   John Maynard Keynes, *Essays in Biography* (London: R. Hart-Davis, 1951), 259.

9.   Mario Giampietro and Kozo Mayumi, "Another View of Development, Ecological Degradation, and North-South Trade," *Review of Social Economy*, 56, no. 1 (1998): 24-26.

10.   Jevons, *The Coal Question*, 140–42.

11   Jevons, *The Coal Question*, 152–53.

12.   Jevons, *The Coal Question*, 15–16, 189–90, 221.

13.   Jevons, *The Coal Question*, 163.

14.   Jevons, *The Coal Question*, 164–71.

15.   Nicholas Georgescu-Roegen, *The Entropy Law and the Economic Process* (Cambridge, Massachusetts: Harvard University Press, 1971), 2.

16.   See chapter 9 below.

17.   Karl Marx and Frederick Engels, *Collected Works*, vol. 46, (New York: International Publishers, 1975), 411.

18.   Frederick Engels, *Dialectics of Nature* (Moscow: Progress, 1966), 180–83.

19.   Jevons, *The Coal Question*, 459–60.

CHAPTER SEVEN: A PLANETARY DEFEAT:
THE FAILURE OF GLOBAL ENVIRONMENTAL REFORM

This chapter has been adapted and revised for this book based on an article that appeared under the same title in *Monthly Review* 54, no. 8 (January 2003): 1–9. It was based on notes for several talks delivered by the author in Johannesburg, South Africa, during events leading up to the World Summit on Sustainable Development, August-September 2002.

1.   Wolfgang Sachs, *The Jo'burg Memo: Fairness in a Fragile World— Memorandum for the World Summit on Sustainable Development*, Heinrich Böll Foundation, 2002, http://www.worldsummit2002.org. In addition to Sachs, such well-known environmentalists as Hilary French, Paul Hawken, Hazel Henderson, and Anita Roddick (of The Body Shop) were among the sixteen contributors to *The Jo'burg Memo*.

2.   Stephan Schmidheiny, *Changing Course* (Cambridge, Massachusetts: MIT Press, 2002).

3.   United Nations Environment Programme, *Global Outlook 3* (Sterling, VA: Earthscan, 2002), 150–52; Worldwatch Institute, *State of the World 2002* (New York: W. W. Norton, 2002), 5–12; International Forum on Globalization, *Intrinsic Consequences of Economic Globalization on the Environment: Interim Report* (San Francisco: IFG, 2002), 101, 146; Lester R. Brown, *Eco-Economy* (New York: W .W. Norton, 2001), 9, 27, 71.

4.   United Nations, *Human Development Report, 2002* (New York: Oxford University Press, 2002), 17–19.

5.   The Worldwatch Institute also argued for a "global fair deal" in its report pre-
      pared for the Johannesburg summit. In Worldwatch's case this meant forging new
      "partnerships" between multinational corporations, NGOs, governments, and
      international organizations. See Worldwatch, *State of the World 2002*, 183, 198.
6.   See Ted Nordhaus and Michael Shellenberger, *Break Through* (Boston:
      Houghton Mifflin, 2007); Thomas Friedman, *Hot, Flat, and Crowded* (New
      York: Farrar, Straus and Giroux, 2008).
7.   "Climate Warming Gases Rising Faster than Expected," *Guardian*, February
      15, 2009.
8.   Naomi Klein, *The Shock Doctrine: The Rise of Disaster Capitalism* (New York:
      Henry Holt, 2007). On the global economic crisis see John Bellamy Foster and
      Fred Magdoff, *The Great Financial Crisis* (New York: Monthly Review Press,
      2009). On the new imperialist wars see John Bellamy Foster, *Naked
      Imperialism* (New York: Monthly Review Press, 2006).

CHAPTER EIGHT: MARX'S ECOLOGY IN HISTORICAL PERSPECTIVE

This chapter has been adapted and revised for this book based on an article
that first appeared under this title in *International Socialism* 96 (Autumn
2002): 71–86. It was based on a talk delivered at the Marxism 2002 conference,
London, July 6, 2002.

1.   George Lichtheim, *Marxism: An Historical and Critical Study* (New York:
      Praeger, 1961), 245.
2.   On the strengths of Marx's ecological analysis see John Bellamy Foster, *Marx's
      Ecology* (New York: Monthly Review Press, 2000), and Paul Burkett, *Marx and
      Nature* (New York: St. Martin's Press, 1999).
3.   For a detailed breakdown of the various criticisms of Marx on the environment
      see the following chapter.
4.   Maarten de Kadt and Salvatore Engel-Di Mauro, "Marx's Ecology or
      Ecological Marxism: Failed Promise," *Capitalism, Nature, Socialism*, 12, no. 2
      (June 2001): 52–55.
5.   Foster, *Marx's Ecology*.
6.   E. P. Thompson, *The Essential E. P. Thompson* (New York: New Press, 2001), 6.
7.   Except where otherwise indicated, all of the brief quotes from Liebig in the text
      below are taken from an unpublished English translation of the 1862 German
      edition of his *Agricultural Chemistry* by Lady Gilbert contained in the archives
      of the Rothamsted Experimental Station (now IACR-Rothamsted) outside
      London.
8.   The translation of this passage from the introduction to the 1862 edition of
      Liebig's work follows Erland Mårold in "Everything Circulates: Agricultural
      Chemistry and Recycling Theories in the Second Half of the Nineteenth
      Century," *Environment and History* 8 (2002): 74.
9.   Lord Ernle, *English Farming Past and Present* (Chicago: Quadrangle, 1961),
      369. For a fuller discussion of Marx's ecological argument and its relation to the
      nineteenth-century guano trade see John Bellamy Foster and Brett Clark,

"Ecological Imperialism," in *Socialist Register, 2004* (New York: Monthly Review Press, 2003), 186–201.

10.   Karl Marx, *Capital*, vol. 1 (New York: Vintage, 1976), 638.

11.   Marx, *Capital*, vol. 1, 636–639; Karl Marx, *Capital*, vol. 3 (New York: Vintage, 1981), 948–950, 959.

12.   Marx, *Capital*, vol. 1, 283, 290.

13.   Marx, *Capital*, vol. 3, 911.

14.   Marx, *Capital*, vol. 1, 637; *Capital*, vol. 3, 959.

15.   Documentation of Marx's various ecological concerns can be found in the following chapter and in Foster, *Marx's Ecology* and Burkett, *Marx and Nature*. In their time, Marx and Engels raised the problem of local climate change (speculation on temperature changes due to deforestation). See Engels's notes on Fraas in Marx and Engels, *MEGA* IV, 31 (Amsterdam: Akadamie Verlag, 1999), 512–15.

16.   Frederick Engels, *Ludwig Feuerbach and the Outcome of Classical German Philosophy* (New York: International Publishers, 1941), 67.

17.   The phrase "the revolution in ethnological time" is taken from T. R. Trautmann, *Lewis Henry Morgan and the Invention of Kinship* (Berkeley: University of California Press, 1987), 35, 220.

18.   See Foster, *Marx's Ecology*, 49–51.

19.   Ibid., 196–207, 212–221.

20.   Karl Marx, *Theories of Surplus Value*, vol. 3 (Moscow: Progress Publishers, 1971), 294–295.

21.   Karl Marx, *Early Writings* (New York: Vintage, 1974), 328; *Capital*, vol. 1, 285–286. See also John Bellamy Foster and Paul Burkett, "The Dialectic of Organic/Inorganic Relations: Marx and the Hegelian Philosophy of Nature," *Organization and Environment*, 13, no. 4 (December 2000): 403–425.

22.   Frederick Engels, *Dialectics of Nature* (New York, 1940), 281.

23.   Stephen J. Gould, *An Urchin in the Storm* (New York: 1987), 111–112.

24.   See Noel Castree, "Marxism and the Production of Nature," *Capital and Class* 72 (Autumn 2000): 14; John Bellamy Foster, "Review of Special Issue of Capital and Class," *Historical Materialism* 8 (Summer 2001): 465–467.

25.   Nikolai Bukharin, *Philosophical Arabesques* (New York: Monthly Review Press, 2005), 101.

26.   See the discussion in Foster, *Marx's Ecology*, 241–244; Rachel Carson, *Lost Woods* (Boston: Beacon Press, 1998), 229–230.

27.   On the dialectics of nature and ecology in Marx and Lukács see John Bellamy Foster, "The Dialectics of Nature and Marxist Ecology," in Bertell Ollman and Tony Smith, eds., *Dialectics for the New Century* (London: Palgrave Macmillan, 2008), 50–82.

28.   Neal Wood, *Communism and British Intellectuals* (New York: Columbia University Press, 1959), 145.

29.   Lysenkoism was an erroneous doctrine associated with the work of the Russian agronomist Trofim Denisovich Lysenko that deemphasized genetic inheritance in favor of a notion of the plasticity of the life cycle. For a balanced discussion of

Lysenkoism see Richard Levins and Richard Lewontin, *The Dialectical Biologist* (Cambridge, Massachusetts: Harvard University Press, 1985), 163-96.

30.   See the more detailed discussions of Lankester in Foster, *Marx's Ecology*, 221–225; and John Bellamy, "E. Ray Lankester, Ecological Materialist: An Introduction to Lankester's 'Effacement of Nature by Man,'" *Organization and Environment* 13, no. 2 (June 2000): 233–235.

31.   For biographical information on Tansley see Peder Anker, *Imperial Ecology: Environmental Order in the British Empire* (Cambridge, Massachusetts: Harvard University Press, 2001), 7–40.

32.   Anker, *Imperial Ecology*, 41–75, 118–149; Jan C. Smuts, *Holism and Evolution* (London: Macmillan, 1926); Lancelot Hogben, *The Nature of Living Matter* (London: Kegan Paul, Trench, Trubner and Co., 1930); Hyman Levy, *The Universe of Science* (New York: The Century Co., 1933). For Smuts's racial views see Jan Christian Smuts, *Africa and Some World Problems* (Oxford: Oxford University Press, 1930), 92–94.

33.   Anker, *Imperial Ecology*, 152–156; Arthur G. Tansley, "The Use and Abuse of Vegetational Concepts and Terms," *Ecology* 16, no 3 (July 1935): 284–307.

34.   Karl Marx and Frederick Engels, *Collected Works*, vol. 5 (New York: International Publishers, 1975), 39–41.

CHAPTER NINE: MARX'S THEORY OF METABOLIC RIFT:
CLASSICAL FOUNDATIONS FOR ENVIRONMENTAL SOCIOLOGY

This chapter is a revised and adapted version of an article published under the same title in the *American Journal of Sociology* 105, no. 2 (September 1999): 366–405.

1.   See Carl Sauer, *Land and Life* (Berkeley: University of California Press, 1963).

2.   See Clifford Geertz, *Agricultural Involution: The Processes of Ecological Change in Indonesia* (Berkeley: University of California Press, 1963); Kay Milton, *Environmentalism and Cultural Theory* (New York: Routledge, 1996).

3.   A. C. Pigou, *The Economics of Welfare* (London: Macmillan, 1920); Michael Jacobs, "The Limits of Neoclassicism," in Michael Redclift and Ted Benton, eds., *Social Theory and the Global Environment* (New York: Routledge, 1994), 67.

4.   John Dryzek, *The Politics of the Earth* (Oxford: Oxford University Press, 1997).

5.   Riley Dunlap, "The Evolution of Environmental Sociology," in Michael Redclift and Graham Woodgate, eds., *International Handbook of Environmental Sociology* (Northampton, Massachusetts: Edward Elgar, 1997), 21-39.

6.   William Burch, *Daydreams and Nightmares* (New York: Harper and Row, 1971), 14–20; Riley Dunlap and William Catton, "Environmental Sociology," in Timothy O'Riordan and Ralph D'Arge, eds., *Progress in Resource Management and Environmental Planning*, vol. 1 (New York: John Wiley and Sons, 1979), 57–85; Ted Benton, "Biology and Social Theory in the Environmental Debate," in Redclift and Benton, *Social Theory and the Global Environment*, 28–30; Raymond Murphy, *Rationality and Nature* (Boulder,

Colorado: Westview, 1994), ix–x; Frederick Buttel, "Environmental and Resource Sociology," *Rural Sociology* 61, no. 1 (1996): 56–76.

7.   Frederick Buttel, "Sociology and the Environment," *International Social Science Journal*, 109 (1986): 338.

8.   Buttel, "Environmental and Resource Sociology," 57.

9.   Benton, "Biology and Social Theory in the Environmental Debate," 29.

10. Raymond Murphy, *Sociology and Nature* (Boulder, Colorado: Westview, 1996), 10.

11. Riley Dunlap and Kenneth Martin, "Bringing Environment into the Study of Agriculture," *Rural Sociology* 48, no. 2 (1983): 201–18; Dunlap, "The Evolution of Environmental Sociology," 23; Riley Dunlap and William Catton, "Struggling with Human Exemptionalism," *American Sociologist* 25, no. 1 (1994): 8.

12. William Catton, Jr., and Riley Dunlap, "Environmental Sociology: A New Paradigm," *American Sociologist* 13 (1978), 41–49; Frederick Buttel, "Environmental Sociology: A New Paradigm?," *American Sociologist* 13 (1978): 252–56; Dunlap and Catton, "Struggling with Human Exemptionalism," 5–30.

13. Benton and Redclift, "Introduction," Redclift and Benton, *Social Theory and the Global Environment*, 3; Dunlap and Catton, "Environmental Sociology," 58; David Goldblatt, *Social Theory and the Environment* (Boulder, Colorado: Westview, 1996), 3.

14. Dunlap and Martin, "Bringing Environment into the Study of Agriculture," 204; Dunlap and Catton, "Struggling with Human Exemptionalism," 6.

15. Frederick Buttel, "New Directions in Environmental Sociology," *Annual Review of Sociology* 13 (1987): 466.

16. William Catton, *Overshoot* (Urbana: University of Illinois Press, 1982).

17. Murphy, *Rationality and Nature*.

18. Timo Järvikoski, "The Relation of Nature and Society in Marx and Durkheim," *Acta Sociologica* 39, no. 1 (1996): 73–86.

19. Buttel, "Sociology and the Environment," 341–42.

20. Alfred Schmidt, *The Concept of Nature in Marx* (London: New Left Books, 1971); Howard Parsons, ed., *Marx and Engels on Ecology* (Westport, Conn.: Greenwood, 1977); Anthony Giddens, *A Contemporary Critique of Historical Materialism* (Berkeley: University of California Press, 1981); Michael Redclift, *Development and the Environmental Crisis* (New York: Methuen, 1984); John Clark, "Marx's Inorganic Body," *Environmental Ethics* 11 (1989): 243–58; Ted Benton, "Marxism and Natural Limits," *New Left Review* 178 (1989): 51–86; Andrew McLaughlin, "Ecology, Capitalism, and Socialism," *Socialism and Democracy* 10 (1990): 69–102; Kozo Mayumi, "Temporary Emancipation from the Land," *Ecological Economics* 4, no. 1 (1991): 35–56; Reiner Grundmann, *Marxism and Ecology* (Oxford: Oxford University Press, 1991); Robyn Eckersley, *Environmentalism and Political Theory* (New York: State University of New York Press, 1992); Michael Perelman, "Marx and Resource Scarcity," *Capitalism, Nature, Socialism* 4, no. 2 (1993): 65–88; Tim Hayward,

Ecological Thought (Cambridge, Massachusetts: Polity, 1994); David Harvey, *Justice, Nature and the Geography of Difference* (New York: Blackwell, 1996); Paul Burkett, "Nature in Marx Reconsidered," *Organization and Environment* 10, no. 2 (1997): 164-83; John Bellamy Foster, "The Crisis of the Earth," *Organization and Environment* 10, no. 3 (1997): 278-95; Peter Dickens, "Beyond Sociology," in Redclift and Woodgate, eds., *International Handbook of Environmental Sociology*; James O'Connor, *Natural Causes* (New York: Guilford, 1998).

21. Buttel, "Sociology and the Environment," 340-41.

22. Juan Martinez-Alier, *Ecological Economics* (Oxford: Blackwell, 1987), 183-92.

23. The issue of sustainability, or the notion that basic ecological conditions need to be maintained so that the ability of future generations to fulfill their needs will not be compromised, is the leitmotif of most contemporary environmental thought.

24. Buttel, "Environmental and Resource Sociology," 61.

25. Environmentalists sometimes use the terms "dark green" and "light green" to refer to the same division as that between "deep ecology" and so-called "shallow ecology." In both cases, the nature of the distinction is the same: between what is thought of as an "anthropocentric" perspective versus a more "ecocentric" one—though such distinctions are notoriously difficult to define. For a sympathetic account of deep ecology, see McLaughlin, "Ecology, Capitalism, and Socialism."

26. Clark, "Marx's Inorganic Body"; Victor Ferkiss, *Nature, Technology and Society* (New York: New York University Press, 193).

27. Giddens, *A Contemporary Critique of Historical Materialism*; Alec Nove, "Socialism," in John Eatwell, Murray Milgate, and Peter Newman, eds., *The New Palgrave Dictionary of Economics*, vol. 4 (New York: Stockton, 1987), 398-407; Redclift, *Development and the Environmental Crisis*; Benton, "Marxism and Natural Limits"; McLaughlin, "Ecology, Capitalism, and Socialism"; Eckersley, *Environmentalism and Political Theory*; Jean-Paul Deléage, "Eco-Marxist Critique of Political Economy," in Martin O'Connor, ed., *Is Capitalism Sustainable?* (New York: Guilford, 1994), 37-52; Goldblatt, *Social Theory and the Environment*, 3.

28. O'Connor, *Natural Causes*.

29. Parsons, ed., *Marx and Engels on Ecology*; Perelman, "Marx and Resource Scarcity"; Mayumi, "Temporary Emancipation from the Land"; Michael Lebowitz, *Beyond Capital* (London: Macmillan, 1992); Elmar Altvater, *The Future of the Market* (London: Verso, 1993); Foster, "The Crisis of the Earth"; and Burkett, "Nature in Marx Reconsidered."

30. Giddens, *A Contemporary Critique of Historical Materialism*, 59-60.

31. Redclift, *Development and the Environmental Crisis*, 7.

32. Michael Redclift and Graham Woodgate, "Sociology and the Environment," in Redclift and Benton, eds., *Social Theory and the Global Environment*, 53.

33. Nove, "Socialism," 399.

34. F. M. L. Thompson, "The Second Agricultural Revolution, 1815-1880,"

Economic History Review 21, no. 1 (1968): 62–77. Thompson designates the second agricultural revolution as occurring over the years 1815–1880, that is, commencing with the agricultural crisis that immediately followed the Napoleonic Wars. I have narrowed the period down to 1830–1880 here in order to distinguish more fully between the crisis that to some extent preceded the second agricultural revolution and the revolution proper, for which the turning point was the publication of Liebig's *Organic Chemistry* in 1840 followed by J. B. Lawes's building of the first factory for the production of synthetic fertilizer (superphosphates) a few years later.

35. Karl Marx, *Capital*, vol. 3 (New York: Vintage, 1981).

36. David Ricardo, *Principles of Political Economy and Taxation* (Cambridge: Cambridge University Press, 1951), 67.

37. Frederick Engels, "Outlines of a Critique of Political Economy," in Karl Marx, *The Economic and Philosophic Manuscripts of 1884*, ed. Dirk J. Struik (New York: International Publishers, 1964), 197–226.

38. Karl Marx, *The Poverty of Philosophy* (New York: International Publishers, 1963), 162–63.

39. Foster, *The Crisis of the Earth*; O'Connor, *Natural Causes*, 3.

40. Lord Ernle, *English Farming Past and Present* (Chicago: Quadrangle, 1961), 369; Daniel Hillel, *Out of the Earth* (Berkeley: University of California Press, 1991), 131-32.

41. William H. Brock, *Justus von Liebig* (Cambridge: Cambridge University Press, 1997), 149–50.

42. J. M. Skaggs, *The Great Guano Rush* (New York: St. Martin's Press, 1994).

43. Liebig quoted in Karl Kautsky, *The Agrarian Question*, vol. 1 (Winchester, Massachusetts: Zwan, 1988), 53.

44. Karl Marx and Frederick Engels, *Collected Works*, vol. 38 (New York: International Publishers, 1975), 476; James F. W. Johnston, *Notes on North America* (London: William Blackwood and Sons, 1851), 356-65.

45. Henry Carey, *The Past, the Present and the Future* (New York: Augustus M. Kelley, 1967), 298–99, 304–308; *Principles of Social Science*, vol. 2 (Philadelphia: J.B. Lippincott, 1867), 215; and *The Slave Trade Domestic and Foreign* (New York: Augustus M. Kelley, 1967).

46. Justus von Liebig, *Letters on Modern Agriculture* (London: Walton and Maberly, 1859), 175-78, 183, 220.

47. Justus von Liebig, *The Natural Laws of Husbandry* (New York: D. Appleton, 1863), 261.

48. Justus von Liebig, *Letters on the Subject of the Utilisation of the Metropolitan Sewage* (London: W.H. Collingridge, 1865).

49. Marx and Engels, *Collected Works*, vol. 42, 227.

50. Karl Marx, *Capital*, vol. 1 (New York: Vintage, 1976), 638.

51. Marx, *Capital*, vol. 3, 949–50.

52. Marx, *Capital*, vol. 1, 637–38.

53. Ibid., 348.

54. Ibid., 283, 290.

55. Marx and Engels, *Collected Works*, vol. 30, 40. Marx highlighted the method-ological importance of the concept of "material exchange [*Stoffwechsel*] between man and nature" in his *Notes on Adolph Wagner,* his last economic work, written in 1880. As early as 1857–1858, in the *Grundrisse,* Marx had referred to the concept of metabolism (*Stoffwechsel*) in the wider sense of "a system of general social metabolism, of universal relations, of all-round needs and universal capacities . . . formed for the first time" under generalized com-modity production. Throughout his later economic works, he employed the concept to refer both to the actual metabolic interaction between nature and society through human labor, and also in a wider sense to describe the com-plex, dynamic, interdependent set of needs and relations brought into being and constantly reproduced in alienated form under capitalism, and the ques-tion of human freedom that this raised—all of which could be seen as being connected to the way in which the human metabolism with nature was expressed through the organization of human labor. Marx thus gave the con-cept of metabolism both a specific ecological meaning and a wider social mean-ing. It makes sense therefore to speak of the "socioecological" nature of his con-cept. See Karl Marx, *Texts on Method* (Oxford: Basil Blackwell, 1975), 209; Karl Marx, *Grundrisse* (New York: Vintage, 1973), 158.

56. Karl Marx, *Early Writings* (New York: Vintage, 1974), 328.

57. Hayward, *Ecological Thought,* 116.

58. Marx, *Capital,* vol. 3, 959.

59. Franklin C. Bing, "The History of the Word 'Metabolism,'" *Journal of the History of Medicine and Allied Sciences,* 26, no. 2 (1971): 158–80; Kenneth Caneva, *Robert Mayer and the Conservation of Energy* (Princeton: Princeton University Press, 1993).

60. Liebig, *Animal Chemistry or Organic Chemistry in Its Application to Physiology and Pathology* (New York: Johnson Reprint, 1964); Brock, *Justus von Liebig,* 193; Caneva, *Robert Mayer and the Conservation of Energy,* 117.

61. Marina Fischer-Kowalski, "Society's Metabolism," in Redclift and Woodgate, eds., *International Handbook of Environmental Sociology,* 120.

62. Eugene Odum, "The Strategy of Ecosystem Development," *Science* 164 (1969): 262–70.

63. Fischer-Kowalski, "Society's Metabolism," 119–20; Hayward, *Ecological Thought,* 116–17; Allen Schnaiberg, *The Environment* (Oxford: Oxford University Press, 1980); Dunlap and Catton, "Environmental Sociology."

64. Abel Wolman, "The Metabolism of Cities," *Scientific American* 213, no. 3 (1965): 179–90; Herbert Giradet, "Sustainable Cities," *Architectural Design* 67 (1997): 9–13.

65. Fischer-Kowalski, "Society's Metabolism," 122.

66. Fischer-Kowalski, "Society's Metabolism," 121, 131.

67. Karl Marx, *Theories of Surplus Value,* part 3 (Moscow: Progress Publishers, 1971), 301.

68. Karl Marx, *Capital,* vol. 3, 195.

69. Frederick Engels, *The Housing Question* (Moscow: Progress Publishers, 1975), 92.

70. Marx, *Capital*, vol. 3, 195.

71. Marx, *Capital*, vol. 1, 860.

72. Marx, *Capital*, vol. 3, 754.

73. World Commission on Environment and Development (the Brundtland Commission), *Our Common Future* (New York: Oxford University Press, 1987), 43.

74. Marx, *Capital*, vol. 3, 948–49.

75. Marx, *Capital*, vol. 3, 911.

76. Marx and Engels, *Collected Works*, vol. 24, 356.

77. On this later phase of Marx's analysis, in which he addressed the agricultural concerns of the Russian populists, see Teodor Shanin, *Late Marx and the Russian Road: Marx and the Peripheries of Capitalism* (New York: Monthly Review Press, 1983).

78. Marx and Engels, *Collected Works*, vol. 46, 411.

79. Marx and Engels, *Collected Works*, vol. 42, 559; Karl Marx, *Capital*, vol. 2 (New York: Vintage, 1978), 322.

80. Marx, *Capital*, vol. 1, 892–93.

81. Karl Marx and Frederick Engels, *Selected Correspondence* (Moscow: Progress Publishers, 1975).

82. Nove, "Socialism," 399.

83. Marx and Engels, *Selected Correspondence*, 190.

84. Marx, *Capital*, vol. 3, 195–97.

85. McLaughlin, "Ecology, Capitalism and Socialism," 95.

86. Karl Marx and Frederick Engels, *The Communist Manifesto* (New York: Monthly Review Press, 1967), 40–41.

87. Marx, *Capital*, vol. 1, 637.

88. Marx, *Capital*, vol. 3, 959; *Capital*, vol. 1, 637–38.

89. Jean-Paul Deléage, "Eco-Marxist Critique of Political Economy," in Martin O'Connor, ed., *Is Capitalism Sustainable?* (New York: Guilford Press, 1994), 48; Ward Churchill, *From a Native Son* (Boston: South End Press, 1996), 467–68; Nicholas Georgescu-Roegen, *The Entropy Law and the Economic Process* (Cambridge, Massachusetts: Harvard University Press, 1971), 2. Ten years after this essay was first published, this error continues to be repeated in the literature. Thus, Luiz Barbosa has written that Marx "believed raw materials are given to us gratis (for free) by nature and that it is human labor that gives it value. Thus Marx failed to notice the intrinsic value of nature." Luiz C. Barbosa, "Theories in Environmental Sociology," in Kenneth A. Gould and Tammy Lewis, eds., *Twenty Lessons in Environmental Sociology* (New York: Oxford University Press, 2009), 28. Barbosa is undoubtedly unaware of the fact (explained in the following discussion) that the notion that nature was a "free gift" was proposed first by Malthus and has been viewed as an economic law of orthodox economics up to the present. Nor does he seem to be aware of the fact that Marx, in referring to this deeply entrenched notion (arising out of the workings of capitalism itself), was engaged in a *critique* of the labor value system under capitalism, insisting that wealth had to be understood as arising from

nature as well as labor. The misinterpretation arises from seeing Marx as an adherent of the labor theory of value *as a transhistorical law*, rather than as the root of the specifically capitalist law of value, which needed, in his view, to be transcended. Nothing could be more absurd, therefore, than arguing on this basis alone, as Barbosa does, that Marx rejected the notion of "intrinsic value"—a concept which raises issues far outside the purview of economic value analysis. For a useful discussion see Paul Burkett, "On Some Misconceptions about Nature and Marx's Critique of Political Economy," *Capitalism, Nature, Socialism* 7 (September 1996): 64–66.

90.   Thomas Malthus, *Pamphlets* (New York: Augustus M. Kelley, 1970), 185.

91.   Campbell McConnell, *Economics* (New York: McGraw Hill, 1970), 20, 672.

92.   Marx and Engels, *Collected Works*, vol. 34, 151–59.

93.   Marx, *Capital*, vol. 3, 955.

94.   Marx, *Capital*, vol. 1, 323.

95.   Marx, *Capital*, vol. 1, 134.

96.   Karl Marx, *Critique of the Gotha Programme* (Moscow: Progress Publishers, 1971), 11.

97.   Karl Marx, *Grundrisse* (New York: Vintage, 1973), 325.

98.   Marx, *Grundrisse*, 409–10; Francis Bacon, *Novum Organum* (Chicago: Open Court, 1994), 29, 43.

99.   Frederick Engels, *Dialectics of Nature* (New York: International Publishers, 1940), 291–92.

100. Marx, *Capital*, vol. 1, 461; Marx and Engels, *Collected Works*, vol. 41, 246–47.

101. Marx and Engels's complex relation to Darwin's work—which neither denied a relation between society and biology nor reduced one to the other—may also have something to say about why they never utilized the term "ecology," coined by Darwin's leading German follower Ernst Haeckel in 1866, the year before the publication of volume 1 of *Capital*. Although the concept of ecology only gradually came into common usage, Marx and Engels were very familiar with Haeckel's work and so may have been aware of his coinage of this concept. Yet the way that Haeckel, a strong social Darwinist, originally defined the term was unlikely to have predisposed them to its acceptance. "By ecology," Haeckel had written, "we mean the body of knowledge concerning the economy of nature . . . in a word, ecology is the study of all those complex interrelations referred to by Darwin as the conditions of the struggle for existence." Haeckel quoted in Frank Golley, *A History of the Ecosystem Concept in Ecology* (New Haven: Yale University Press, 1993), 207.

102. Dunlap, "The Evolution of Environmental Sociology," 31–32.

103. Marx, *Capital*, vol. 1, 493.

104. Anton Pannekoek, *Marxism and Darwinism* (Chicago: Charles H. Kerr, 1912); Charles Darwin, *The Origin of Species* (Middlesex: Penguin, 1968), 187–88.

105. Engels, *Dialectics of Nature*, 279–96.

106. Stephen Jay Gould, *An Urchin in the Storm* (New York: W.W. Norton, 1987), 111–12.

107. Richard Norgaard, *Development Betrayed* (New York: Routledge, 1994).

108. Engels, *Dialectics of Nature*, 172.

109. Marx, *Capital*, vol. 3, 213–16.

110. Marx, *Capital*, vol. 1, 133–34.

111. Redclift and Woodgate, "Sociology and the Environment," 53.

112. Engels, *Dialectics of Nature*, 6.

113. Massimo Quaini, *Marxism and Geography* (Totowa, New Jersey: Barnes and Noble, 1982), 136.

114. Karl Kautsky, *The Agrarian Question*, vol. 2 (Winchester, Massachusetts: Zwan, 1988), 214. In saying there was no exploitation of agriculture in terms of the law of value, Kautsky was arguing that transactions here, as in other areas of the economy, were based on equal exchange. Nonetheless, he insisted that "material exploitation" (related to use-values) was present insofar as the soil was being impoverished. Marx too argued that the soil was being "robbed" or "exploited" in the latter sense and connected this to the fact that the land under capitalism was regarded as a "free gift" (as Malthus had contended) so that the full costs of its reproduction never entered into the law of value under capitalism.

115. Kautsky, *The Agrarian Question*, vol. 2, 214–15.

116. V. I. Lenin, *Collected Works*, vol. 5 (Moscow: Progress Publishers, 1961), 155–56.

117. Stephen Cohen, *Bukharin and the Bolshevik Revolution* (Oxford: Oxford University Press, 1980), 118.

118. Nikolai Bukharin, *Historical Materialism: A System of Sociology* (New York: International Publishers, 1925), 108–12.

119. Ibid., 77, 111–13.

120. Ibid., 89, 104.

121. Ibid., 75, 89, 104.

122. Nikolai Bukharin, "Theory and Practice from the Standpoint of Dialectical Materialism," in Nikolai Bukharin et al., *Science at the Crossroads* (London: Frank Cass, 1971), 17. In referring to the "biosphere," Bukharin drew upon V. I. Vernadsky's *The Biosphere,* first published in 1922, which was one of the great works in ecological science of the twentieth century and was extremely influential in Soviet scientific circles in the 1920s and early1930s. Vernadsky was "the first person in history to come [to] grips with the real implications of the fact that the Earth is a self-contained sphere." He achieved international renown both for his analysis of the biosphere and as the founder of the science of geochemistry (or biogeochemistry). V. I. Vernadsky, *The Biosphere* (New York: Copernicus, 1998); Lynn Margulis et al., "Foreword," in Vernadsky, *The Biosphere*, 15.

123. V. L. Komarov, "Marx and Engels on Biology" in before Bukharin et al., *Marxism and Modern Thought* (New York: Harcourt, Brace, 1935), 230–32; Y. M. Uranovsky in ibid., 147. Uranovsky was one of the first scientists to be arrested, in 1936, in the Stalinist purges. Accompanying Bukharin as a member of the Soviet delegation to the Second International Conference of the History of Science and Technology, London, 1931, was also the brilliant plant geneti-

cist N. I. Vavilov (one of the greatest figures in the history of ecological science), founder and first president of the Lenin Agricultural Academy, who applied a materialist method to the question of the origins of agriculture with the support of early Soviet science. Like Bukharin and Uranovsky, he fell prey to the Stalinist purges. Roy Medvedev, *Let History Judge* (New York: Columbia University Press, 1989), 441; N. I. Vavilov, "The Problem of the Origin of the World's Agriculture in the Light of the Latest Investigations," in Bukharin et al., *Science at the Crossroads*, 95–106.

124. Murray Feshbach and Arthur Friendly, Jr., *Ecocide in the U.S.S.R.* (New York: Basic Books, 1992); D. J. Peterson, *Troubled Lands* (Boulder, Colorado: Westview, 1993).

125. Douglas Weiner, *Models of Nature* (Bloomington: Indiana University Press, 1988), 4, 22–28, 259; and "The Changing Face of Soviet Conservation," in Donald Worster, ed., *The Ends of the Earth* (New York: Cambridge University Press, 1988), 254–56; Kendall Bailes, *Science and Russian Culture in an Age of Revolutions* (Bloomington: Indiana University Press, 1990), 127, 151–58.

126. Max Horkheimer and Theodor Adorno, *The Dialectic of Enlightenment* (New York: Continuum, 1972).

127. Schmidt, *The Concept of Nature in Marx*; Leiss, *The Domination of Nature*.

128. Perelman, "Marx and Resources," *Environment, Technology, and Society* 51 (Winter 1988): 15–19; Hayward, *Ecological Thought*; Foster, "The Crisis of the Earth"; Fischer-Kowalski, "Society's Metabolism."

129. Mayumi, "Temporary Emancipation from the Land"; Fred Magdoff, Les Lanyon, and Bill Liebhardt, "Nutrient Cycling, Transformations, and Flows," *Advances in Agronomy* 60 (1997): 1–73; Gary Gardner, *Recycling Organic Wastes* (Washington, D.C.: Worldwatch, 1997).

130. Peter Dickens, *Society and Nature* (Philadelphia: Temple University Press, 1992).

131. Martinez-Alier, *Ecological Economics*, 183–92.

132. Émile Durkheim and Marcel Mauss, *Primitive Classification* (Chicago; University of Chicago Press, 1963), 81–88; Émile Durkheim, *The Division of Labor in Society* (New York: Free Press, 1984), 208–209; *Pragmatism and Sociology* (Cambridge: Cambridge University Press, 1983), 21–27, 69–70.

133. Durkheim, *Pragmatism and Sociology*, 69–70.

134. Catton and Dunlap, "Environmental Sociology," 42–43.

135. Ibid., 45.

136. Eckersley, *Environmentalism and Political Theory*, 75–95.

137. Murphy, *Sociology and Nature*, 10.

138. Marx, *Capital*, vol. 1, 92.

139. See Magdoff et al., "Nutrient Cycling, Transformations and Flows"; Mayumi, "Temporary Emancipation from the Land"; Gardner, *Recycling Organic Wastes*.

140. Wolman, "The Metabolism of Cities"; Giradet, "Sustainable Cities"; Fischer-Kowalski, "Societies Metabolism"; J. B. Opschoor, "Industrial Metabolism, Economic Growth, and Institutional Change," in Redclift and Woodgate,

International Handbook of Environmental Sociology, 274–86.

141. Max Weber, *The Protestant Ethic and the Spirit of Capitalism* (London; Unwin Hyman, 1930), 181-82.

142. Dunlap, "The Evolution of Environmental Sociology," 34.

143. Ibid., 31–32, 35; Peter Dickens, *Reconstructing Nature* (New York: Routledge, 1996), 71.

CHAPTER TEN: CAPITALISM AND ECOLOGY:
THE NATURE OF THE CONTRADICTION

This chapter was adapted and revised for this book from an article by the same title that appeared in *Monthly Review* 54, no. 4 (September 2002): 6–16. It was based on a talk presented to the Socialism 2002 conference in Chicago on June 15, 2002.

1. See chapter 9 and John Bellamy Foster, *Marx's Ecology* (New York: Monthly Review Press, 2000), 141–77.

2. Karl Marx and Frederick Engels, *Collected Works*, vol. 3 (New York: International Publishers, 1975), 172; Thomas Müntzer, *Collected Works* (Edinburgh: T & T Clark, 1988), 335. See also Frederick Engels, *The Peasant War in Germany* (New York: International Publishers, 1926), 68.

3. Alan Rudy, "Marx's Ecology and Rift Analysis," *Capitalism, Nature, Socialism* 12 (June 2001): 61; James O'Connor, *Natural Causes* (New York: Guilford Press, 1998), 160, 165, 173. In the context in which he makes the statement quoted above, Rudy attributes the very same criticism of Marx for failing to integrate the metabolic rift with his theory of capitalist economic crisis, to me. My outlook, however, is different, as this chapter should make clear.

4. Kovel, *The Enemy of Nature* (London: Zed Press, 2002), 39–40.

5. Alan Rudy, contribution to "Marx's Ecology or Ecological Marxism," *Capitalism, Nature, Socialism* 12 (September 2001): 143.

6. See Elmar Altvater, "Ecological and Economic Modalities of Time and Space," in Martin O'Connor, ed., *Is Sustainable Capitalism Possible?* (New York: Guilford Press, 1994), 88–89.

7. The closest thing to a cyclical theory in this regard is Karl Polanyi's theory of the "double movement," which refers to a political cycle of regulation-deregulation associated with capitalism's attempt to regulate its "fictitious commodities" (conditions of production). The double movement, however, plays no role in the "second contradiction" theory.

8. U.S. Environmental Protection Agency, *Climate Protection Report, 2002*, http://www.gcrio.org/CAR2002/.

9. Karl Marx, *Theories of Surplus Value,* part 3 (Moscow: Progress Publishers, 1971), 368.

10. Kovel, *The Enemy of Nature*, 218. For criticisms of the "second contradiction" thesis that are similar to the ones offered in this chapter see Paul Burkett, "Fusing Red and Green," *Monthly Review* 50 (February 1999): 47–56 and his *Marx and Nature* (New York: St. Martin's Press, 1999), 193–97.

11.   It would, of course, be wrong to say that Marx never dealt with ecological costs as a possible source of economic crisis under capitalism. For example, his treatment of the tendency of the rate of profit to fall viewed rising raw material costs as a potential factor in a general crisis of profitability. See Michael Lebowitz, "The General and Specific in Marx's Theory of Crisis," *Studies in Political Economy*, no. 7 (Winter 1982): 9–13.

12.   Rosa Luxemburg, *Letters* (Atlantic Highlands, N.J.: Humanities Press, 1993), 202–03 (Luxemburg to Sonja Liebknecht, May 2, 1917).

13.   Stephen Jay Gould, *The Structure of Evolutionary Theory* (Cambridge, Massachusetts: Harvard University Press, 2002), 1018.

CHAPTER ELEVEN: *THE COMMUNIST MANIFESTO* AND THE ENVIRONMENT

This chapter is adapted and revised for this book from an article with the same title that first appeared in Leo Panitch and Colin Leys, eds., *The Socialist Register, 1998* (New York: Monthly Review Press, 1998), 169–89.

1.   The first of these three positions can be seen in the interpretations of such thinkers as Victor Ferkiss and John Clark; the second in the work of Anthony Giddens, Ted Benton, Kate Soper, Robyn Eckersley, Murray Bookchin, and David Goldblatt (the reference to "illuminating asides" can be found in Goldblatt's book *Social Theory and the Environment* [Boulder, CO: Westview], 1961, 5); the third in the writings of Elmar Altvater, Paul Burkett, Michael Perelman, Michael Lebowitz, David Harvey, and the present author. For more specific references see the discussion in this chapter below and chapter 9.

2.   Frederick Engels, "Outlines of a Critique of Political Economy," in Karl Marx, *Economic and Philosophical Manuscripts of 1844* (New York: International Publishers, 1964), 210.

3.   Karl Marx, *Early Writings* (New York: Vintage, 1974), 328, 359–60.

4.   Karl Marx, *Capital*, vol. 1 (New York: Vintage, 1976), 638.

5.   William Leiss, *The Domination of Nature* (Boston: Beacon Press, 1975), 85, 198.

6.   Karl Marx, "Feelings," in Karl Marx and Friedrich Engels, *Collected Works*, vol. 1 (New York: International Publishers, 1975), 525.

7.   John Clark, "Marx's Inorganic Body," *Environmental Ethics* 11, no. 3 (Fall 1989): 258. For a reply to Clark's suggestion that in referring to "inorganic body" rather than organic body Marx was somehow being anti-ecological see John Bellamy Foster and Paul Burkett, "The Dialectic of Organic/Inorganic Relations: Marx and the Hegelian Philosophy of Nature," *Organization and Environment* 13, no. 4 (December 2000): 403–25.

8.   Frederick Engels, *Anti-Dühring* (New York: International Publishers, 1939), 309–310.

9.   Ted Benton, "Marxism and Natural Limits," *New Left Review*, no. 178 (November–December 1989): 75. For other green criticisms of Marx and Engels in this respect see Robyn Eckersley, *Environmentalism and Political*

Theory (Albany: State University of New York Press, 1992), 80–81; and Murray Bookchin, *Toward an Ecological Society* (Montreal: Black Rose Books, 1980), 204–206.

10. Frederick Engels, *Dialectics of Nature* (New York: International Publishers, 1940), 293 (emphasis added).

11. Karl Marx, *Capital*, vol. 3 (New York: Vintage, 1981), 959.

12. Paul Burkett, "Nature in Marx Reconsidered," *Organization &Environment* 10, no. 2 (June 1997): 172.

13. Engels, *Dialectics of Nature*, 291–92; and *The Housing Question* (Moscow: Progress Publishers, 1975), 92.

14. See René Dubos, *The Wooing of the Earth* (New York: Charles Scribner's Sons, 1980); David Harvey, "The Nature of Environment," in Ralph Miliband and Leo Panitch, eds., *The Socialist Register, 1993* (New York: Monthly Review Press, 1993), 26; Richard B. Norgaard, *Development Betrayed* (New York: Routledge, 1994). For an example of the dualistic approach to environmental problems focusing on the " anthropocentric" vs. "ecocentric" distinction and criticizing Marx and Engels for belonging allegedly to the former camp see Robyn Eckersley, *Environmentalism and Political Theory* (Albany: State University of New York Press, 1992).

15. Victor Ferkiss, *Nature, Technology, and Society* (New York: New York University Press, 1993); Gary Snyder, "Nature as Seen from Kitkitdizze is No 'Social Construction,'" *Wild Earth* 6, no. 4 (Winter 1996/97): 8.

16. Marx and Engels, *The Communist Manifesto* (New York: Monthly Review Press, 1964), 9. Unless otherwise indicated, all further references to *The Communist Manifesto* in this chapter are to the 1998 Monthly Review Press edition.

17. Hal Draper, *The Adventures of the Communist Manifesto* (Berkeley: Center for Socialist History, 1998), 117, 211; Karl Marx and Frederick Engels, *The Communist Manifesto* (Chicago: Haymarket Books, 2005), 46. See also Engels, *The Housing Question*, 92, where he refers to delivering the "rural population" from its "isolation and stupor."

18. Engels, *The Housing Question*, 92.

19. Marx, *Capital*, vol. 1, 636–39.

20. Karl Marx, *The Eighteenth Brumaire of Louis Bonaparte* (New York: International Publishers, 1963), 125. Cevennes, a mountainous region in France, was the site of a large uprising of Protestant peasants at the beginning of the eighteenth century. Teodor Shanin, ed., *Peasants and Peasant Societies* (New York: Blackwell, 1987), 336–37. On Marx and Engels's views of Thomas Müntzer see John Bellamy Foster, *Marx's Ecology* (New York: Monthly Review Press, 2000), 74; Frederick Engels, *The Peasant War in Germany* (New York: International Publishers, 1926), 68.

21. Engels, *Anti-Dühring*, 195–96.

22. Williams, *The Country and the City* (London: Hogarth Press, 1973), 37–38.

23. Marx, *Capital*, vol. 1; Karl Marx, *Capital*, vol. 2 (New York: Vintage, 1978), 322. In *Anti-Dühring* Engels too complained of how large landowners in

Scotland "robbed" the peasants of their common land and turned "arable land into sheep-runs and eventually even into mere tracts for deer hunting." Engels, *Anti-Dühring*, 196. Marx's approach to nature tended to emphasize the fact that much of what we call "nature" has been socially constructed. As he and Engels wrote in *The German Ideology*, in response to the abstract, ahistorical notion of nature propounded by Feuerbach: "[N]ature, the nature that preceded human history, is not by any means the nature in which Feuerbach lives, it is nature which today no longer exists anywhere (except perhaps on a few Australian coral islands of recent origin), and which, therefore, does not exist for Feuerbach either." Marx and Engels, *Collected Works*, vol. 5, 39–40.

24. Marx and Engels, *The Communist Manifesto*, 40.

25. The meaning given in Marx and Engels's day to the notion of the "improvement" of the soil was well expressed by the U.S. agriculturist (and later sanitary engineer) George Waring, in his *Elements of Agriculture*, in which he states: "From what has now been said of the character of the soil, it must be evident that, as we know the *causes* of fertility and barrenness, we may by the proper means improve the character of all soils which are not now in the highest state of fertility." Waring, *Elements of Agriculture* (New York: D. Appleton and Co., 1854), 88.

26. Karl Marx, "The Chartists," in Marx and Engels, *Collected Works*, vol. 11 (New York: International Publishers, 1979), 333.

27. Justus von Liebig, *Lectures on Modern Industry* (London: Walton and Mabery, 1859), 171–83, 220.

28. Marx, *Capital*, vol. 3, 950.

29. World Commission on Environment and Development, *Our Common Future* (New York: Oxford University Press, 1987), 43.

30. Marx, *Capital*, vol. 3, 754.

31. Marx, *Capital*, vol. 3, 948–49. The continuing relevance of the ecological analysis of the soil nutrient cycle and its relation to the development of capitalist industry can be seen today in the work of Kozo Mayumi, "Temporary Emancipation from Land," *Ecological Economics* 4, no. 1 (October 1991): 35–56. See also Fred Magdoff, Les Lanyon, and Bill Liebhardt, "Nutrient Cycling, Transformations and Flows: Implications for a More Sustainable Agriculture," *Advances in Agronomy* 60 (1997): 1–73.

32. Marx, *Capital*, vol. 3, 911.

33. Marx, *Capital*, vol. 3, 754, 963.

34. Anthony Giddens, *A Contemporary Critique of Historical Materialism* (Berkeley: University of California Press, 1981), 59–60.

35. Massimo Quaini, *Marxism and Geography* (Totowa, New Jersey: Barnes and Noble Books, 1982), 136.

36. See, for example, Kate Soper, "Greening Prometheus," in Ted Benton, ed., *Greening Marxism* (New York: Guilford, 1996), 81–99.

37. Marx and Engels, *The Communist Manifesto*, 10.

38. Ibid., 11.

39. Eckersley, *Environmentalism and Political Theory*, 80.

40. Karl Marx, "Speech at the Anniversary of *The People's Paper*," in Karl Marx and Friedrich Engels, *Collected Works*, vol. 14 (New York: International Publishers, 1980), 655–56.

41. Marx, *Capital*, vol. 1, 637.

42. Joseph A. Schumpeter, *Essays* (Cambridge, Massachusetts: Addison-Wesley Press, 1951), 293–94.

43. Karl Marx, *Grundrisse* (New York: Vintage, 1973), 409–10.

44. The reference to "general barriers" to capital is taken from Michael Lebowitz, who has demonstrated that Marx pointed to two kinds of barriers to capital leading to contradictions in capital accumulation and crises: general barriers common to production in general, and thus having to do with natural conditions, and more specific historical barriers immanent to capital itself. See Lebowitz, "The General and Specific in Marx's Theory of Crisis," *Studies in Political Economy* 7 (Winter 1982): 5–25.

45. Francis Bacon, *Novum Organum* (Chicago: Open Court, 1994), 43, 29.

46. On the shift from post-materialist to materialist ecology see Juan Martinez-Alier, "Political Ecology, Distributional Conflicts and Incommensurability," *New Left Review*, no. 211 (May-June 1995): 70–88.

47. The relation of sustainability to communism, as conceived in the work of Marx and Engels, can be seen in the young Engels's response to the Malthusian issue of overpopulation. "For even if Malthus were completely right, this transformation [i.e., social revolution] would have to be undertaken on the spot, for only this transformation and the education of the masses which it alone provides makes possible the moral restraint of the propagative instinct which Malthus himself presents as the most effective and easiest remedy for over-population." Engels, "Outlines of a Critique of Political Economy," in Marx, *Economic and Philosophic Manuscripts*, 221.

48. Eugene Pottier, "The International," in John Bowditch and Clement Ramsland, eds., *Voices of the Industrial Revolution* (Ann Arbor: University of Michigan Press, 1961), 187.

CHAPTER TWELVE: ECOLOGICAL IMPERIALISM:
THE CURSE OF CAPITALISM

This chapter is adapted and revised for this book from an article by the same title, coauthored with Brett Clark, that appeared in Leo Panitch and Colin Leys, eds., *The Socialist Register, 2004* (New York: Monthly Review Press, 2004), 186–201.

1. Alfred W. Crosby, *Ecological Imperialism: The Biological Expansion of Europe, 900-1900* (Cambridge: Cambridge University Press, 1986).

2. The importance of ecological materialism is highlighted in John Bellamy Foster, *Marx's Ecology: Materialism and Nature* (New York: Monthly Review Press, 2000).

3. For a detailed analysis of the relationship between material-ecological flows (usually expressed in terms of use-values) and value flows in Marx's analysis,

see Paul Burkett, *Marx and Nature* (New York: St. Martin's Press, 1999).

4.   Karl Marx, *Capital*, vol. 1 (New York: Vintage, 1976), 896; Malthus to Ricardo, August 17, 1817, in David Ricardo, *Works and Correspondence,* vol. 7, (Cambridge: Cambridge University Press, 1952), 175.

5.   Karl Marx, *Early Writings* (New York: Vintage, 1974), 318–19.

6.   For an elaboration of Liebig's argument and its influence on Marx see chapter 11,

7.   Based on these observations, Marx developed a view of the necessity of a sustainable relation between human beings and nature (going beyond the issue of the soil)—a relation that had to be governed by the principle of maintaining (or improving) the earth for the sake of future generations. See Karl Marx, *Capital*, vol. 1 (London: Penguin Books, 1976), 636–38; and vol. 3, 949–50 and 911.

8.   Marx, *Capital*, vol. 1, 915.

9.   Ibid., 914–30.

10.   Karl Marx, *The Poverty of Philosophy* (New York: International Publishers, 1963), 223.

11.   Eduardo Galeano, *Open Veins of Latin America* (New York: Monthly Review Press, 1973), 72–73.

12.   Jason W. Moore, "Environmental Crises and the Metabolic Rift in World-Historical Perspective," *Organization & Environment*, 13, no. 2 (2000): 124.

13.   Galeano, *Open Veins of Latin America*, 191–92.

14.   Bruce W. Farcau, *The Ten Cents War: Chile, Peru and Bolivia in the War of the Pacific, 1879–1884* (Westport, Connecticut: Praeger, 2000), 8–10; William Jefferson Dennis, *Tacna and Arica* (New Haven: Yale University Press, 1931), 27, 34–37.

15.   Farcau, *The Ten Cents War*, 10.

16.   See Dennis, *Tacna and Arica*; Farcau, *The Ten Cents War;* John Mayo, *British Merchants and Chilean Development, 1851–1886* (Boulder: Westview Press, 1987), 157–87; William F. Sater, *Chile and the War of the Pacific* (Lincoln: University of Nebraska Press, 1986); Dr. I. Alzamora (former Vice President of Peru), *Peru and Chile* (pamphlet [publisher unknown], no date [around 1908]); Harold Blakemore, *British Nitrates and Chilean Politics, 1886–1896: Balmaceda and North* (London: University of London, 1974), 14–22; Michael Montéon, *Chile in the Nitrate Era* (Madison, Wisconsin: University of Wisconsin Press, 1982), 19–20, 27; Henry Clay Evans, *Chile and Its Relations with the United States* (Durham, North Carolina: Duke University Press, 1927), 97–119.

17.   John Mayo, *British Merchants and Chilean Development*, 181.

18.   United States House of Representatives, 47th Congress, 1st Session, House Reports, report no. 1790, *Chili-Peru*, 217–18. See also Perry Belmont, *An American Democrat* (New York: Columbia University Press, 1941), 255–62. Blaine's claims regarding the clandestine role of Britain in fomenting the War of the Pacific have been denied by Victor Kiernan, who, based on a careful perusal of British Foreign Office records, delivered a verdict of "not guilty." Kiernan's argument, however, rested on the contrary claim that no actual smoking-gun evidence had been located proving that the British Foreign Office had directly

instigated the war. The support of British investors and the British government for Chile in the war itself is not in doubt, nor is the division of the loot during and after the war (so strongly emphasized by Blaine). Kiernan also indicates that the British influence was exercised more directly from Valparaiso and Santiago, rather than directly from the Foreign Office in London. The one factual point in Kiernan's argument that is most doubtful is his insistence that there were no restrictions on the Peruvian purchase of British armaments. Representatives of both the Chilean and American governments claimed otherwise. See V. G. Kiernan, "Foreign Interests in the War of the Pacific," *Hispanic American Historical Review* 35, no. 1(1955): 14–36.

19. José Carlos Mariátegui, *Seven Interpretive Essays on Peruvian Reality* (Austin: University of Texas Press, 1971), 9–13; Paul Gootenberg, *Imagining Development: Economic Ideas in Peru's "Fictitious Prosperity" of Guano, 1840–1880* (Berkeley: University of California Press, 1993), 183–84.

20. Farcau, *The Ten Cents War*, 14.

21. Galeano, *Open Veins of Latin America*, 157–58; Blakemore, *British Nitrates and Chilean Politics*; Andre Gunder Frank, The Development of Underdevelopment in Latin America (New York: Monthly Review Press, 1969), 73–93; Evans, *Chile and its Relations with the United States*; Montéon, *Chile in the Nitrate Era*; J. R. McNeill, *Something New Under the Sun* (New York: W. W. Norton, 2000), 24–25. During the events leading up to the civil war in Chile, U.S. foreign policy, headed by Blaine, who was again secretary of state, was sympathetic toward Balmaceda, whose nationalism was seen as a curb on British power.

22. See John Bellamy Foster and Fred Magdoff, "Liebig, Marx, and the Depletion of Soil Fertility: Relevance for Today's Agriculture," in Fred Magdoff, John Bellamy Foster and Frederick H. Buttel, eds., *Hungry for Profit* (New York: Monthly Review Press, 2000), 54; National Public Radio, "The Tragedy of Fritz Haber," July 11, 2002, www.npr.org/programs/morning/features/2002/jul/fritzhaber/.

23. Michael Perelman, "Myths of the Market: Economics and the Environment," *Organization & Environment* 16, no. 2 (2003): 199–202.

24. Acción Ecológica, "Ecological Debt: South Tells North 'Time to Pay Up,'" www.cosmovisiones.com/DeudaEcologica/a_timetopay.html.

25. Aurora Donoso, "Who Owes Who?: Collecting the Ecological Debt," http://www.foe.org.au/resources/publications/cams-stuff/international-solidarity/external-debt-ecological-debt-who-owes-who.

26. Acción Ecológica, "No More Plunder, They Owe Us the Ecological Debt!," www.cosmovisiones.com/ DeudaEcologica/a_averde78in.html.

27. Georg Borgstrom, *The Hungry Planet* (New York: The Macmillan Company, 1965); Mathis Wackernagel and William Rees, *Our Ecological Footprint* (Gabriola Island, B. C.: New Society, 1996); Richard York, Eugene A. Rosa and Thomas Dietz, "Footprints on the Earth," *American Sociological Review* 68 (April 2003): 279–300.

28. Donoso, "Who Owes Who?"

29.   Aurora Donoso, "No More Looting!: Third World Owed an Ecological Debt,"
      www.cosmovisiones.com/DeudaEcologica/a_looting.html. The increase is
      measured in terms of volume not price because of the tendency of the prices of
      goods from the South to decline.

30.   Paul A. Baran and Paul Sweezy, *Monopoly Capital: An Essay on the American
      Economic and Social Order* (New York: Monthly Review Press, 1966).

31.   Donald Worster, "Transformations of the Earth: Toward an Agroecological
      Perspective in History," *The Journal of American History* 76, no. 4 (1990):
      1087–1106.

32.   Josué de Castro, *The Geography of Hunger* (Boston: Little, Brown and
      Company, 1952), 7, 212.

33.   For a discussion of the commons and struggles to maintain environmental
      space free from capitalist intrusion see The Ecologist, *Whose Common Future?
      Reclaiming the Commons* (Philadelphia: New Society Publishers, 1993).

34.   Andrew Simms, Aubrey Meyer, and Nick Robins, *Who Owes Who? Climate
      Change, Debt, Equity and Survival*, www.jubilee2000uk.org/ecological_debt/
      Reports/Who_owes_who.htm.

35.   John Bellamy Foster, *Ecology Against Capitalism* (New York: Monthly Review
      Press, 2002), 21, 64.

36.   Acción Ecológica, "Trade, Climate Change and the Ecological Debt,"
      www.cosmovisiones.com/DeudaEcologica/a_averdetrade.html; Anil Agarwal
      and Sunita Narain, *Global Warming in an Unequal World: A Case of
      Environmental Colonialism* (New Delhi: Centre for Science and Environment,
      1991). While efficiencies vary between nations, the poorest nations are the
      most efficient users of energy in terms of GDP. See Simms, Meyer, and Robins,
      Who Owes Who? and Tom Athanasiou and Paul Baer, *Dead Heat: Global
      Justice and Global Warming* (New York: Seven Stories Press, 2002).

37.   Simms, Meyer, and Robins, *Who Owes Who?*

38.   See Marten Scheffer, Steve Carpenter, Jonathan A. Foley et al., "Catastrophic
      Shifts in Ecosystems," *Nature* 403 (2001): 591–596; Roldan Muradian,
      "Ecological Thresholds: A Survey," *Ecological Economics* 38 (2001): 7–24.

39.   A relationship has been established such that $3,000 of GDP produces on aver-
      age a ton of carbon emissions. See Simms, Meyer, and Robins, *Who Owes
      Who?*; Acción Ecológica, "Trade, Climate Change and the Ecological Debt."

40.   Athanasiou and Baer, *Dead Heat*, 84. Also see Andrew Simms, *An
      Environmental War Economy: The Lessons of Ecological Debt and Global
      Warming* (London: New Economics Foundation, 2001); Acción Ecológica,
      "Ecological Debt."

41.   Acción Ecológica, "No More Plunder."

42.   http://web.archive.org/web/20060127223742/http://www.globalclimate.org//

CHAPTER 13: ENVISIONING ECOLOGICAL REVOLUTION

This chapter has been revised and adapted for this book from an article originally published under the title "Organizing Ecological Revolution," in *Monthly
Review* 57, no. 5 (October 2005): 1–10. It was based on an address delivered

to the Critical Management Studies section of the Academy of Management, Honolulu, Hawaii, August 8, 2005.

1. Paul M. Sweezy, "Capitalism and the Environment," *Monthly Review* 41, no. 2 (June 1989), 4.

2. International Climate Change Task Force, *Meeting the Climate Challenge*, January 2005, http://www.americanprogress.org.

3. *The Times* (London), January 27, 2005.

4. See chapter 4.

5. Bill McKibben, "Our Thirsty Future," *New York Review of Books*, September 25, 2003.

6. Worldwatch, *Vital Signs 2005*, www.worldwatch.org; Brett Clark and Rebecca Clausen, "The Oceanic Crisis," *Monthly Review* 60, no. 3 (July-August 2008): 91, 94–97.

7. Stuart L. Pimm and Clinton Jenkins, "Sustaining the Variety of Life," *Scientific American*, September 2005, 66–73; Stuart L. Pimm and Peter Raven, "Extinction by Numbers," *Nature*, February 24, 2000, 843–45.

8. Mathis Wackernagel et al., "Tracking the Ecological Overshoot of the Human Economy," *Proceedings of the National Academy of Sciences* 99, no. 14 (July 9, 2002): 9268.

9. Jared Diamond, *Collapse* (New York: Viking, 2005),10. Paul Raskin, Tariq Banuri, Gilberto Gallopín et al., *Great Transition: The Promise and Lure of the Times Ahead* (Boston: Stockholm Environment Institute, 2002), http://www.gsg.org.

10. Raskin et al., *The Great Transition*, 17–18.

12. Raskin et al., *Great Transition*, 7.

13. Karl Marx, *Capital*, vol. 1 (New York: Vintage, 1976), 247–57; Paul M. Sweezy, *Four Lectures on Marxism* (New York: Monthly Review Press, 1981), 26–36. Much of Marx's analysis in *Capital* is concerned with where $\triangle$m or surplus-value comes from. To answer this question, he argues, it is necessary to go beneath the process of exchange and to explore the hidden recesses of capitalist production—where it is revealed that the source of surplus-value is to be found in the process of class exploitation.

14. Lester Brown, *Outgrowing the Earth* (New York: W. W. Norton, 2004).

15. Raskin et al., *Great Transition*, 22.

16. See chapter 6.

17. Raskin et al., *Great Transition*, 22–24, 29.

18. Ibid., 33.

19. Ibid., 41, 77.

20. Ibid., 25.

21. Ibid., 27.

22. See chapter 5.

23. John Bellamy Foster, *Naked Imperialism* (New York: Monthly Review Press, 2006), 147–60.

24. Raskin et al., *Great Transition*, 47.

25. Ibid., 71–90.

26. To be sure, Mill at this time thought of himself as something of a socialist. See John Stuart Mill, *Principles of Political Economy* (New York: Longmans, Green, and Co., 1904), 452–55.

27. See Bertell Ollman's discussion in "The Utopian Vision of the Future (Then and Now)," *Monthly Review* 57, no. 3 (July-August 2005): 78–102.

28. Epicurus, *The Extant Remains*, translated by Cyril Bailey (New York: Limited Editions Club, 1947), 161. On Marx's relation to Epicurus see John Bellamy Foster, *Marx's Ecology* (New York: Monthly Review Press, 2000).

29. Marx and Engels, *Collected* Works, vol. 24 (New York: International Publishers, 1975), 519; Paul Burkett, "Marx's Vision of Sustainable Human Development" in *Monthly Review* 57, no. 5 (October 2005): 34–62.

30. Roy Morrison, *Ecological Democracy* (Boston: South End Press, 1995), 80, 188.

CHAPTER 14: ECOLOGY AND THE TRANSITION FROM CAPITALISM TO SOCIALISM

This concluding chapter is adapted and revised from an article by the same title that appeared in *Monthly Review* 60, no. 6 (November 2008): 1–12. It was based on an address delivered at the "Climate Change, Social Change" conference, Sydney, Australia, April 12, 2008, organized by *Green Left Weekly*.

1. Karl Marx, *Capital*, vol. 3 (New York: Vintage, 1981), 959.

2. Karl Marx, *Capital*, vol. 1 (New York: Vintage, 1976), 636–39; *Capital*, vol. 3, 754, 911, 948–49.

3. Karl Marx, *Early Writings* (New York: Vintage, 1974), 328. Documentation of Marx and Engels's ecological concerns listed above can be found in the following works: Paul Burkett, *Marx and Nature* (New York: St. Martin's Press, 1999); John Bellamy Foster, *Marx's Ecology* (New York: Monthly Review Press, 2000); and Paul Burkett and John Bellamy Foster, "Metabolism, Energy, and Entropy in Marx's Critique of Political Economy," *Theory & Society* 35 (2006): 109–56. On the problem of local climate change as it was raised by Engels and Marx in their time (speculations on temperature changes due to deforestation) see Engels's notes on Fraas in Marx and Engels, *MEGA* IV, 31 (Amsterdam: Akadamie Verlag, 1999), 512–15.

4. Marx, *Capital*, vol. 3, 911.

5. On the ecological insights of socialists after Marx see Foster, *Marx's Ecology*, 236–54. On early Soviet ecology see also Douglas R. Weiner, *Models of Nature* (Bloomington: Indiana University Press, 1988). On Podolinsky see John Bellamy Foster and Paul Burkett, "Ecological Economics and Classical Marxism," *Organization & Environment* 17, no. 1 (March 2004): 32–60.

6. Karl Marx, *Grundrisse* (London: Penguin, 1973), 471–79; and *Capital*, vol. 1, 915.

7. On precarious work see Fatma Ülkü Selçuk, "Dressing the Wound," *Monthly Review* 57, no. 1 (May 2005): 37–44.

8. Joseph Needham, *Moulds of Understanding* (London: George Allen and Unwin, 1976), 301.

9. Branko Milanovic, *Worlds Apart* (Princeton: Princeton University Press, 2005); John Bellamy Foster, "The Imperialist World System," *Monthly Review* 59, no. 1 (May 2007): 1–16.

10. Hannah Arendt, *The Human Condition* (Chicago: University of Chicago Press, 1958), 248–73; Karl Marx and Frederick Engels, *Collected Works*, vol. 1 (New York: International Publishers, 1975), 224–63.

11. Michael R. Raupach et al., "Global and Regional Drivers of Accelerating CO_2 Emissions," *Proceedings of the National Academy of Sciences* 104, no. 24 (June 12, 2007): 10288–10289; Associated Press, "Global Warming: It's the Humidity," October 10, 2007.

12. See Paul Burkett's "Marx's Vision of Sustainable Human Development," *Monthly Review* 57, no. 5 (October 2005): 34–62.

13. Ernesto "Che" Guevara, "Man and Socialism in Cuba," http://www.marxists.org/archive/guevara/1965/03/man-socialism-alt.htm. Che was referring to bourgeois criticisms of socialist transition, but it was clear that he saw this problem as an actual contradiction of early socialist experiments that had to be transcended. See also Michael Löwy, *The Marxism of Che Guevara* (New York: Monthly Review Press, 1973), 59–73.

14. Rodríguez quoted in Richard Gott, *In the Shadow of the Liberator* (London: Verso, 2000), 116; Simón Bolívar, "Message to the Congress of Bolivia," May 25, 1826, *Selected Works*, vol. 2 (New York: The Colonial Press, 1951), 603.

15. Karl Marx, *The Poverty of Philosophy* (New York: International Publishers, 1963), 146; and *Early Writings* (New York: Vintage, 1974), 348, 353.

16. István Mészáros, *Socialism or Barbarism* (New York: Monthly Review Press, 2002), 23.

17. A powerful critique of biofuel production has been authored by Fidel Castro Ruiz in a series of reflections over the past years. See http://www.monthlyreview.org/castro/index.php.

18. See Paul M. Sweezy, "The Transition to Socialism," in Sweezy and Charles Bettelheim, *On the Transition to Socialism* (New York: Monthly Review Press, 1971), 112, 115; Michael Lebowitz, *Build It Now* (New York: Monthly Review Press, 2006), 13–14.

19. G. W. F. Hegel, *Introductory Lectures on Aesthetics* (London: Penguin, 1993), 51; Karl Marx, "Confessions," in Teodor Shanin, *Late Marx and the Russian Road: Marx and the Peripheries of Capitalism* (New York: Monthly Review Press, 1983), 140.

20. See Bill McKibben, *Hope, Human and Wild* (Minneapolis: Milkweed Editions, 1995); and *Deep Economy* (New York: Henry Holt, 2007).

21. Michael A. Lebowitz, "An Alternative Worth Struggling For," *Monthly Review* 60, no. 5 (October 2008): 20–21.

22. McKibben, *Deep Economy*, 73. See also Richard Levins, "How Cuba Is Going Ecological," in Richard Lewontin and Richard Levins, *Biology Under the Influence* (New York: Monthly Review Press, 2007), 343–64; Rebecca Clausen, "Healing the Rift: Metabolic Restoration in Cuban Agriculture," *Monthly Review* 59, no. 1 (May 2007): 40–52; World Wildlife Fund, *Living*

Planet Report 2006, http://assets.panda.org/downloads/living_planet_report.pdf, 19; Peter M. Rosset, "Cuba: A Successful Case Study of Sustainable Agriculture," in Fred Magdoff, John Bellamy Foster, and Frederick H. Buttel, eds., *Hungry for Profit* (New York: Monthly Review Press, 1999), 203–14.

23. Levins, "How Cuba Is Going Ecological," in Lewontin and Levins, *Biology Under the Influence*, 367.

24. Lebowitz, *Build it Now*, 107–109. On the theory of communal exchange that influenced Chávez see István Mészáros, *Beyond Capital* (New York: Monthly Review Press, 1995), 758–60. On "socialist time accountancy" see Mészáros's *Crisis and Burden of Historical Time* (New York: Monthly Review Press, 2008).

25. David Raby, "The Greening of Venezuela," *Monthly Review* 56, no. 5 (November 2004): 49–52.

26. McKibben, *Hope*, 62, 154.

INDEX

Abrupt Climate Change Scenario and its Implications for United States National Security, An (Schwartz and Randall), 107, 113–116, 260

Acción Ecológica, 242–243

Afghanistan, 85, 91, 130

Africa, 102

Agarwal, Anil, 245–246

Agenda 21, 42, 130, 132

Agreement on Forest Principles, 132

agriculture, 49–50; British high farming, 237; *Communist Manifesto* on, 219–223; impact of climate change on, 113, 114, 254; Kautsky on, 189, 305n114; Lenin on, 189–190; Liebig on, 145–146; Marx on, 147, 163, 167, 175–176, 180–183, 187, 193, 210, 224–225; metabolic rift in, 236; pesticides used in, 68, 76–77, 82; second and third agricultural revolutions in, 169–171, 198–199; soil depletion and, 171–174

albedo flip, 56

alienation, 34; capitalism and, 268–271; Engels on, 217; Marx on, 32, 148–149, 197

Alley, Richard, 111

Al-Rodhan, Khalid R., 99

Anderson, James, 224

animals, agricultural, 82

anthropocentricism, 195–196, 218

anthropology, 162

antibiotics, 82

apartheid, 157

appropriation problem, 188–194

Arctic Ocean, 56

Arendt, Hannah, 269

Babeuf, François, 32

Baby Tooth Survey, 74

Bacon, Francis, 150, 185, 230

Bahro, Rudolf, 28

Baker Institute (James Baker III Institute for Public Policy), 88–89, 100–101

Balmaceda, José Manuel, 240–241, 313n21

Barbosa, Luiz C., 303–304n89

basic communism, 29, 30, 32

Bauer, Bruno, 160

Benton, Ted, 163, 217

Bergson, Henri, 157

Bethune, Norman, 71

bioaccumulation, 72–73

biocides (pesticides), 68

biofuels, 273

biogeography, 162

biological control, 68
biological magnification, 72–73
biosphere, 154, 305n122
Blaine, James G., 239–240, 312–313n18,
    313n21
Bloch, Ernst, 7
Bolivarian Alternative for the Americas
    (ALBA), 275
Bolivia, 239, 276
Bookchin, Murray (Lewis Herber), 76
Borgstrom, Georg, 243
Bourdieu, Pierre, 283n48
bourgeoisie, 224, 227, 268
Bowles, Samuel, 62
brain, human, 152, 187
Brando, Marlon, 39
Brecht, Bertolt, 7
Britain, see United Kingdom
Brodine, Virginia, 73
Brooks, Paul, 80
Brown, Lester R., 56, 99, 286n6
Brundtland Commission (World
    Commission on Environment and
    Development), 181, 225, 259
Bukharin, Nikolai, 154, 155, 190–191,
    305n122
Burkett, Paul, 9, 218
Burn! (film, Pontecorvo), 39–40, 51–53,
    283n1
Bush, George W., 43, 87, 89, 92, 99, 130
Bush administration (GWB), 90–92, 207,
    247–248
Business Council for Sustainable
    Development, 132
Buttel, Frederick, 163, 165

Cambridge Energy Research Associates, 96
Campbell, Colin J., 86, 88
cancers, 69
capital, 204, 230, 257–258, 311n44
capitalism, 184; accumulation under,
    62–63; alienation and, 268–271; antago-
    nistic to environment, 144; as business-
    as-usual, 46–47; climate change and,

117–119; Commoner on, 7; destructive
    uncontrollability in, 40–41; dynamism of
    production under, 229–230; ecological
    contradictions of, 231–232; ecological
    destruction under, 127; ecology and,
    201–212; ecology in transition to social-
    ism from, 265; globalization of, 133;
    Global Scenario Group on, 257–258;
    labor theory of value in, 184–185; Marx
    on material contradictions of, 32; meta-
    bolic rift in, 50, 236; Mumford on fail-
    ures of, 31; natural capitalism, 135; prim-
    itive accumulation in, 235; sustainability
    compatible with, 14–15, 19; Sweezy on,
    61; as unpaid costs, 23
carbon emissions (carbon and CO_2), 271;
    carbon debt, 245–246; concentration in
    atmosphere of, 108, 117, 133; increase in
    rate of, 26; IPCC report on, 116; neo-
    classical economists on, 23–25; Stern
    Review on, 57–60; see also climate
    change; global warming
Carey, Henry, 173–174
Carson, Rachel, 67–83, 105, 154, 192
Castro, Josué de, 244
Catton, William, 164, 194–195
Caudwell, Christopher, 155–156
Cavanagh, John, 136
Center for Strategic and International
    Studies (CSIS), 88, 99
cesium-137 (isotope), 72, 73
Cevennes (France), 222, 309n20
Cheney, Dick, 89
Chatterjee, Pratap, 132
Chávez, Hugo, 33, 100, 103, 104, 272, 275
chemicals: mutations caused by, 70; pesti-
    cides, 67–69, 75–76, 82
Chile, 239–241, 313n21
China, 104
Christian, David, 14
Clark, Brett, 8–9
Clark, John, 216–217
Clements, Frederick, 74, 157
climate change: abrupt, 109–114; accelerated,

116–117; Bush administration on, 207; capitalism and, 117–119; coal plants and, 21; economics of, 57–60; fossil fuels as cause of, 105; global warming in, 108–109; Intergovernmental Panel on Climate Change on, 42; neoclassical economists on, 23–25; Nordhaus and Shellenberger on, 18; Pentagon report on, 112–116; social effects of, 107; tipping point in, 56; *see also* global warming

Cline, William, 23

coal, 20–21, 122–127, 208, 258

Cobb, John, 32, 262

Cochet, Alexandre, 238

coevolution, 218–219; gene-culture coevolution, 152, 187

Colombia, 103

Committee for Environmental Information, 74

Commoner, Barry, 7, 72–74

communism, 217

Communist Manifesto, The (Marx and Engels), 213–219, 231–232; Prometheanism in, 226–229; on rural society and agriculture, 219–223; on sustainability, 223–226

conservation movement: in Soviet Union, 192

Contract with the Earth, A (Gingrich and Maple), 18

conventional (crude) oil, 94

Convention on Biological Diversity, 130–132

Cordesman, Anthony, 99

Council on Foreign Relations, 88–89, 100

Crosby, Alfred, 233–234

crude (conventional) oil, 94

CSIS, *see* Center for Strategic and International Studies

Cuba, 274–275

culture, 194

Daly, Herman, 31–32, 262

"dark green" environmentalism, 300n25

Darwin, Charles, 78, 150–151, 156; Durkheim on, 165, 193, 199; Marx and Engels on, 183, 186, 197, 304n101

debts, ecological, 242–247

"deep ecology," 300n25

Defense, U.S. Department of: on climate change, 107, 112–117, 120, 260

definitional problem, 194–196

deforestations, 182–183, 255

Deutch, John, 100

dialectical materialism, 197

Diamond, Jared, 120, 255

disaster capitalism, 139

Dunlap, Riley, 164, 194–195

Durkheim, Émile, 163, 165, 193–194, 199

Dyson, Freeman, 27

earth summits (1992 and 2002), 41–43, 259; Johannesburg (2002), 134–138; Rio (1992), 129–134

Easter Island, 119–120

Eckersley, Robyn, 228

Eco-communalism, 261, 264

eco-industrial revolution, 12

ecological debts, 242–247

ecological imperialism, 118–119, 233–235; debts and, 242–247; metabolic rift and, 235–238; opposition to, 247–249

ecological Marxism, 209

ecological materialism, 153–156

ecological moderation, 19

ecological revolutions, 28–32, 253–264, 282n41; green industrial revolution, 14–22; Merchant on, 11–12

ecological-social revolution, 263–264

ecological succession, 157

ecology: capitalism and, 201–212; Carson's, 67–69, 80–83; coined by Haeckel, 304n101; of Easter Island, 119–120; ecosystem ecology, 74–80; Marx on, 143–144, 266–268, 316n3; materialist thought in, 153–160; radiation and, 69–74; in transition from capitalism to socialism, 265

economics, 23; climate change and, 117–119; environmental concerns in, 162

ecosystem ecology, 74–80; materialism in, 156–160

Edwards, Richard, 62

EIA, *see* Energy Information Administration

Eldredge, Niles, 11

electricity: Friedman on, 17–18, 20

Elton, Charles, 75

energy: climate change tied to fossil fuels, 105, 293n43; Engels on misuse of, 182; Jevons Paradox in, 124–128; new energy regime, 289n1; from unconventional sources of oil, 93; U.S. policy objectives on, 99–104; *see also* oil

Energy, U.S. Department of, 89–90, 96–98

Energy Information Administration (EIA), 87, 291n25

Energy Watch Group (Germany), 96

Engels, Frederick, 144; on agricultural productivity, 170–172; *Communist Manifesto* by, 213–219, 231–232; on Darwin and evolution, 150–152, 183, 186–187, 304n101; dialectical materialism of, 197; on ecology, 126–127, 266, 316n3; on energy use, 182; on Malthus, 311n47; materialism of, 149, 153; on nature, 185–186, 188; on pollution, 180–181; on revenge of nature, 52; on rural society and agriculture, 219–223; on sustainability, 223–226; on technology, 227–228

England, *see* United Kingdom

entropy, law of, 20, 280n16

environment: *Communist Manifesto* and, 213–219; Marx on, 167–169; metabolism in relation of organisms to, 179; in scholarly disciplines, 162

environmentalism, 57, 139, 205, 274; "dark green" and "light green" perspectives in, 300n25; post-environmentalism and, 18

Environmental Protection Agency, 207

environmental sociology, 196–200; appropriation problem in, 188–194; based in Marx, 48–49; classical barriers to, 161–167; debate over Marx in, 167–169; definitional problem in, 194–196

Epicurus, 149–150, 156, 159, 263–264

ethanol fuel, 99

evolution: in Carson's ecology, 80; Darwin on, 150–151; Durkheim on, 193; ecosystem ecology and, 78; of humans, 186–187; Marx on, 152; *see also* Darwin, Charles

exterminism, 22–28

extinctions, 25, 285–286n3; global warming as cause of, 108–109; mass extinctions, 45; rate of, 255

Farcau, Bruce, 240

feminism, 205

Ferkiss, Victor, 219, 222

Fersman, E. A., 192

fertilizer, 171, 198; Kautsky on, 189; Lenin on, 189–190; nitrates in, 238–241; synthetic, 172, 202, 210

feudalism, 268

Feuerbach, Ludwig, 149, 309–310n23

Field, Christopher, 26

Finger, Matthias, 132

Fischer-Kowalski, Marina, 179, 180

fish stocks, 255

forests (trees; woods): Agreement on Forest Principles on, 132; deforestation of, 182–183, 255; on Easter Island, 120; Engels on, 127; genetically engineered, 27; Jevons on, 123; Marx on, 223; tropical, 207

France, 60

Frankfurt School, 153, 155, 192, 268

Friedman, Thomas, 16–18, 21, 139, 280n19; l, 20

Frosch, Robert, 26–27

Gaia hypothesis, 284n7

Galbraith, John Kenneth, 23, 80

Galeano, Eduardo, 237, 238

Galileo, 269

Gandhi, Mohandas, 157, 264

gasoline, *see* oil

gene-culture coevolution, 152, 187

General Agreement on Tariffs and Trade (GATT), 133

geoengineering, 26–27

geography, 162

Georgescu-Roegen, 165

Germany, 241

Giddens, Anthony, 167, 226–227

Gingrich, Newt, 16, 18

Global Climate Coalition, 247–248

global fair deal, 295–296n5

globalization, 17, 130, 133, 136, 282n41

Global Scenario Group, 63, 256–264

global warming, 14, 108–109, 245, 269, 271; albedo flip and, 56; Bush administration on, 207; as business-as-usual, 46; capitalism and, 117–119; curse of oil and, 242; Friedman on, 17; geoengineering solutions to, 26–27; Lovelock on, 44–45; neoclassical economists on, 23–25; tipping point in, 55, 285n2; warnings of, 254; *see also* climate change

Goldblatt, David, 163

Gould, Stephen Jay, 152, 187, 212

Government Accountability Office, U.S. (GEO), 98

Gramsci, Antonio, 155

Great Britain, *see* United Kingdom

Greater St. Louis Citizens Committee for Nuclear Information (CNI), 74

Greece, 270

green capitalism, 139

greenhouse effect, 108

greenhouse gases, 57–60, 108, 118; *see also* carbon emissions

green industrial revolution, 12, 14–22, 28–29, 279n3

Greenspan, Alan, 91–92

growth, 23, 125–126

guano, 49–50, 146, 171, 173, 210; Marx on, 177; nitrates in, 238–240

Guano Islands Act (U.S., 1903), 49

Guevera, Ernesto "Che," 271–272, 274, 317n13

Haber, Fritz, 241

Haeckel, Ernst, 152, 304n101

Haldane, J. B. S., 78, 154

Hanford (Washington), 72–73

Hansen, James: on carbon dioxide levels, 58, 59, 293n43; on coal, 21; on destabilization of ice sheets, 45; on extinctions, 25; on global warming, 41; on oil-based CO_2 emissions, 291n21; on tipping point, 56

Hawken, Paul, 135

Hayward, Tim, 178

Hegel, Georg Wilhelm Friedrich, 149, 150, 197

Heinberg, Richard, 94–95

Hirsch, Robert L., 97

historical materialism, 7

Hogben, Lancelot, 158

Holdren, John P., 27

holism, 157–160

Hubbert, M. King, 92

Hull, Edward, 123

human exemptionalist paradigm, 163, 194–195

humans: Bukharin on, 190–191; in classical sociology, 163; culture of, 194; evolution of, 151–152, 186–187; impact of climate change on, 107, 109, 111–116; in new environmental paradigm, 195; relation to nature of, Marx on, 51, 126–127, 143, 160, 168, 177, 301–302n55

Hume, David, 23

Hussein, Saddam, 89, 91

Huxley, Thomas Henry, 151, 156

Hyatt, Joe, 112

hydrogen bomb tests, 73

hydrological cycle, 116

IEA, *see* International Energy Agency

imperialism, 105, 211; in control over oil

supplies, 85–86; ecological imperialism, 118–119, 233–249; energy imperialism, 103–104; following September eleventh terrorist attacks, 130

India, 237

industrial metabolism, 179–180

industrial revolution, 12, 268–269, 279n3

information: profits from, 15

Intergovernmental Panel on Climate Change (IPCC), 113; on CO_2 emissions, 116, 271; creation of, 42; on global warming, 47, 245, 254; on thermohaline circulation, 110

International Energy Agency (IEA), 86, 94, 97–99

International Forum on Globalization, 136

International Monetary Fund (IMF), 136

iodine-131 (isotope), 72

Iran, 90, 100, 102

Iraq: invasion of, 130, 233; oil production in, 85, 89–92, 101

Iraq War, 91, 104, 233

Järvikoski, Timo, 165

Jenkins, Clinton, 255

Jennings, H. S., 70

Jevons, William Stanley, 121–128, 258

Jevons Paradox, 19, 124–128, 258

Jo'burg Memo, The (Sachs), 131, 134–136

Johannesburg (South Africa): earth summit at (2002), 41–43, 129–131, 134–138

Johnston, James F. W., 173, 226

Kant, Immanuel, 149

Kapp, K. William, 23

Kautsky, Karl, 154, 189, 305n114

Kazakhstan, 98, 102

Keynes, John Maynard, 22, 63, 123

Kharecha, Pushker, 291n21, 293n43

Kiernan, Victor, 312–313n18

Klare, Michael, 85, 90

Klein, Naomi, 139

Komrov, V. L., 191

Korsch, 155

Korten, David, 282n41

Kovel, Joel, 204, 209

Kunstler, James Howard, 102

Kurlantzick, Joshua, 104

Kyoto Protocol, 25; Global Scenario Group on, 259; U.S. failure to ratify, 42–43, 118, 130, 132, 233, 247–248

labor: alienation of, 197; in human evolution, 151, 152; Marx on, 32; metabolism and, 177

labor theory of value, 184–185

Laherrère, Jean H., 86, 88

Lankester, E. Ray, 74, 156–157

Lasalle, Ferdinand, 186

Latin America, 103; nitrates in, 238–241; socialism in, 272, 275–276

Lawes, J. B., 172, 300–301n34

law of restitution, 146

Lebowitz, Michael, 311n44

Leiss, William, 216

Lenin, V. I., 154, 189–192, 267

Leopold, Aldo, 32, 75

Levins, Richard, 275

Levy, Hyman, 158, 159, 288n10

Leyden, Peter, 112

Lichtheim, George, 143

Liebig, Justus von, 124, 224; on agriculture, 49, 236; Marx and, 145–149, 166, 175, 197, 266; on metabolism, 50, 179; second agricultural revolution and, 169, 300–301n34; on soil depletion, 171–174, 201–202, 224

life, origins of, 78–79

"light green" environmentalism, 300n25

Litvin, David, 104

Lovelock, James, 44–46, 52, 284n7

Lubbock, John, 151

Lucretius, 159, 185

Lukács, Georg, 152, 155

Lunacharskii, Anatolii Vasil'evich, 192

Luxemburg, Rosa, 154, 211–212

Lyell, Charles, 151

Lynas, Mark, 14, 25

Lysenko, Trofim Denisovich, 192, 297–298n29

Lysenkoism, 156, 297–298n29

Malthus, Thomas Robert, 149, 164, 235; Engels on, 311n47; Marx on, 169–170, 202; on nature, 184, 303–304n89

Mander, Jerry, 136

Maple, Terry, 18

Mariátegui, José Carlos, 240

Marshall, Alfred, 184

Marshall, Andrew, 112, 113, 115

Marshall Islands, 73

Martinez-Alier, Juan, 193

Marx, Eleanor, 156

Marx, Karl, 264; on agricultural economics, 163, 172; appropriation problem in, 188–194; on coal, 208; *Communist Manifesto* by, 213–219, 231–232; on Darwin and evolution, 150–152, 304n101; definitional problem in, 194–196; on ecological ruin, 28; on ecology, 144, 266–267, 316n3; on environment, 167–169; environmental sociology based on, 48–49, 165, 166, 196–200; general formula of capital of, 257–258; on humans' relation with nature, 51, 126–127, 143, 160; Lankester and, 74, 156; Liebig and, 147–148; on material contradictions of capitalism, 32; materialism of, 149–150, 153; on metabolic rift, 49–50, 201–203, 210, 236–238; on metabolism, 175–180, 301–302n55; on primitive accumulation, 235; on production for social needs, 33; Prometheanism of, 226–229; on revolutionary situations, 13–14; on revolutionizing production, 256; on rural society and agriculture, 219–223; on second agricultural revolution, 169–171; second contradiction of capitalism and, 203–206; on socialism, 272; on surplus value, 258, 313n13; on sustainability, 180–188, 223–226; on technology, 20; on utopian socialism, 282n43

Marxism, 33; ecological materialism in, 153–156; ecology and, 192–193, 266–268; sustainable human development in, 34

mass extinctions, 45

materialism, 149–150; ecological materialism, 153–156; in ecosystem ecology, 156–160

McCay, Mary, 78–79

McKibben, Bill, 44, 274–276

McLaughlin, Andrew, 183

Merchant, Carolyn, 11–12

Mészáros, István, 22, 41, 275, 283n48

metabolic restoration, 50, 52–53

metabolic rift: alienation of nature in, 197; ecological imperialism and, 235–238; Marx on, 32, 49–50, 126, 147–148, 175–180, 201–203, 210; second agricultural revolution and, 169–171

metabolism, 50, 177–179, 301–302n55

methane, 44

Mill, John Stuart, 29–30, 262, 282n43, 283n53, 315–316n26

Miller, Stanley, 78

Mol, Arthur P. J., 19

Montreal Protocol, 42

Moore, Jason, 237–238

Moore, Samuel, 219

Morales, Evo, 35, 276

Morgan, Lewis Henry, 151

Morris, William, 63–65, 144, 211, 264

Morrison, Roy, 29, 264

Morse, Edward L., 88

Mossadeq, Mohammed, 91

Muller, H. J., 70–72

multinational corporations, 132

Mumford, Lewis, 13, 28–32, 283n53

Müntzer, Thomas, 202, 222

Murphy, Raymond, 164–165

mutagens, 70

mutations, 70

Narain, Sunita, 245–246

natural capitalism, 135

nature, humans' relation with: absent from
    classical sociology, 163–166; Bacon on,
    230; Bukharin on, 190–191; as "free
    gift," 184–186; Jevons on, 126; Marx and
    Engels on, 51, 126–127, 143, 147, 160,
    168, 178, 187–188, 193, 197–198,
    215–218; in Marxist ecological material-
    ism, 153, 155; Marx on metabolism and,
    177, 301–302n55; in transition from
    capitalism to socialism, 265
Neanderthals, 151
Needleham, Joseph, 269
neoliberalism, 133–138
New Economy, 112–113, 130
new environmental paradigm, 194, 195
New Partnership for Africa's Development
    (NEPAD), 138
New Sustainability Paradigm, 261
nitrates, 238–241
Nordhaus, Ted, 18–19
Nordhaus, William, 23–25, 286n8
Nove, Alec, 168, 183
nuclear power, 20, 45, 280n19
nuclear weapons, 69, 71–73, 273
Nunn, Sam, 88

Obama, Barack, 21
O'Connor, James, 203–205, 208–210
Odum, Eugene, 73, 179
oil: ecological imperialism and, 241–242;
    geopolitics of production of, 86–92;
    imperialism in control of supply of,
    85–86; increases in price of, 208; Iraq
    War over, 233; in new energy regime,
    289n1; peaks in production of, 92–99,
    105, 254, 291n19; U.S. policy objectives
    on production of, 99–104
Oliver, Francis Wall, 157
Oparin, Alexander I., 78, 154, 267
Ostwald, Wilhelm, 165, 193
overpopulation, see population
Owen, Robert, 282n43

paperless office, myth of, 15

Pascual, Carlos, 103
Pauling, Linus, 72
peak oil, 92–99, 105, 208, 254, 291n19
peasantry, 219–223, 235
Pentagon, see Defense, U.S. Department of
Perelman, Michael, 242
Persian Gulf, 100; oil production in, 85,
    88, 90, 92
Peru, 238–240
pesticides, 67–69, 75–78, 82
Pesticides and a Living Landscape (Rudd), 77
petroleum, see oil
petro-socialism, 274
Petty, William, 185
Philips, Kevin, 289n1, 291n24
Phillips, John, 158
Pickens, T. Boone, 96
Pigou, A. C., 162
Podolinsky, Sergei, 267
Polanyi, Karl, 204, 307n7
political science, 162
pollution, 180–181
Pontecorvo, Gillo, 39–40, 52–53, 283n1
population: Engels on, 311n47; Friedman
    on, 17; Malthus on, 170; Marx on, 202;
    Mumford on, 31
possessive individualism, 279–280n4
primitive accumulation, 235, 236
Primm, Stephen, 255
private property, 148, 226
profits: sustainable economics and, 14–15
proletarianized peasantry, 235, 269
Prometheanism, 143, 167, 192, 214,
    226–229
property, Marx on, 51, 226; communal,
    225–226
Proudhon, Pierre-Joseph, 144

Quaini, Massimo, 188–189, 226–227

racism, 157–158
radiation, 69–74
Randall, Doug, 112–115, 117
Redclift, Michael, 167–168, 188

Ricardo, David, 169–170, 184
Rio de Janeiro (Brazil), earth summit at
  (1992), 41, 42, 129–134
Rodriguez, Carlos Rafael, 275
Rodríguez, Simón, 272
Royal Agricultural Society of England, 172
Rudd, Robert, 75–78, 81
Rudy, Alan, 203, 205, 307n3
Rumsfield, Donald, 91
Running, Steve, 21
rural society: *Communist Manifesto* on,
  219–223; *see also* agriculture
Russian agricultural communes, 182

Sachs, Wolfgang, 131
Saint-Simon, Claude-Henri de Rouvroy,
  282n43
Samuelson, Paul, 62
Saudi Arabia, 87, 90, 91, 97–99, 101–102
Schlesinger, James R., 88, 100
Schmidheiny, Stephan, 132
Schmidt, Alfred, 153
Schneider, Stephen H., 24–27
Schumpeter, Joseph, 40, 229
Schwartz, Peter, 112–115, 117, 294n10
science, 22, 215, 227, 268
Sea Around Us, The (Carson), 73, 78
second agricultural revolution, 169–172,
  198, 300–301n34
second contradiction of capitalism, 48,
  203–206, 209–210
September eleventh terrorist attacks, 91, 130
"shallow ecology," 300n25
Shellenberger, Michael, 18–19
Shelley, Percy Bysshe, 31
Silent Spring (Carson), 67–72, 75, 80, 81
Simmons, Matthew R., 86–88, 96–99, 103
Simms, Andrew, 246
Smith, Adam, 33
Smuts, Jan Christian, 74, 157–158
Snyder, Gary, 219
social Darwinists, 186, 304n101
social-ecological metabolism, 177–179
social ecology, 230–231

socialism, 33–34; ecology in transition
  from capitalism to, 265; J.S. Mill and,
  29–30, 282n43, 315–316n26; Speth's
  rejection of, 63; sustainability and,
  183–184, 271–277
social movements, 205, 209
social sciences, 162
sociology, 161–167; *see also* environmental
  sociology
soil fertility, 170–171; Liebig on, 236;
  Marx on exploitation of, 224; soil depletion and, 171–174, 202
solar power, 20
Solow, Robert, 26
South Africa, 131, 138, 139, 157–158
Soviet Union, 33–34, 272, 283n52; agriculture in, 199; ecology in, 154–155,
  267; environmentalism in, 191–192;
  Lysenkoism in, 297–298n29; Muller in,
  71; rejection of Marx's ecological analysis in, 189
Speth, James Gustave, 61–63
Stalin, Josef, 71
Stalinism, 155, 192, 267, 305–306n123
stationary state, 29–30, 283n53
Stern, Nicholas, 23, 57
*Stern Review, The (The Economics of
  Climate Change,* Stern), 57–60, 286n8
Strategic Energy Initiative (CSIS), 88
*Strategic Energy Policy Challenges for the
  21st Century* (Council on Foreign
  Relations), 88–89
strong sustainability hypothesis, 26
strontium-90 (isotope), 72–74
Summers, Lawrence, 23
Sumner, William G., 164
surplus value, 258, 313n13
sustainability, 139, 300n23; capitalism com-
  patible with, 14–15; *Communist Manifesto*
  on, 223–226; *Jo'burg Memo* on, 135–136;
  Marx on, 167, 180–188, 202, 210, 312n7;
  socialism and, 271–277; weak sustainability hypothesis, 26
Sweezy, Paul, 34, 43, 61, 253

Tansley, Arthur, 74–75, 156–160
technology: as "black box," 15–16;
    Bukharin on, 190; as cure-all, 22; in
    human evolution, 151–152, 186; Marx
    and Engels on, 20, 227–229; in metabol-
    ic relation of humans to nature, 187–188;
    solutions to global warming in, 26–27; in
    weak sustainability hypothesis, 26
Terence, 273
Thatcher, Margaret, 137
thermohaline circulation, 110–111, 114,
    294n10
third agricultural revolution, 169, 198
Thompson, Edward P., 27–28, 144
Thompson, F. M. L., 300–301n34
tipping points, 55–56, 285n2
town and country antagonisms, 32, 168,
    172, 180–184, 189, 197, 201, 210–211,
    221–222
transportation: peaking oil production and,
    93, 97
treadmill of production, 48
trees, see forests

unconventional oil, 94
United Kingdom, 60; agriculture in,
    145–146, 169, 237; coal consumption in,
    122–123, 125–127; industrial revolution
    in, 268–269; Marxism in, 155–156; soil
    depletion in, 171, 177; in War of the
    Pacific, 239–241, 312–313n18
United Nations, 261
United Nations Conference on
    Environment and Development, 41
United Nations Framework for Climate
    Change (Kyoto Protocol), 132
United States: carbon emissions of, 119;
    control over world oil supply by, 85–86,
    89; Convention on Biological Diversity
    opposed by, 132; energy policy objec-
    tives of, 99–104; Iraq invaded by, 233;
    Kyoto Protocol rejected by, 42–43, 118,
    130, 247–248; oil imports into, 86;
    Pentagon report on impact of climate

change on, 115; soil depletion on, 173;
    during War of the Pacific, 239–240,
    312–313n18
Uranovsky, Y. M., 191, 305–306n123
urban movements, 205
Urey, Harold, 78
Urquhart, David, 221
utopian socialism, 33, 210, 282n43

van der Veer, Jeroen, 98
Vavilov, N. I., 154, 155, 267, 305–306n123
Veblen, Thorstein, 22
Venezuela, 33, 275; oil production in, 98,
    100; petro-socialism in, 274; U.S. policy
    on, 103, 104
Vernadsky, V. I., 78, 154, 192, 267,
    305n122
Verri, Pietro, 187–188

Waring, George, 310n25
War of the Pacific (Nitrate War), 239–241,
    312–313n18
War on Terrorism, 91, 260, 261
water shortages, 254
weak sustainability hypothesis, 26
Weber, Max, 163, 165, 193, 199
Williams, Raymond, 7, 223
Wolfowitz, Paul, 91
Woodgate, Graham, 168, 188
woods, see forests
Works Progress Administration (WPA), 30
world alienation, 269
World Bank, 136
World Summit on Sustainable
    Development (Johannesburg, South
    Africa; 2002), 42–43, 129–131, 134–137
World Trade Organization (WTO), 133,
    135–137
Worldwatch Institute, 295–296n5

Yergin, Daniel, 88
York, Richard, 9
Younger Dryas, 110